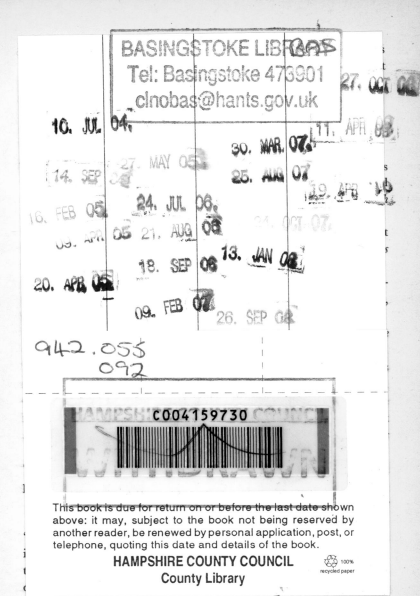
'Green's rendering, for all its h   nd
intelligently written'   ent

D1419155

The Double Life of Doctor Lopez

*Spies, Shakespeare and the Plot
to Poison Elizabeth I*

Dominic Green

arrow books

Published by Arrow Books in 2004

3 5 7 9 10 8 6 4 2

Copyright © Dominic Green 2003

Dominic Green has asserted his right under the Copyright, Designs and
Patents Act, 1988, to be identified as the author of this work

First published in the United Kingdom in 2003 by Century

Arrow Books Limited
The Random House Group Limited
20 Vauxhall Bridge Road, London SW1V 2SA

Random House Australia (Pty) Limited
20 Alfred Street, Milsons Point, Sydney,
New South Wales 2061, Australia

Random House New Zealand Limited
18 Poland Road, Glenfield
Auckland 10, New Zealand

Random House South Africa (Pty) Limited
Edulini, 5a Jubilee Road, Parktown, 2193, South Africa

The Random House Group Limited Reg. No. 954009

www.randomhouse.co.uk
www.dominicgreen.net

A CIP catalogue record for this book is available from the British Library

Papers used by Random House are natural, recyclable products made
from wood grown in sustainable forests. The manufacturing processes
conform to the environmental regulations of the country of origin

ISBN 0 09 943189 0

Typeset in Baskerville MT by Palimpsest Book Production Ltd,
Polmont, Stirlingshire
Printed and bound in the United Kingdom by
Bookmarque Ltd, Croydon, Surrey

To Betty

Contents

Acknowledgements

For their help with research, I would like to thank Marion Rea and Samantha Searle, Archivists at the Clerk's House, St Bartholomew's Hospital; Robin Harcourt Williams, Archivist at Hatfield House; the staff of Lambeth Palace Library; Sarah Westwood, Archivist, and Theresa Thom, Librarian of Gray's Inn; Chris Thompson and Martin Wood at St Katharine Creechurch; the Museo Maritimo, Macau; Leigh Saville at Theobald's Park; the staff of the London Library; the staffs of the Humanities 1, Rare Books, and Manuscripts Rooms of the British Library; the staffs of the Manuscript and Print Rooms of the Guildhall Library; the staff of the Public Record Office, Kew; and Melanie Blake at the Courtauld Library.

I owe more personal thanks to Maja Löfdahl and Giles Coren, who read the manuscript and gave valued advice; Joseph and Guida Teles, for their hospitable assistance with translations from Portuguese; and Doctor Lisa Löfdahl, for medical advice.

My agent, Lizzy Kremer at Ed Victor Ltd., developed an idea into a story, and my editor, Anna Cherrett at Century, turned a manuscript into a book. I would like to thank them both for their patience and enthusiasm; I am also grateful to Grainne Fox at Ed Victor Ltd., for her help in the final stages; and to Lindsay Davies at Arrow, who prepared the paperback edition.

My wife, Maja Löfdahl, encouraged me when I had given up, advised me when I was stuck, and edited the manuscript too. For all of those things, and for so much more, I thank her in love and admiration.

'Gracious and great, that we so boldly dare
('Mongst other plays that now in fashion are)
To present this, writ many years agone,
And in that age thought second unto none,
We humbly crave your pardon. We pursue
The story of a rich and famous Jew
Who lived in Malta. You shall find him still,
In all his projects, a sound Machiavell;
And that's his character. He that hath passed
So many censures is now come at last
To have your princely ears. Grace you him; then
You crown the action and renown the pen.'

Christopher Marlowe, *The Prologue Spoken
at Court* from *The Jew of Malta*

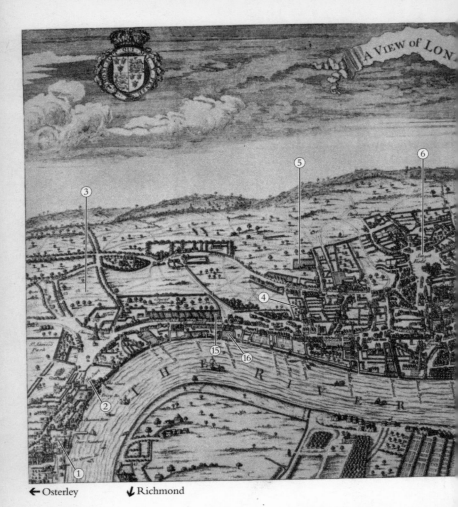

← Osterley   ↓ Richmond

The Remarkable Places in this Antient View of LONDON
are referr'd to by Figures

1 Westminster Hall
2 The Court
3 Tyburn Fields
4 Southampton House (probable location)
5 Gray's Inn

6 West Smithfield
7 St. Paul's Church
8 Wood Street
9 Guildhall
10 Fisher's Folly

about the Year 1560.

that are not distinguished by Words in the Body thereof;
as hereunder specified:

Prologue

S *aturday 7 June 1594.* His penultimate view of the world was from the perpendicular, almost flat on his back, inches above the ground, moving forward but looking backwards and upwards. Directly above him the sky, the weather clear enough to have drawn a crowd of thousands. Below that, the gables and spires of the City of London, retreating as his procession drew eastwards along Holborn into the fields. And beneath that, within inches of his face, more faces. Thousands of them, mouths open in careless display of carious Tudor dentistry, faces distorted by anger and joy, fascination and hatred, faces twisted in the act of screaming an insult whose sense was lost in the swirl of noise, faces pursed in the pout of spitting, faces slack in loose-jawed gawp, all pushing forward to lean over and take a look. The tumbling humanity of a Brueghel carnival, a surging sea of people parting and closing before and after him as if he were a caravel carving a path through the Atlantic waves, and he the pilot on its poop, astrolabe held up to the skies in calculation of invisible distance to an unseen destination.

Even from his inverted, foreshortened perspective, he knew just where he was and how much further there was to go. The journey had begun at the Queen's Bench in Southwark, the law court near the theatres, where the Sheriff of London's men had tied him and the other two men to the hurdles, wooden frames like a stretcher for the wounded, but with handles at one end only. The handles serving as carriage shafts, the three hurdles were hauled off in procession, their trailing ends raising a dry cloud of June dust around the Sheriff's men. After involuntarily crossing London Bridge, he had been dragged through the City, past Leadenhall and westwards. Now, he was being taken along the street where he lived. Over the City ditch, past Hatton House and its famous garden, to Gray's Inn and the parish church of St Andrew's. When he passed Mountjoy's Inn – the home where his wife and children still lived, where the long hours of a summer Sabbath were being counted – he knew there remained little more than twenty minutes.

As the houses at the roadside thinned and the procession entered the City's country fringe, his body on the hurdle cast a shadow like the finger of a sundial, the seconds falling away like sand grains. The last minutes of a long life roughly attaining the promised three score years and ten, but elliptically, ricocheting on to unforeseen routes in response to sudden forces. The predictable, preordained tangent of family, faith and work had met the random forces of rupture, violence and politics. Like a Galileo experiment: a ball was rolled down a plane, but its direction and velocity were altered permanently by the shifting of that plane. This was the final stages of motion, where the forces were great enough to counter the original velocity. He slowed to a stop in Tyburn Fields, his ellipse complete.

His hurdle halted before the scaffold and he was lowered to the ground. They cut his bonds, pulled him upright and pushed him up the ladder steps. His legs weak from imprisonment, constriction and fear, he stood before the noose. Restored to the vertical, he looked at the surging crowd over the heads and pikes of the Sheriff's men, like an actor or a king. The profane comedy of a city at play on a hot summer Saturday, thousands subsumed into a single form, a mob milling and churning, a miasma cloud made flesh, preyed upon by the perennial festive parasites, hawkers and singers, thieves and whores. Above the crowd were the rich and the highborn, who had bought seats on temporary banks, and beyond them, across the fields by the river, were the towers of the palace of Westminster and the spire of Edward the Confessor's abbey. The air was scented with sweat and drink, and the smell of burning wood.

From the fields, the old man on the stage was a thin figure. His lips moved as he made to speak, yet the crowd was too great and too aroused for a soliloquy, and they would not hear him. Its factions fell into comic dispute, some calling, 'Speak out, speak out!', as others called, 'Hold your peace, hold your peace!'.

His words were lost in the tumult. The only response was a bellowing hatred, a call for his blood. Trying again, he chose his last words.

'I love the Queen as well as I love Our Lord.'

They laughed as if he were a stage clown like Richard Tarleton or Tom Kemp, delivering some choice item of ironic foolery. It was common knowledge that behind his public observance of Christian rites he was a Jew, and that when a Jew claimed to love the Queen as well as he loved Jesus Christ, he proved how he did not love her at all. After the laughter, more anger and mockery, the hissing fury of the mob at the arrogance of the renegade.

'He is a Jew!'

Other tiny figures pinioned him with strong arms and placed the noose round his neck. To a surge of acclaim, they tore his shirt from him. He stood naked before the storm of voices, and then they hanged him. Not by the sudden opening of a trapdoor but gradually, so that his neck might not be broken, winching him into the air until his legs kicked for the ground and he choked into unconsciousness.

Then they cut him down. They were experienced and they timed the hanging with professional pride, taking him to the edge of death and reviving him roughly. They held him down and the crowd surged closer, and its noise grew frenzied as the executioner kneeled over him, one hand holding a long butcher's knife. To the rapture of the mob, the executioner castrated him, slashed his torso open, eviscerated his internal organs and cut out his heart, raising it with a bloodied forearm like an Aztec priest. Taking an axe, he severed the head and, heaving his hatchet like a butcher jointing a chicken, hacked the body into rough quarters, each with its useless limb and transection of internal cavity. The head and quarters were piled up, preserved for exhibition on the southern gatehouse of London Bridge, under which crowds would pass heading for the other kind of theatre in Southwark, and the bloody thrills of *The Jew of Malta* and *Titus Andronicus*. Delirious for more, the crowd called for the next victim to be brought on to the scaffold.

This was the traitor's death of Doctor Roderigo Lopez. Convicted of plotting to poison Elizabeth I, Queen of England, he was hung, drawn and quartered at Tyburn. The two men tied to the other hurdles were his alleged co-conspirators, both of them nondescript members of the shifting cast of spies and intriguers barnacled to the underbelly of Elizabethan politics, obscurities who came to public notice only at their deaths and were then forgotten. Lopez was different.

A society physician possessed of a suave Italianate manner, for more than thirty years the Doctor had been a familiar figure in the streets of the City and the ante-rooms of its great houses. A Fellow of the Royal College of Physicians and active in the City as a fund-raiser for shipping ventures, he lived in a suburban mansion near the fashionable Inns of Court. His practice had taken him into the homes and confidences of Elizabeth I's closest advisers: Sir Francis Walsingham; Robert Dudley, Earl of Leicester, and his stepson Robert Devereux, Earl of Essex; William Cecil, Lord Burghley, and his son, Sir Robert Cecil. Lopez was well-trusted, well-paid and well-known. His handy way with the enema pump and the high fees he charged for his 'purgations' had been satirised on the London stage. Christopher Marlowe had joked about him in *Doctor Faustus* (1588). A horse dealer comes to Faustus, hoping to buy his horse. Tutored by Mephistopheles, Faustus tricks the 'horse-courser' of his money. The dealer returns to Faustus crying, 'Alas, alas! Doctor Lopus was never such a doctor. He has given me a purgation, he has purged me of forty dollars!'

For thirteen years, Lopez had been the Queen's personal doctor. This was a position of unique trust in a time of great danger. Protestant England was at war with Catholic Spain, and the summer of *Doctor Faustus* had also been the summer when the Spanish Armada had sailed into the Channel. The pious Philip II of Spain concurred with the Pope's analysis of Elizabeth I: she was illegitimate by birth and by religion, and her displacement was a moral and spiritual obligation. Apart from military means, there were other, cruder ways of returning England to the Catholic fold. Discreetly distanced from Philip by a bureaucratic web of secretaries, but acting with an implicit royal licence, were suicidal would-be assassins, either desperate English Catholics or ideologically charged graduates of Jesuit seminaries on the Continent. As the Queen's physician, Lopez had been charged with a dual task, the preservation of a body that existed on two planes at once: human and sacred, physical and metaphysical, the gout and neuralgia of a childless sexagenarian in uneasy cohabitation with the divinity of an anointed monarch. The survival of the Elizabethan State had been Lopez's personal responsibility. It was hard to imagine a more elaborate mask for treason, or a more dangerous position from which to launch it.

Yet it appeared that Roderigo Lopez had used this trust and his high profile to mask the worst crime of all: treason. It seemed that the Doctor had been leading a double life: physician and spy, Jew and Christian, servant of the Queen of England and agent of the King of Spain. This hidden corruption had been revealed by one of the Doctor's patients, the Earl of Essex. Over several months, the Earl had peeled back the layers of the Doctor's public image, discovering a foul complex of treason, its tendrils winding from London to the courts and ministries of Europe, to Madrid, Brussels, Paris, Antwerp and Constantinople.

For years Lopez had successfully partitioned his life into two spheres, known and unknown. Comfortably resident in the bright world of the Court, he had also been a secret actor in the sleazy world of espionage, a shadow play of Catholic hunters and ciphered mails, of assignations in Antwerp potrooms and confessions extracted on the rack. Essex claimed that Lopez had sold his services to Philip II as a spy and had accepted a jewelled ring in payment. He had offered to murder the Queen with poison, haggling over the price of his regicide like a merchant at an auction. Conducting a long correspondence with the Count of Fuentes, leader of the Spanish army of occupation in the Netherlands, Lopez had passed secrets about the state of the navy and the Court. He had arranged an offshore account in Antwerp for the money to be paid into and had laid plans to flee the country for the Court of the Great Turk at Constantinople as soon as he had murdered the Queen.

Now everything tumbled out: tales of botched abortions and murder by physic, safe houses and mail drops, secret synagogues and ciphered letters, double agents and triple identities. The fallout was enough to cause one of his patients, Don Antonio, the exiled King of Portugal, to flee London for Paris in fear of his life, and the resulting circus of trial and interrogation transfixed the public's imagination.

The playwrights and theatre managers responded in greedy sympathy. In the decades following his death, Lopez gave wicked cameo appearances in Thomas Middleton's *A Game at Chess*, Thomas Dekker's *The Whore of Babylon*, and was also poetically resurrected in Thomas Nashe's *Lenten Stuff*. One play in particular seemed to go further than easy references to treason and poison: Shakespeare's *The Merchant of Venice*. In the figure of Shylock, the vindictive Jewish moneylender who seeks a pound of flesh when his debtor cannot repay in cash, Shakespeare drew a character saturated in echoes of the Lopez affair.

Yet despite his theatrical celebrity, Lopez's notoriety faded with time. The name 'Roderigo Lopez' became one among many, an Elizabethan footnote, a minor figure on the roll of Tudor treasons and, like a popular but tired repertory piece, his story became hackneyed and archaic. Nine years after his execution, the Tudor dynasty expired with Elizabeth I, and two years after that the Lopez Affair's remaining topicality was obscured by a far more spectacular attempt at regicide, the Gunpowder Plot. A century after his violent death before the mob at Tyburn, Roderigo Lopez was forgotten and *The Merchant of Venice* was a minor play by an unfashionable playwright.

Lopez lay undisturbed in the mass grave of historical anonymity for nearly 300 years until 1879, when the actor-managers Henry Irving and Ellen Terry revived *The Merchant of Venice* at London's Lyceum

Theatre. Among the audience was an Oxford undergraduate named Sidney Lee, a future biographer of Shakespeare. When Lee saw Irving's Shylock, he felt that Shylock seemed so real that he must have been drawn from life.

Henry Irving as Shylock.

Yet the history books were adamant that there were no Jews in Shakespeare's London. So Lee took to the archives, where he found Doctor Roderigo Lopez. In the spring of 1880 Lee published his findings under the provocative title *The Original of Shylock*, igniting a long-running Shakespearean controversy. In James Joyce's *Ulysses*, when a group of loafers gather in the library to contest theories of Shakespearean authorship, the young hero Stephen Dedalus repeats Lee's Lopez-Shylock thesis in his reflections on the Shakespearean imagination.

All events brought grist to his mill. Shylock chimes with the jewbaiting that followed the hanging and quartering of the queen's leech Lopez, his jew's heart being plucked forth while the sheeny was yet alive.

But just as there is more to Shylock than Lopez, so there is more to Lopez than Shylock. They cannot be the same, but they cannot be wholly disconnected. In delineating their relationship, the obstacles are not logical, but technical. The Elizabethan archives are an irregular blend, where a lush thickness suddenly thins to an almost imperceptible sheen(y), and there are no 'smoking guns' in Shakespeare studies: no diaries or working papers, no play scripts flamboyantly autographed at the stage door, no 'To be or not be?' scribbled on the reverse of an ale-stained, tobacco-scented scrap snatched from behind the bar in a moment of inspiration. In his later years as businessman and impresario, Shakespeare was a minority shareholder in another Bankside venture, the Globe. If a cache of personal papers existed in some backstage nook, they would not have survived the afternoon performance of *Henry VIII* on 29 June 1613. In Act I, the firing of a cannon to mark Henry's arrival at the house of Cardinal Wolsey released a spark which tindered in the dry thatch of the Globe's roof. Within an hour the theatre burnt to the ground. No one died, although one man's breeches caught light, and they 'would perhaps have broiled him, if he had not, by the benefit of a provident wit, put it out with a bottled ale'. The documentary loss was less easily replaced than the scorched breeches.

Lopez is a different case. Although we must climb back past the impressive but hollow bulk of Shylock to reach it, the double life of Doctor Lopez has waited there for centuries, an unquiet ghost from the last nervous years of Elizabethan England. Its fractured traces survive in State Papers and private letters, legal cases and domestic inventories, interrogations and debriefings, dainty requests for patronage and a mystical Hebrew manuscript found in 'the coffers of the kitchen at Pipe Hall'. There can be no absolute proof, only a mosaic of fragments, many of them circumstantial, but by laying those fragments in their proper place, piece by piece, it is possible to assemble a portrait, and to deduce the shape and colour of the missing pieces from the surrounding pattern. Doctor Lopez worked for the government, as both physician and intelligence agent, and the last, ambiguous phase of his life was memorialised by the mountainous paperwork of a treason inquiry and trial. A shambles of information survives, the shattered evidence of a long career and its disastrous finale. It is also a transection of the Elizabethan State, for unlike similar trials, the Lopez Affair reached to the heights of the political system, and eventually to the Queen herself.

The focus of the inquiry was on Doctor Lopez. But what if the case is reopened and the microscope is turned not just on the suspect, but also on his examiners? The evidence against Lopez was adjudicated by Lord Burghley, pre-eminent politician of the day. It was prosecuted by Sir Edward Coke, the most acute legal mind in an age of lawyers. It was analysed by another lawyer, the young Francis Bacon, and it fascinated William Shakespeare. It set the two rising stars of contemporary politics, Sir Robert Cecil and the Earl of Essex, against each other. Finally, it dragged the Queen herself into the case. How did a routine spy trial evolve into the most sensational political event since the defeat of the Spanish Armada? The Lopez Affair reached from the sleaziest to the noblest, from City lodging houses to the apex of power. In its wake, it left a thick trail of paper. Some documents are obscure, some describe the same events from different perspectives, and some are forgeries, deliberate falsifications of the record. Others were purposely withheld from his trial and the official accounts that followed. Many of these documents have never been published and many others have never been linked to Lopez. But even the thinnest shard is a piece of the pot and even the most mute document can speak.

In Elizabethan England, a self-made man knew he had arrived in society when the College of Arms approved his request to use a coat of arms. Shakespeare's father John applied in 1569, but the guardians of heraldic privilege turned him down; this slight was rectified in October 1596, when his son William launched a successful application. In the records of the College of Arms, there is a page titled 'Lopez' in its top right corner. The rest of the page is blank.

No explanation is given, yet the empty page tells its own story of omission. It seems that the Queen's physician had begun the process of obtaining his escutcheon, but that its granting had been suddenly abandoned. Lopez is an expanse of silence, symbolically absent in a ledger of symbols.

There is a greater mystery to Doctor Roderigo Lopez than the imponderables of his relationship to Shylock and Shakespeare. Who was Doctor Lopez? Was he a Spanish spy who plotted the assassination of Elizabeth I? If not, who sent him to Tyburn, and who gained from his butchery? And if Lopez resists compression into Shylock, where does William Shakespeare fit into the Lopez story? These questions have lain unresolved for over four centuries. This book attempts to answer them and to fill in the blank page marked 'Lopez'.

London, 2003

I

I

The Anatomist

All physicians are destined for Gehenna.
The Talmud

From the sea to the river, and the river to the city. Two days out of Antwerp, the grey North Sea gives way to the muddy mouth of an estuary. A rising tide carries the ship and its passenger westwards through the cries of gulls. From the deck, he sees a flat countryside of smudged green and brown. Haphazard low shacks, homes of shipwrights and sailors, straggle along the banks in ragged escort. Sentinel forts and beacons mark the progress to the dockyards, Chatham to port, Tilbury to starboard. At Greenwich a royal palace rises over a palisade of trees, then a third dock at Deptford, where the air is sticky with tar and the craft flock like swans by the shore. The high-pooped warships back from the great oceans lie careened on their sides, skeletal oak masts stencilled against a low winter sky.

A smear of workshops and shacks appears along the waterside, the shambling fringe of a city, and then his destination, London. The halls of the City livery companies loom like castles over a crush of wood and stone. Jumbled squat houses huddle against the east wind, chimneys wheezing into an empty sky pricked by the spires of parish churches. The City has burst the banks of its medieval walls, its mud hovels puddling against the old stones and trickling along the fore-shore, where the dockers unload carracks and caravelles. Behind them, his eyes trace the City's tributary roads, back from the wharves to open fields and distant villages, the sweet waters and windmills of Hackney and Hampstead.

A fortress guards the river approach, the White Tower rising sternly over the tide that licks slickly at the teeth of the water gates. Before it, the City's only bridge blocks the watery highway of the Thames like a stockade, the flood boiling through its arches. Above, high thin houses jostle along its length, their diamond-shaped window-panes catching weak light like watery gemstones. At the southern end of the bridge the towers of a massive gate are crowned with bare poles, their spiked tips waiting for the heads of traitors. From the gate the City debouches on to the southern bank, pooling into a slummy afterthought of brothels, taverns and pleasure gardens, a patch beyond the City's jurisdiction, the haunt of thieves and prostitutes, gamblers and bear baiters. From the windows of his palace to the west, the Archbishop of Canterbury can see the lost sheep.

A lighter vessel, like the wherries and rowboats scudding back and forth between the legs of London Bridge, might wait for the ebb tide and shoot beneath the arches, following the parade of great mansions lining the northern bank as it curves slowly south towards Westminster. But a ponderous merchant carrack, built to ride the green malice of the North Sea and the Atlantic seaboard, is too big. It docks just short of the City, at the half-mile of wharves and warehouses in the shadow of the Tower. The deck planks shudder as his ship is roped to the wharf.

On the dockside, the ancient rhythm of port life plays out to the toll of church bells and the cries of sailors. A diurnal tide of goods and money washes back and forth through the Customs House. Unfinished wool, lifeblood of the island economy, sits stacked in bales, ready for shipping to Antwerp, the biggest port in the world. From there, the rough kersies will be distributed across the Low Countries and Germany, to be finished by nimbler hands. In return the desic-cated, granulated gold of the storehouses of Antwerp is unloaded, winched bale by lucrative bale out of the hold and on to the dock. Movement stirs the dormant contents and the cold, damp air of a northern port in winter is touched by the dry, smarting scent of the Indies. The improbable exotica of the East, condi-ments and medicines for the tables of the wealthy and the cabinets of apothe-caries. Cloves, cinnamon, nutmeg and mace mingle with the local bouquet of salted herring and unwashed bodies.

As the loading continues, the human cargo disembarks. As a port, London has its community of foreign traders, a gaggle collectively grouped as the Merchant Strangers, agents and distributors for the great houses of Genoa, Antwerp and Lisbon. But it is also a city of refuge, a city of exile for dissenting Protestants of all shades. For a price, the payment of a tax levied on aliens, they can make a new life in London. When the Lord Mayor's assessors tour the lodging houses of the City noting the 'Returns of Strangers', they find that London has become discreetly international, a city that is home to 3000 Strangers. Jewellers from Paris live alongside clothworkers from Antwerp, musicians from Milan and merchants from Venice, and each nation has its own church, with services in its native tongue. In the swirl of goods and bodies, individuals become unremarkable, lost in the crowd, one transit among thousands.

A short man in an age of short people, with a close-cropped black beard and a Mediterranean cast, he could be a modest merchant watching the delivery of his cargo, or he could be a seminary graduate, protégé of the Calvinists of Antwerp or the Jesuits of Reims. The impression is educated and well-travelled, Iberia via the Low Countries, with a waft of the exotic like the spices in the bales. He has a contact in London, maybe a face in the crowd at the dockside. There is an opacity to him, a sense of something that does not fit, a scent that hangs in the air long after he has disappeared into the narrow alleys in the shadow of the Tower.

Roderigo Lopez Gallo was born around the year 1525 in Crato, a small town in the Alentejo region of Portugal. He only used the 'Gallo' if he wanted to be associated with his relatives, the Lopez Gallo family of Antwerp merchants, and he preferred the diminutive 'Ruy' to 'Roderigo'. In 1538 he entered the University of Coimbra, the 'Oxford of Portugal', one hundred miles north-west of Crato. Studying 'Artes', or Sciences, he graduated three years later. After studying anatomy in Spain at the University of Salamanca, he returned to Coimbra to practise medicine. Shortly after the accession of Elizabeth I in November 1558, he settled in London. He found work as house physician at St Bartholomew's Hospital and married Sara Añes, daughter of a London Portuguese merchant.

These are the facts of Lopez's prehistory, brief but eloquent. They are the thumbnail biography of a typical Iberian doctor of the period: the truncated childhood of a professional man's son, long hours spent in rote learning; early adolescence in the monastic, Latinate world of the university, heavy on theology and Aristotle; later teens spent in professional specialisation, swapping 'Artes' for anatomy. By modern standards, he was remarkable not for the trajectory, but only for the velocity with which he shot through his education. This, though, was not an era of magic bullets, mineral water and mass vaccination. A child of the sixteenth century was an investment against the short odds of infant mortality and a parent's only hedge against old age.

Ordinarily exceptional, notable but not remarkable, young Lopez left no deeper imprint on the record. A few further details can be spied in the background, like the distant hills over the shoulder of the Mona Lisa. The landscape of childhood, a habitual shaper of memory, was the empty, austere Alentejo, the territory 'over the Tejo river', an underdeveloped inland appendix to a seafaring state. A gentle countryside of endless wheat, cork and olive farms, their backwater monotony enlivened by fallen dolmens and Roman ruins, sleepily watched over by walled market towns. The world had not yet gathered itself into cities and even the greatest began as provincials. The journey of Sir Francis Drake, circumnavigator of the globe, began in the village of Crowndale, Devon. William Tyndale, translator of the Bible into English, learned to read in the hamlet of Slimbridge, Gloucestershire. By contrast, William Shakespeare, raised among the wheeler-dealer wool dealers of Stratford-upon-Avon, was a veritable urbanite.

Crato, the scene of Lopez's childhood, was one of the Alentejo's few claims to national significance. It was a garrison town, seat of the thoroughly medieval Grand Priory of the Order of Crato, whose gardens were laid out in the shape of a Maltese cross. The Order was the Portuguese branch of the Knights Hospitaller, the chivalric military society rooted in twin traditions of providing shelter to Christian pilgrims and fighting the Muslim enemies of Christendom in the Mediterranean. Aristocratic in membership, it was headed by a member of Portugal's ruling House of Avis. When Lopez was born, the Grand Prior of the Order was Luis, Duke of Beja, second son of King Emanuel of Portugal. In 1530, when Lopez was about five years old, Duke Luis fathered a son by his mistress Yolanda Gomez, a Jewish beauty known to her admirers as 'The White Pelican' for her prematurely whitened hair. Her baby, named Don Antonio, would become the next Grand Prior. Lopez, the future physician, and Don Antonio, his future patient, were childhood contemporaries in the military monastery at Crato. Later, they would be distantly related by bonds of marriage and their fates would become entangled like ivy on a monastery wall, each shoot strangling the next.

Lopez's father was probably a physician attached to the Order of Crato, perhaps attending to Duke Luis himself. Medicine was a profession which tended to run in families, and there were few other reasons to live in Crato. Lopez grew up among the protocols of Court life and the subtle phrases of a royal physician. At thirteen he left Crato for Coimbra, and at sixteen he moved east across the Spanish border to Salamanca. From the wooden benches of an anatomy theatre he observed the inner secrets of the human body, a ringside spectator of the Renaissance.

Covering two centuries in more than a dozen countries, the Renaissance bridged the medieval and the modern. The rediscovery of ancient art and thought, lost to most of Europe in the Dark Ages, prompted a reassessment of their sources. In religion, Luther called for the purification of Christianity by uprooting it from corrupt papal politics and replanting it in an authentic reading of the Old Testament. In art, the sculptors and painters of northern Italy returned to the relics of ancient Greece and Rome. In literature and philosophy, Greek and Latin texts were reprinted in accurate translation and used as models. The founding text preceded theology and the evidence of the eye preceded habit; when the text and the eye did not accord, a reinvention followed. As with religion and art, so with medicine: a period of recovery, of restoring the tarnished images and tampered texts, preceded a period of reinvention.

Lopez was a medical hybrid, his education coinciding with the advent of modern medicine. The principles of ancient medicine had become lost and corrupt in the northern Europe of the Dark Ages, but they had survived in Lopez's native Iberia, where Greek writings had been preserved in the aspic of Hebrew and Arabic. Hippocrates of Cos, the Ancient father of medicine, had proposed that the body was a balanced system. Sickness was an imbalance and healing was the restoration of equilibrium by the rebalancing of the body's *chymoi*, or fluids. In the second century CE, Galen of Pergamon filtered the Hippocratic system through the subsequent Roman and Alexandrian schools to form a unified theory of ancient medicine: the complete physical, philosophical and ethical structure of the Theory of Humours. The play of the Humours was as central to life as sap was to plants, and their continual flux was an echo of cosmic process. The four Humours of Phlegm, Yellow Bile, Black Bile and Blood correlated to the four primary qualities: hot, dry, wet and cold; to the four elements: air, fire, earth and water; to the four temperaments: Phlegmatic, Melancholy, Sanguine and Choleric; the four seasons; and the four points of the compass. When the excess fluids of one or another Humour gathered in the body, they stagnated. The answer was to remove the blockage. There were three methods: the alimentary canal was dosed at its antipodes with emetics and enemas, and the liver and circulatory system were unblocked with generous bloodletting.

Dissecting a human body was immoral and illegal, because a damaged corpse hindered the deceased's prospects in the afterlife. Galen had obtained some opportunistic insights from the damaged bodies of defeated gladiators, but for further detail he was forced to rely upon animal substitutes. After dissecting pigs and apes, whose livers were shaped differently from those of humans, he concluded that the human liver possessed five lobes that gripped the stomach like fingers. Examining a dog's jaw, he deduced that the human jaw also was composed of two bones.

Galenic anatomy reigned for over a millennium, until the Renaissance. Inspired by ancient statuary, Italian artists seeking absolute physical verisimilitude became the accidental godfathers of modern anatomy. The medieval shadow still hung heavily, though. In the years after 1506, Leonardo da Vinci, 'passing the night hours in the company of these corpses, quartered and flayed and horrible to behold', produced more than 750 anatomical drawings, but he deformed the evidence of his eye to fit Galenic theory, producing grotesques where perfect human embryos floated in canine wombs. In *On the Statue* (1535), Leon Battista Alberti theorised that anatomical knowledge was vital to the artist because human proportion echoed the macrocosm, a position which supported Aristotle and Galen philosophically while it undermined them aesthetically.

Modern translations of Galen and Hippocrates were printed in 1525, the year of Lopez's birth. Combined with the interest of artists, the subsequent examination of the ancients produced a reassessment of the Galenic legacy. Its agent was Andreas Vesalius, whose earliest anatomical experiment had involved abducting the corpse of a criminal from a roadside gibbet and reassembling the skeleton at home. In 1543, while Lopez was studying anatomy at Salamanca and Nicholas Copernicus was completing his theory that the earth orbited the sun, Vesalius produced the masterwork of Renaissance anatomy, *On the Fabric of the Human Body*. He resurrected the executed criminals of Padua's underclass as flayed Greek statues, their muscles and sinews laid bare for analysis.

Galen's pigs and puppies had been returned to the veterinary zoo, yet it took time for theory to adapt to technical progress. Galen's defenders offered the rearguard defence that Vesalius contradicted Galen because his subject had fallen from anatomical Eden. 'These dissections are of doubtful morality,' protested Thomas Vicary, Lopez's employer at St Bartholomew's. 'Mankind must have altered since old times and, as Aristotle is but the rubbish of an Adam, so our muscles and bones and arteries have degenerated from their comparative perfection in the times of Aristotle and Galen.'

As traditionalists ignored Vesalius, and progressives saw the new anatomy as a sideshow in the circus of Humours, physicians continued to chase stagnant *chymoi* from the body with emetics, clister pumps and leeches. Lopez was a beneficiary of the Renaissance, but he was burdened by a medieval inheritance.

Not much more can be known about Lopez's early life. Of course, there was more. The imperatives of mortality that fired him through university with such decent haste also commanded that he married quickly. There would have been parents, too, grandparents, siblings and cousins, friends from Coimbra and Salamanca, conversationalists and controversialists, theologians and logicians, Paracelsians and Galenists, patients and rivals – all of them equally evanescent, faceless people and nameless traces. The records are partial, unsystematic and maddeningly brief. Birth names, city names, markings on university registers: indistinct, faded line drawings from a vanished world. Crato was a small town, and the scholastic and medical worlds were little bigger. People lived and died in social intimacy. There was no need to write down much more than a name or a date, and it was hard to keep a secret. There seemed to be no reason to trail Roderigo Lopez, to follow him around the towns of his youth and record whom he spoke to or what he said. There is nothing about the facts of his early life to suggest that posterity might take an interest in him and wonder what he liked to eat, whether he preferred Portuguese *fado* to Spanish *flamenco*, or whether he slept on the right side or the left.

A typical life, then, if not for the missing fragment of information, the hub that holds together the spoke of the biographical wheel. When Roderigo Lopez began a new life in London in the winter of 1558, he was in his middle thirties. According to the lines on which his life hitherto had run, this was a disastrous rupture. He was well established in Coimbra, an ancient and wealthy city with plenty of rich patients whose gouty veins might be bled for regular, fat fees. His destiny should have been a comfortable, toothless retirement, the just reward of a life spent sweetening the stenches of sickness. Instead, he had been forced from his homeland and deprived of his livelihood. All the time that Roderigo Lopez had been ascending studiously the ladder of Portuguese life, he had been very conscious of one biographical detail in particular, one which he had hidden all his life with the utmost care, a matter of life and death whose public revelation might be his ruin. He was Jewish, and secretly so.

The most neutral – and possibly most accurate – description is 'crypto-Jewish'. The term has satisfying associations of subterranean life, unnoticed and encrypted, decodable only to those holding the right cipher key. But it is also a modern coinage, an anachronistic attempt to clarify the unclarifiable and resolve the irresoluble. It is tidy, but unfair. If a generic term did not exist, then historians would have to invent one, but in this case there is already an excess of options from which to choose. Four contemporary classifications attempted to describe Lopez's identity. Each was created according to the interest of its coiners, intended as a legal definition to trump all others, a final interpretation of who and what they preferred him to be. Then and now, they struggle together like snakes in a basket, symptoms of the Iberian condition: Converso, New Christian, Marrano, Annus.

As the bridge between Europe and Africa, medieval Iberia had been home to three groups: Muslims, Christians and Jews. For centuries, the Muslims and Christians had fought each other for supremacy over the peninsula. The Jews, who were numerically smaller and lacked a territorial motive, had attempted to find a middle path between the two and consequently had earned the enmity of both sides. In an age when religion was politics and war was its dialogue, forced conversion was the political price of being conquered. So when there were violent riots in the Christian north of Spain in 1391 and mass forced conversions of the Jewish population, there was little cause for alarm in the long term. The Christians were in the middle of a holy war to reclaim their land from Islam, and this latest persecution was one of its symptoms. Jews had lived in Iberia since Roman times, and had already survived brief forced conversions to Christianity in 611 CE and to Islam in 1148 CE. Like others before it, this persecution would pass when peace came to the peninsula and its economic life recovered.

This was a grievous misreading of the two varieties of holy war that had buffeted Iberian Jewry. The Islamic law of the Moors had tolerated those who did not believe in Mohammed, albeit only as *dhimmis*, a legal underclass. Under the Moors, the Jews had taken an active part in the cultural synthesis of the Golden Age, as urban artisans and professionals, businessmen and royal advisers. But the Christians had no such provision in their legal code and their tolerance declined as their Iberian kingdom grew. As the Moors were pushed south and the various Christian kingdoms were welded together by war and marriage, the Jews were left in legal and religious limbo. Some of the Conversos of 1391 and their descendants were sincere in their new faith, but many had only adopted a show of Christianity in order to save their necks and continued as Jews in private. Combining this ambiguity with the traditional Iberian obsession with pedigree and *limpieza de sangre*, purity of blood, resulted in chaos and still greater fanaticism.

The trajectory of Iberian Jewish life now followed a path that was re-enacted five centuries later in post-Enlightenment Europe. Conversion was the equivalent of a passport stamp that allowed its holder access to parts of society that had been blocked by the religious bar. Suddenly the religious, legal, administrative, university and military worlds were open to any Converso, regardless of his private belief and practice, so long as he claimed to be a 'New Christian'; in one extreme, but not unique, example from the early fifteenth century, the rabbi formerly known as Solomon Levi became Pablo de Santa Maria, Bishop of Burgos. The sudden advent of competition in previously protected areas of civil life caused great resentment among the Old Christians, who could no longer depend on their historic religious privilege. The most successful among the arrivistes intermarried with the Old Christian aristocracy, so that within two generations hardly a single ancient line remained unpolluted by a New Christian infusion. The removal of the legal barrier did not remove the taboo, but only shifted it from religion to ethnicity. Blood had replaced conscience as the arbiter of identity.

Caught between old and new allegiances, the New Christians persisted as an identifiable caste, incubating an alternative response to the Converso predicament: a double identity, publicly Christian and privately Jewish. The Moors, who had their own crypto-Islamic cults, gave such Jews the satirical nickname *Alboraycos*, after Mohammed's fantastical steed Al-Burak, who was neither horse nor mule, male nor female. Given that the Moors were also being expunged from Iberia, this Koranic quip did not catch on with the Christian population. They called the crypto-Jews *Marranos*. The etymology has been controversial. *Marrano* has been variously suggested as coming from Hebrew – *marat ayin*, 'the appearance of the eye', or the punning *mar annus*, 'Mr Forced Convert'; from Aramaic – *maranatha*, used in a New Testament curse against heretics; or the elaborate *mumarano*, in which the Arabic *mumar*, 'apostate', acquired a Spanish ending in a linguistic death rattle of the Golden Age. Generally, these suggestions have come from Jewish scholars seeking to avoid the most obvious and least pleasant conclusion: *marrano* was originally a dialect term in medieval Spanish, vulgar slang for 'pig'. It was a perfect derisory epithet for people who did not eat pork, but were held to be theologically swinish. Hence the joke made by Shylock's daughter Jessica after her conversion to Christianity, 'In converting Jews to Christians, you raise the price of pork.'

In the simplest formulation, Marranos were Jews in all but name and Christians in name only. They adapted to their new public habit, but continued as Jews in private, leading a complete double life. In the bicameral world of Lopez's childhood, a household might marry, baptise its children, make irregular confession and be buried in church, but it might also wash off the baptismal chrism when it returned home, circumcise its sons and conduct a second, Jewish, marriage ceremony behind closed doors. Still living in the same *juderias* and the same communities as they had before their nominal change in status, many Marranos kept traditional Jewish rites. Meat could be slaughtered according to kosher practice in the privacy of a courtyard. Two dishes could be prepared for the Friday night Sabbath meal, a meat dish for the celebrants and a fish dish, to be produced in case of the unplanned arrival of Christian neighbours. Furtive synagogues were established in the homes of the old *juderia*. Later, when great numbers of Marranos escaped to the Americas, they would often scatter the floors of their synagogues with sand. The romantic notion that this was done in identification with Moses's wanderings in the Sinai contends with the more pragmatic analysis that this was a vestigial Marrano habit, as the sand muffled the sound of footsteps and prayer. Lopez grew up fluent in two social languages, Christian and Jewish, every audible step masking its muffled echo.

If the Spanish had intended to cripple Judaism in Spain, they had succeeded; but if they had also attempted to separate Christians, Jews and Muslims, they had achieved the opposite effect. The logical end point came in 1492, a year of movement, almost all of it invol-untary. The Moors were expelled from Granada, their last strong-hold in Spain, and were pushed past the Pillars of Hercules into the wastes of the Maghreb. Three days after Columbus sailed west, the

Jews were expelled. Many fled to neighbouring Portugal, buying admittance at eight cruzados per head; their number included Abraham Zacuto of Salamanca, who was soon appointed astronomer to the House of Avis. Others fled to the Muslim kingdoms of North Africa, or to the other end of the Mediterranean, to the Ottoman cities of Constantinople, Salonika and the Holy Land. Some, including many of Lopez's cousins, went to Antwerp, the northern clearing house for Portuguese exports. Those who remained undercover in Spain were subject to detection and persecution by the Inquisition.

If Roderigo Lopez's parents were among the refugees who had bought their way into Portugal in 1492, they found no haven. In 1497, the Spanish monarchs Ferdinand and Isabella placed a condition upon the dynastic marriage between their daughter Isabella and Manuel, heir to King João of Portugal: Portugal must expel or convert its Jews. A catalogue of horrors followed. On the first day of Passover 1497, all Jews between the ages of four and twenty were seized for forcible conversion. The tactic was intended to force their parents to stay, but instead it produced cruel scenes of martyrdom and suicide. Of 20,000 Jews stranded on the dock at Lisbon offered a choice between conversion or slavery, most chose slavery. Others attempted to flee. And some, like Lopez's parents, went underground, adhering to the fatal Iberian habit of staying in their homes and waiting for the storm to abate.

The hoped-for reversal of the 1497 order never came. In 1531, when Lopez was six years old, the Inquisition was extended to Portugal. The hunt for Marranos became systematic and sadistic. Lopez was educated in the rites of his secret faith against a background of informers and spies, torture and confession, the public burning of books and bodies, the raised passions and fiery end of false messiahs. This was a challenge to faith, and in their distress overt and covert Jews alike became prone to the consolations of mysticism. At Safed in the Holy Land, a colony of mystics formulated the Kabbalah, a mystical recasting of Judaism, magical and superstitious, where the destruction of Iberian Jewry presaged the end of the world and the triumphal advent of the Messiah. Elaborate fantasies of power and restoration were composed in the cities of exile, and were smuggled into Iberia. In *halachah*, Jewish law, the categories of Converso, New Christian and Marrano were irrelevant. Jews converted against their will, by force or threat, were a variety of victim familiar from Jewish history, and precedent existed for their reassimilation into the Jewish people and faith when conditions eased. They were *Annusim*, 'forced ones', and pending their return, they were considered to be Jews living under temporary constraint, in historical suspension. But what happened when the temporary became permanent?

The accumulated disasters of the fifteenth century had distilled the Jews of Iberia down to their most determined and faithful core, and then poured them into Portugal, but perseverance alone was not enough. Cut off from the Jewish world outside Portugal, with education and worship rendered dangerous by the presence of the Inquisition, Marrano faith became diluted and diverged from Jewish tradition. At its most extreme, it became a theological phantasm, blending confused memories of Judaism with strands of the Christianity that concealed it. Even the mainstream of Marranism was adulterated. Where other Jews retold the story of Esther, who had saved the Jews of ancient Babylon from the wicked king Haman, Marranos venerated her as St Esther through a Catholic-style cult. A fully fledged Marrano represents as much of a taxonomical challenge to the historian as the duck-billed platypus did to a Victorian naturalist. All Conversos were New Christians, but some New Christians were really Marranos, and both New Christians and Marranos were in fact *Annusim*.

North of the Pyrenees, this morbid Iberian obsession with the fine-grading of identity seemed confusing and dangerous. A fifth term developed as a way of jamming the snakes back into their basket, a catch-all to denote the treacherous knot of ethnic and religious tension that lurked beneath: 'Portuguese', or as the English had it, 'Portingall'. The term was a shield against religious antagonism, a prophylaxis against the contaminatory vapours of the Inquisition, and it was neutral enough to allow international trade, which was the Portingall speciality, to continue without adding religious conscience to the complexities of international credit, leaky ships and bad maps. A sixteenth-century Portingall was a displaced collection of overlapping identities. The language of his mother tongue had soured in his mouth as the language of his persecutors, and his country had become a land of his enemies and memory. Protected by the trading rights of a member of 'the Portuguese nation', he had often been specifically excluded from that nation.

In the late 1550s, the Portuguese Inquisition caught up with Roderigo Lopez and turned him into a Portingall. The goods of 'Rui Lopes' the false New Christian were confiscated by the Inquisition of Coimbra. By the hand-chopping, public-burning standards of the Inquisition, this was a relatively light punishment, but its implications were clear and frightening. Convicted of secret Judaism, his professional future was destroyed. He might be tortured for information and forced into collaboration. If he became a mole for the Inquisition and was detected by his fellow Marranos, he might be murdered. He was now permanently marked as a suspect, and a further conviction meant prison or death. He had to leave Portugal at once, for his own sake and the sake of his community.

Roderigo Lopez, courtly physician and religio-legal anomaly, became a refugee, a traveller in a world of ghosts, a wanderer on a lost continent of memory called *Sepharad*, the vanished land preserved in food and language, in the garlicky scents of the kitchen and the Hebrew-inflected Spanish of Ladino dialect. The families of his world passed down the keys to their ancestral home from generation to generation without knowing if the house was still there. Regrouping in rented houses in Constantinople, Alexandria or Antwerp, the exiles waited for word from Lisbon that history had thrown itself into precipitous reverse and that they could return. Lopez was a survivor, one of the last thousands to have maintained their identity, but that identity was being distorted by the world, bent into new shapes. An exile enchanted by songs from the lost homeland, a dreamer consoled by fantasies of power and redemption, supposed never to have existed or not to exist, he represents a recurrent human condition, Homeric and Judaic. His notes can be heard in the long music of exile, in the song of the Israelites by the rivers of Babylon, in the wanderings of Odysseus, in the laments of Moors thrown from their *Al-Andalus*.

An anatomist by training, accidents of birth and history turned Lopez into a living experiment in the anatomy of personality. His was a hybrid character, in a transitional age. Lopez was cast into a Europe torn by political and religious confusion. Led by Luther and Calvin, a creeping reaction against the corruption of the Catholic Church and its interference in local politics had triggered the Reformation, an open rebellion against Rome. Nations and city states declared their Protestantism and their independence, launching a crisis of politics and faith. In England, Henry VIII had appointed himself head of the Anglican Church, but the reigns of his first two heirs had swung so wildly between the extremes of Catholicism and Puritanism that by 1558 a thirty-five-year-old Englishman or woman had experienced the Reformation as a disorientating sequence of contradictory dispensations. They had been Catholic and then Anglican under Henry VIII, had headed towards Calvinism and then away from it under the boy king Edward VI, had returned to Rome under Mary, and would now depart from it again under Elizabeth.

Combined with the rationalist implications of the new science, these political and religious switchbacks created confused social and spiritual hybrids with wavering religious convictions. Without faith, what remained was the evidence of the eye, and that reinforced the empirical confidence of the scientist. '*Que sais-je?*' asked Michel de Montaigne, the lawyer son of a Bordeaux Catholic and a Lopez Marrano, and nephew of Calvinist merchants in Antwerp, 'What do I know?' William Shakespeare, whose Hamlet suffers intellectual indigestion from a surfeit of Montaigne, was raised in a Protestant country as the son of a Catholic mother related to a Gunpowder Plotter and a father who hid Catholic tracts in the rafters of the family house. Shakespeare's contemporary Francis Bacon was a thorough product of the new Protestant elite. Like Isaac Newton two generations later, he could only reconcile Protestant theology with the scientific method by bridging the gap with alchemy and mysticism.

Into the gap left by faith there poured a new morality: *politique*, or the imperative of ethnic self-interest. In 1532, Niccolò Machiavelli produced a manual for the politicians of the frightened new world, *The Prince*; in 1561 the Elizabethan Sir Thomas Hoby translated into English a similar handbook, Castiglione's *The Courtier*. The Christendom of the Middle Ages was shattering into nation states, and their needs overrode traditional religious morality and loyalty. In 1570, when news reached London that a Spanish fleet had turned back the Turks at the Battle of Lepanto, celebratory bonfires were lit in the streets. Yet ten years later, when Protestant England needed allies against Catholic Spain, it made common cause with the same Muslim Turks, and used Jews to pass intelligence between London and Constantinople.

The paths of the Jewish dispersion from Iberia had been the shipping lanes of the European economy. In an age of primitive banking, untrustworthy mail and unsafe credit, the extended family networks of the Marranos became a pan-European communications structure, serving espionage and trade alike. Lopez had relatives in the major ports of Europe – Antwerp, Lisbon, Venice and Constantinople – and his prized commercial links could easily be adapted to valuable covert use.

The most lucrative business in Europe was the spice trade, and its biggest outlets were at either end of the Mediterranean. To the east was Constantinople, seat of the Ottoman Empire and major terminus of the overland route; by becoming middlemen between the Turks and their European customers, fourteenth-century Genoa and fifteenth-century Venice became the successive commercial hubs of Europe and imperial powers in the Mediterranean. To the west was Portugal, a fringe nation in Mediterranean affairs, but one whose seat on the edge of the Atlantic became a springboard to empire. In the late fifteenth and early sixteenth centuries, Portuguese sailors pioneered an alternative route to the East that had broken the Turkish monopoly and turned Lisbon into a vast warehouse for 'Indian pepper'. In 1501, the first shipment from Lisbon reached Antwerp, turning the little port on the Scheldt estuary into the clearing house of northern Europe. London, already tied to Antwerp by the wool industry, became its satellite.

The opening of the Indian Ocean and the discovery of the New World of the Americas moved European economic competition away from the Mediterranean basin and on to the high seas. The Portuguese became a global power, swiftly followed by the Spanish, who squandered silver from the mines of South America to build an even greater dominion of their own. The English, peripheral to the Mediterranean heart of affairs since Roman times, now found themselves at the centre of a watery new map of the world. Forced by their religious isolation to seek economic alternatives, and possessed of seamanship honed on the rough North Sea and Atlantic, the Elizabethans joined the race. As international competition moved on to the oceans and into new markets in new continents, the seed of the British Empire was planted in the trading settlements of adventurous merchants.

Roderigo Lopez's world lacked the certainties of the medieval world of faith or the Enlightenment world of science. His was a time of extended transition, relentlessly fluid, turning from the Mediterranean to the Atlantic, a balancing act between medieval and modern, after the Crusades but before imperialism; between feudalism and the nation state, religion and rationalism, the telescope and the microscope. The modern age dawned ambiguously, urgent and blind as the flight of a migrant.

2

A House in Paradise

All idiots, priests, Jews, actors, monks,
barbers and old women think they are physicians.
Medieval Latin proverb

There once lived a merchant of Venice named Ansaldo, and Giannetto was his godson. When Giannetto's friends asked him on a trading expedition to Belmont, he went along. Ansaldo entrusted him with him a cargo of goods to sell when he got there. At Belmont, Giannetto fell in love with the Lady of Belmont. After selling his cargo and loading up for the return journey, he sailed for Venice, but was shipwrecked en route. Although a valuable cargo had been lost, Ansaldo was only relieved that his godson was alive. Realising that Giannetto was in love, Ansaldo spent every ducat he had to equip another ship. Soon, Giannetto returned to Belmont. After eating and drinking heavily, he lay down in the Lady's bed and fell asleep next to her. When he returned to his ship the next morning, he found that the locals had stolen its cargo.

Ansaldo was sanguine about that loss too, but he could not afford any more like it. Giannetto, however, was oblivious. He was besotted with the Lady and could not wait to return to Belmont. To help his cherished godson, Ansaldo borrowed 10,000 ducats from a Jewish moneylender. As he had no credit left, the terms of the loan were that if repayment was not made by St John's Day next, the Jew could take a pound of flesh from whatever part of Ansaldo's body he pleased. After informing Giannetto of these terms, Ansaldo despatched Giannetto to Belmont with a third cargo. Giannetto promised to be back by St John's Day.

When Giannetto got to Belmont, the Lady tested her lover. When it was time for them to retire, the Lady's attendants offered him a cup of wine. One of the ladies in waiting whispered to Giannetto that he should only pretend to drink. So he poured the wine into his shirt, allowing the Lady to believe he had drunk it. He went to bed and pretended to be asleep. When she came to bed he embraced her and they made love all night. In the morning, the Lady announced that they were to be married. After their wedding, Giannetto settled into married life in Belmont and forgot about Ansaldo and the loan.

One day, Giannetto looked out of the palace window to see a group of Belmont craftsmen bearing flaming torches, on their way to make a St John's Day offering. Suddenly he remembered his vow to Ansaldo. Giannetto and the Lady hurried to Venice.

Repayment being overdue, the Jew was suing Ansaldo for a pound of his flesh. Giannetto offered the Jew 20,000 ducats, but the loan shark was adamant: he would be satisfied in court. Ansaldo was saved by the Lady of Belmont. Disguised as a lawyer, she argued in court that the laws of Venice did not allow the Jew to shed a single drop of blood, or to take more or less than an exact pound of flesh. Furious, the Jew tore up his bond. When Giannetto offered the mysterious lawyer payment, he/she refused money, but asked for his wedding band. Tormented but grateful, Giannetto gave away his ring.

Giannetto and Ansaldo sailed to Belmont, unaware that Giannetto's love for his Lady had been tested. Meanwhile, the Lady hurried back before them and shed her legal robes. When the two men arrived at Belmont, she affected anger at Giannetto for losing his ring. Accused of having squandered it on one of his Venetian mistresses, Giannetto burst into tears. Cut to the heart by the authenticity of his passion, she embraced him, showed him the ring and explained that she was the lawyer. The couple were reunited, and lived in happiness and joy all the days of their life. Giannetto made up for letting down Ansaldo by marrying off his godfather to one of the Lady's damsels in waiting.

The model for the plot of *The Merchant of Venice* was an ancient story, with roots in religious tales from Persia and India. This Venetian version of the story also pre-dates Doctor Lopez. It is from Ser Giovanni's *Il Pecorone*, a fourteenth-century collection modelled on another more influential collection, Boccaccio's *Decameron*. Lopez's English contemporaries could have read the story of Ansaldo and Gianetto in an edition of *Il Pecorone* reprinted at Milan in 1558: in the year of Lopez's new beginning in London, the plot of *The Merchant of Venice* reappeared in chrysalis, ready to hatch in the 1590s.

Frontispiece of the 1558 Milan edition of Il Pecorone.

What Lopez did in the three years between 1559 and 1562 is a mystery. By definition, a successful Marrano left no trace, and any archival footprints are evidences of failure. Aided by the anonymity of a new life in a big city, Lopez stepped off the boat and vanished. He reappeared in the early 1560s with a teenage bride and the post of house physician at St Bartholomew's Hospital. Friends had been waiting for him in London, and they had taken care of him.

They lived there secretly. Officially, no Jews lived in England between the violent expulsion of a medieval community in 1290 by Edward I, and Oliver Cromwell's grant of resettlement in 1656. Yet in the intervening period the historical separation between Englishmen and Jews was neither clear nor total. A trickle of Jews passed through England in the later Middle Ages, mostly physicians or pedlars, and after the wrecking of Iberian Jewish life in 1492 and 1497, the trickle became a steady stream. Portuguese Jews took flight on the caravelles plying between Lisbon and Antwerp, and London was a stop on the way. Most refugees went on to Antwerp and beyond, but some stayed in London, forming a small community whose numbers never exceeded one hundred adults. The Lopez name and its Portuguese analogue 'Lopes' were constant threads in that story, and always in connection with the trilogy of medicine, Marranos and Antwerp, as though pre-echoing Roderigo.

'Magister Hernando Lopez is a most distinguished doctor,' a satisfied Henry VIII reported to King Ferdinand of Spain on 20 October 1515. In London, Hernando's career took an alarming tangent. Thirty-five years later, Hernando, 'a Jew born, by report, who should have been burnt in Portugal', was convicted of 'whoredom' – most probably pimping in the stews of Bankside. For his 'naughty lying and devilish practices', lascivious Lopez was paraded through the City's streets on a cart wearing a striped hood and then ejected from England.

By this time, merchant Lopezes were in London as middlemen in the spice trade. After 1512, the pepper business at Antwerp was the monopoly of the Spice Trust, an intermarrying group of Portuguese Marranos headed by the banking brothers Diego and Francisco Mendes. Profits on the distribution of pepper in the London market were used to subsidise the Marrano exodus. By 1540, the London home of a Mendes cousin named Alves Lopes was a stop on an underground railroad linking Portugal, Antwerp and Constantinople. Alves lived 'in the Hebrew manner, though in secret' and used his house as a secret synagogue, where he was joined on the Sabbath 'by other false Christians to the number of about twenty'. Congregants travelled to Southampton and Plymouth, where ships sailing from Portugal to Antwerp docked, and informed any Marranos on board as to whether it was safe to proceed directly to Antwerp, or whether they should disembark, travel overland to London and await passage there. The Lopes house was used as a hostel and clearing house for the refugees, with Alves dispensing Mendes money for their onward journey to Antwerp.

When Roderigo Lopez arrived in London, the twin pillars of the secret community reflected its brief secret history. Dunstan Añes was the Spice Trust's local agent, a member of the Grocers' Company and Grocer to the Queen's household. Doctor Hector Nuñez was equally respectable, a Fellow of the Royal College of Physicians and a businessman specialising in direct import from Spain and Portugal. Between the two of them, they found a place for Roderigo Lopez in London. It was probably Hector Nuñez who introduced Lopez to St Bartholomew's and proposed his election to the College of Physicians.

The Hospital of St Bartholomew the Less sat on an equilateral triangle of land based on the rubbish-filled ditch running along the medieval City wall. At the apex of the triangle was the hospital church, whose square Norman tower gave a northern vista over the orchards of Islington, where Henry VIII had hunted. Turning to the eastern face of the triangle, the viewer looked over a tangle of streets leading to Aldersgate, the breach in the City wall for traffic from the north. Opening before the western face of the triangle was

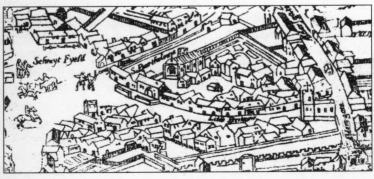

West Smithfield and St. Bartholomew's Hospital in the 1560s.

the counterpoint to medical East Smithfield, the open plain of West Smithfield, London's meat market.

West Smithfield had been London's original stage for public executions, and though the executions had long since moved to Tyburn by the time Doctor Lopez moved in, he worked to their eerie animal counterpoint. Every day a tide of mooing cattle and bleating sheep was driven into the ten acres of open space before the hospital walls. It was penned and tethered, auctioned off to a mob of butchers, and driven around the corner for slaughter in the abattoirs of Newgate Street. From their beds the patients of St Bartholomew's and the prisoners of Newgate Jail heard a daily chorus of protesting animals and bullying butchers' boys, urgent sellers and wrangling buyers, despatching over 600 sheep and fifty bullocks per day. The streets around the hospital were a gastronomic geography of the slaughterhouse district: Chicken Lane, Cock Lane, Duck Lane, Cowcross Lane – where cattle entered West Smithfield – and Pie Corner, where they left it.

In September 1562, 'Ruy de Lopes' was engaged by St Bartholomew's 'for one year from next Christmas in curing, helping and comforting the sick and sore in the House of the Poor'. Lopez was the hospital's first resident physician. Twice a week, he sat in the hospital cloisters and held a surgery for the 'poor, sick and impotent' of the City.

The hospital's outlook was still essentially medieval. Its all-purpose remedy was the Plaster of Bartholomew, a miraculous concoction whose recipe had remained unaltered for 200 years, and when in 1558 the Governors bought soap for Matron, it was for her clothes, not her patients. Several of Lopez's assistants did not pretend to medical expertise: a priest and four chaplains, doubled this duty with shifts at the monument to typhoid that was Newgate Jail. There were also twelve sisters who, though untrained, had picked up functional skills through practice, and a Matron whose duties included ensuring that the sisters stayed in their rooms at night. Lopez's only professional accomplices were a trio of surgeons, who ensured that the standards of butchery pertaining in the shambles of Newgate Street were maintained inside the walls.

The Governors of the hospital were wealthy City aldermen and they took pride in driving a hard bargain. 'Without any salary save his house,' noted the Clerk of the Hospital. St Bartholomew's had a plentiful stock of properties, but most were decrepit. 'Mr Renter' the estate agent reported that many were 'in great decay', some were 'rotten ruinous', and others had been so ransacked by tenants that the remaining furniture barely sufficed the 'three or four harlots then lying in childbed, and no more'. Having economised on Lopez's salary, the Governors skimped on his accommodation.

In January 1561, an intimation of wintry mortality had prompted Lopez's predecessor, Thomas Vicary, to prepare his will. The Governors knew that Vicary was ailing and they wanted to make provision for his wife, Alice. They leased a property to the couple, inspiring the Clerk of the Hospital to add a modest witticism to his minutes, 'Mr Vicary, for a house in Paradise'. Apart from being Mr Vicary's imminent destination, 'Paradise' was the local nickname for Duck Lane, an alley behind the hospital whose houses had once been the refectory and dormitories of a medieval priory. Six months after the Governors paid Vicary this fatal compliment he was dead. The Governors billeted his replacement in the morbid company of Widow Vicary and her husband's legacy of two human skulls, a text-book by 'Guido' – probably the valuable *Cyrurgia* – and an arsenal of souvenirs from his time as a military surgeon: 'two bows, two sheaves of arrows, two bracers, two shooting gloves, two bills, one handgun, and one jack'.

There was no privacy for Lopez among the skulls and armoury of the 'house in Paradise'. Dispensing in the cloisters with Matron and her twelve sisters or resting at home, there was no moment when the alien newcomer was not under observation, when he might relax the mask. Religious observance was conducted elsewhere, in the opposite corner of the City, in Tower and Aldgate Wards, where the Añes and Nuñez families had congregated. The focus of the community was an improvised arrangement in a private home, an echo of Alves Lopes's synagogue-cum-communal office, adapting the standard architecture of an Elizabethan merchant's house to Jewish worship, the rush-strewn hall for the men, the minstrel gallery for the women.

References from cousins in Antwerp, a recognition of professional or personal qualities, a familiarity deepened by the rhythm of the ritual year and the perennial shortage of eligible partners for the community's children all pointed to one conclusion: marriage. In the spring of 1563, within months of his engagement by St Bartholomew's, Lopez married Sara, the teenage daughter of Dunstan Añes, patriarch of the London Marranos. Invisibly he had settled into a new life in a different city, forming the bonds of work and marriage which would support him for the rest of his life.

When Sara Lopez became pregnant, it was time to move. The Governors had profited by the terms of their contract with Lopez and it cost them little to shunt him round the corner to Little Britain, a short street connecting the hospital with West Smithfield. The houses in Little Britain were grander and they had private city gardens, but they were still old and downwind of seamy West Smithfield, where the vagrants gathered around the spitroasts of Pie Corner for 'a meal of steam'. The free 'billets and coals' provided for heating failed to subdue the draughts whistling through the warped boards and crumbling plaster, and Lopez's appearances before the Court of the Hospital became a series of increasingly sour negotiations over improvements to his home.

Lopez was nearly forty years old when Ellen, his first daughter, was born in late December 1563 or early January 1564. When she was baptised in the hospital church, the registrar recorded her father's identity as 'Master Doctor Lopus', using the smooth Anglicisation of his name that would, with variation into a rurally twanging 'Lopas', become standard among his English contemporaries. Ellen was joined by two brothers; Ambrose, baptised on 6 May 1565; and John, who made his sole mark in the world when he left it on 12 December 1567. This third pregnancy and the death of the baby may have affected Sara Lopez's health or her husband's uxorious vigour, as she was not to bear another child for six years.

After five probationary years in the cloisters, in 1567 Lopez succeeded in extracting a token salary of forty shillings from the Governors. The first time he received it, he had to pay most of it back: on 8 December 1567 the Court of the Hospital ordered that

Lopez pay thirty shillings for a deputy to cover for his absence. While his sick new baby John was dying round the corner in Little Britain, Doctor Lopez was away from London, drifting in and out of the hospital as lightly as he drifted in and out of the records.

As well as his medical ability, Lopez's exotic past and family connections had led him into government service. In the late 1560s, the entente that had marked the first Elizabethan decade deteriorated into a cold war. The causes were religion and trade, or rather that Spain insisted on a monopoly of both. A conflict of interests developed. A Protestant England was unacceptable to the passionately Catholic Philip II; it would only be a matter of time before he accepted that Elizabeth's Protestantism was not an aberration, but permanent. To defer a direct confrontation with powerful Philip, the English attempted to tie Spain down in two spheres. On the oceans, the Queen licensed freelance English privateers to hunt for Spanish treasure ships and force themselves into protected Spanish markets; three times in the 1560s, John Hawkins launched trading expeditions which, having bought slaves in the Portuguese entrepôts of the West African coast, carried them across the Atlantic and intimidated the local Spanish governors into buying them. On the Continent, the English offered support and sanctuary to Protestants of all varieties, especially the Huguenots of France and the Calvinists of the Low Countries.

The Low Countries were seventeen small provinces speaking Dutch, Flemish or French, and unified by the prickly independent spirit of the Protestant merchant. They were also the property of Philip II of Spain, who hoped to turn them into a citadel from which he might police Europe. Radical religion collided with excessive taxation and a crude Spanish attitude. In 1566, there were iconoclastic riots in Antwerp, with mobs of Calvinists smashing the icons of the old religion, and there was talk of a Protestant federation between the Low Countries, the Huguenots of France and the Protestant princes of Germany. Philip II responded with an army of 10,000 'blackbeards' under the Duke of Alba, who began a brutal and unsuccessful repression. It was the start of three decades of war.

Apart from its religious implications, war in the Low Countries threatened the English economy. Antwerp was the prime outlet for English wool and, as an ally in Protestantism, it was the only Continental money market willing to lend cash to the English treasury. In a climate of revolt in the Netherlands, English piracy in the Atlantic and the retaliatory impounding of English ships in Spanish ports, mutual suspicion between English and Spanish politicians deepened. The Duke of Alba detected a Jewish conspiracy in London and Antwerp. 'I am told', he warned, 'that some of the Portuguese in Antwerp are in secret league with those of their race in England, to whom they will transfer the spice trade thither, and so encourage the English in their evil intentions. I have no doubt that many of them would like to go thither [England] to live in the law of Moses.'

The English had little more faith in Spanish intentions. By August 1568, and probably earlier, Elizabeth's Principal Secretary, Sir William Cecil, had engaged a thirty-four-year-old lawyer named Francis Walsingham to snoop for Spanish agents among the immigrants in London. After graduating from Gray's Inn, Walsingham had studied at Padua in Italy, where he had contracted the fanatical world-view of Continental Protestantism. For Elizabeth and Cecil he would build an intelligence service in his image: a cruel, labyrinthine creature dedicated in its hatred of Spain and Catholicism. A conspiracist, he saw conspiracy everywhere. His first report warned that the Queen should 'look well to her food, her bedding and other furniture, lest poison be secretly administered'.

With trade and foreign policy already synchronised, it was inevitable that the third component – espionage – should be added. This was where Roderigo Lopez and the London Marranos came in. Tightly knit by secrecy, exile and intermarriage, less than one hundred in number, their horizons were the boundaries of the known world. They were well-educated, with a surfeit of doctors among their ranks. They were well-organised, with communal facilities secreted in their homes and an intelligence system that reached over the borders of Spain and beyond the frontiers of Christendom. And they were well-connected, with family and business links in Lisbon, Antwerp, Hamburg, Salonika, Milan, Genoa and Constantinople.

The trade between these ports already served as a secret Marrano postal system and as a carrier of human traffic. It was simple to use the same network to smuggle propaganda and espionage. It was an open secret at the Court of Queen Elizabeth that London was host to this illicit gaggle of medico-merchant-spies, but their potential in diplomacy, finance and medicine overrode the illegality of their position. Ambition and reward drew Lopez out from behind the walls of St Bartholomew's and into the service of three of the Queen's Privy Councillors: Lord Burghley, Sir Francis Walsingham and the Earl of Leicester.

Lopez entered a Court world that was like the Copernican solar system, its orbits plotted by the gravity of power and patronage. At its heliocentric heart was the Queen. Around her were the major planets, great landowning dynasties like the Howards of Norfolk and the Percys of Northumberland, a densely intertwined cousinhood with finer pedigrees than the Tudors they served. Beyond the planets, the stars: a constellation of new men who, lacking the history and power that made the old families threatening to a new dynasty, found their fate tied to their Queen and her religion as surely as she found herself bound to their support. In the portraits lining the long gallery of Elizabethan memory, it is these new men who dominate, and usually Elizabeth's notorious crew of piratical sailors, the Drake, Hawkins and Raleigh of salty legend, sprung from the minor gentry of the West Country and unleashed on the unsuspecting oceans in a glorious riot of theft, destruction and epic voyages.

Yet among the flashy ruffs, pearled doublets and golden earrings of the sailors, there hang the faces of another less flamboyant class. Their clothes are a Puritan black. Their faces are pale, baggy-eyed from reading by candlelight, alternately puffy or gaunt from the relentless cares of the Renaissance state. They are another variety of new man, which through self-replication became the most adaptive of all political species: the bureaucrat. The Tudor century was a time of transition between the medieval and the modern, as the old feudalism gave way to a society based on the nation state, and this change required its negotiators. Politics was becoming professionalised, the monopoly of one profession in particular. Elizabeth's key Privy Councillors had all trained as lawyers. It was inevitable that a cornucopia as rich as the Elizabethan should have required its cataloguers and overseers, and that a reign so threatened from within by religious strife and from without by imperial envy should have needed its enforcers and strategists. Elizabeth's hold on her throne as an unmarried, excommunicated Protestant owed as much to her civil servants as to the sailors who defended her.

Elizabeth's closest advisers were drawn from recently elevated families. The architect of the Elizabethan State, Sir William Cecil, Lord Burghley, was the son of a Lincolnshire farmer who had served Henry VII. Sir Nicholas Bacon, her first Lord Keeper, was the son of a Suffolk estate official. Courtly Sir Christopher Hatton, who rose to the office of Lord Chancellor, was the son of titleless North-amptonshire gentry. Sir Francis Walsingham, creator of England's first systematic intelligence service, was the grandson of a minor Kentish gentleman whose highest appointment had been that of Sewer Commissioner of the Thames. All of them had risen via the Inns of Court. A Catholic restoration would cost them more than religious liberty; it would be the undoing of their personal ambi-tions. Consequently, they built up a power base through marriage and patronage that imitated the social fortifications of the old fami-lies. Burghley and Nicholas Bacon were brothers-in-law, each having married daughters of the humanist tutor to Edward VI, Sir Anthony Cooke; Walsingham's daughter Frances married the Earl of Leicester's nephew, Sir Philip Sidney, icon of military Protestantism and fashionable poetry.

If Court life was a solar system, then Lopez's niche was beyond the constellated new men, with the *stella nebulae*, the cast of servants and suppliers, entertainers and facilitators. Most benign among the nebulae were the actors. Aristocrats maintained pet companies like horses in a stable, liveried in proprietorial titles such as the Queen's Men or Lord Strange's Men, on hand to elevate seasonal feasts and diplomatic banquets with the Elizabethan stage's giddy mixture of slapstick and slaughter, farce and scholastics.

Less prominent, but more numerous than the actors, were the 'intelligencers': the couriers and spies, the unseen eyes behind the arras. In this colder region of the Elizabethan universe, presided over by the dark star of Sir Francis Walsingham and rarely warmed by the sun of royal favour, the principle of the Renaissance man found its debased corollary, the polymath whose variety was driven by necessity, rather than refinement. For Lopez, serving the national interest was another way to make a living and advance himself in the patronage system.

There was no government budget for a spy service, only occasional royal grants to cover Walsingham's expenses. Apart from a core of professional agents, most of Walsingham's sources were also suppliers of other types of knowledge: sea captains and businessmen, doctors and well-connected immigrants. Their pay, if any, was small. In Elizabethan England, doctor or actor, alchemist or artist, financial survival meant finding a powerful patron.

As an even newer man, Lopez's loyalty was with the new ascendancy. By 1571, he had entered the service of Lord Burghley; an embarrassing note in the Annals of the Royal College of Physicians records that Lopez was directed to return a fee to Burghley, after neglecting the swollen shinbone of one of his Lordship's servants. By then, Lopez also attended upon the spymaster Sir Francis Walsingham.

Shortly after Walsingham had been promoted to the Paris embassy, his health had collapsed due to overwork, kidney stones and his inveterate self-medicating experimentation with 'physic' – pseudo-alchemical potations involving opium and metals. 'My disease grows so dangerously upon me,' he reported, 'as I most humbly desire Her Majesty to take some speedy order for some to supply my place.' Elizabeth sent a new ambassador and Walsingham's physician, Doctor Lopez. Negotiating the Normandy roads in winter, and beset by a seasonal lack of horses, the Doctor arrived in Paris on Tuesday, 21 November 1571.

Lopez found a chaotic scene in the Paris embassy: a prostrate ambassador inducting his replacement from his sickbed, confidential mails from London delayed by the horse shortage, couriers hurrying in the hallways. Walsingham squeezed his consultation with Doctor Lopez between audiences with a courier and a spy. Twenty-two years after he passed Lopez in Walsingham's doorway, the courier, Nicholas Faunt, would assist in Lopez's prosecution. The spy was Captain Thomas Franchiotti, who shared an interest in covert Spanish activities in London with Doctors Nuñez and Lopez, and had been the source of Walsingham's 1568 report of Spanish poison plots against the Queen. Lopez was now a fixture of the ambiguous, espionage-soaked circle around Sir Francis Walsingham.

The physicians patched up Walsingham over the winter, and Lopez exchanged Parisian glamour for the sores and fractures of the London poor. He was back by March 1572, but once again he disappeared to Antwerp. This time, his name appears on a list of investors in the pepper trade; he bought four *amas de servuesa*, just over half a ton of spices.

The roll of Lopez's fellow speculators is an inventory of Marrano intrigue. Roderigo and his brother Luis, an occasional courier for the English government, were joined by their cousins Diego and Jeronimo Lopez Soiero; Diego ran a secret synagogue in Antwerp, while Jeronimo, like Roderigo, floated back and forth across the Channel on a government passport. The Nuñez family was also represented. There were the merchant brothers Estevan and Bernaldo Nuñez, who hid secret letters in their bales of dry goods; and Doctor Hector's notorious brother-in-law, the daredevil agent provocateur Bernaldo Luis. There was also Roderigo Lopez's distant relative Alvaro Mendes, who would shortly flee to Constantinople, revert to Judaism and become an intimate adviser to the Ottoman Sultan. From there, he and his Lopez kinsmen in London and Antwerp would correspond and plot across the breadth of Europe.

Lopez now had two masters, the Court and the City. Through the 1570s he tacked between the two, usually at the expense of St Bartholomew's. Having powerful new patrons gave him influence over his old employers, and he used it to intensify his campaign of home improvements. First, he persuaded the Court of the Hospital to board his draughty hall with deal panelling, then his parlour. Next, he replaced his rotten garden fence with planks from their stores, before crowning his renovations by retiling the roof. While these works were taking place, he continued to flit between the hospital, the Court, and Secretary Walsingham's house at Barn Elms, west of London near Richmond Palace.

'I am at my own house, under the hands of the physicians, of whom I hope shortly to be rid,' complained Walsingham, while Lopez prepared to bleed him again.

'Doctor Lopez shall be the more painful in looking to the poor,' the Court of the Hospital reminded their wayward physician after another of his brazen demands for free building materials.

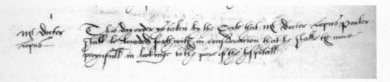

5 November 1575: Lopez is promised that his parlour will be reboarded, but only if he is 'more painful in looking to the poor'.

'I have an indisposition in my body,' came the cry from Barn Elms two weeks later, and off went Lopez, even though the carpenters were still at work on his new parlour.

If ambition was not enough of a motivation, the rapid expansion of Lopez's family impelled him to take private patients. After six barren years, in the decade after 1573 Roderigo and Sara Lopez presented the vicar of the hospital church with a barrage of new infants for baptism. Many died in infancy: from at least nine live births, the adult aggregate of the Lopez brood would stand at three daughters and two sons.

By the end of the 1570s, Lopez's combination of medicine and espionage had carried him to the top of his profession. He now completed his triumvirate of Privy Council patrons by ministering to a more controversial patient, the Earl of Leicester.

No courtier better exemplified the uneasy Elizabethan mixture of repressed old and assertive new than Robert Dudley, Earl of Leicester. The most powerful nobleman of the age, he was the grandson of Henry VII's finance minister. Fascinated by the Machiavellian model of politics, he studied law at the Inner Temple. Ambitious for the

highest place of all – that of royal consort – he engaged in an elaborate courtship of the Queen, but persisted in conducting further
furtive romances. Wealthy and ostentatious, but a convinced Puritan;
cultured and humanist, but an accomplished manipulator of the
levers of state, Robert Dudley was a living contradiction, a volatile
mirror image of a shifting age.

To his Catholic enemies he was the wickedness of Protestant
England personified. A scandalous Jesuit pamphlet of 1584, *Leicester's
Commonwealth*, accuses him of greed, cowardice, conspiracy, irreli-
gion, and being 'extremely hated in Wales', as well as 'Murder . . .
in secret, committed upon divers occasions at divers times, in sundry
persons, of different calling in both sexes, by most variable means
of killing, poisoning, charming, enchanting, conjuring and the like'.
His assistants in this homicidal programme were named as the
Queen's physician, Doctor Bailey, who advised on the administering
of slow poison; the alchemist John Dee, practitioner of the black
arts of 'Figuring and Conjuring'; two physicians, 'Julio the Italian
and Lopas the Jew', whose specialities were 'Poisoning' and 'the art
of destroying children in women's bellies'; and Messrs Verney and
Digby who, when not assisting with 'Murdering', provided the Earl
with 'Bawds'.

The maintenance of the Earl's sagging libido was another of his
doctors' tasks. Despite 'a broke belly on both sides of his bowels'
and recurrent malaria the ageing Leicester was 'more libidinous'
than ever and in order to 'move his flesh at all times', he swigged
an 'Italian ointment'. One of 'his Physicians' quipped that the Earl
kept a full supply of his love potion at hand and that, instead of a
pillow, he 'had a bottle for his bedhead, of £10 the pint'.

This might be the real substance of the *Commonwealth*: that
Leicester was a cruel and ambitious courtier, who acquired mistresses
from his fellow aristocrats with the same devotion with which he
amassed carpets from Turkey, portraits from France and skilled
servants from the professions. Greedy but well-educated and progres-
sive, he was enormously wealthy and used his position in the Queen's
trust to press aggressively for a Protestant crusade against the
Spanish. These were good enough reasons for a Jesuit propagan-

dist to fear and hate him. The allegations of murder were an extension of his political cynicism to its logical ends, but there is no real evidence to suggest that he commissioned anything more from his doctors than abortions, purges and pints of love philtre to 'make dead flesh arise'.

So Doctor Lopez's work for the Earl of Leicester was the routine of a rich roué's physician: curing his festal hangovers with purgatives, assisting his love-making with a pinch of cantharides, easing his regular malarial relapses with bloodletting; scenting, flattering and stirring the inflated ego of a hard-living, middle-aged aristocrat. But also supplying snippets of news from Antwerp or Lisbon or Constantinople, stoking the fire of English militarism, and skimming contracts to supply the English army in Ireland with wheat.

'All rising to great place is by a winding stair,' wrote Francis Bacon. Step by step, Lopez worked his way up, maintaining the health of the body politic and the bodies political, his steps patterned on kidney stones and neuralgia, and geared to the stately decline of Anglo-Spanish relations. The higher he rose, the further he saw. On 9 May 1579, he took time from his busy schedule to ask the Court of the Hospital if he 'might let his house to another man'. The dung and gore of West Smithfield had lost their charm. He wanted 'better air', suitable for inhalation by a rising man and his young children. Hiring a deputy to handle his charity cases, Lopez

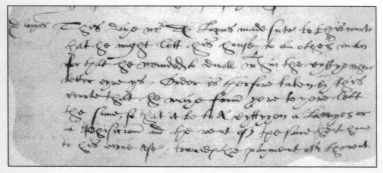

'This day Mr. Doctor Lopus made suit to this court that he might let his house to another man, for that he wanted to dwell in the City, where better air is.'

moved his family to fashionable Wood Street in the City.

Roderigo Lopez Gallo, the immigrant doctor, had morphosed into Roger Lopas the society physician, importer of spice and intelligence. He had built a new existence on the ruins of his old life, and the scars of the past were covered by a fractionated gloss like the varnish on an oil portrait, its surface cracked into jagged panels. Luxurious obscurity beckoned. He might have achieved it, had it not been for the apparition of a ghost from Crato.

3
The Lord Ambassador

A sovereign should always regard an ambassador as a spy.

The Hitopadesa, III, c.50 CE

Don Antonio, Prior of Crato and King of Portugal.

I n his portrait Don Antonio waits on a balcony, proud in his armour. A squat, muscular man with a strong jawline hedged with black beard, his dark eyes are lambent with purpose and his chest swells in martial glory, assisted by a steel breastplate and a ruff the size of a dinner plate. Half-soldier, half-cleric, his right hand toys with a royal medallion as his left grips his Prior's staff; his elbow almost rests on the top of his crown. Behind him is the ocean, on whose storm-racked waves warships pitch with billowed sails. Though the sky is dark with storm clouds and lightning strikes the black water, he is resolute: he will return to Portugal, his by right and force. A slight ripple on his forehead, the hint of a raised right eyebrow, and the lips almost curling into a smile beneath the fronds of his goatee suggest ironic detachment. Sceptical as Montaigne, he is used to the vagaries of fate and rides them out like an experienced mariner.

The artist has placed Antonio in two places – two states – at once. Waiting to board his flagship, Antonio is determined; in the struggle of his ships against cosmic forces we see his resolution in effect. At the same time as the exile prepares for battle on the shore, the returnee sails in conquest on the water. There is a difference between these two states. Antonio on the shore is a concrete figure, the Prior of Crato and the heir to the House of Avis, acknowledged as a king in exile by the Courts of England and France. Antonio at sea is as fluid as water, prospecting for the path of least resistance, a hypothesis of kingship who had ruled for a few weeks and then spent the rest of his life trying to return to that state.

Just after Antonio took the crown in 1580, his forces were routed outside Lisbon by the Spanish. He fled to the hills for a brief guerrilla war and then became a fugitive. Hiding in safe houses – 'he was hidden for three days in a tavern' – and chased through olive groves by Spanish horsemen, Antonio, his adviser Diego de Botello and the Bishop of Guardia attempted to escape from Portugal. One night on a road near Lisbon the trio became a duo when, after diving into the bushes to avoid meeting other travellers, Antonio and Botello lost the Bishop in the shrubbery. In January 1581, Antonio slipped from the port of Bayona, credibly disguised as a man 'in great want of money', but carrying the Portuguese crown jewels. He washed up on the coast of Brittany, joined by other Avis loyalists, all 'in very bad case, and without a *real*'.

Possessed of a gracious manner and a slew of bastards 'by base women, most of them by New Christians', Antonio's generosity was unaffected by his new poverty. Dissolute and feckless, he dispensed other people's money as wildly as he had wasted his own. To Antonio kingship was a right and dissipation was its prerogative. He was similarly dutiful in his religious offices and always travelled with his clerical paraphernalia. Between masses he passed the *longueurs* of exile by composing his own translation of the Psalms, somewhat heavier on remorse than the original.

To the English and the French, his claim was a political tool to be used according to their needs, and the privileges he could grant as a crowned monarch were the price of their hospitality. Strategists in both London and Paris saw the danger in Spain absorbing Portugal and its empire unopposed. 'If King Philip had Portugal in quiet, and their East Indies with his West Indies, he might (as with his arms) embrace and crush the world.' Conversely, if Portugal was not 'quiet', Philip might be diverted from global supremacy. His troops were already tied down in the Netherlands. They would be stretched further by an insurgency in his Iberian backyard.

If the English and French acknowledged Antonio as King of Portugal, he could grant them trading concessions in his colonies. The spice markets of Goa, the slave markets of West Africa and the silver mines of Brazil would be opened, and every profit for English or French merchants would be a loss to Philip II. That Antonio ruled only in the distant, mid-Atlantic Azores meant little. He was a pawn, a speck of a ship on the wide ocean. His patrons were more interested in money than justice, and his protestations of legality were the perfect fig leaf for their *politique* and mercantile opportunism. Strength was the momentum of the wind in his sails, but his course was in the teeth of the wind. Antonio sought sanctuary in England.

When Roderigo Lopez heard that his childhood companion had arrived in London, he was presented with irresistible temptations. Lopez saw grander economic and political opportunities in Antonio:

a monopoly instead of a slice of the market, and restoration instead of rebellion. The Spice Trust in Antwerp had a long history of economic co-operation with the House of Avis. They were partners in monopoly: every year, when the merchantmen brought East Indies spice to Lisbon, the cargoes were sold to the King of Portugal and he sold them on to the highest bidders. If this trade passed into the hands of Philip II, they would lose their monopoly and the power it gave them in Antwerp. In purely economic terms, the Portuguese exiles of London and Antwerp were natural agents for Antonio's cause: the greater his success, the greater their profit.

Lopez had sentimental reasons too. Marrano hopes were pinned on Don Antonio as their man, in more than one sense. Spanish control over Portugal meant greater power for the Inquisition and the further crushing of any hopes of return. Antonio was the only claimant to the Portuguese throne who might be expected to pursue a policy independent of Spain. Although he was the Prior of Crato, he was also the part-Jewish son of 'The White Pelican', and when he shed his clerical regalia, he preferred his mistresses to be New Christians. He was sympathetic to crypto-Jews. If he was returned to his throne by non-Catholic powers and funded by non-Catholic bankers in Antwerp, his policies would reflect the interests of his investors. Portuguese Jews and English merchants would benefit.

Roderigo Lopez was in both of these categories and, as an agent of Leicester and Walsingham, he had access to the Privy Councillors most sympathetic to Antonio. Antonio needed a well-connected, trustworthy representative in England, and Lopez was his best choice. The Doctor became Antonio's English ambassador, an emissary from a presumed kingdom, an accidental parodist of diplomacy. In August 1580, Lopez went to Walsingham at Barn Elms with Antonio's offer: complete loyalty for total support. The secretary and the ambassador cooked up a shopping list for an invasion: a dozen warships, 2000 arquebusiers, 1000 quintals of gunpowder, 2000 quintals of cannonballs and 'as much bronze ordnance' as the Queen could spare. Funds would be offered by 'the Antwerp merchants' and further payment would come from the loot of Portugal, 'in coin, jewels, or specie, as the Queen shall please'. Then they sent it to

Leicester, who would sponsor the scheme to the Queen and Privy Council.

'I pray you herein to show yourself a true Portuguese,' Lopez begged Leicester, 'and I promise to be not only, as I am, your doctor and servant, but your slave.' He also promised that Portugal under Antonio would be 'ever devoted with all its might to the service of this realm'.

The following night, Lopez's proposal was discussed over dinner at Leicester House. To remind Leicester of Antonio's commercial potential, he was given some of the Portuguese crown jewels, 'among the best of them a diamond, a belt and collar'.

Lopez and Walsingham had convinced Leicester, but they could not sway the Queen and Lord Burghley. The difference was not the analysis, but its response. It was clear that England and Spain were drifting towards war. Leicester and Walsingham considered open hostilities to be inevitable and therefore best initiated pre-emptively on English terms. The Queen and Burghley hoped that war might be delayed or even averted by playing for time, entangling the Spanish giant with minor irritations while maintaining diplomatic contact. The Portuguese proposal offered the most extreme scenario of all: a land war with Spain, on Philip's doorstep. There was no guarantee apart from Ambassador Lopez's promises that the Portuguese would welcome Don Antonio, or that the English army would be able to maintain its extended maritime supply lines. It was a recipe for division in the Privy Council, and an unwinnable war.

A typically Elizabethan compromise was reached. Elizabeth sent Antonio a letter, drafted by Walsingham, that recognised him as the King of Portugal. This allowed the Privy Council to make money from the trading licences that Antonio dispensed in return. Within weeks, Antonio's supporters in the Azores were loading 2000 quintals of woad on to the *White Falcon*, with the intention of selling the goods in London or Antwerp to raise munitions for Antonio. Further expeditions were financed in a deal brokered by Leicester and Burghley, who arranged the pawning £12,000 worth of Antonio's jewels to 'the richest aldermen and merchants of London'. Antonio's hosts were determined to make a profit from him, whether in the Azores or in the City.

This was a triumph for Lopez. Almost overnight, the Doctor had become a diplomatic playmaker. As the international situation ripened and relations with Spain worsened, ambition and opportunism dovetailed with patriotism. The old physician possessed charm enough to convince Privy Councillors of their interest, and vision enough to ensure his own profit. A cosmopolitan in an age of monolithic nationalism, he balanced Portuguese and English interests as easily as he moved between languages. The double identity that might have made the English suspicious of him was now a source of confidence.

But Lopez could not convince the Queen and Lord Burghley that Don Antonio represented anything more than a commercial opportunity. After a year in London, Antonio realised that his English friends preferred fleecing him for his jewels to restoring him to his throne. While the English offered only fine words and a hungry eye on the Azores, the French offered a fleet that would claim the islands for Antonio, so he decided to move to Paris. But his hosts did not want to lose their asset. In the first week of September 1581, a surprised Spanish spy observed Antonio starting out 'booted and spurred after dinner, with all his Portuguese, hastily putting his baggage into a boat', and setting out 'to take leave of the Queen'. She talked him round 'tenderly', so that he missed the ebb tide. That night, she sent Lord Admiral Howard and Sir Philip Sidney to flatter Antonio further, and in case he resisted their charm, she ordered that no ships be allowed to leave English ports. Naturally, diplomatic vessels were exempt. Just over a week later, Antonio boarded the French ambassador's barge at the Strand, and its oarsmen rowed for Gravesend. As he was smuggled past the palace at Greenwich, a party cast off from the shore to intercept him. Sir Philip Sidney and Doctor Lopez drew alongside and boarded the barge with an appeal from the Queen. But Antonio was already in French hands, and nothing could be done that would not cause offence. To save face, the Queen provided 'a coach and four Hungarian horses' to take him to Dover. Lopez's ticket to power fluttered from his fingers and away to Paris.

In the habit of exile politics, Antonio's camp now devoted itself to factional squabbling. Most of his Court followed him to Paris, leaving Ambassador Lopez on a limb in London at the head of a smaller faction. Accusations of treachery were slung between the capitals. When William Wade, Clerk of the Privy Council, went to Paris with 'letters for the King from Doctor Lopez', he was humiliated before Don Antonio. The King's advisers said that Wade should be ignored, as 'doubtless Lopez was an Englishman' and 'would depend more to their side than to Portugal'. Lopez, a Jew in Portugal and a Portingall in London, was now an Englishman in Paris.

The Paris faction had exaggerated, but not by much. Lopez 'depended' more to Portugal than England or France, but he also depended more to England than France. Although the two countries shared an interest in obstructing Spain, they were rivals. Lopez served the English interpretation of Antonio's interest, not the French interpretation or Antonio's own, and the Doctor never forgot self-interest. While the French prepared a war fleet for the Azores, Lopez organised a joint-stock expedition to the islands with Sir Henry Cobham, Sir Francis Drake and Sir John Hawkins. While Don Antonio worked with the French, Lopez maintained a complementary policy in London.

And while Lopez served Antonio, he also served his English patrons. Through Lopez, Sir Francis Walsingham could follow Portuguese exile politics and French Court politics, and keep track of Spanish agents in London. One of the techniques of the new art of intelligencing was 'projecting', where an agent provocateur feigned sympathy in order to draw out an enemy agent. This was dangerous work in low company and it involved leaving a trail of treasonable statements. In an age when merely to think of treason was a capital crime, a Privy Councillor could not afford the risk of direct contact with his sources. But a Portingall immigrant of ambiguous nation and faith could pass between the Court and the espionage underworld, fluent in both vernaculars. And Walsingham, who placed his health in Lopez's hands, had a patient's trust in Lopez.

Lopez also served as a diplomatic lightning conductor, to dignify England's piratical trade policies. In December 1581, a cargo of 'sugar, ginger, and other merchandise' from the rebels of the Azores arrived at Lyme. Claiming that the goods belonged to Philip II, the Spanish ambassador, Bernadino de Mendoza, obtained a 'stop' from the Court of Admiralty. Pending the resolution of the case, the Queen ordered that the impounded goods be held 'in the name of Doctor Lopez'. Leicester and Walsingham then secretly lifted the embargo, and 20,000 crowns' worth of spices were sold on the London market, to Don Antonio's profit and Mendoza's fury.

As tensions with Spain rose, information became more valuable and Lopez made himself the centre of an espionage network. Its skeleton was the sea lanes, and its vehicle was the cargo carried upon them, interweaving an almost invisible thread of espionage into the broad cloth of business and communal life. Lopez enlisted his Añes in-laws, his Lopez cousins and his Nuñez friends as spies for Walsingham, and their intelligences poured into Barn Elms from all over Europe. All Portuguese roads led to the Doctor's door.

There was the Nuñez family: Doctor Hector, whose peppermint cordials calmed the anxious digestion of Lord Burghley and who, when asked why he did not minister to the Queen, replied, 'I would rather be free'; Hector's uncle Doctor Henrique, who transcribed a smuggled copy of the Marrano classic *A Consolation for the Tribulation of Israel* and passed it around the community; and Hector's brother-in-law Bernaldo Luis, who went to Madrid for Walsingham, was arrested, but talked his way out of the lion's den.

There was the Añes family: venerable Dunstan, spicing the Queen's supper with cinnamon from Calcutta and snippets from Antwerp, and his four sons: Jacob, the family agent at Lisbon, operating under the nose of the enemy; Benjamin, who went to the Azores for Walsingham and came back alive; William, who went to Spain for Walsingham and nearly died in a prison cell; and little Erasmus, apprenticed as a boy to the Court musician Augustine Bassano, a Venetian Jew whose sultry daughter Emilia wrote secret poetry and became a candidate for the 'dark lady' of Shakespeare's sonnets.

Beyond the inner circle, an interleaved group of sympathisers: the wealthy merchant Francisco Pinto and his partner Antonio da Costa;

Peter Lopo, the Venetian musician, and Karen, his wife from Antwerp; the Fernandes brothers, international businessmen with a sideline in spying; and, further out on the fringes of respectability, the *ménage à trois* that was Francis Alvarez and his African servants Gratia and Elizabeth Negro, frequenters of the English Church.

And then there was the Lopez family. In Antwerp, Roderigo's cousin Diego Lopez Soiero slipped intelligences into the 'ordinary post', the bundle of merchants' letters passed to departing ships as they left the port. In London, Diego's brother Jeronimo Lopez Soiero threshed the wheat of intelligence from the chaff of commerce and then forwarded Diego's mails to Roderigo. The same system was used in the reverse direction, to connect Walsingham and Leicester with the rebels and financiers of the Low Countries. Jeronimo, older, wiser and wealthier than Roderigo, with a counting house near the Tower and the luxury of a 'blackamoor' servant, was an adept projector.

Posing as a disaffected follower of Don Antonio, Jeronimo Lopez insinuated himself into the trust of Don Bernadino de Mendoza. When Jeronimo offered to send Spanish intelligence by the 'ordinary post' under the cover of his business dealings, Mendoza accepted. Before the mails reached Dover, Jeronimo and Roderigo Lopez had prised them open, copied them for Secretary Walsingham, and resealed them for delivery. This allowed Walsingham to discover Mendoza's sources in London and 'turn' them back to English service as double agents. And because of the four- to six-week journey of mail between London and Madrid, and the equivalent time taken by Philip II's instructions to reach London, it gave the English a telling advantage in the intelligence war.

Mails from Paris came via Calais, where the shop of the jeweller-merchant Bernardo Nuñez was used as a mail drop and meeting point. Mails from Spain came via Doctor Hector Nuñez, whose channel was used in the mid-1580s by Lord Burghley to sound out the possibility of peace with Philip II. All three of the Añes, Lopez and Nuñez families had relatives in the eastern Mediterranean, in Venice, Genoa, Salonika and Constantinople, where the chief adviser to Sultan Murad III was a Jew named Joseph Nasi, Duke of Naxos.

Constantinople was crucial. If Turkey allied with Spain, Spanish ships would control the Mediterranean, and Spanish soldiers could be concentrated against England and the Low Countries. If Turkey leant towards England, Philip II would have to maintain a garrison and a fleet in the Mediterranean, and his forces would be split between the northern and southern theatres. In 1579, Philip's Protestant and Muslim enemies made common cause against him. Turkey would divert Philip's forces, intelligence would be shared between the Courts of London and Constantinople, and trade would be opened. The following year the Levant Company was founded for the purpose, funded by City merchants and the speculators of the City and Privy Council. To protect their interests, they despatched an ambassador to the barbarian court.

The Pope had decreed that any Catholic who sold the infidel goods which had military applications would be excommunicated. The Levant Company stepped in, exporting English leather and tin, the latter essential for the smelting of cannon. In return, Constantinople offered spices via the overland route from Asia. Philip II now controlled the Portuguese pepper trade; the Ottoman loophole allowed English merchants to break the Spanish monopoly without piracy or subterfuge. The deal between the English Queen and the Ottoman Sultan declared a shared interest but fell short of full alliance. It was *politique* of the crudest kind and an affront to (Catholic) Christendom; the English had allied with their fellow heretics in Constantinople. It was an alliance sustained via the cousins Roderigo Lopez in London and Alvaro Mendes in Constantinople.

Roderigo Lopez and Alvaro Mendes were related twice over by a double threads of Marrano intermarriage in Antwerp. Alvaro was related to the banking Mendes brothers, and Roderigo was related to the Lopez Gallos. The two prominent Antwerp families had intermarried; the link had been confirmed by the union of Alvaro's sister Esther and Roderigo's cousin Diego Lopez Soeiro, brother of Jeronimo the merchant-spy. Alvaro Mendes and Roderigo Lopez were in same generation of an extended Marrano family, 'cousins' by sympathy if not blood. Alvaro was also a cousin to Don Antonio; both their mothers were Gomezes. In the elaborate genealogy of

Marranism, Doctor Lopez could claim kinship with Don Antonio – Lopez's cousin's wife's brother was Don Antonio's cousin.

Trained as a goldsmith, Alvaro Mendes had become a diamond expert after his Mendes uncles sent him to the diamond mines of India in 1545. He had returned ten years later with a fortune that launched a virtuoso, vagabond career. Mendes was a constant Marrano intriguer: adviser to King João III of Portugal; freelance diplomat in Madrid and Florence; adviser to Catherine de Medici, the French Queen Mother; Parisian host of Don Antonio; merchant of Venice, Antwerp, Lyons and London. After floating around Europe for more than twenty years, he reached Salonika in 1585, where he reverted to Judaism under the name Solomon Abenaish. Moving on to Constantinople, he assumed his final incarnation as an adviser to Sultan Murad III, who added the titles of Duke of Metilli, Grand Commissary of the Court and Lord of Tiberias to Mendes' collection. The ships of the Levant Company carried the correspondence of Doctor Lopez and Alvaro Mendes in their cargoes of Turkish spices.

Signature of Alvaro Mendes, using the name Don Solomon Abenaish, from a letter written to Elizabeth I in 1592.

Yet smuggled mails and the ordinary post were leaky methods. The most sensitive or urgent intelligence was carried not on parchment but in the human memory, where it was less visible than onion water or lemon juice, and more obscure than code or cipher. It was dangerous work. When Lopez's brother Luis couriered between London and Paris in the winter of 1581, he had to dodge marauding gangs of deserting soldiers in the Normandy countryside. Spanish surveillance of the 'fickle Portuguese' was intense and funded by a constant supply of South American silver. When William Añes went to Spain with his cargo of wheat, he raced against a letter from Mendoza which detailed his mission and supplied a description to ease his arrest: 'He is a young fellow of twenty, well built, with a fair and handsome face and a small fair beard.' The letter reached Spain in time, and William was captured.

In the spring of 1583, Lopez conducted his own undercover mission. Don Antonio had raised a French-sponsored fleet for the Azores, and Walsingham sent Lopez across the Channel to co-ordinate the English contribution to the venture, which was ready to sail from Plymouth. On 13 March 1583, Lopez docked at Dieppe, a letter from the Secretary hidden on his person. He went on to Rouen and spent ten days there with Antonio. Before Antonio sailed, he gave his reply, so sensitive that he did not write it down. 'You will know from the Doctor the state of my affairs, and my resolution therein,' he wrote in a covering note. When the second French fleet met with as little success as the first, Antonio accepted Walsingham's offer. His 'resolution' was to move to London. It had taken four years for Antonio to tire of Paris, and less for Paris to tire of Antonio. Lopez was waiting for him.

'Pardon me if I am tedious to you,' Lopez genuflected to Walsingham in his best Italian, 'for I can do no less, your Lordship being the person who has always aided and favoured me, through your courtesy and not through my deserts.'

This was courtly flummery, in language and sentiment. Walsingham's 'aid and favour' were bought with nuggets of information: medical, political and financial. The reimbursements were precisely weighted according to value, and the account was never paid in cash. Just as the Queen gave grants and gifts to Walsingham for his work, so in turn the Secretary disbursed patronage to Lopez and his casual army of spies. The Doctor became a familiar figure on the fringes of the Court, a hissing, sibilant accent whispering in the shadows, grey-bearded and worldly.

A circle of mutual backscratchers had formed, motivated by trade and politics. Antonio's supporters among the militant Calvinists and crypto-Jews of Antwerp were also lenders of cash and importers of spices. English privateers who harassed Spanish shipping under licence from Elizabeth or Don Antonio added silver to the English treasury while they stretched the patience and infrastructure of Spanish power. The Privy Council were rarely impartial. They were also speculators, and they eyed their investments as keenly as they protected the national interest. The Portuguese exiles shared a common interest with the English, and Lopez was the pivot between their agendas. The Queen could lodge disputed goods in his name, so that the Privy Council and the Antwerp merchants might benefit from their sale. When Antonio sailed for the Azores for the second time, Lopez could ensure that the status of English traders in the islands would not be affected if they fell under French control.

The Doctor had profited from the English flirtation with Antonio, but he suffered from its fallout. William Wade, Clerk of the Privy Council, had been humiliated in Paris because of the feud between the Portingall factions in London and Paris. A 1581 venture cooked up by Lopez and Sir Francis Drake had lost £1000 for Sir Henry Cobham, the ambassador to Paris. And the Governors of St Bartholomew's were left short-staffed. When their physician was there at all, he was conceited, standing on the shaky dignity of his pseudo-diplomatic status. He insisted on being referred to as the 'Lord Ambassador', a rank somewhat higher than that of Governor of the Hospital. Vanity was its own reward.

Lopez the Lord Ambassador was not Lopez the physician to the poor: the needy immigrant had become an unmanageable courtier. The Governors had pared his wage at every turn, and now he revenged himself on them with equal pettiness, ending his time at the hospital on a magisterially bitter note. The Governors had engaged a replacement, Doctor William Turner, and groomed him for Lopez's departure. This took longer in coming than they hoped. Eight months after Lopez had grandly requested 'better air', he was still in Little Britain. Two years after that, when Doctor Turner had long since taken over Lopez's duties, Lopez remained in the house that was meant to be Turner's salary. The Governors gave him three weeks' notice, but three months later he was still there. A 'destitute' Doctor Turner appealed to the court, who issued another demand, but it took nearly six months for Turner to obtain the key to his house. When he finally entered the house in paradise, he found that the Lopez family had stripped it, leaving it as bare as they had found it.

On the upward spiral of the winding stair, Lopez did not care on whose shoulders he climbed, but his cruder steps did not go unheard: Wade humiliated, Cobham gulled, the Governors insulted. He was protected by his patrons, but outside the shade cast by powerful masters, the climate was unforgiving to speculator and social climber alike. Stephen Gosson, a failed playwright turned Puritan critic, had recently written *The School of Abuse*. Scanning the debauched London stage for work of moral merit, Gosson approved of only two plays. Both foreshadow Lopez's twin fates, historical and literary.

> *The Jew* and *Ptolemy*, shown at the Bull, the one representing the greed-iness of wordly choosers, and bloody minds of Usurers; the other very lively describing how seditious states, with their own devises, false friends, with their own swords, and rebellious commons, in their own snares are overthrown.

But Lopez felt protected, diplomatically immune. Now, he had the greatest patron of all. On 3 October 1581, he became more than Lopez the mere Lord Ambassador.

> Grant for life to Roger Lopius, MD, of the office of Physician to the Queen and her Household, from the death of Julius Borgarutius, the last holder; with an annuity of £50, payable at the Exchequer.

'Julius Borgarutius' was 'Doctor Julio', the royal doctor named in *Leicester's Commonwealth* as Lopez's fellow abortionist. Slander being a peculiar accolade of medical success, Lopez had reached the heights. The higher he climbed, the greater the distortion of his name – from 'Ruy de Lopes' to 'Roderigo Lopus' to 'Roger Lopius' – as though each upward step was a further development of his invented persona.

Meanwhile, the crumbs of reward dropped from the table: the £50 annual payment from the Exchequer; leases on properties in the City of London; shares in joint-stock fleets headed by Sir Francis

Drake; shares in ventures cobbled together in London or Antwerp in the name of Don Antonio, a free Portugal, and free markets; commissions for distributing imports, commissions on commissions, interest on loans; the same bale unlocking rewards for the spices and the letters it contained, the multifarious perplexity of Elizabethan commerce opening before him like a New World. And in June 1584, the stamp of favour, of proximity to power: a monopoly, or tax-farming concession, whose holder paid heavy customs duties on the bulk import of goods and was then entitled to sell them for further distribution, thus making a profit.

Lopez was already a regular visitor to the Customs House by the Tower, haggling with the officers who were only following orders from the Privy Council when they impounded the latest Spanish prize, paying duties on Don Antonio's goods, meeting couriers off the boat from Antwerp, Calais or Dieppe. Now he arrived there less as adversary than as partner, holder of the aniseed and sumach monopoly.

Aniseed and sumach – a dark-blue plant dye – were both imported to London from Turkey. They were luxurious by-products of the Anglo-Turkish entente. It was apt that the Doctor, midwife of the supply, should be the monopolist of its distribution. Further varieties of payment and commission, proxy and service. By rewarding Lopez with a monopoly, the Queen saved cash; just as he had generated his use, he must generate his payment. By dealing with the 'rene-gade' Turk via their Court Jew, the Privy Council dodged the papal charge of unchristian behaviour. And by trading with Alvaro Mendes they obtained espionage about the eastern Mediterranean.

The value of information rose as Anglo-Spanish relations declined, and Lopez was an informational node. As the cold war with Spain heated up, his contacts became more and more valuable. In October and November 1585, Lopez's smart new house in Wood Street was the scene of four secret meetings between Elizabeth and Don Antonio.

With an English army under the Earl of Leicester now fighting the Spanish in the Netherlands, Antonio's value as an antagonist and a diversion had soared. To keep him in London, he had to be pampered. Elizabeth gave Antonio money – '1000 or 2000 crowns a time' – dressed his household 'in London cloth', fed them 'on beef and beer', and at Christmas gave his sons 'a great quantity of silk and cloth of gold'. But the romance soured as Antonio realised that he was a card to be held, not played. Elizabeth was wary of the proxy war in the Netherlands, and she could not afford a second involvement in Portugal. Antonio would have to wait.

Antonio took his sidelining with regal bad grace, and sank back into his usual round of over-indulgence and extravagance. By summer 1586 he was lodged in a less grand setting in London, 'needy and in want of money', and by November he had been shunted to an ex-monastery at Eton, near Windsor Castle, but far from Elizabeth's mind. The Portuguese King emitted bitter complaints that he could not maintain his household. The English Queen replied that he 'should not burden himself with so many people, as she could not feed them'.

Antonio was riding the current of events, but pushing against English policy. Lopez had provided Antonio with the assurances of Walsingham, Leicester and Drake – who blustered that he 'would either place him in Portugal, or lose his life in the attempt' – but Elizabeth and Burghley were more cautious. The Netherlands campaign had become bogged down in winter mud. It was expensive and it threatened to spill into a general European war. While Leicester fought, Burghley negotiated secretly with the Spanish. Using Doctor Hector's factors – Jeronimo Pardo in Lisbon and Bernaldo Luis in Madrid – as channels, Burghley sounded out whether the Spanish would consider negotiation. Although both sides addressed the question with profound bad faith – Pardo's runs to Spain gathered more espionage than they did Spanish letters – the mere mention of peace talks was enough to terrify Antonio.

Antonio knew that in wartime the Queen considered him a last card, to be played in counter-attack. However, in peace talks he would be her first card. She would hand him to Philip II as a sweetener, exchanging Portugal for peace. That would mean death, exile upon some Atlantic atoll, or permanent immuration in a monastery. His debauchery augmented by anxiety, Antonio's health suffered. He was 'much grieved' and 'constantly unwell', moping in his cloisters, stricken with depression and digestive irregularities. He prepared escape routes to the Low Countries, Paris or Morocco in case Burghley's initiative came off, and he bitterly blamed his ambassador-physician for his plight.

Despite the sour atmosphere, Lopez paid court regularly at Eton. Perhaps the only ambassador in history to visit his monarch with an enema pump, he could relieve Antonio's ravaged digestion with solutions brewed from senna leaves, but he had no answer for the King's political problems. It was not the right time to invade Portugal. Lopez tried to steer a middle path between Don Antonio and the Privy Council, organising commercial instead of military ventures, and accumulating goodwill for future use. Expeditions to Brazil and the East Indies were launched with funds from Antwerp, the Privy Council and the City of London. A propaganda pamphlet was printed at Leiden to advertise Antonio's claim to kingship among potential investors. Sir Francis Drake took Antonio to the Low Countries, to raise funds and talk with Leicester. In December 1586, Drake and Lopez presented a case to the Privy Council for an invasion of Portugal or the Azores. The absent Leicester, they claimed, was in agreement, and the rebel States of the Low Countries had offered forty ships to accompany Drake's and Antonio's seven.

In debate, Walsingham was outgunned by the more cautious Councillors. England stuck with its old policy of piracy and economic antagonism. Drake was licensed only to sail for the Portuguese Indies, and Lopez had to settle for the smaller profits of a stockholder. Antonio, expected to maintain 150 displaced and disgruntled Portuguese aristocrats, found that no amount of money was sufficient to keep them loyal or hopeful. Already 'overburdened with debt' and 'almost starving', his supply of jewels was running out. His hosts were toying with him, and his followers were visibly disenchanted, their ranks thinned by desertion. Even Thomas, his barber of twenty-seven years, absconded to Paris. He felt in constant danger of his life, and not without reason.

The common interests and origins among the London Portuguese meant that the Marrano underground had become overlain by Don

Antonio's Court. Never impermeable, that Court became honeycombed with intrigue. Don Bernadino de Mendoza had been expelled from London in 1586 for his encouragement of the Babington Plot, which had sought to replace Elizabeth with her Catholic cousin Mary, Queen of Scots. Retreating to Paris, Mendoza had stepped up his use of spies. His most fecund sources were both trusted aides to Don Antonio. In Paris, Antonio d'Escobar forwarded digests of all Portuguese mail to Mendoza under the codename 'Sampson'. From London, Antonio da Vega corresponded directly with Mendoza via the ordinary post. Unfortunately for Mendoza, da Vega's letters were sneaked across the Channel in the commercial packets of Jeronimo Lopez, who passed copies to his cousin Roderigo.

Secretary Walsingham knew that Antonio da Vega was a traitor, but permitted him to continue spying for Mendoza. This allowed him to gauge just how far the Spanish had penetrated Don Antonio's Court, and which secrets were still secret. A conduit between London and Paris could as easily be used for disinformation as information; with Mendoza in Paris, the Spanish had no way of corroborating their intelligence.

By early 1587, Doctor Hector Nuñez's agents had supplied clear intelligence that the Spanish were preparing an invasion fleet, to be launched that summer from Cadiz. From da Vega's reports of military preparations in the ports of southern England, the Spanish expected an English counter-move, but did not know where in their vast empire it would strike. Walsingham devised a counter-intelligence scheme that used Mendoza's source against his paymaster. Roderigo Lopez turned da Vega into a fount of lies, feeding him a succession of false stories that Mendoza relayed to Madrid. Drake and Don Antonio were about to sail for Portugal. Or for the Barbary Coast. Or for Brazil. Or for the Azores. Or Goa. Or was Antonio about to return to the fleshpots of Paris?

Mendoza was so engrossed in dissecting these speculations that he missed the real English plan. In March 1587, while the English fleet completed its preparations, Mendoza was engrossed in an offer from Doctor Lopez to resolve the Portuguese succession on Philip II's behalf by murdering Don Antonio with a poisoned enema. By 12 April 1587, when Sir Francis Drake cast off at Plymouth, Antonio da Vega had been arrested in London by Walsingham's men. Da Vega was held for a week and then released without charge. Mendoza's source had been silenced at the moment he was most needed, but not held so long that Mendoza might suspect his man had been detected.

When da Vega was released, his first action was to send an urgent mail to Mendoza: the English were sailing to Cadiz, not Lisbon, and to destroy the Armada, not to crown Don Antonio. A race ensued between Drake's ships and da Vega's letter. Five days after da Vega passed the mail to Jeronimo Lopez, Mendoza had read it and sent a copy to Philip II. The letter was couriered across France and Spain with remarkable speed, taking only five more days to reach the palace of Aranjuez, where the master of much of the known world read it in bed while resting a gouty knee. The letter and the ships had reached their destinations on the same day, but that was too late for the Spanish.

At four in the afternoon of 30 April 1587, Drake's flagship, the *Elizabeth Bonaventura*, led the fleet through the narrow channel protecting Cadiz harbour. His ships surprised more than sixty merchantmen that were in the process of being converted into warships. As Philip II read Mendoza's letter, his fleet was torched in its harbour. The English withdrew at dusk, leaving the harbour lit by burning ships, and returned for further attacks in the next days. By the time Drake withdrew on 10 May, nearly half the invasion fleet had been destroyed. The 'singeing of the King of Spain's beard' meant that the Armada would not be ready for the summer of 1587. Philip, getting dizzily out of bed after having been bled twice, sent a sarcastic note to Mendoza, suggesting that he double-check his source in London.

Falling back on her Tudor parsimony and her habitual caution, after Cadiz the Queen ordered Drake back to England. If she had not, he could have proceeded to Lisbon – where the remainder of the Spanish fleet sat defenceless – and destroyed the rest of the Armada. She settled for the 60,000 ducats that Drake towed into Dartmouth harbour on his prize, the treasure ship *San Felipe*. The

Spanish assault had been delayed, not averted, and Secretary Walsingham had won an intelligence battle at Cadiz, but not the war. One summer evening early in May 1588, Walsingham was surprised by the appearance of a breathless Doctor Hector. Nuñez had been at home in Mark Lane, eating his dinner as he listened to a report from the latest ship to arrive at the docks. When he heard the news, he had hurried on arthritic legs to Walsingham's house. Walsingham had dreaded this report for years. The restored Spanish Armada had sailed for England.

4

The Pretender

So may the outward shows be least themselves –
The world is still deceived with ornament.

Bassanio, in *The Merchant of Venice*

Along the coasts of England the militias drilled. The ports were sealed and the beacons were stacked for the flame. As the two fleets converged, a courier from Don Antonio slipped across the Channel for Paris. Travelling on a diplomatic passport from Antonio's hypothetical kingdom, on 24 July 1588 he presented himself to the Spanish embassy at Paris and offered his services to Don Bernadino de Mendoza. His name was Manuel d'Andrada.

Andrada was the apocryphal Portuguese aristocrat. A patriotic *fidalgo*, he had fought for Don Antonio in 1580. While Antonio jumped into bushes and ran through olive groves, Andrada had hidden Antonio's sons in his own house. Andrada had been organising the escape of Antonio's daughter, Doña Louisa, from Portugal when Philip II had summoned her to Spain and imprisoned her. Offered a Spanish pardon, Andrada refused. He followed his King into exile, first in Paris and then in London. Unconscionable poverty ensued. He became a courier for Antonio. Picking up Flemish from the rebels of Antwerp and reporting to Walsingham on his return, he became an intelligence specialist on the Low Countries, an agent in the Lopez network. After the Paris mission, he was to base himself at Rouen, a link in the intelligence chain.

Andrada's circumstances were ripe for his corruption: his fall into poverty and exile; his connections and his ear for languages; the soliloquies of self-doubt in the long missions of a courier; the constant shadow of Spanish agents and the constant temptation of Spanish silver. He had forfeited his wife, his children and his estates for nothing. His honour might command a better price. For money, he told Mendoza, he would draw Don Antonio to the Low Countries and betray him into Spanish hands.

Manuel d'Andrada's signature.

Andrada's offer was premature. He had gone to Paris assuming that a great Spanish victory was imminent: when the English were defeated and sued for peace, Andrada would be a useful adviser to Mendoza. But the English were not defeated in the Channel. Instead, a combination of superior seamanship, familiarity with the battlefield and a lucky turn of weather sent the Armada scattering into the North Sea. Suddenly, Andrada seemed no more valuable than any other Portuguese traitor.

Mendoza's advanced cataracts did not prevent him from assessing his interviewee as 'shabby'. Using an official passport, Andrada had exited an English port at the height of invasion hysteria. He might be a Walsingham spy sent to infiltrate Mendoza's network. Mendoza engaged Andrada, but cautiously, as a petty informer. For small change, Andrada would pass Antonio's mails to Mendoza, as well as any other morsels he might snap up while hanging around the Prior of Crato and his menagerie of heretics and traitors. Mendoza gave Andrada the codename 'David' and referred the kidnapping offer to Philip II. Abducting a monarch was morally complex, even if the abductee was not recognised as a monarch by the kidnappers. The matter was best referred to the royal conscience.

Andrada went on to Rouen, where he acted as postmaster for Antonio's communication between London, Paris and the Low Countries, and copied all Portuguese mails for Mendoza including, in September 1588, the welcome news that the Earl of Leicester had died. After three months, he received a summons from Don Antonio: Andrada and Escobar were needed in London. Philip II worried that his 'David' and 'Sampson' had been detected, but something else was afoot. The greater the concentration of Portuguese, the greater the concentration of spies, and Philip soon received details. The English were raising a fleet, a Counter-Armada to invade Portugal for Don Antonio. 'Ojo!' wrote Philip in the margin of one report.

The development of an invasion fleet in England changed Andrada from a minor informer to a prized asset. His luck seemed to have turned, and his intelligences from London had won the trust of Philip II and Mendoza. 'With regard to employing David in one place or another,' Philip told Mendoza, 'you will use your own discretion, and use him where you think he may be most profitable.' Andrada became braver and greedier. He enticed Mendoza with an offer to poison Don Antonio should kidnapping prove too complex.

In London, Doctor Lopez had no idea that Andrada was a traitor, and neither did Walsingham and Don Antonio. They were pre-occupied with dusting off their old plans for invading Portugal. The advent and defeat of the Armada had validated the analysis of the warriors on the Privy Council over that of the diplomats. Philip had chosen war over negotiation, yet his fleet had been routed. There were rumours from Iberia that Philip was preparing a second Armada to avenge the first. There was a need for another pre-emptive strike, the old nexus of commercial and strategic ambition still underpinned all 'Portingall matters', and the 'fullbellied' mood in both country and Council was nationalistic and triumphalist.

Lopez saw that there might never be another opportunity.

Bookended by the defeat of the Armada and the death of the old campaigner Leicester, the summer of 1588 marked the beginning of a new phase of Elizabethan politics. The actors were ageing. Elizabeth was past childbearing age and Philip II was working himself to death in his monkish cubicle in the Escorial palace. Lopez and Don Antonio were both in their sixties. Of the twin pillars of their support, Leicester was dead and Walsingham was terminally ill. King Antonio and his Lord Ambassador had one last throw of the dice before they would have to abandon their titles and admit the pretence. Either Portugal could be freed from the Inquisition, Jewish life in Iberia could recover and the Lord Ambassador could retire to the land of his birth, the restorer of the House of Avis; or Lopez, Antonio and the Marranos faced a slow slide into irrelevance as the Anglo-Spanish war petered out, taking with it their usefulness and sources of patronage, a slow tangent whose conclusion would be death in exile. A final, glorious transformation was at stake, an irresistible blend of profit and redemption. Having made the transition from doctor to ambassador, Lopez now turned military strategist.

While the Armada was in the Channel in June 1588, Lord Admiral Howard had suggested that an English victory would be the perfect springboard for an attack on Portugal. Over a summer charged with anxiety and its victorious catharsis, the spark of this idea grew from a punitive 'beard-singeing' to a full-scale invasion that would restore Don Antonio to the Portuguese throne. The scheme was the work of Walsingham, Lopez, Sir Francis Drake, and the veteran soldier Sir John Norris. To allay the Queen's financial anxiety, they suggested the formation of a joint-stock company. Of the £40,000 capital required, the Queen would contribute only £5000; the rest would come from private investors in the City and on the Council. In late September Lord Burghley, more usually prone to verbose variation in the manner of Polonius, jotted a laconic 'Articles of offers from King Antonio':

1. To attempt to burn the ships in Lisbon and Seville.
2. To take Lisbon.
3. To take the Islands [the Azores].

These gnomic notes were a strategy for destroying the Spanish empire by economic strangulation. Lisbon was the home port of the pepper trade from the East Indies. The trade would pass into English hands with the city. The Azores would be turned into an advance base for English privateers. With limitless food and fresh water from the islands, they could pick off Spanish slave ships from West Africa and Spanish treasure ships from South America. Deprived of the twin rivers of spice and metal running from the East and West Indies to the treasury in the Escorial, the Spanish economy would collapse. To preserve some part of his empire, Philip would be forced to cede other parts. England, with its soldiers in the warehouses of Lisbon, its sailors controlling the sea lanes, and its treasury flooded with silver and gold, would dictate terms. An amphibious invasion was daunting, but the potential rewards tempted even Burghley. Yet the Lord Treasurer made certain to insure England against military failure.

Elizabeth's terms were merciless. After allowing the English army to sack his new capital for the first ten days of his reign, Antonio would have to pay her 500,000 ducats 'in gold', and an additional 300,000 ducats annually, equivalent to a *San Felipe* docking in London every year. Portugal would become an English province. English merchants would have full trading rights in the Portuguese East Indies. Portuguese ports were to be used to 'fit out a fleet against the King of Spain' and all the major castles of Portugal were to have English garrisons, all to be maintained at Antonio's expense.

Antonio was expected to sell the substance of his kingship for military support. It was an almost Shylockian bond, calculated against his palpable desperation. He had no choice but to accept. He was now so hopeless that in March 1588 he had attempted to flee to Paris, rather than risk being handed to the Spanish to stave off the Armada. After vanishing to 'a pleasure house' at Brentford, he and Captain Edward Perrin had sneaked to Dover in disguise. They were arrested as they boarded a ship for the Low Countries. One of Lord Admiral Howard's men had recognised Antonio by his pet lapdog, and the King had been arrested by his hosts. To calm Antonio, the Queen 'caressed' him and made the usual promises. To show he bore no grudge, Lord Admiral Howard fired off a royal salute when Antonio reviewed the fleet. But Antonio remained as miserable as ever, an unwilling, neglected lapdog.

Sir John Norris (left) and Sir Francis Drake (right).

On 23 February 1589 a royal warrant for the expedition was issued to Norris and Drake, accompanied by a second bond from Antonio, promising a nervous Elizabeth that he would reimburse all costs immediately upon taking possession of Portugal. Desperate for money, Don Antonio pawned his last diamond and sold trading rights to his nominal possessions in West Africa to a merchant consortium. Lopez had already supported Antonio with cash advances totalling £4000. To this debt further expenses were added. Antonio offered Lopez 5 per cent of the proceeds from the African franchise. To repay Lopez for obtaining the Queen's miraculous warrant, he gave the Doctor a credit note for 50,000 crowns, to be paid from the future income of the Crown of Portugal. Antonio was now wholly in the hands of his creditors. They had ransacked his title like pirates in an entrepôt.

After decades of caution, Elizabeth had finally been tempted into the kind of aggressive, expensive adventure she distrusted instinctively. Yet the plan was detailed, it had the qualified support of Lord

Burghley, and it would be carried out by her most expert land and sea captains. Naturally, everything unravelled from that day on.

An army of 16,000 soldiers was raised, mostly the unemployed, desperate and criminal of all classes, attracted by promises of easy loot. They gathered on the shore at Plymouth and Southampton, gambling and grousing their way through a mountain of stores while their commanders awaited the arrival of a contingent from the Low Countries. Costs spiralled from £40,000 to over £50,000, and the Queen's share quadrupled to £20,000. After consuming its sea rations, the mob on the shore ran up credit with the innkeepers of the south coast and sent the bills to London. When their credit was stopped, the soldiers stole dried herrings from a Flemish ship that had had the misfortune to enter Plymouth harbour. They grew riotous and threatened to rampage across the countryside.

While Drake and Norris corralled their army on to the ships, a final bitter complication was provided by the Queen's favourite, Robert Devereux, 2nd Earl of Essex. Banned by royal order from joining the expedition, Essex had slipped out of London and hurried to Plymouth. Although he had to avoid the expedition's commanders and anybody else who might recognise him, security was so lax in the port that Essex easily discovered the fleet's planned departure date, rendezvous points and objectives. He rode to nearby Falmouth, boarded the *Swiftsure* and sailed on the first tide. On the same morning, the rest of the fleet left Plymouth with a fluttering of sails and invoices, nearly three weeks behind schedule.

The wind blew them straight back into the arms of the search party sent from London by the furious Queen. Drake, the circum-navigator of the world, was bottled up in his home port, 'disconso-late' as the rain poured down, fearing 'dishonour' and worse, 'loss'. After a further twelve days the fractious, damp, hungry, under-supplied and under-equipped Counter-Armada finally escaped from Plymouth and the wrath of the Queen, tacking into open water under low, unforgiving skies, Drake's *Revenge* in the van, Don Antonio's *Victory* behind.

That April, when the Royal College of Physicians conducted its annual census, two of the College's four 'Strangers' were recorded as being *peregrinus*: travelling. Doctors Hector Nuñez and Roderigo Lopez were somewhere on the Atlantic Ocean. Drake the pirate, Norris the soldier, Antonio the King over the water and Lopez, his government of one, neared the climax of their scheme.

For two days Lopez's ship was battered by cross-winds in the Channel, but on the third the weather cleared and the fleet caught a fresh north-easterly across the Bay of Biscay. From the deck of the *Victory*, Lopez surveyed a stirring hopeful spectacle of more than 150 ships under full sail. But as Cape Finisterre brought Iberia in sight on the sixth day, supplies of food and drink ran out. The untrained soldiery, without 'wine to mix with their water, nor bread to eat with their meat', began to fight among themselves. To avoid mutiny, Drake and Norris decided to change course, to the alarm of their Portuguese passengers, in order to make a diversion for fresh supplies and plunder. All thought of fulfilling the Queen's orders and landing Don Antonio in Portugal was abandoned as the fleet bore down on the remote north-western corner of Spain and the port of Coruña. To the total surprise of the inhabitants and the Cortes of Galicia, whose session was interrupted with the terrifying news that the diabolical Drake had chosen the port as the site of his next outrage, 7000 men landed a mile from the city walls.

The garrison of Coruña abandoned the port and fled to the walled upper town, leaving the English army in the promised circumstances of their recruitment. The warehouses of Coruña groaned with supplies. Every cellar in the port seemed stacked with drink. An ocean of wine, a lake of oil, whole herds of beef, mounds of sea biscuit and three shiploads of ammunition: the stores of an Armada-in-waiting. An orgy of looting and murder began, the troops so drunk that they staggered oblivious to the barrage of shot coming from the upper town and forgot to seize a galleon sitting at the dock. Its crew blew it up, casting an apocalyptic pall of wood and tar smoke over the bay.

If the expedition had proceeded to Lisbon at this point, it would have lost only forty-eight hours and could still have claimed to be within its original orders. But having established a toehold on the peninsula, and having gauged the quality of their army, Drake and

Norris opted to make Coruña, not Lisbon, their base. This meant taking the upper town. The expedition had been assembled with a different mission in mind – the gates of Lisbon were to be opened by Don Antonio's delirious subjects, not by cannon – and consequently had only carried light artillery. After taking four days to sober up, Norris's gunners began battering at the walls with their small ordnance. While the volunteer troops were felled by drink, shrapnel and exotic food, the regular troops threw themselves heroically and fruitlessly at the breach, where falling masonry pinned poor Captain Sydenham to the ground with 'three or four great stones upon his lower parts'. He died the next day, after a further dozen men had died trying to rescue him. Outside the walls, the English army burnt down a monastery and declared a great victory over the local cattle. The smoke from their barbecues joined that rising from the burning villages of the district, whose inhabitants were chased across the countryside and hacked to pieces as they hid in the hedgerows.

Lopez and Don Antonio watched the columns of smoke spread across the Galician sky from the deck of the *Victory*. This was an English show. The Portuguese Court had been not invited and was powerless to protest. The invasion had begun as Antonio's and Lopez's dream, and the closer it had come to reality, the more control they had lost. Now, they were prisoners of the English stock company they had helped create. Lopez knew that this diversion had cost the fleet any element of surprise it still possessed. The English generals had agreed a plan with their Queen, they had wrecked it at the first opportunity, and the odds of failure increased with every day. After two wasted weeks, the army rowed what it could steal out to the ships and destroyed the rest. The fleet sailed for Portugal, Drake and Norris despatching exaggerated accounts of military valour to London. Sir John Norris's brother Edward had provided an appropriate metaphor for the Coruña diversion when he had tripped over his own pike and mortally wounded himself in the head with its blade.

After four days at sea, the wild card in Drake's pack of jokers turned up. The *Swiftsure* joined the fleet, and with it the Earl of Essex. Drake and Norris gave the Earl furious mails from Elizabeth.

'If the Earl of Essex has joined the fleet, they are to send him home instantly,' she ordered. 'If they do not, they shall truly answer for the same at their smart, for as we have authority to rule, so we look to be obeyed, and these be no childish actions.'

Instead of sending Essex home, Drake and Norris appointed him commander of the next troops to be landed, and pressed on for Lisbon. They had little to lose. They had exhausted the Queen's patience before leaving England. If they returned with enough loot – and the warehouses of Lisbon called the sailors like sirens – their buccaneering indiscretion would be forgiven. If they did not, they would be disgraced anyway.

Lopez and Antonio were embroiled in this treasonable disobedience, passengers hijacked by privateers. The doctor had become trapped in a hand of *monte*, the Spanish card game. Having dealt the entire pack, the players took turns to trump each other with cards of successively higher value, forming a small hill, or *monte*, of discarded cards. Eventually, one player could not find a card of sufficiently high value in his hand. He had to pick up the whole pile, the full *monte*, as the English called it. The winner was the player who got rid of all his cards. Having dissipated its strength at Coruña and adopted wayward Essex, the expedition now possessed only one trump. Antonio must be recognised by enough Portuguese to constitute a popular rejection of Spanish control over Portugal. Otherwise the expedition would fold.

Treasonable north-easterlies carried the *Swiftsure* and the fleet round Cape Finisterre and south to Lisbon. A week after leaving Coruña, they were only sixty miles from their target. Lopez saw the rocky coast of his homeland, the villages clinging to its inlets with their painted fishing boats, the scrubby hills behind. On the salty tang, his old life appeared before his eyes. He was only a day from the Tejo estuary and Lisbon, but once again Drake and Norris took a greedy diversion. From captured fishermen they had picked up rumours of a Spanish treasure ship loaded with 1 million crowns in gold, hiding by the fortress of Peniche. The ship had fled to Lisbon by the time they got there, but they landed anyway. While the troops agitated for loot and the Earl of Essex exercised antiquarian dreams of chivalry, Lopez was desperate to touch native soil. With the expedition turning into a nightmare, Peniche was as good a place as any to begin Antonio's *reconquista*.

At the edge of the bay, 2000 English soldiers decanted into longboats and rowed towards the harbour. The fortress was garrisoned by Portuguese troops, stiffened by Spanish reinforcements. Leaving the Portuguese to hold the fort, the Spanish gathered before the most likely place for a landing, a sheltered stage in front of the fortress. The other option was a bleak, wave-racked spot a mile away, the Beach of Consolation, where 'the wind was great and the sea was high' enough for no human defence to be needed.

As the Spanish fired from the sheltered side of the bay, the longboats veered towards Consolation and attempted a landing. The Earl of Essex was determined to be first ashore. Not waiting to reach the shallows, he leapt into the surf in his armour and went in up to his neck. He was followed by the rest of his boat, most of whom were not as tall as the lanky Earl. To the concerted thunder of cannon and breakers, with boats overturning and armoured men flailing in the waves, the English staggered ashore and chased the garrison from the foreshore at 'the push of the pike'. The rest of Norris's troops landed before the fortress and demanded its surrender. Its commander, Captain Aruajo, turned out to be an admirer of Don Antonio and insisted on surrendering to his rightful King.

A message was brought to the *Victory* out in the bay. Lopez followed Antonio into a heaving longboat. Slowly, they were rowed to the fort. With no fanfare but the drumming of the surf on Consolation Beach, King Antonio summoned the small dignity available to a short man stepping from a bobbing boat, and stood on Portuguese soil for the first time in nine years. Lopez, whose elderly legs would have found the jump no easier, followed him. Captain Aruajo and his garrison kneeled before them.

After the years of waiting, an interlude of bizarre normality. The carpet knights from London entered the fortress to find that all was as if King Antonio had never left. A canopy shaded his empty throne. Silver plate from the Indies adorned his dining table, and prostrate servants awaited his whim. For two days Antonio held court as if on a summer progress, casting benedictions upon supplicant peasants who came in from the country.

But while Antonio revelled in harmonious privilege, Lopez heard a repetitive, discordant note. Priests and goatherds might view Antonio as their saviour, but to raise a convincing revolt, he needed the support of the Portuguese nobility. Spies in London and deserters from Coruña had provided Philip II with a list of Antonio's potential backers in Lisbon, and the Spanish King had executed them all. This had a discouraging effect on those Portuguese nobles not already in Philip's hands. But now the expedition was on Portuguese soil, it had to press on to Lisbon. Norris the soldier was for an overland march. They were only forty miles from the capital and, judging from Peniche, they could depend on the locals for succour. Drake the sailor was for storming Lisbon as he had Cadiz, by sailing along the coast, up the Tejo estuary and grabbing that elusive treasure ship, whose million crowns were now tied up on the India House wharf. Antonio, no doubt backed by Lopez, was determined to stay on land. Overruling Drake, they settled on an overland march. Drake followed them to the first hill, wished them luck and returned to the *Revenge*. They would meet at Cascais, eleven miles down the Tejo from Lisbon.

By mid-May, the baking Portuguese summer had begun. Without food, drink or transport, the soldiers carried their munitions on their backs. On the second day they ran out of bread, but the need to charm the local population into rising for Antonio meant that looting was banned. Instead, Norris asked Antonio to raise supplies. The King bought what food had not been stolen by the retreating Spanish on credit from the peasantry. Hankering after 'their own fat meats and birds', the English found it 'dry and tasteless', and complained about the heat. With no more than a dozen Portuguese volunteers joining Antonio's army, it dwindled before his eyes. The officers had private surgeons, but the soldiery, debilitated by drink, wounds and dysentery, died by the roadside. On the fourth night, they were ambushed in the dark by Spanish troops. The next morning, they drank 'standing waters' and cholera broke out. A paranoid theory circulated in the camp that they had been fed poisoned honey by the peasants. That morning, Lopez surveyed the walls of Lisbon from a hilltop three miles away. Behind the walls were warehouses loaded with East Indies spice, the key to Portugal's power. But apart from Essex and some bravoes who raced up to the city walls and banged on the gates, the soldiers were too tired and sick to do more than sleep.

Inside the walls, all was panic. It was rumoured that Drake was on the rampage with 900 blood-crazed Irish wolfhounds. 'We are in great alarm, and have passed a very bad night. God help us!' wrote a Spanish commander. As the Spanish dug in and held regular public executions of Don Antonio sympathisers, priests loyal to Antonio passed from house to house whispering that the English were not the heretics the Spanish claimed them to be, and that some were even good Catholics. To the rich they offered Antonio's favour, and to the poor they offered the pescatorial metaphor that 'fishing in troubled waters was profitable to the fishermen'. But the populace, cowed by the twin threats of execution by the Spanish or digestion by Drake's wolfhounds, would not fight. Every night, anyone who could fled to the other side of the Tejo.

Without heavy artillery or siege equipment, the walls of Lisbon were impenetrable. A monk who offered to open the gates by subterfuge slipped into the city, only for his tonsured head to appear on a spike on the walls. In the suburbs before the walls, the English found only 'old folks and beggars, crying "*Viva el rey Don Antonio*", and the houses shut up'. There was nothing to eat and nobody to fight. After two days, Antonio attempted to transfer his Court to the house of a Portuguese gentleman on the road to Cascais. But his putative host rejected his King, and Antonio's party barely escaped unhurt. With the people too scared to assist them, Lopez and Antonio were now forced to stick close to the English for their own safety. The Doctor had become a prisoner of his scheme.

Down at Cascais, Drake had better luck. The port had surrendered at the mention of his name. If he had sailed up the Tejo to Lisbon, his intervention might have tipped the balance, but his ships were undermanned and had no soldiers, so he rested at Cascais while Norris and his colonels squabbled about what to do next. After three days before the walls of Lisbon, they told Lopez and Antonio they had had enough. Their men were hungry and sick, and Antonio's promised support had not appeared. Having acquitted themselves honourably, they should retreat to Cascais.

Lopez and Antonio pleaded for more time. They were at the handles of the lock, at the very gates of their capital. Lisbon was weakening, and a mirage of an army might yet appear. Unconvinced and fearful of mutiny, Norris gave them twelve hours. The Portuguese company passed a long night of desperation before the walls. That night, Lopez waited for the army of pitchfork-wielding peasants and armoured nobles to appear but, like every other night since he had splashed ashore at Peniche, he heard only crickets. Just before dawn, the English crawled from their trenches and began the trek to Cascais. Hardly a month after leaving Plymouth, the Counter-Armada's troops abandoned their siege of Lisbon and with it the cause of Don Antonio. Last to leave was the Earl of Essex. Not finding a wind-mill worth tilting at, he rode up to the walls and embedded his lance in the gates, offering to defend his Queen's honour in single combat with any of the defenders who wished to come out. No one accepted his challenge to medieval theatricals. Lopez turned his back on Lisbon for the last time, heading back to exile.

At Cascais, Drake blamed Norris, Norris blamed Drake, and both blamed Lopez and Antonio. Mails from the Queen caught up with the expedition. She was furious about the Coruña episode and ordered Essex back at his 'uttermost peril'. Drake and Norris sent reports back, explaining that they had been 'reduced by the heat' and that the Portuguese were 'the greatest cowards ever seen'. They admitted Essex had been with them the whole time, excusing their betrayal with technical flannel about 'the wind being east and northerly ever since His Lordship's being in these parts'. They did not explain why they had given Essex a command in the army.

Essex was sent home, where his apologies might smooth the way for the fleet's return. Drake and Norris had failed to destroy Philip's ships and to establish Don Antonio in Portugal. Only the third element of the plan remained: to take the Azores. Of the 16,000 soldiers who had embarked at Plymouth, only 4000 remained alive. Taking the healthiest among them and the remainder of the stores, Drake and twenty ships would head for the Azores. Norris and the Portuguese would sail home. Lopez and Antonio endured a purgatorial last chapter, ten days without food or water, the bodies of the dead being thrown overboard as the ships struggled in 'the greatest storm we had all the time we were out'. On 2 July, Norris's ships crawled into Plymouth Sound to find that Drake, having taken all the supplies so that he might raid the Azores, had changed his mind and reached Plymouth a day earlier. Having double-crossed the Queen, Walsingham, Lopez and Antonio, Drake had cheated Norris too.

The Counter-Armada was a total failure, and Lopez was liable. Just 5000 of the original 23,000 adventurers had survived. Drake and Norris were disgraced. Don Antonio was a laughing stock, heckled as a 'dog' by the people of Plymouth as he stepped off the *Victory*. When the booty was auctioned on the quayside, an expedition costing more than £50,000 turned out to have generated only £30,000 in prize money. A terrible financial imbroglio followed while the investors fought over the small spoils. The Queen, most of her Council and the most important City merchants were all out of pocket. Incensed shareholders in London alleged that the captains had offloaded further loot on the Continent and kept the proceeds for themselves, and that the Mayor of Plymouth had deliberately depressed the sale prices of the booty at the quayside auction, so that his friends could resell the goods at a higher price. Drake put to sea again as soon as he could, leaving Norris and Lopez to clear up the financial and political mess. The soldiers were paid off with a miserable five shillings each.

The only beneficiary of the Counter-Armada was the Earl of Essex, a lion in a campaign of donkeyish incompetence. His chivalric courage caught the imagination of both the public and those politicians who favoured an aggressive policy towards Spain. One poem making the rounds that summer, *An Eclogue Congratulatory*, cast him in the role of a mythic and militant swain, the 'Shepherd of England's Arcadia'. The defeat of the Counter-Armada became the platform for a political career. Essex stepped into the role of his late stepfather, the Earl of Leicester, as the totem of the 'war party'.

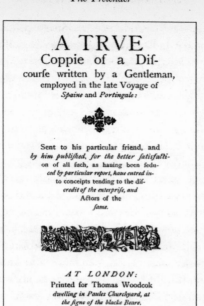

A TRVE
Coppie of a Dif-
courfe written by a Gentleman,
employed in the late Voyage of
Spaine and *Portingale*:

Sent to his particular friend, and
by him publifhed, for the better fatisfacti-
on of all fuch, as hauing been fedu-
ced by particular report, haue entred in-
to conceipts tending to the dif-
credit of the enterprife, and
Actors of the
fame.

AT LONDON:
Printed for Thomas Woodcok
dwelling in Paules Churchyard, at
the figne of the blacke Beare.
1589.

Frontispiece of A True Copy of a Discourse, *a pro-Essex account of the Portuguese expedition written by one of its survivors, Captain Anthony Wingfield.*

Lopez was ruined. To raise money for the fleet, the Doctor had used his patients' trust. Its failure had squandered capital accumulated in decades of work. Instead of restoring him to Portugal, it had reduced him to being a permanent exile. There would be no comfortable retirement in the Alentejo. He was an old man, washed up in a northern port. The Counter-Armada had been riddled with spies, funding problems and the egotism of its hydra-headed leadership. The carefully built image of Don Antonio as a credible king in exile had been tested and found wanting, revealing Antonio as a pretender in the worst sense. The Queen was furious with the Doctor, Walsingham would not speak to him, and Don Antonio blamed him for the elaborate humiliation that their supposed triumphant return had become.

After lying low for a few days, Lopez wrote to Walsingham, offering

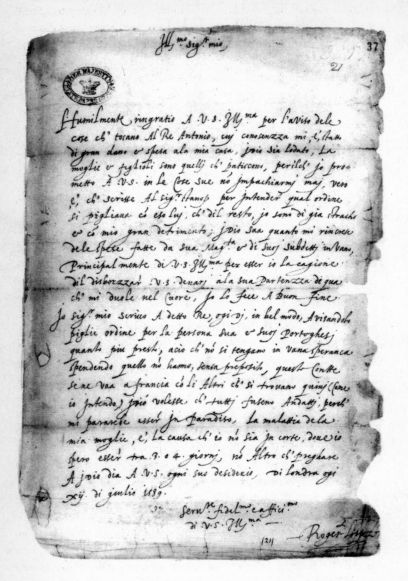

July 1589: Lopez apologises to the Privy Council, writing in Italian, the language of diplomacy and the new learning.

abject apologies 'that his advice had induced Her Majesty to spend so much money to so little purpose'. Giving the transparent excuse that he would have come to court and apologised personally, but his wife had been ill, he promised to write to Don Antonio. The London Portuguese were supposed to be an intelligence asset to England, but they had proved corrupt and useful only to the Spanish. Antonio must 'take some order for himself and his Portuguese', and root out the traitors in his Court.

Lopez's financial plight could not be eased by apologies in Italian and promises of service. Like all the other investors, he had extracted every possible concession from Don Antonio and had lost almost every penny he had invested. But unlike the other investors, Lopez was also the recipient of these investments; he was Don Antonio's financial agent and ambassador. Consequently, he was liable for the losses. Antonio had issued two bonds to the Queen, promising Portuguese revenues in perpetuity and the immediate refund of the expedition's costs, but had failed to pay either. Antonio's creditors came to Lopez, and Lopez was unable to pay them.

He sent another letter to Walsingham. His aniseed and sumach licence was due for renewal, but the Queen withheld her signature. He pleaded his need for 'relief' from 'his present necessity'. Would Walsingham intervene on her Doctor's behalf? The Secretary did not reply. Ambassador for a king of a pretend kingdom, Lopez was out of credit and out of favour. The spring of patronage ran dry as suddenly as it had flowered.

5

A Kind of Jewish Practice

Which is the merchant here, and which the Jew?

Portia in *The Merchant of Venice*

There once lived a merchant of Venice named Antonio, and Bassanio was his friend. They were both noblemen, but Bassanio was poor. On a trading venture to Belmont, Bassanio fell in love with Portia, a lady of Belmont. To win her hand he needed money. He asked Antonio to lend him 3000 ducats. Antonio had tied up his capital in half a dozen different trading expeditions and had no cash. Although he was very possessive of Bassanio, such was Antonio's love for his friend that he went to a Jewish loan shark called Shylock. Antonio had often upbraided Shylock for the sin of lending money at interest. Shylock had not forgotten this insult. When Antonio came to him without collateral and asked for a loan, Shylock suggested a bond: if the money was not repaid within three months, Shylock would be entitled to cut a pound of flesh from Antonio's body. Shylock gave no explanation for the origin of this bizarre proposal. Perhaps it was a metaphor for castration anxiety caused by the Jewish practice of circumcision. Perhaps he had read it in the popular Italian collection *Il Pecorone*.

Antonio gave Bassanio his 3000 ducats. Confident that at least some of his numerous investments would pay off, he forgot about the old Jew and his loan. Bassanio went to Belmont, apparently unconcerned that by pretending the money was his own, he was misrepresenting himself to his beloved. Although he now had money, he still had to pass the test stipulated in the will of Portia's father. Portia was to marry the man who, when presented with three caskets – one of gold, one of silver, one of lead – picked the one containing her portrait. Bassanio, a poor man pretending to be rich, knew that appearances could be deceiving. Unlike his competitors, the Prince of Morocco and the Prince of Aragon, he picked the right casket: the leaden one. Bassanio and Portia were married, and his friend Antonio married her maid Nerissa.

Back in Venice, reports arrived that all of Antonio's ventures had ended in disaster. The loan was overdue, and Shylock wanted his pound of flesh. The Jew brought his suit before the Doge of Venice, with Antonio in the dock and Bassanio in the gallery.

Portia and Nerissa disguised themselves as a lawyer called Balthazar and his clerk, and went to the court to defend Antonio. They made such convincing men that neither of their husbands recognised them. Portia appealed to Shylock to show mercy, but he refused and insisted upon the letter of the law. So she admitted the validity of his claim – Antonio had given his word as a gentleman, after all – but defeated Shylock with the same technical adherence to the code that he had demanded. His bond was for a pound of flesh. If he spilt the tiniest drop of blood while cutting it then, under the laws of Venice, his life would be forfeit. And for having conspired against the life of a Venetian citizen, Shylock – who, as a Jew, could not be a citizen – had committed a further capital crime.

The Doge spared Shylock's life, but ordered that in compensation he must give half his wealth to Antonio and half to the State. Antonio offered to let Shylock keep his half of the money, but on two conditions. Shylock must convert to Christianity, and on his death all his property must pass to his daughter Jessica, whom he had disinherited for eloping with a Christian friend of Antonio's called Lorenzo. Shylock agreed. Ruined and broken, he disappears from the story.

In return for saving Antonio, the lawyer and his clerk asked for Antonio's and Bassanio's wedding rings. The two men had promised never to give them away, but in their gratitude they did just that. Then they sailed for Belmont to see their wives.

Portia and Nerissa had hurried there before them, and reverted to female dress. They pretended to be distraught that their husbands had given away their rings. After Antonio and Bassanio had protested their love for their wives, they were let in on the joke. Antonio's friend Lorenzo and Shylock's daughter Jessica were there too. When news came that Antonio's ships had not been wrecked after all, but had all arrived safely in Venice, everyone lived even more happily ever after.

This is the plot of *The Merchant of Venice* in its oldest published form, a quarto from the year 1600. Shakespeare's basis was probably the pound of flesh story from *Il Pecorone*. He was not the first Elizabethan to use it. In 1580, the hack writer Anthony Munday set it in Verona for *Zelauto, or The Fountain of Fame*, featuring a gentile usurer named Signor Truculento. Shakespeare combined the 'pound of flesh' and 'Lady of Belmont' strands with a story from another collection: the casket plot from the thirty-second story in the Latin compilation *Gesta Romanorum*. Compiled in England in the thirteenth century, the *Gesta* was a staple of European literature, an influence upon Boccaccio and Chaucer. If Shakespeare needed reminding, a new edition of the *Gesta Romanorum* was 'translated and newly perused and corrected by R. Robinson' in 1595.

The title-page of the 1600 folio reads, 'The most excellent History of the Merchant of Venice. With the extreme cruelty of Shylock the Jew toward the said Merchant, in cutting a just pound of his flesh; and the obtaining of Portia by the choice of three chests. As it hath been divers times acted by the Lord Chamberlain his Servants. Written by William Shakespeare. At London, printed by I. R. for Thomas Hayes, and are to be sold in Paul's Churchyard at the sign of the Green Dragon. 1600.'

'I. R.' the printer was James Roberts, who printed several other plays performed by the Lord Chamberlain's Men, including Shakespeare's *Troilus and Cressida* and *Hamlet*. Two years before printing *The Merchant*, Roberts had entered the play in the Stationers' Register, paying sixpence for the rights. The Register for 22 July 1598 reads, 'Entered for his copy, under the hands of both the wardens, a book of the Merchant of Venice, or otherwise called the Jew of Venice. Provided that it be not printed by the said James Roberts,

THE EXCELLENT

History of the Mer-
chant of Venice.

With the extreme cruelty of *Shylocke*
the Iew towards the saide Merchant, in cutting a iust pound of his flesh. And the obtaining
of *Portia*, by the choyse of
three Caskets.

Written by W. Shakespeare.

Printed by *J. Roberts*, 1600.

Frontispiece of the 1600 folio of The Merchant of Venice.

or any other whatsoever, without licence first had from the Right
Honourable the Lord Chamberlain.'

When combined with topical texual references, this scrappy information on the genesis of *The Merchant* provides a rough chronology
for its composition. The latest date is July 1598, when James Roberts
registered 'a book of the Merchant'. The reference to a 'book'
suggests that Roberts may have registered a text drawn from the
'prompt book' used to remind the Lord Chamberlain's Men of their
lines.

The earliest date for *The Merchant*'s composition is less easy to
define. The oldest surviving text of a Shakespeare play is not always
its original version. If it was drawn from a prompt book, it would
have undergone modifications through performance. If it was drawn

from a pirated copy, or 'reconstructed' from the memories of its actors, inaccuracies will have entered the text; as in the 1603 'bad quarto' of *Hamlet*, whose protagonist utters the undying question, 'To be, or not to be, I there's the point.' There is also the possibility that the 1600 quarto is a revision of an earlier work; apart from the 'bad' quarto and three surviving 'good' quartos, *Hamlet* also existed in an early version, now lost and known as the Ur-*Hamlet*. So the text of the 1600 quarto of *The Merchant* can only date the text, and not the plot or the play.

The earliest date for the 1600 quarto appears to be the summer of 1596. That July, an English raiding party attacked the Spanish port of Cadiz and, in the chaos, a Spanish galleon named the *Andrew* ran aground in the harbour and was captured. In the opening act of *The Merchant*, when Salerio talks of a merchant's worries, he says:

> I should not see the sandy hour-glass run,
> But I should think of shallows and flats,
> And see my wealthy Andrew dock'd in sand.

The news of the *Andrew*'s capture reached the Court on 30 July 1596. This gives a window of just under two years for the 1600 quarto's composition – after 30 July 1596 and before 22 July 1598 – but it does not preclude the possibility that Shakespeare revised the play in that period, rather than wrote it from scratch.

In this scenario, *The Merchant*'s roots are in the summer of 1594 and the scandal surrounding Doctor Lopez. Two references in particular suggest a nod to the Doctor and his cruel death. When Antonio is in the dock, his friend Gratiano accuses Shylock of having been possessed by the soul of an executed wolf.

> Thou almost mak'st me waver in my faith,
> To hold opinion with Pythagoras,
> That souls of animals infuse themselves
> Into the trunks of men: thy currish spirit
> Govern'd a wolf, who hang'd for human slaughter –

Even from the gallows did his fell soul fleet,
And whilst thou layest in thy unhallowed dam,
Infus'd itself in thee: for thy desires
Are wolvish, bloody, starv'd and ravenous.'

Is Shakespeare punning on 'Lopus', the name by which Lopez was known in London, and which derived, like 'Lopez', from the Latin *lupus*, a 'wolf'? If so, there might be a reference to the rumours surrounding the interrogation of Doctor Lopez in Act III of *The Merchant*, when love-struck Bassanio compares the torture of his love for Portia to lying 'upon the rack', and Portia rejoins, 'Ay, but I fear you speak upon the rack, where men enforced do speak any thing.'

Of course, both these references to Lopez – if that is indeed what they are – could have been written in the July 1596–July 1598 period; Lopez was a popular reference point in 1599, when Nashe wrote *Lenten Stuff*, and remained so as late as 1624, when Middleton wrote *A Game at Chess*. The most that they indicate is topicality and an imaginative link that enriched *The Merchant* for its original audience.

What that audience thought, and what Shakespeare intended it to think, are impossible to define. Combined with ambiguities of origin are ambiguities of interpretation, both contemporary and modern. James Roberts's first registration of *The Merchant* in July 1598 records that it was played and known under two titles. This suggests an ambivalence about the play's focus: is it about Antonio 'the Merchant of Venice', or Shylock 'the Jew of Venice'? The play is a comedy in the Shakespearean sense, of restored cosmic order rather than laughter. It ends with three happy couples romping in the moonlight at Belmont. Under the same moon in Venice is Shylock, whose expulsion from the play and their lives restores that order. Shylock was written to be comical in the cruder sense. There was a long heritage of comic Jews on the medieval stage, part theological caricature, part slapstick. Marlowe's Barabas is a homage to these antecedents. Shylock's comedy was meant to dignify Antonio, the protagonist of the play. If Elizabethan audiences found Shylock more memorable than Antonio, it was because he derived from a familiar comic ancestry, Barabas via the Mystery Plays. But that did not make him more important. The usurer was a sub-plot.

Shylock appears in five of *The Merchant*'s twenty scenes, and speaks only 360 of the play's lines. Yet Shakespeare found a potential in Shylock that made his character meatier than that of anodyne Antonio. Like Al-Burak, the androgyne horse-mule that Muslim tradition tethered to the Western Wall in Jerusalem, Shylock the forced convert is left just outside the ghetto wall of Venice. Shakespeare's Marrano is a new social form, neither Jew nor Christian. This tension makes him a complex character, fuller than the medieval cliché or Marlowe's 'Machiavell'. The modern preference for Shylock over Antonio prizes this aspect – a tragedy of identity – over Shylock's original comic characterisation.

This has distorted *The Merchant* into almost unrecognisable shapes, making the original intent nearly irrecoverable. Modern interpreters and audiences alike have found a morbid fascination in a simultaneous loathing and sympathy for Shylock, an interest intensified by the evident comfort of the young couples at Shylock's annihilation, and Shakespeare's implicit assumption that the successive scenes in which Shylock is tormented by the Christians, and his daughter is spooning in the moonlight with their friend, would jar as little with the sensibilities of his audience as it did with the characters themselves. When the play is skewed towards Shylock, its resolution pulls it back towards Antonio. When it is Antonio's play, Shylock upstages him. The Jew and the Merchant are tied by more than a usurer's bond.

After the failure of the Counter-Armada, Lopez held Don Antonio within his bond as Shylock held his Antonio. And, like the Doge and Court of Venice with Shylock, the Queen and Privy Council held Lopez in their bond. But to what end? Don Antonio had nothing to give either Lopez or the Queen and Council, and Lopez had little more. If Antonio's creditors severed themselves completely from him, they would lose any chance of regaining their money. To hold on to their investments, the Privy Council had to throw good money after bad. And so they threw a lifeline to Lopez, architect of the Antonine disaster.

After three months of penury, Lopez received a royal grant, conferring upon him the revenues from Tredington and Blockley, two small estates in the Midlands, for the term of nineteen years. Inspecting his domain, the new man of property could not have seemed more incongruous: an absurd figure, stepping through the boggy furrows of autumnal England in his dapper cloak and flopping ruff; to a local war veteran, some Pistol or Nym or Bardolph returned from the Netherlands, suspicious too, with his soft Iberian manner and Hispanic lisp. The new landlord was determined to extract the maximum value from the backs of the sheep in his fields. Well-connected and foreign, Lopez was a gift to tavern gossips and debt-struck merchants across the district. In springtime his tenants would deliver their wool to the local market town, Stratford-Upon-Avon, along with grumbled reports of sharp dealings by their new landlord, the alien urbanite foisted upon them by a decree from the distant capital.

After giving Lopez his reprieve, the Privy Council gave another to Don Antonio. The pretender had washed up in the London house of his mistress, Elena Figuera. His clothes were full of holes and his Court had contracted to a trio: his longtime councillor Diego de Botello; his spiritual adviser Brother Diego Carlos; and a nobleman called Cipriano de Figueredo. All of them were on 'very bad terms' with each other, and Figueredo was a Spanish agent. Lopez sent Antonio money for a new doublet and a set of velvet breeches, and the Privy Council issued Antonio a monthly stipend of £100, pragmatically and 'with a very ill grace'. He still possessed titular value as a king and, if they abandoned him, he would take his new doublet and breeches to new creditors in Paris or Constantinople. Kept in London, he was a bargaining chip for future negotiations with Philip II. Giving just enough support to stop the whole London Portuguese apparatus from collapsing, they kept Antonio captive in order to trade him away.

Like the Privy Council, Lopez had profited by the conceit that Antonio was a king, not a pretext. He had also lost money wagered on the success of that conceit. As the financial pressure mounted, Lopez saw a way of recovering his £4000 from Antonio. Lopez's and Antonio's return to Plymouth in July 1589 had coincided with

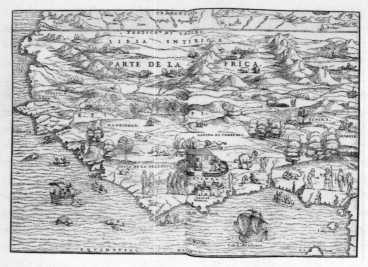

The Guinea coast of West Africa circa 1550, by Giacomo Gastaldi.

the return of a more successful venture. The Guinea merchants to whom Antonio had sold a licence to trade on the West African coast had landed a profitable cargo on the quayside. Noticing Don Antonio's unpopularity, the Plymouth merchants had kept his 5 per cent of the profits for themselves. Antonio had already signed over this 5 per cent to Lopez against his debt of £4000. Lopez sued for the commission in a letter to the Privy Council, prosecuting the merchants and, by extension, Don Antonio. A Jew, and a Portingall at that, was attempting to use English justice to gain satisfaction from a king.

When the Privy Council convened at the palace of Richmond on the morning of 21 December 1589, Lopez's suit was the first item on their agenda. It was a common type of request – the Council had been untangling similar suits resulting from the Counter-Armada for months – but what made it remarkable were the identities of its plaintiff and defendant. King Antonio was being sued by his own ambassador. It was an insult to Antonio's dignity, but the precise nature of the offence was hard to quantify. The status of both parties was debateable. Antonio was not a real king, and Lopez was not a real ambassador. The ambiguity of this constructively obscure arrangement had suited the Council for nearly a decade, but now it created a problem.

What was Lopez's status? King Antonio recognised Lopez as a Portuguese subject and had appointed him as his ambassador, but Lopez was also an endenizened English subject. In effect, he had dual nationality. If Lopez sued Antonio as a naturalised Englishman, he had the right to appeal to the Council, but they had no right to hear his suit. A foreign monarch was immune to the suits of another monarch's subjects, even if one of the monarchs lived at Elena Figuera's and lacked a spare pair of hose. The dispute would have to be resolved between the monarchs. Conversely, if Lopez sued Antonio as a Portuguese ambassador, it was an entirely Portuguese matter. If Antonio was a king, then the Privy Council were only empowered to judge Lopez's complaint against the Guinea merchants, regardless of whether Antonio was central to the suit.

Yet Antonio's status was no clearer. The Queen had recognised him as a king in order to pick off trade concessions, hijack ships and invade Portugal. But if her Council judged his affairs, that would suggest they did not consider him to be a king, merely a Portuguese subject. It would fall to the King of Portugal to enforce any verdict, and if Antonio was not the King of Portugal, then somebody else must be. This opened a realm of unpleasant speculation, as the alternatives to Antonio were his own sons Emanuel and Cristovão; the Spanish puppet João, Duke of Braganza; and the puppeteer himself, Philip II of Spain.

Lopez put the Council in an impossible position. Like Shylock, he sought 'the due and forfeit' of his bond from Antonio via the mechanism of the law. And like Shylock with the laws of Venice, Lopez had a case. Regardless of the unorthodox diplomatic terms prevailing between Lopez and Antonio, the Privy Council held Lopez responsible for Antonio. They awarded in Lopez's favour but – like Portia before the Doge of Venice – they showed the sword of law to be double-edged.

Among Antonio's biggest creditors were the Councillors at

Richmond that Sunday, including Lord Burghley, Sir Francis Walsingham and Lord Admiral Howard. Apart from a decade of subventions and the £100 per month they now paid to Antonio, they had all invested and lost in the Counter-Armada. Lopez had 'induced' these investments, yet he brazenly asked for his debt to be considered ahead of the debts of his betters and patrons. In Shylockian terms, he put his legal right ahead of his social duty.

Both Lopez and Shylock advanced suits that they could not be allowed to win. Both possessed bonds that had been extracted at the borrower's greatest necessity and which could not possibly be repaid: Lopez's 50,000 crowns and Shylock's pound of flesh. Though technically valid, both contracts were morally invalid. If Lopez's contract was enforced, the debts of a Portuguese Jew would take precedence over the debts of the Privy Council and City investors. If Shylock's contract was enforced, the laws of Venice would be amenable to barbarism. While Shylock's failure is one of compassion, Lopez's was one of taste. The Council rewarded him in kind. He might be entitled to his pound of flesh from Antonio, but they would make him earn it.

Tiptoeing around the question of Antonio's status, they ordered that two letters be despatched. The first informed the recalcitrant Guinea merchants that not only was Don Antonio's 5 per cent due, but it was to be paid 'only to Doctor Lopas or his lawful deputies', until Lopez had collected all of the £4000 that Antonio owed him. The second letter was to Lopez. He was to exert 'his utmost endeavour' to recover the commissions. When he had recouped his money, he was to continue endeavouring and collecting until all of Antonio's debts were cleared. At the time Antonio had taken the £4000 loan, he had plenty of other debts to other, more influential creditors. When Antonio had pawned his financial affairs to the Doctor, Lopez had taken on Antonio's liabilities as well as his assets. Responsibility for the repayment of these debts also fell to Lopez.

The royal physician had been commanded to behave like a common debt collector, a Shylockian loan shark. Lopez was ordered to keep a 'perfect reckoning and account' of how 'he received and disbursed' the incomes he collected for Antonio, so that 'it might appear what money did come into his hands, and how the same was employed' to the discharge of Antonio's debts. As Don Antonio was bankrupt, the clearance of his debts was as unlikely as discovering the North-East Passage to Cathay. Lopez had been appointed as Antonio's official receiver, lifelong accountant to the King of Portugal. Through greed and ambition, Lopez and Antonio had tied themselves in a knot of bitterness. The Council tightened it into a stranglehold, turning Lopez's bond into a permanent contract. Like Shylock before the Doge and magnificoes of Venice, Lopez had brought a suit before Lord Burghley and the Lords of the Council and, like Shylock, he had been punished even though his claim was not disproved.

The Doctor, of all people, knew how slim his chances of recompense were. A king whose wardrobe required subsidy had no chance of repaying £4000, let alone £50,000, from a lost kingdom. The Guinea revenues were more accessible than the Portuguese revenues, but for Lopez to pursue them when Antonio's penury was visible in the holes in his doublet smacked of vindictiveness. Yet revenge was stronger than reason. Lopez had ruined himself in the cause of Antonio, so Antonio must be ruined in the cause of Lopez.

The suit had backfired on its suitor. As the recently appointed government lawyer Francis Bacon was to write, revenge was 'a kind of rough justice, which the more a man's nature runs to, the more ought the law to weed it out'. The Council were exasperated with both Lopez and Antonio. Both needed to be reminded of the real order of things. The law was not a neutral tool to be wielded in vendetta against a man's betters. Before the great patrons, Lopez's role was that of the patronised. His duty, if not his due, was to do their will and collect the money that Antonio owed. If Antonio could be called 'dog' to his face, then Lopez could expect no favours.

The circumstantial similarities between Lopez's real suit against Don Antonio and Shylock's fictional suit against Antonio the merchant are so strong that the differences between the two cases are more remarkable than their similarities. Lopez and Shylock: both aliens, both traders in a great port city, both well-connected at home and abroad, both known in commercial and political circles as Jews, both issuing loans to a high-born Antonio on unreasonable terms, both bringing a suit before the aristocracy of their cities, and both thwarted by verdicts that support their claims but mock the claimants. The only element present in Shylock's story but absent in Lopez's is the exact terms of the loan.

Shylock, impelled by theological hatred, lent 3000 ducats for three months, and received as security the promise of a pound of flesh, a metaphor for usury made horribly real. When Antonio borrowed from Shylock, he had an exact idea of how and when he should repay the Jew, and he confidently told Bassanio not to worry.

> Why fear not man, I will not forfeit it, –
> Within these two months, that's a month before
> This bond expires, I do expect return
> Of twice three times the value of this bond.

If all Antonio's argosies returned with their cargoes intact, he expected to make 18,000 ducats, and well within the time scale he agreed with Shylock. From a usurer's point of view, there was not much chance of catching an enemy 'upon the hip' in such an arrangement.

Lopez's loan to Don Antonio was bigger and riskier. The loan was secured on speculative revenues, and if there was a timescale for repayment, it depended upon the invasion of Portugal, a much more risky venture than sending argosies to Mexico or India. Antonio might have taken both pounds and flesh to Paris or Constantinople at any moment, taking Lopez's money with him. By Elizabethan standards, Lopez's £4000 was a colossal sum for a private citizen. In current terms, £4000 would be equivalent to more than £2 million. The Elizabethan economy depended upon the wool trade. Periodically disrupted by war on the Continent, it was prone to extended periods of high inflation. To lend such an amount without insuring against depreciation was folly. It was certainly not the behaviour of an experienced merchant, an aniseed and sumach monopolist who dealt in several currencies and was active in the Spice Trust. So what was Lopez's pound of flesh?

In London, Lopez sought £4000. In Venice, Shylock sought 3000 ducats. The ducat had originated in Italy in 1140 as the personal coinage of the Duke of Apulia, but by Shakespeare's and Lopez's day, there were many different ducats in circulation on the Continent, each minted by different dukes and each of different relative value. Shakespeare's reference to the ducat as the currency of Venice was no more significant in itself than other naturalistic touches, like his references to the Rialto or the carnival. There is no reason to believe that Shakespeare ever saw the Rialto at Venice; if he had been to Italy, he might not have made Verona a port in *Romeo and Juliet*. Neither is there any reason to believe that he arrived at Shylock's loan by calculating Don Antonio's debt in Venetian ducats. By the rates of exchange offered in the City of London, 3000 Venetian ducats was, at approximately 15 ducats to the English pound, equivalent to £2250. The significance of Antonio's debt to Shylock lies not in its currency, but in its quantity.

Why 3000 ducats, instead of the 10,000 ducats cited in *Il Pecorone*? Antonio was sure he would shortly make six times that amount. He could have borrowed 12,000 ducats for Bassanio's dowry, or 20,000. There is only one contemporary reason why Lopez's £4000 might have turned into Shylock's 3000 ducats, and that is in the nature of Elizabethan moneylending. Historically, Christianity had been characterised by a detestation of usury. The Gospels and the early Church Fathers had condemned it, and medieval legal authorities had denounced it – albeit at a length that suggests its unofficial prevalence. Jews, denied access to any professional fields in which they might compete or mingle with Christians, became synonymous with usury. When Henry VIII experimented with its legalisation in 1545, virtuous Catholics everywhere found confirmation of their worst suspicions about the portly heretic, led into Jewish practices by greed and contempt for Roman tradition. Henry's experiment was revoked in 1552, but economic pressure forced the legalisation of usury in a Parliamentary Act of 1571. Usury was essential to agriculture, industry and foreign trade; the English economy could not develop without a system of short-term loans and their proscription only encouraged illegal loan sharking. The year before, John Shakespeare, father of William had been fined forty shillings for charging £20 interest on an £80 loan, an interest rate of 25 per cent.

The Usury Act specified that 'all usury, being forbidden by the law of God, is sin and detestable'. In *The Merchant of Venice*, Shylock's main reason for hating the honourable Antonio is rooted in the refusal of Antonio, a good Christian, to profit by moneylending.

> He lends out money gratis, and brings down
> The rate of usuance here with us in Venice.
> If I catch him once upon the hip,
> I will feed fat the ancient grudge I bear him.
> He hates our sacred nation, and he rails
> (Even there where merchants most do congregate)
> On me, my bargains, and my well-won thrift,
> Which he calls interest. Cursed be my tribe
> If I forgive him!

Under the Usury Act, if money had to be lent at all, the rate of interest should be no greater than 10 per cent. A usorious contract, which spoke specifically of punitive conditions and interest rates higher than 10 per cent, could be proven legally invalid, and anyone who was caught charging higher rates was liable to prosecution. Although it was an improvement, the Act created impossible situations in the Elizabethan economy. The finances of extended, credit-driven ventures such as the spice trade or the invasion of foreign countries could be ruined by inflation. Yet there was still great demand for loans, as the economy could not expand without them. If a way could be found to issue them without suffering from inflation, there was also a great willingness to issue them and make an easy profit. A second, illegal, market developed in the shadow of the Usury Act. It hid its tracks with three simple fictions.

The first trick was that when the borrower signed a receipt for his money, the sum named on the receipt was not the sum borrowed, but the sum to be repaid. In other words, the loan, plus hidden interest. A usurer who lent £20 might issue a receipt for £30, thus hiding a 50 per cent interest in the contract with the connivance of both parties. If the borrower defaulted, the receipt was the usurer's guarantee of legal redress. If the borrower attempted to escape the debt by confessing that the contract was illegal, he was condemned by his own signature on the receipt. The second trick was that if goods were bought on credit, the buyer would take a small 'loan' at the same time. He signed a receipt for both amounts: the value of the goods and the 'loan', which was really the interest on his credit. The third option was to combine the receipt with a verbal agreement, so that a hidden high interest rate accompanied a low visible one.

If Lopez was a usurer as well as a physician, businessman and landlord, it might explain how Shylock's 3000 ducats grew into Lopez's £4000. Don Antonio had no collateral, so if Lopez had lent him money, it would have been at an illegally high rate of interest. The figure of £4000 on their contract would have been a cumulative sum: the £3000 loan plus interest. When Antonio defaulted on his debt, Lopez sued him. The Privy Council knew that Lopez, having issued an illegal loan, was asking for an excessive return. Their punishment was to accept Lopez's inflated figure of £4000, and then to turn it against him. He would get his 33.33 per cent, but at a price: he would have to take permanent responsibility for Don Antonio's finances.

A similar whiff of skulduggery rises from William Shakespeare's adventures in credit. In the spring of 1605, Shakespeare sued one of his Stratford neighbours, an apothecary named Philip Rogers, for an unpaid debt. The amount was not enormous: £2. 2s., of which 6s. had already been paid. The £2 was for the twenty bushels of malt which Shakespeare had sold to Rogers, and the 2s. were a loan that Shakespeare claimed to have given him. This was a legal fiction in the classic model of Elizabethan moneylending. The 2s. were not a loan at all, but interest on the outstanding 40s. at a rate of 5 per cent. This was 5 per cent more than the interest-free loans of Antonio, Shakespeare's Merchant of Christian conscience, but it was 5 per cent less than the legal maximum. It would have been a modest, ethical piece of speculation, were it not for the damages. For apart from interest, Shakespeare sought a further 10s., or 20 per cent, from

Rogers in compensation. That would have raised his profit to 12s. on a loan of 40s: a Shylockian return of 30 per cent, and the same return that John Shakespeare had been fined for extracting in 1570. There is no record of how the court ruled in Shakespeare versus Rogers, but in 1608 Shakespeare tried the same approach in another case of credit turned sour. That time his Antonio was one John Addenbrooke, from whom the Stratford Shylock sought £6 and damages of 24s. The claim gave a return of 20 per cent, plus whatever profit might have been hidden in the original contract.

A contemporary witness attests to Lopez's reputation as a usurer. Gabriel Harvey was a friend of the poet Edmund Spenser and a small versifier in his own right. He was also a leering gargoyle on the cathedral of Elizabethan letters, an ambitious man 'who came ruffling it out hufty-tufty in his suit of velvet', a picker of literary brawls, a compulsive medico-legal carper and incontinent pamphleteer. Tipped at Cambridge as a leader of his generation, he had entered the Earl of Leicester's service as a secretary at a time when the habitués of Leicester House included the poet-diplomats Edmund Spenser and Sir Philip Sidney, as well as Doctors Roderigo Lopez and John Dee. But Harvey lacked the feel for patronage that would convert brilliance into success. Overtaken by greater and lesser minds, he retreated to misanthropic obscurity as a provincial doctor in small-town Cambridgeshire.

Harvey was an inveterate annotator. He contributed less to posterity through his own work than he did through his marginalia on other people's. One of the items in his library was *A Calumny on Jewish Physicians and their Murders: An Exhortation to Christian Faith* by Johannes Thomas Fregius, printed at Basle in 1570. Harvey, the frustrated suitor and country doctor, chose this imbalanced diatribe as the repository of his own medical reflections and his conspiracy theories about why his peers had succeeded where he had failed. 'Francis I, King of France, could not be cured by any physician but a Jew,' he wrote across the title page. 'Doctor Julio the Italian, beside his courtly finesse, had wit and learning in him, and for his gallant practise, deserved to be a Prince's physician.' Naturally he recorded his impression of England's current 'Prince's physician'.

Doctor Lopus, the Queen's Physician, is descended of Jews, but himself a Christian, and Portugall. He none of the learnedest, or expertest Physicians in the Court; but one that maketh a great account of himself as the best; and, by a kind of Jewish practice, hath grown to much Wealth, and some reputation, as well with the Queen herself, as with some of the greatest Lords and Ladies.

Gabriel Harvey's impression of Lopez.

Through a 'kind of Jewish practice', Lopez had grown to 'much Wealth'. There was little substance to this claim. Lopez owed his success and failure to his talents as physician and intelligencer. In his rise, Lopez had profited from his ambiguity; in his fall, it would harm him. Harvey's marginalia was undated, although it must have been written in or after 1594, as he cited that year elsewhere in these jottings. Either previously or contemporaneously with Shakespeare, Harvey blended the images of a physician and a usurer in Lopez. Just as a physician cut his patient's vein to let blood, so a usurer scalped his clients for a pound of flesh. Both were assumed to be Jewish – and if not, to be in 'Jewish practice' – and in England both were exemplified in Lopez. Like Drake's fleet and Norris's soldiers, the Doctor's celebrity had run out of his control.

II

Torne Papers blowne into the Ship.

F.H. sc.

6

The Double Bond

From the physician and the lawyer keep not the truth hidden.

John Florio, *First Fruits* (1578)

At Eton, Don Antonio mouldered in his monastery, an antique theological treatise in a library of lost causes. Antonio identified with the biblical King David. He too had enjoyed brief happiness on his throne and suffered a long coda of divine vengeance. Reflecting on his life in old age, David realised that his ruin had been precipitated by his lust for Bathsheba. Antonio considered his ruin to be Lopez's work. He had trusted his physician and had been led into a trap of debt. Like David in his disappointed years, Antonio the psalmist drank and fornicated by the rivers of Berkshire, alternating between debauchery and remorse. 'I have always been an Artist in iniquity,' he admitted in a moment of wry clarity, 'I have always proceeded with impiety, and its documents hath been ever most delightful to me.'

Antonio wanted to escape from London and his debts, but the Queen and her agent Lopez kept him leashed in England. He was a debtor in the hands of his creditors, a king in the hands of his ambassador, but he still needed the Doctor, because Lopez was his connection to the Privy Council and the Queen. The Council had tied them together like a crabby married couple, forcing them to maintain the pretence of doctor–patient and king–ambassador relations, to ensure that Portugal remained a thorn in Philip II's side, and to maintain the flow of exotic imports to English ports. Once a week, the Doctor attended upon Antonio at Eton to administer an easeful senna enema. The King's servant had become his bitter master, and relations were overshadowed by their double bond of financial and diplomatic obligation. 'O how great hath my misfortune been, having incensed him against me, who could have made me most happy.'

Once again, Antonio attempted to flee England. He turned to one of the few followers he could trust. Manuel d'Andrada had stayed with him through all his vicissitudes, had followed him to the gates of Lisbon and back to Plymouth. Andrada spoke Flemish and had underworld connections in the Low Countries, so Antonio asked him to go there and find a captain willing to smuggle him to Dieppe. Once he was on 'the other side', the pretender could begin again and head for the Courts of Constantinople or Morocco, or even sail for Brazil with Sir Francis Drake.

Antonio did not know that Andrada was a Spanish spy and was behind Bernadino de Mendoza's recent attempt to slip an assassin into Eton. The plan had been thwarted by Monsieur de la Chastres, the Governor of Dieppe, who had arrested the killer as he took ship for England and warned Walsingham that a 'David' was 'haunting' Don Antonio. Oblivious to the closing net, Andrada continued his scheme. He crossed the Channel, found his smuggler and sailed to Plymouth to wait for Antonio. From there, he wrote as 'David' to Bernadino de Mendoza in Paris. For 2000 crowns Andrada would hijack Antonio, divert his ship to a Spanish-held Channel port, such as Dunkirk or Gravelines, and pass Antonio to Mendoza's men. 'I am environed with a thousand evils,' wrote Antonio the psalmist.

But Andrada's letter was intercepted at Calais, where Portuguese mails passed through the shop of the Walsingham agent Estevan Nuñez. Although it was pseudonymous, ciphered and 'written in blank with a certain water', Walsingham's cryptologist Thomas Phelippes made fast work of it. As 'David' had written from Plymouth, he could only be Andrada. The double agent was unmasked and Antonio's escape was cancelled. The Flemish captain sailed home unpaid.

In prison, Andrada waited for his death, a traitor caught in the act. But instead of an executioner, he received a visitor. Doctor Lopez appeared in his cell. The old Doctor had pulled some strings with his patients on the Privy Council and had secured a reprieve. Andrada was free to go. Or almost free. The Doctor had some work for Andrada. Lopez was landlord of a house near Aldgate, in the eastern City parish of St Katharine Creechurch, leased from the Bishop of Winchester. The Doctor used it as a lodging house for passing couriers and penurious Portuguese aristocrats. Andrada should go there, take to his bed and feign illness. That would be a suitable cover for the Doctor to visit him with further instructions.

Resurrected from the near-dead, Andrada was cast from his dungeon into the chill, bright streets of a London January like Orpheus escaped from the underworld. He had hardly found his bearings before he ran into another Portuguese intelligencer, Lopez's brother-in-law Bernaldo Luis, who also had some work for Andrada. Luis was a graduate of Walsingham's intelligence service and an able agent. He told Andrada that he was 'scandalised at Don Antonio' because the King 'had used harsh words' towards Lopez's father-in-law, old Dunstan Añes the grocer; so scandalised that he wanted to kill him. In return for Andrada's assistance, Luis offered to 'advise Don Bernadino de Mendoza with all that should pass in England'. Reeling from his release and the twin interventions of Lopez and Luis, Andrada staggered across the City to St Katharine Creechurch and went to bed.

As promised, the Doctor made his house call a few days later. His prognosis was blunt. Andrada's arrest and release were like an illness and its treatment. God had ordained the sickness of imprisonment and God, through his divine instrument Roderigo Lopez, had ordained the patient's release. Lopez had personally begged Andrada's small life from the Queen. He was a man of great influence, and not only the Queen appreciated his uses. Mendoza had already sent Bernaldo Luis to the Doctor with a plan to get Don Antonio out of the way. Lopez had only refused because he did not want to deal with Bernaldo Luis, whom he considered to be a double agent. Perhaps there was another way, one in which Andrada could begin to repay Lopez for saving his life. Perhaps Andrada could deliver a message to Mendoza. If Mendoza had Philip II's permission to deal 'in concerts and agreements' about peace, then 'this was the time'. Lopez worked for Secretary Walsingham and had the ear of the Queen, who was in such 'great fear' of another Spanish Armada that she would 'grant all that should be requested', including the abandonment of Don Antonio and the withdrawal of support from the rebels of the Low Countries.

The Doctor loomed over his healthy patient's pallet, making messianic announcements about his purpose in life, boasting of his powerful connections, and declaring that he possessed the power of life and death over Andrada. The patient accepted. Lopez had known he would; he had no choice. The Doctor issued the prescription that would save Andrada. After taking the message to Mendoza in Paris, Andrada was to reply to Lopez from Calais. Lopez would send him a passport issued by Sir Francis Walsingham, so that when negotiations began Andrada could freely cross the Channel as a courier. When he came to London, Andrada was to stay secretly at Lopez's safe house, where he would be debriefed by Lopez and Walsingham. If the peace talks did not transpire, Lopez could still use his influence to have Don Antonio expelled from or kept captive in England, whichever Philip II desired. If peace talks did develop, Lopez would be the channel for the Privy Council's 'determinations' and would tell Mendoza when the time was right 'to make the contracts' of a treaty.

Lopez had one final instruction for Andrada. If everything went to plan, he would need to prove to the Privy Council that the Spanish intended to negotiate sincerely and considered him to be an acceptable intermediary. He needed a token, something valuable enough to indicate sincerity, but small enough to be carried into England discreetly. A jewel, for instance. Of course, if Andrada returned with the token, but the talks never happened, then he and Lopez could scam the jewel for themselves. Apart from negotiating with the Spanish, Lopez was negotiating the marriage of his daughter Anne to the son of Pero Rodrigues, a Marrano banker from Lyons. He could use it for her dowry.

As a frequenter of taverns on both sides of the Channel, Andrada was familiar with the new, fashionable game of billiards. The English were obsessed with it, although Edmund Spenser thought it a 'thriftless game'. Mary, Queen of Scots had wiled away her incarceration at the table; after her execution, her doctor had wrapped her corpse in its green baize. Shakespeare slipped an anachronistic reference to the cue and balls into *Antony and Cleopatra*: 'Let it alone, let's to billiards.' If Andrada had been more alert or less desperate, he might have realised that in the days after his release from prison he had been spun all over the table in the trajectories of a double cannon shot. After Andrada had been propelled from his cell, first Bernaldo Luis made one offer, then Lopez made another. Between them, they offered everything that Philip II might desire: peace in the Netherlands and an end to Don Antonio. Unable to control his own movement, Andrada ricocheted from prison to Luis to Lopez, and then over the Channel to Paris.

It was treason to talk of negotiations and treaties with Spain, but both Lopez and Bernaldo Luis could pose as double agents in safety, as the hand that drove the cue belonged to Secretary Walsingham. They had both served the Secretary for years, posing as traitors to intercept mails and detect spies. Knowing Andrada's desperation, Walsingham had squeezed him between two claws, Luis and Lopez, and loaded him up with promises, each studded with a hook. The Queen and Burghley wanted peace, but Walsingham was an unlikely midwife. He was a lifelong ideological enemy of Spain, to whom any accommodation was anathema. The ailing Secretary put out his feelers less in the hope of opening peace talks with his lifelong enemies than in sneaking a spy into the Escorial. That was why his proposal was less substantial than it seemed. It was nothing for Lopez to 'offer' that Don Antonio be imprisoned in London, as he was already a financial and political hostage. And the rebels of the Netherlands would fight the Spanish occupation with or without English aid. Andrada's mission was Walsingham's last flourish, an attempt to gull the King of Spain in his own Court. Acting his part, Lopez added his own commission to the sting, the jewel. The whole plan was an intelligencer's 'projection', designed to draw out Spanish agents and intelligence.

On 5 March 1590, Andrada left London for Paris, bearing a full

menu of diplomatic temptations. To let him know he was on proba-
tion, he was arrested on the road to Dover and the letter he carried
for Mendoza was copied. It was returned to him and he was sent
on his way. Having cannoned off Bernaldo Luis and Doctor Lopez,
Andrada spun softly into the pocket. When he reached Paris, he did
not tell Mendoza that the letter in his hand had already been read
by Secretary Walsingham. Andrada had begun as a servant of Don
Antonio. He had become a double agent for Mendoza. And now he
was a triple agent for Walsingham.

Mendoza had worried about Andrada after his letters had dried
up inexplicably, so when the spy appeared in Paris, the ambassador's
first reaction was relief. This turned to fascination when he heard
Andrada's report. Mendoza knew of Lopez's long service to
Walsingham, but he was sufficiently intrigued by the Doctor's offer
to pass it on to Philip II at the Escorial. At the very least, it was an
opportunity to send Andrada 'backwards and forwards to England
under cover of the negotiations'; Mendoza had seen the same
malleable purpose in Andrada as Lopez and Walsingham. Since
Mendoza did not trust the post – he suspected that the English had
obtained copies of the current set of ciphers – he sent Andrada in
person. As he packed in Paris, Andrada sent word to Lopez that the
first part of his mission had succeeded.

But while Andrada crossed France, he did not know that the
controller of his mission was dead. His mind exhausted by overwork
and his body ruined by 'physic', Secretary Walsingham died in his
London home at midnight on 6 April 1590. Around 'ten of the clock
in the next night following', his family interred the Queen's tireless
servant in secret 'in Paul's church without solemnity', before his creditors could impound his corpse. His private papers, the accumulation of more than two decades of intelligencing, were stolen from
his home immediately after his death. The identity of the thief is
unknown. Walsingham's death was to impart an unforeseen spin to
events, like a tear in the green baize. Lopez and Luis had pretended
to be traitors in order to entrap Andrada. When Walsingham died,
so did their proof of innocence. To another eye, their projecting
might look like treason.

Oblivious, Andrada went to Spain. News of Walsingham's death delayed his case because Philip II was unsure of whether it would moderate the English stance. It was not until 4 April 1591 – over a year after receiving his orders from Lopez – that Andrada reached the Escorial, Philip's fortress-monastery near Madrid.

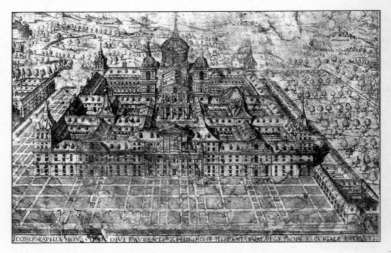

San Lorenzo del Escorial, in a 17th Century engraving.

In the cool, thick-walled chambers of the Escorial, the mighty emperor was 'much tormented with gout in his legs'. The pain was so bad that his doctors had bled him four times, leaving him exhausted and anaemic. He was steered into the room in a wheelchair trimmed with black velvet. Andrada screwed up his courage and delivered Lopez's offer. In return, he received immediate hope of 'going to see his wife' and obtaining a pardon for supporting Don Antonio.

A summary of the interview was prepared for Philip's reference.

By means of Doctor Lopez, [Andrada] was opening negotiations for peace with England, if permission be given for him to do so. He believes that he could carry these through successfully, as he understands that they desire it, and Doctor Lopez assures him of success. By means of the same Doctor Lopez, he will undertake, if so desired, that Don Antonio shall never leave the country. Or otherwise, that he shall be expelled at once, if that course be preferred. Besides these three things, which are the main objects of his coming, he says that he has an understanding with an Englishman, a brother-in-law of the said Dr Lopez [Bernaldo Luis], who undertakes to send him advices of events there, and will also attempt to do another secret service which he recommended to him.

Andrada had delivered Lopez's message to the letter, and Walsingham's plan to pass an agent into the Escorial had succeeded posthumously. But Philip had seen the intent behind the offer and was determined to play Walsingham's ghost at his own game. The hermit of the Escorial responded in the duplicitous terms of Lopez's offer. Philip ordered Andrada to return to England and obtain a passport from Lopez as planned. He was to encourage the Doctor with 'hopes of success', but was to use them as 'an excuse for remaining there safely for some time'. With his cover established, Andrada was to urge Bernaldo Luis to kill Don Antonio, or at least to persuade Lopez to exile him. For this service, Andrada received 300 *reals*, plus a monthly stipend of 30 *reals*. It would be necessary to convince Lopez that the Spanish were genuinely interested in negotiations. In accordance with Doctor Lopez's request, Andrada left with 'one of the old jewels from His Majesty's caskets'.

Philip had repaid Walsingham in his own coin. If Andrada could enter the Escorial with a peace offer, then he could also enter the palace of Whitehall with one, and he could enter both places as a spy. Philip knew that the dazzling reflection of the jewel and the promise of further reward would blind the greedy Doctor to Andrada's intelligence gathering in London.

After surviving a shipwreck in the Bay of Biscay, Andrada wrote to Lopez from Dieppe on 1 July 1591. He requested that Lopez send a 'safe conduct' to Calais, care of Estevan Nuñez's jewellery shop, so that he might 'come disguised' into England on their matter of 'great importance'.

Lopez had not heard from Andrada for over a year. In that time the political scene in London had changed, and he did not feel that this was an opportune moment for Andrada to resurface. Leicester and Walsingham, the warrior and the strategist, were dead, and had left an army of spies and handlers without patronage or employment, suddenly exposed to the predatory competition of their rivals. Lopez had to be careful. He had despatched Andrada on a mission for Walsingham. Andrada had returned bearing a jewel from Philip II. Only Walsingham had known the terms of Andrada's mission and Lopez's reward. Lopez was aware that he might be mistaken for a Spanish agent taking his pay, rather than an English projector tricking Philip out of a commission. It was clear that he needed the sanctuary of a new patron, but whom?

Before the early 1590s, Elizabethan politicians had shared a common perception – England had a conflict of interest with Spain – and differed only on the appropriate response. But a generational and political watershed had been passed. England and Spain had each launched a failed attack on the other, producing a balance of failure. The next steps in the long dance were uncertain. The drawn-out, expensive conflict had drained both countries, and the dancers were faltering. Philip II was a sick, elderly man, seemingly intent on dying at his desk. Though her portraitists flattered her with a young girl's looks, Elizabeth was balding, with blackened teeth and sour breath. Of her old circle, Lord Burghley was the last survivor, erratic in his dotage, his flowing script crabbed by arthritis. Like bare-knuckle boxers in a Southwark booth, England and Spain staggered in an embrace that kept both on their feet, unsure if their balance was an opportunity to declare a draw or to launch a knockout punch. A new generation arose, and domestic politics became a struggle for influence over the Queen, played out in foreign policy.

Two parties formed. One was the governing faction, led by Lord Burghley. The Chancellor wanted to bequeath a stable State, steered by his family. He advocated compromise with Spain and groomed his pale, hunchbacked son Robert Cecil as the heir to his 'peace party'. The other faction was outside the citadel of power. It favoured an aggressive military policy towards Spain, for without patronage, loot was the best way for an aristocrat to pay his debts. This faction, the 'war party', possessed as its totem the hyperbolic blend of chivalry and cynicism, passion and falsity that was Robert Devereux, second Earl of Essex, the last great courtier of the age, and one whose greatness resounded all the louder for its hollowness.

A tall man with square shoulders and an adolescent stoop, Essex had the pale, gingery cast prized by his time, and a wide, pale face bisected by a long nose and a wispy red beard. He had inherited his title at the age of nine and had been appointed a ward of the Crown. His guardian, the Master of the Court of Wards, was Lord Burghley. At one point in Essex's irregular childhood, he lived in Burghley's London home where he met his future political adversary, Robert Cecil, Burghley's brilliant but crippled son. After becoming the Earl of Leicester's stepson, the Hamlet of Kenilworth arrived at Court at the age of seventeen, possessed of the appropriate graces and a good dose of Cambridge classicism. He was a melodious singer, a light dancer, a reader of Renaissance handbooks like *The Courtier* and a writer of romantic verses. He combined a stylish wardrobe with spontaneous vulgarity, cultivating both the foppish wit of the carpet knight and the hearty, hard-drinking manner of the professional soldier.

After the death of the Earl of Leicester, the prior champion at casting such poses, Essex began an exhibitionistic simulacrum of a love affair with Elizabeth, politics disguised as romance. She was a sexagenarian virgin, he was in his teens. He was also penniless. The debts that he had inherited with his title had made Essex the poorest earl in England. His largest creditor was the Queen. The romantic pose covered financial necessity as well as political ambition. He could afford nothing less.

Andrada resurfaced just as the first round of Essex's joust with Robert Cecil came to a head. While Andrada was being shipwrecked and saved in the Bay of Biscay, Lopez had been following the Queen around England on her annual progress. The tour had been a vehicle for intense factional competition. In early May, when Elizabeth stayed at Burghley's country seat of Theobalds in Essex, she had conferred an advantage on the peace party, by knighting Robert Cecil. Yet on 19 July she chose a reception at Burghley House as the moment to reward the war party, by appointing Essex to the Privy Council as Master of the Horse. And on 2 August, when Lopez was with the Court at the country retreat of Nonsuch, she adroitly balanced that gift by elevating Sir Robert Cecil to the Council.

The two factions were neck and neck, but they did not have the same resources. It was the meeting of a novice and a master. Burghley was the most experienced and most senior Privy Councillor, the architect of the Elizabethan State. His portrait in old age shows the Lord Treasurer as a haggard, fur-swagged old man, sagging beneath the golden garland of his chain of office. There are puffy dark pouches beneath his eyes, but they still possess a piercing, interrogatory vision. Another portrait shows Burghley balanced on the back of a mule like a Chaucerian pilgrim, legs stiff with gout, inspecting every foot of his estates for himself, leaving nothing to chance. He plodded through his papers with deceptive determination, a copy of Cicero's *Offices* tucked into his sleeve, modesty concealing purpose, a vicious kick concealed by a calm manner.

Essex was an immature newcomer, spoilt and unproven. Distracted by vanity, he swung between inertia and obsession, and was crude in his handling of Queen and Council alike. Meanwhile his nemesis, Robert Cecil, crept up on him, a pale, flush-cheeked hunchback with a mind sharp as a stiletto. Crippled from birth, sickly Robert Cecil could not flatter the Queen by playing the besotted swain, but he could appeal to the same instinct for caution and self-preservation that she shared with his father. Father or son, one of the Cecils was the most likely suspect in the case of Walsingham's missing files.

Intelligence was a theatre for factional competition, and Lopez knew that Andrada was an intelligence asset. The Doctor had to choose which faction he would join. On past form, he should have been a member of the war party and sided with Essex, heir to Leicester and Walsingham. But as far back as 1571 and the embarrassing episode of the servant's shinbone, Lopez had always taken care to balance that allegiance with a complementary allegiance to

Lord Burghley. And now, casting his experienced eye over the Cecil–Essex struggle, Lopez thought that the Cecils were most likely to win. So he decided to take Andrada's letter to the Cecils. He had known Burghley for more than twenty years. Also, Andrada's mission had been initiated under cover of a peace overture. Admittedly, the original value of the mission had lain in its fakery, but in the new climate of factional jockeying it would be more valuable if it were genuine. If Andrada's report of a Spanish interest in negotiations were true, it would be a coup for the peace party. If it was not, then Andrada could be prevented from falling into the war party's hands. The value of information lay as much in its control and application as in the facts.

To Lopez's relief, Lord Burghley recognised Andrada's potential. He told Monsieur de la Chastres at Dieppe to arrest Andrada and send him under guard to Rye. The next morning, Burghley ordered the interrogation of Andrada at the Customs House in Rye. The chief examiner was to be Thomas Mills, a shady figure who had handled agents for Walsingham in the Low Countries and Calais. Doctor Lopez and Diego Botello, adviser to Don Antonio, were to assist 'Mr Mills', as they called him, by interpreting from Portuguese. Travelling down to Rye, Lopez realised he was under a new, tenuous patronage. His future prosperity depended on its success.

Burghley wanted the truth from Andrada and had given Mr Mills detailed orders about obtaining it. Mr Mills opened the interrogation 'in a friendly manner', but when Andrada did not co-operate, he was dealt with 'strongly . . . as with a traitor', threatened and mishandled 'so very thoroughly as to be afraid of his life'. As he built up his new position, Lopez was in the piquant position of assisting at the torture of his own agent.

Andrada offered no more resistance. His first concern was not to be mistaken for a Spanish agent – or only for a Spanish agent – and his second was to replace Walsingham's patronage with Burghley's. He had already written to Don Antonio begging that his misdemeanours be 'scruffed off'. In his interrogation by Mr Mills, and in a letter to Burghley, he stressed that his mission to Philip II had been at Walsingham's and Lopez's instigation. Lopez left Rye bearing this

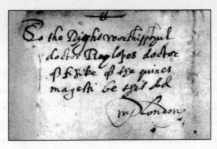

'To the right worshippful doctor Ruy Lopes doctor of fisike of the quines majestie be this delivered in London': Lopez's postal address, as written by Manuel d'Andrada, 11 July 1591.

letter and followed the road along the south coast to Chichester, where the Court now resided. Burghley read Andrada's letter and Mills's report, and he heard Lopez's own account. They all matched: Andrada had been acting for Lopez on Walsingham's instructions.

Lopez had escaped disaster. His dealings with Andrada had been confirmed as the intelligencing of a patriot, not a traitor. In his relief and ambition, he attempted to convince Burghley that Andrada's direct link to Philip II might be a channel for peace talks. Burghley wanted peace and Lopez claimed to offer it, but the careful Lord Treasurer distrusted espionage. He was generally suspicious of Andrada and found it hard to believe that formal, snobbish Philip II would have considered such a dramatic overture from a 'shabby' like Andrada. Burghley had intuited that the Spanish had divined Walsingham's intention and had decided to play the English at their own game, by sending Andrada to England as an emissary and using him as a spy, a projector to catch a projector. But Lopez's agent, and the Doctor himself, both had other uses.

Burghley had already acquired part of Walsingham's network. Monsieur de la Chastres at Dieppe, Mr Mills in London and now Doctor Lopez had all entered his employ. Andrada was an experienced field operative. Because he had been caught acting as a double agent, his life depended on his usefulness. Fluent in Flemish, he would be more productive as an intelligencer in the Low Countries than as a bearer of deceptive vagaries from Madrid. In particular, Burghley wanted intelligence about the collaboration between the

Spanish vizier in the Low Countries, Don Pedro Enriques e Toledo, Count of Fuentes, and the English Catholic exile Sir William Stanley, around whom there swirled a maelstrom of regicidal plots.

A cousin to the Earl of Derby, Stanley had been a captain in Leicester's army in the Low Countries when he had succumbed to the 'golden bullets' of Spanish bribery and deserted. His betrayal was preceded by a long history of failed ambition. The Stanleys had a distant claim to the English throne. This claim, combined with their Catholicism, made them a focus of English Catholic aspirations and of Spanish intrigue. By the 1590s, it was apparent that Elizabeth I would neither marry nor bear children. Open speculation was treasonable, but the Cecils were in covert contact with her cousin James VI of Scotland. A Catholic initiative was also attempted.

In 1591, Stanley and the leading Jesuit exile, Father Robert Persons, were attempting to sound out whether the Derby heir, Ferdinando, Lord Strange, might allow himself to be suggested as a Catholic candidate for the English Crown. Ferdinando was no stranger to intrigue; in the same year, when Christopher Marlowe was charged with counterfeiting in the Low Countries port of Flushing, one of character references he gave was the weighty name of Lord Strange. Ferdinando's father was the Lord Strange who patronised the theatre company at the Rose that bore his name. The repertory of Lord Strange's Men included Marlowe's *Jew of Malta*. They were probably the first London employers of William Shakespeare.

It was this knot of Catholic exiles and their apparently regicidal intent that Burghley wanted Andrada to sniff out. He instructed Lopez to retain Andrada. This did not make Andrada useless, merely smaller. A grand peace could not be negotiated only through Andrada, but the Queen's enemies might be pre-empted through his intelligence. By doing so, Burghley continued Walsingham's arrangement. On the last day of August 1591, Lopez sent Andrada to Calais. Andrada's instructions were to write from there to Burghley 'with such news as he found in the streets, and that from there he might run with the Count of Fuentes' in order to penetrate Sir William Stanley's circle. Burghley paid him '100 cruzados' in advance. A month later Andrada returned and delivered his first mails for

Burghley to Lopez at the house in St Katharine Creechurch.

Adrift after Walsingham's death, Lopez had been forced to move with the times. Walsingham's scheme to trick Philip II had loomed up from the Secretary's grave, and Lopez had regrafted it on to Lord Burghley. Like Mr Mills, he had shifted between patrons with different agendas without missing a beat. He might not have assayed the base metal of Walsingham's proposal into the diplomatic gold of peace talks, but he had fixed himself and his agent in Burghley's service, and in the process had changed political tack. For nearly twenty years, Lopez had been closest to those members of the Privy Council favouring confrontation with Spain. While Leicester and Walsingham had used Lopez as physician and intelligencer, the moderate Burghley had preferred the peppermint cordials and pepper-bale espionage of the comparably moderate Hector Nuñez. But the ground had shifted. Leicester and Walsingham were dead, Don Antonio's hand had been revealed as a bluff, and Burghley had been vindicated by the failure of the Counter-Armada. By handing Andrada to Burghley, Lopez cast in his lot with the peace party over the war party. His dreams of grandeur had collapsed outside the walls of Lisbon. His concern now was not a revolution in Portugal, but to salvage a nego-tiated compromise and recover financially. Despite Essex's romantic postures, Burghley was winning the factional battle. By supplying Burghley with Low Countries intelligence, Lopez improved the Cecils' position and began the slow work of improving his own.

But Andrada was still the slipperiest of fish. Lopez had saved Andrada's life before Burghley, yet Andrada insisted that Philip II had refused to give him the jewel 'for his daughter's dowry'. When Lopez discovered that Andrada had kept the jewel for himself, he was furious and forced the ungrateful courier to give him his reward. On the last day of November 1591, as London shivered in a winter of exceptional harshness, Andrada came to Lopez's house and surrendered a ring, a fat ruby stone set in gold. It would have been ideal for a bride's dowry, as in a superstition dating from Babylonian times, Jews believed that wearing a red gem such as ruby, coral or cornelian would cure infertility. But despite his claims, Lopez had no intention of giving it to his daughter Anne. It spoke not of marriage, but of another, less public kind of bond.

The ring connected Philip II and Lopez in two mutual understandings. One was that Lopez's role in the Andrada mission had not gone unappreciated. The second was that Spain was open to negotiation, in which case Lopez might produce the jewel to the Queen and Privy Council as proof of Spanish sincerity, and that Philip II wished to conduct negotiations through the Lopez channel. Lopez decided to keep it hidden until that day. If he cashed it in, questions would be asked about its provenance. If he declared its receipt to the Privy Council, the current climate of factional instability might make his commission seem more like a bribe. The ring was best kept secret, the cut of its stone best admired privately in candlelight, a bond holding Philip II, Andrada, Lopez and Burghley in a circle of close, unacknowledged proximity. Lopez hoped that one day he might bring it into the light, where its faces could be admired and its message understood, and some of its riches would refract back on to him, but now was not that time. Just as there was much to be won, there was much to be lost.

Back Andrada went across the Channel, a servant of the Queen and Doctor Lopez, making contact with Estevan Nuñez in Calais or Monsieur de la Chastres in Dieppe, then disappearing into the Low Countries, where Spanish *reals* waited if Doctor Lopez's English crowns ran out. When Andrada returned, Lopez kept him tucked away like the ring. The house in St Katharine Creechurch was in the eastern City, just north of the Marrano focus of Hart Street, far from the prying eyes of Wood Street. From Aldgate, Lopez could walk in a straight line along Aldgate Street, Cornhill and Poultry to West Cheap; past his house on Wood Street to Newgate, where he left the City after travelling little more than a mile. Up Snow Hill, over the stinking Fleet Ditch, and then another mile along Holborn, past the Inns of Court and the open fields to the Palace of Westminster: a straight line like the flight of an arrow. An hour's stroll, and faster if, instead of heading west, he cut south from Aldgate through the scimitar curve of Poor Jewry, Crutched Friars and Hart Street, then down to Thames Street and the fragrant cargoes of Fish

Wharf, where the wherrymen waited at Old Swan Steps to taxi him up the great river. An hour by foot or minutes by boat, connecting the slum where Manuel Andrada lay fearful and confused on a straw pallet, to the palace where the Queen and her Councillors ruled in luxury and anxiety.

7

A World of Words

He who serves two masters has to lie to one of them.

Portuguese proverb

The miserable winter of 1591 had forced the plague into abeyance in time for the first day of the new term. The Court, scattered to country retreats by the epidemic, had returned gingerly to the capital. On Saturday 19 February 1592, Parliament risked a sitting at Westminster after rural exile at Hertford. Across the river at Philip Henslowe's Rose Theatre, Ned Alleyn and Lord Strange's Men began their new season with a hit from the previous year, Robert Greene's *Friar Bungay and Friar Bacon*, played to a half-empty house. Persevering through the foot-stomping, hand-blowing chill of a Thameside February, the players achieved their first full house of the season the following Saturday with Marlowe's *The Jew of Malta*. On Friday, 3 March, warmed up after a winter of lay-offs, private performances and country tours, Alleyn and his company launched a new three-part history play by William Shakespeare, *Henry VI*. It sold out, generating £3.16s.8d for a delighted Philip Henslowe.

The next morning, Roderigo Lopez also had money on his mind. Unlike Henslowe, his financial worries had not declined with the plague. While the court had been wintering at Hertford, Lopez had come across a nearby estate called Hatfield Broadoak, which belonged to St Bartholomew's Hospital. It would be an ideal reward for his service to Lord Burghley, a ripened fruit of patronage ready to fall from the tree. In time for the new term, Lopez obtained a letter from the Privy Council, requesting that he be granted the lease. Too grand to deliver it personally after the embarrassments of his departure from St Bartholomew's, Lopez sent it by messenger to Sir Rowland Hayward, head of the Court of the Hospital. The Privy Council's request arrived as the Court convened on the morning of Saturday, 4 March. While Lopez waited at home and his messenger waited in the hospital for a reply, the Governors deliberated.

Resting on the Hertfordshire–Essex border, Hatfield Broadoak's lease was in the hands of Widow Bright, the relict of Thomas Bright, a hospital stalwart in Lopez's time. In 1587, Ralph Treswell, the hospital's surveyor, had ventured out of London to assess its rural holdings, pencil in hand. Treswell had found an estate covering 167 acres of rich countryside, set around a 'Mansion house' with barns, stabling, and a two-acre garden shaded by pollards, elms and a mixed orchard of plum, apple and filbert trees. Outside the orchard, much of the estate was rented out to local crofters. Most of it was 'grazing land', but another forty acres had barely been touched. This was the hidden value of the estate: timber.

There was a mix of mature maples, ashes and – best of all – oaks. 'Good timber trees,' observed Treswell. Wherever he went, he noted this most lucrative asset down to the last pollarded fruit tree: 'Thirty acres good wood of thirty years' growth . . . some young timber trees . . . one good timber tree . . . wood growing on this mead which would be felled . . . twenty acres lately felled and coppiced.' Even the crofters' lets were covered in 'good wood and some young timber trees'. As a lifelong urbanite shunted to the countryside, the Widow Bright had let her estate run to seed. She did not realise she was sitting on a small fortune.

Industrial expansion and a population boom had caused a surge in demand for wood. It was the primary fuel and building material, as essential for warming the hearth for dinner as for feeding a furnace to smelt iron for cannon. Heat, light and industry consumed vast amounts of wood or charcoal. Government and merchants alike realised that England's commerce and security lay on the oceans, and demand from shipyards for mature oak stripped the forests near English ports. There were still great forests in upland areas, but the terrible Tudor roads made cutting them so uneconomic that in the 1590s the Privy Council asked the merchants of the Muscovy Company to investigate the costs of importing Baltic timber as an alternative.

The English did not live by wood alone. Producing the three staples of the English diet – bread, meat and beer – required the clearing of woodland. In Kent, the forests which had supplied the iron furnaces of the Weald with charcoal since Neolithic times ran short. London's thirst for beer impelled hop farmers to clear the remaining forests, and then accelerate the fermentation process with charcoal-burning oast houses. 'The woods are consumed', reported a tourist in distant Pembrokeshire, 'and the ground converted to corn or pasture'. It was no different in Warwickshire, where Shakespeare invested in pastureland in the 1590s.

Doctor Lopez was not asking for the Hatfield Broadoak lease so that he might retire among the filberts in the final stage of his assimilation, donning the muddy boots and ruddy cheeks of a gentleman farmer and pondering the possibilities of transplanting sturdy Alentejo vines to southern England. He was hoping to strip the estate and convert the timber into brewers' charcoal, building joists and ships' masts. Further, the manor house might serve as a country base of operations. The ageing Doctor was constantly bumping along muddy roads in coaches of dubious suspension. At Hatfield Broadoak he would be just down the road from Burghley's mansion at Theobalds.

Reading the results of Ralph Treswell's exertions, the Court of the Hospital realised the estate's value. They had no intention of letting it fall into the Doctor's hands like an autumnal filbert. Widow Bright had not taken to her final role in life as a country landlady, but the loyal service of the Bright family cast harsh light on Lopez's own career at the hospital. Lopez was the physician obsessed by the state of his lodgings, perpetually absconding from the poor at inopportune moments, whose tenure had ended on a sustained sour note. He had continued to haunt them after his departure, bobbing up to gather subscribers for the Counter-Armada among the City merchants who composed the court, then ducking out of responsibility for its failure while scandalously attempting to sue the King of Portugal. He lacked even the courtesy to appear in person.

Sir Rowland Hill, presiding, tartly told Lopez's messenger, 'This hospital is maintained the better with the fines of such leases.' The hospital preferred a small income from Widow Bright to another speculative entanglement with Lopez. Widow Bright had every legal right to bumble around her unproductive estate for some time. 'There are as yet diverse years to come in the said lease, whereby this court may not let a lease thereof without infringement of the orders of the house.' On this delicate technicality, Sir Rowland asserted the independence of the City over interference from the Privy Council. Next, the court made order that on his next visit Mr Treswell should check that Widow Bright was maintaining the estate properly; the hospital was a charity, run by businessmen.

While Lopez digested the bad news, over at the Rose Philip Henslowe and Ned Alleyn realised that the previous afternoon's success with *Henry VI* might be the sensation of the season. 'The takings continue high,' Henslowe wrote in his diary on 5 April, after a further four performances. He promptly booked another fourteen performances for April, May and June. According to Thomas Nashe, that summer more than 10,000 people – one in every ten Londoners – saw Shakespeare's first complete history cycle at the Rose. More would have seen it had not the plague returned in force.

A familiar figure in Elizabethan London: the ratcatcher.

By July, it was so bad that the Court of Assizes met to the west of London, at St George's Fields, and then 'made haste away, for fear of being infected with the pestilence'. The Privy Council ordered the closure of all London theatres. The Queen and her Court fled for the provinces and the actors followed, for a summer of innyard burlesques and country house masques. By the end of the summer the ban extended to cover all forms of public entertainment within a seven-mile radius of the City, including bear baiting and bowling. Lopez looked for a home outside the dangerous vapours of the City. His youngest son Anthony was about to leave for boarding school at Winchester, where his fees would be paid by the Queen as a reward to her physician. Although Lopez was as entangled with Don Antonio's finances as ever, through the Queen's favour and the patronage of Lord Burghley he had begun to improve his position. The Lopez family moved to Mountjoy's Inn, part of the straggling line of new suburban mansions that lined Holborn, its garden wall abutting Gray's Inn.

William Allington, a Gray's Inn lawyer, had built Mountjoy's Inn like an Inn of Court, constructing it around a central courtyard. In August 1591, his heir, Henry Allington, had died from the plague.

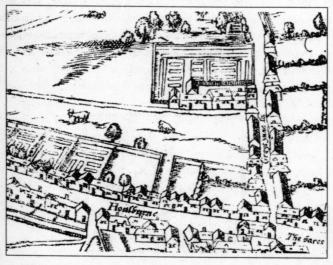

The mansions and gardens of Holborn and Gray's Inn in the 1560s.

The house had passed to his young widow Mary, who became Lopez's landlady. It was an ideal location for Lopez; equidistant between the City, Westminster and the mansions that lay between them, but away from the bad air and prying eyes of the City. Its large walled garden would be perfect for a physic garden, and the view from the rear windows looked past Gray's Inn to open fields.

While the actors wandered the countryside and Lopez retreated to the suburbs, William Shakespeare made his own ambitious arrangements. He had not followed Lord Strange's Men into the country: if he was to make the leap from player to poet, he must follow a poet's course. Like every playwright, he would need a rich, aristocratic patron. And like every other playwright, he would offer dedications of his work to the most fashionable patron of the day, the wealthy, refined and sexually complex Henry Wriothesley, 3rd Earl of Southampton. Unlike them, Shakespeare would succeed. In the plague summer of 1592, he acquired powerful friends.

Southampton was a law student, and the spoilt young men of the Inns of Court flocked to the whore-ridden, word-mad theatres. That was probably where he met Shakespeare, most likely via his tutor John Florio. Not that Southampton was there for Philip Henslowe's jades: it seemed that women did not excite the Earl at all, and men little more. A rival suitor for Southampton's patronage had suggested in a poem dedicated to the Earl that Narcissus was his ideal. Unfortunately, Lord Burghley demurred.

Southampton's father had followed his Catholic faith into the Tower and died there in 1581. Like the young Robert Devereux, the eight-year-old Henry Wriothesley had become a royal ward, which meant that Burghley had been his guardian and had profited from this service. Burghley had processed Southampton through Cambridge by the age of sixteen, then brought him to London for two years' polishing at Gray's Inn. Just as Southampton entered on a postgraduate spree, his mother and stepfather, Lord Montague, pestered him to marry. The plague could strike at any moment and the lineage must be assured. Lord Burghley secured their approval for the match of Southampton to his granddaughter, Elizabeth Vere.

Vain, pretty and nineteen years old, this was not what

Southampton wanted. His model was not Burghley building a dynasty with donkey patience, but his fellow graduate from Burghley's ward-ship, the Earl of Essex. Essex was seven years Southampton's senior, the glamorous, aggressive Master of the Horse. Admittedly, he had married, but his wife was no parvenu's granddaughter. Essex had married the widow of the soldier-poet archetype, Sir Philip Sidney, whose heroism had acquired new topicality in 1591 with the post-humous publication of his sonnet sequence, *Astrophel and Stella*. That year, when Essex had led an expedition to France, all his horsemen kitted out in his personal tangerine and cream livery, Southampton had attempted to join him, but had been barred because he was unmarried and had no heir. His frustration only confirmed his admi-ration. Essex, never noted as a judge of character, was reminded by Southampton of his younger self, and responded in kind.

Sharing generosity, impetuosity, petulance and antipathy towards their ex-guardian Burghley, the two Earls deliberately set about turning Essex House and Southampton House into the twin foci of their generation. The most ambitious, if not the best, of their peers gathered around Essex the leader and Southampton the chief admirer. Their template and their bond were the revered memory of Sir Philip Sidney. Sidney had pined for Essex's sister Penelope, the 'Stella' of his sonnets. Essex married Sidney's widow Mary. Essex's friend the Earl of Rutland married Sidney's daughter. Southampton cultivated Sidney's younger brother Robert like a fetish object. Essex knighted Sidney's page Sir Henry Danvers, and Southampton engaged him as his own retainer. The atmosphere in the inner circle of the set was highly literate, passionately sentimental and exclusively male.

'Sodomites' was the rumour about Southampton and some of his circle. The Elizabethan aristocracy tolerated homosexual urges, but not their acts. Greek philosophy provided impeccable precedents for intimate male friendship, but Elizabethan mores discriminated between a friendship elevated by neo-Platonic thought and one cemented by active homosexuality. Even sentimental attachments were a phase to be grown out of; if society was held together by its aristocracy, an openly homosexual aristocrat was a threat to the social order. Marriage, children and the preservation of a title were the approved destiny.

There were also financial pressures to conform. Essex was a lifelong debtor and Southampton was a wild gambler, once losing £5000 on a tennis match. A canny marriage was the only way to clear debts, but it was also the primary threat to this bond of male friendship.

There may be an echo of the Essex–Southampton relationship in the opening scene of *The Merchant of Venice*. The intended focus of the play is Antonio, not Shylock, and the central relationship is not that of Antonio and Shylock, but Antonio and Bassanio, the fellow nobleman for whom he borrows Shylock's ducats. The play opens with Antonio bemoaning a 'want-wit sadness' whose cause eludes him. His friends Salerio and Solanio suggest that it might be because Antonio is worried about money – he has half a dozen 'argosies' on the oceans – but Antonio discounts their theory. When his 'noble kinsman' Bassanio appears, Antonio's dilemma becomes apparent. Bassanio must marry; not for love, but to escape his debts. For that purpose he has located 'a lady richly left' in Belmont. In *Il Pecorone*, the Lady of Belmont was wooed for love; in *The Merchant*, she is desired for economic necessity. Bassanio promises that marriage will not change his deeper feelings. He will not welch on the loans Antonio has given him – loans which will help push Antonio into Shylock's grasp – nor will he deny his love for Antonio.

> 'Tis not unknown to you Antonio
> How much I have disabled mine estate
> By something showing a more swelling port
> Than my faint means would grant continuance . . .
>
> . . . To you Antonio
> I owe the most in money and in love,
> And from your love I have a warranty
> To unburthen all my plots and purposes
> How to get clear of all the debts I owe.

Responding, Antonio avows his friendship in homoerotic imagery:

> My purse, my person, my extremest means
> Lie all unlock'd to your occasion.

Antonio's dilemma is that if he helps his beloved Bassanio, he will lose him to the Lady of Belmont. The plot of *The Merchant* is resolved not in the vanquishing of Shylock in a Venetian courtroom, but in the subsequent magical resolution by moonlight at Belmont, where Bassanio and Antonio pair off with Portia and Nerissa. It is apt that Shylock's destruction – which opens the way for Antonio's compromise with maturity – is negotiated by Portia and Nerissa donning male dress and masquerading as Balthazar the lawyer and his clerk.

When the theatres were closed, Shakespeare could have retreated to his wife and child in Stratford, but he preferred the fops of Southampton's salon. To be immured with a great patron was a career opportunity. He may have passed the plague season shuttered up at Southampton House in Holborn, but more probably he escaped to Titchfield, the Earl's country seat. While his fellow playwright Robert Greene starved and Lord Strange's Men tramped the countryside, Shakespeare nestled in the luxurious shade of the most desirable patron of all. On the winding stair, the player metamorphosed into an effete poet, like Ganymede, the beautiful Trojan boy who became cupbearer to the gods on Olympus. The atmosphere of Southampton House might have scandalised the stallholders of Stratford market, but it would not have seemed unusual to Shakespeare. The theatre was also exclusively male. Female roles were played by young boys with smooth chins and unbroken voices. Mesmerising Cleopatra, consuming Lady Macbeth and inspiring Desdemona all first stirred the groundlings as boys in drag.

If the motif of Southampton House was decadent posturing, a cynical political agenda was the theme of Essex House. The *politique* model had been an exotic import for Burghley's and Leicester's generation, an ideal to be emulated. Among their heirs, it was thoroughly domesticated. To Robert Cecil and Essex it was a mode of thought, a convention to be turned to advantage. Essex was conscious of his political promise. To fulfil it, he had to build a power base. It would stand on two pillars: his courtship of the Queen, and the political leverage of a faction. Through the Queen he could obtain government posts for his supporters and lucrative monopolies such as the

Farm of Sweet Wines, whose commissions had sustained Leicester, its last holder. On the shared promise of future wealth, he could buy support and create a faction. The combination of royal favour, money and a mass of well-placed supporters would allow him to displace Lord Burghley as the most powerful Privy Councillor, and replace Sir Robert Cecil as Burghley's political heir.

Essex attracted ambitious young men made peripheral by the Burghley ascendancy, in particular the brothers Anthony and Francis Bacon. As Lord Burghley's nephews, they should have been jostling at the trough of favouritism, but Burghley was determined that just as his son Robert Cecil would not be overshadowed physically by Essex, neither would he be overshadowed intellectually by family comparison with the Bacon brothers. Both brothers had passed through Gray's Inn, but their paths had forked in a perfect exegesis of the Elizabethan State. Francis had become a lawyer, ambitious for a place in the government. Anthony, the older brother, had become a spy.

A martyr to gout and kidney stones, Anthony Bacon shared his Cecil cousin's physical feebleness and, by his early thirties, he was a half-blind semi-invalid whose arms were prone to paralysis in cold weather. In 1579, his uncle Burghley had sent Anthony to France. Having steered him out of Sir Robert Cecil's path, Burghley promptly dropped his nephew. Francis Walsingham soon took over Burghley's role. For nearly a decade, Bacon was one of Walsingham's best suppliers of French intelligence. In 1586, Bacon was accused of sodomising a young servant boy at Bearn. The charges were not proven, and he succeeded in keeping the scandal from Walsingham's attention. The case may have explained his lack of haste in returning to England, as he did not come home until April 1592. By then, his younger brother Francis was thick with the Essex set. One of Essex's earliest successes at placing his supporters in office had been Francis's engagement as Clerk of the Prosecutor in the Star Chamber.

Knowledge is power, as Francis would later write. Control over its supply conferred political status. The models of Leicester, Burghley and Walsingham all proved that a successful private intelligence service was the key to influence over foreign policy. Essex hired

Anthony Bacon to build a spy service that would make him omnipotent. Unlike previous services, Essex's was run on a royal budget. The same extravagance Essex showed his tailor was applied to information gathering. Anthony Bacon turned Essex House into an intelligence factory, a paranoid variation on the Renaissance ideal of a fraternal house of intellect.

Essex's friends doubled as Bacon's secretaries, assisted by a cast of underlings. Two experienced field operatives did the dirty work of handling sources, and were Bacon's main suppliers of intelligence: the Anthonies Standen and Rolston. Placed in the Customs House was a recent Essex acquisition, Thomas Phelippes, the cryptologist. Essex also inherited the vestiges of Leicester's household. Leicester's expert secretary Arthur Atey worked by mail from Kenilworth. Don Antonio was passed from Leicester to Essex like an heirloom. Doctor Lopez, the late Earl's physician, became Essex's physician. And, just as he had for Leicester, Lopez became Essex's intelligencer.

Essex inherited Lopez like a household chattel. To the Earl, Lopez was a possession whose use came by right. To the Doctor, Essex was a patient whose custom came by habit. In purely medical terms, Essex was a potential patron like any other. But if that medical service slipped into espionage, the picture would be more complex and Lopez's loyalty would be compromised. Lopez knew that by taking Andrada to Burghley, and running Andrada on Burghley's behalf, he had committed himself to Burghley's policy of seeking peace with Spain. The challenge to Burghley, his policy and his son was headed by Essex. To take commissions from both Burghley and Essex was to serve mutually exclusive causes. To further one was to block the other. If the two factions ever came into direct conflict, Lopez would be in an impossible position.

To advance his political programme, Essex needed the support of the historic allies of the war party's cause – Antwerp bankers, French Protestants and Low Countries rebels – and he needed an intelligence coup to trump the Cecils and seize the foreign policy intiative. For both support and information he needed a regular, safe mail connection between London, Paris and Antwerp. To prove the efficiency of his new spy service, he needed to provide the Queen with an intelligence success, perhaps rooting out a regicidal conspiracy emanating from Father Robert Persons or Sir William Stanley. Resolving 'to make choice of some who should do service in the like kind', he went to London's leading conduit for mail, funding and intelligence from the Low Countries: Doctor Lopez.

It was common knowledge, said Essex, that 'many did practice treason against the Queen'. From his studies in intelligencing, he knew that there was only one way of pre-empting assassination plots: to subvert them from the inside. A conspiracy had to be detected by a double agent, who penetrated the secrecy around a plot by feigning sympathy for its aims. The plotters might even be influenced by the double agent; they might be dissuaded from 'entertaining others' who might be more efficient to join their scheme. This was 'projecting', the dangerous double art of drawing out enemies of the Crown. Essex said that there was no 'fitter man' for this job than Lopez, 'and to this end I would have you to offer yourself, and so to undertake the business'.

Essex was asking Lopez to assume the not unfamiliar position of acting like a traitor in order to be a patriot. Lopez knew that the appearance of the eye could be dangerous. Could he trust Essex? Then again, why should Essex trust him? In Essex's eyes, Lopez was recommended by his long loyalty to Essex's stepfather Leicester. But this might also have been a reason for Essex to distrust Lopez. As that scurrilous book *Leicester's Commonwealth* had claimed, Leicester had been widely suspected of having poisoned Essex's real father in order to pursue his affair with Essex's mother. And it cannot have escaped Lopez's notice that the *Commonwealth* had named him as the poisoner. Lopez could not be certain that Essex's offer was not an elaborate revenge: to place him in a compromised position in order to entrap him as a traitor. Lopez was no fool and had other reasons to suspect Essex's sincerity. Essex had lost money in the Counter-Armada and, as the focus of all anti-Spanish causes, he was now Don Antonio's main patron: two more motives for the Earl to resent Lopez.

Essex's offer had put Lopez in a fraught position, where to accept was little more dangerous than the offence of refusal. The Doctor was tempted, though. Taking Essex's commission might be an insurance policy. Lord Burghley had a contingency plan for a temporary government should the Queen die, but that was no guarantee he would be alive to lead it. Who would be at the royal bedside at the end, proffering an unread paper to be signed in the last, rambling hours, lowering an ear to hear the death-rattle whisper that carried the Queen's final wish? The Lord Treasurer was already in the early mists of senility, Essex was a rising force, and Sir Robert Cecil was unproven. More concerned with retirement than the fate of the nation, Lopez needed money for his old age. So long as he was careful, he could serve both parties and assure himself a share in the victory, whoever the victor might be. But it was vital to protect himself against being stranded patronless in an ambiguous position. He felt he had no choice but to gamble.

'My Lord,' replied Lopez, 'this is a very great business and a dangerous. You are now in favour, but how long you may continue, we know not. You may die, and then the whole treason will be laid upon me. Your Lordship will be pleased to give me some time to advise.'

To protect himself as much as Lopez, Essex went to Elizabeth, seeking her permission to use double agents to detect plotters against her life. She consented, and shortly afterwards, Lopez approached her regarding his role in Essex's plan. 'If it please Your Majesty,' said Lopez, 'My Lord of Essex hath put me upon a business whereof I have little knowledge, and dare not adventure thereon without Your Majesty's approbation.'

This was not entirely accurate. Essex had commissioned Lopez because Lopez was an expert at projecting. The Doctor had conducted just this kind of work for Walsingham in 1587, when he suggested to the double agent Antonio da Vega that Don Antonio might be given a poisoned enema. And at the time of his interview with the Queen, Lopez was using Andrada on 'the other side' to penetrate plots in Calais and the Low Countries for Burghley. Lopez proceeded to tell the Queen what he called 'the whole story', which was not whole at all.

'It is a thing out of your element not to give physic, but to practise in that manner,' Elizabeth pointed out. Of course, this was no more true than Lopez's pretence of naivety. She knew that her physician was a professional intriguer. But in the current unstable climate she would not take sides. It was up to Lopez to decide whether to take Essex's commission, but its success would be noticed. 'If you should do me any service, you should not be unrewarded.'

Lopez thought this gnomic exchange would protect him against the risks implicit in projecting, so he 'undertook the business'. The same network that supplied Burghley with intelligence would be used to supply Essex. Like a gambler watching a dogfight in a Bankside tavern, Lopez had backed both dogs. He would have to balance his loyalties, giving one party the informational edge, but always keeping the other party's confidence. English policy hung between peace and war, Court life had grown into a vicious struggle, and loyalties changed with each round of battle. Andrada had left England in Walsingham's service, but had returned in Burghley's. The future was uncontrollable, but the flow of information was not. The Doctor was keeping his options open. A service for Essex might become a service for the Cecils.

Lopez's engagement as an intelligencer for the 'war party' of Essex and Southampton brought together all the actors in Lopez's fall and fame. Lord Burghley and Sir Robert Cecil were engaged in a factional struggle with Essex, the prize being the Queen's endorsement for their foreign policies. Essex's closest friend was the Earl of Southampton, patron of William Shakespeare. Having successfully placed Cecil's rejected cousin Francis Bacon in government office, Essex had engaged Anthony Bacon to build up a spy service, and engaged Doctor Lopez, an old supporter of war party aims, as an intelligencer. Essex was against Burghley, and Lopez took commissions from both. He was not alone in playing this double game. John Florio, tutor to the Earl of Southampton, kept Burghley informed as to events in Southampton House.

When Lopez delivered information to Essex, he went to Essex House, where Anthony Bacon ran the Earl's spy service and where the Earl of Southampton came with the latest squib from his new marvel, William Shakespeare. Essex was Lopez's patron and Francis Bacon's, too; Southampton was Shakespeare's. The Doctor, the lawyer and the poet were suitors at the same court, witnessing the same intrigues, hearing the same gossip, hovering in the same doorways. Endless intimacies upon intimacies, the small group of players crossed and recrossed paths, each loyal to the other's patrons or set against the other's enemies. And Lopez, like Shakespeare, loyal to all and none.

The circle is complete. Shakespeare to Southampton to Essex to Lopez to Shakespeare: an informational circuit. In their small London, in the smaller orbits of the great houses shuttered against the plague, Lopez and Shakespeare must regularly have crossed paths in the ante-rooms of power. Lopez's old home in Wood Street was a few doors away from the print shop of Shakespeare's Stratford associate, Richard Field, printer of Shakespeare's first work, a kindness Shakespeare apparently repaid by sleeping with Mrs Field. Lopez's new home at Mountjoy's Inn backed on to Francis Bacon's digs at Gray's Inn, and was a stone's throw from Southampton House. They walked the same streets in similar directions, but with different purposes. If Lopez and Shakespeare spoke while waiting for an audience, or to cross the Fleet Ditch to go to St Katharine Creechurch to plot in Portuguese or pass the afternoon in the rank sweat of Mrs Field's unseamèd bed, they would soon have found that they shared more than patrons and faction.

Where to begin? There was the Earl of Leicester, feudal lord of Shakespeare's Stratford childhood and controversial patron of Lopez's rise. There was Leicester's nephew, Sir Philip Sidney, whose sonnets were models for Shakespeare's, and with whom Lopez had rowed out onto the Thames to dissuade Don Antonio from fleeing England. There was the controversial intimacy of the Earls of Essex and Southampton, their common patrons. Perhaps it would have been better to keep to less grand matters and make small talk on the winding stair. They could have discussed the state of the roads at Tredington and Blockley, and the ups and downs of the Stratford wool market. Both the Shakespeare and Lopez families had suffered from financial adventuring. They could have discussed ruefully the perils of lending money in a changeable economy and the flexible boundaries of the Usury Act.

Neither would have been totally alien to the other, neither was without interest to the other. Certainly not for Shakespeare, the Stratford Autolycus who picked up trifles of geography and history from everyone, second-, third-, or fourth-hand. He might have had a question about the task then exercising him, the sonnet. Shakespeare took his rhyme scheme from the medieval Italian poet Petrarch, who had written in Italian. If Shakespeare read Italian at all, it was shakily. In her resting afternoons, Lopez read to Queen Elizabeth in Italian. The Doctor might have provided a phrase or two, some courtly witticism to assist the grammar school boy in his struggle with the university men who dominated his profession. A moment of proximity and a moment of recognition. If it had not been beneath the dignity of the Queen's physician to acknowledge one of Southampton's scented boys – and an obscure yokel poet at that – they might have discovered how much they had in common.

They step into the mire of the roadway, cross the Fleet Ditch and disappear into the City, each towards his own destiny.

8

The Jew of Venice

The marble not yet carved can hold the form
Of every thought the greatest artist has.

Michelangelo, *Sonnet*

There once was a Jew of Venice, but his story is lost. It was written in the early 1590s by the prolific but careless Thomas Dekker, author and co-author of at least forty other lost plays. Dekker called his play *The Jew of Venice*. Presumably, Dekker recounted a story of a Jewish moneylender and a Venetian merchant, and told it along the lines of the various early versions of the story. Nothing can be known for certain beyond his title.

The storyless identity of *The Jew of Venice* floats unsatisfactorily around *The Merchant of Venice*. The two titles have struggled like Shylock and Antonio, or Lopez and Don Antonio. *The Jew* possesses a foggy parallel life to *The Merchant*. Dekker's *Jew* preceded Shakespeare's *Merchant*. Yet subsequently, as evinced by James Roberts's 1598 registration of 'a book of *The Merchant of Venice*, or otherwise called *The Jew of Venice*', Shakespeare's *Merchant* appears to have been acted under the title of *The Jew of Venice*. This creates a double confusion: between Dekker and Shakespeare, and Shakespeare and Shakespeare. Such ambiguities are common in the textual background of the early Shakespeare comedies. A similar confusion attends *The Taming of the Shrew*.

Two months after Roberts registered his *Merchant–Jew*, a percipient critic named Francis Meres registered his *Wits' Treasury*. 'As Plautus and Seneca are accounted the best for comedy and tragedy among the Latins,' wrote Meres, 'so Shakespeare among the English is the most excellent in both kinds for the stage.' Meres listed the six comedies and six tragedies penned by the 'honey-tongued' poet. The comedies were 'his [*Two*] *Gentlemen of Verona*, his [*Comedy of*] *Errors*, his *Love's Labour's Lost*, his *Love's Labour's Won*, his *Midsummer-Night's Dream* and his *Merchant of Venice*'.

Meres did not mention *The Taming of the Shrew*, listed among the early comedies in the collected 'First Folio' of 1623, but he did list *Love's Labour's Won*, a title not featured in the First Folio; the two titles seem to refer to the same play. To add to the confusion, in 1594 another play called *The Taming of a Shrew* – 'sundry times acted by the Right Honourable the Earl of Pembroke his Servants' – was printed. This earlier *Shrew* appears to be a 'memorial reconstruction', assembled from the flawed memories of its actors by an opportunist publisher. So Shakespeare's *Merchant* is not unique in having a confusion of titles.

Shakespeare's play had settled on its official name by the time of its first printing in 1600, resolving the bout between Shylock and Antonio in favour of the 'Comical History' of Antonio, but even then *The Jew* scored a posthumous victory. After its performance at Court on 10 February 1605 by the King's Men, *The Merchant of Venice* vanished from the records for over a century, until Charles Macklin revived it at Drury Lane on 14 February 1741. In the interim, *The Jew of Venice* crept back in for a third appearance. In May 1701, a mutilated adaptation by George Granville debuted at Lincoln's Inn Fields. For four decades Shakespeare's play was performed in this mangled account, until Macklin's revival re-established *The Merchant* over *The Jew*. Ironically, it was Macklin's raging Shylock that permanently established Shylock, not Antonio, as the play's dramatic focus, thus adding a further twist to the Jew–Merchant tension at the root of the play. The *Jew* tracks the *Merchant*, but invisibly, like a shadow at noon.

While Dekker's *Jew* stalked the London stage, Roderigo Lopez assessed the limits of his own performance. By the early 1590s, he knew that he could not escape from the espionage game even if he wanted to. He was the nexus: Portuguese intelligence had converged on him, and had then been distributed to his English patrons. He was known among the Privy Councillors as an intelligencer, a life-long operator, a wheeler of deals. That was why Burghley had retained him, and why Essex had hired him. He knew how the Cecils operated, and he had begun to decipher the private world of Essex House. If Lopez retired he would be free, but to live freely with secrets was a contradiction, as his itching desire for money or status would soon tempt out those secrets. The Cecils did not want Lopez on the open market, and neither did Essex. Lopez had to be kept inside the system, because he knew too much. Like being royal physician, intelligencing was a job for life.

The Doctor was an old man, nearly seventy. He had lost his homeland, had returned to it, and had lost it again. Only his youngest child Anthony was still at school, being trained as an English gentleman at Winchester. The rest were adults now, and the wires of the Marrano telegraph sang with marriage proposals and dowry negotiations that would carry them away to Antwerp, Lyons or Constantinople. He and Sara would be left to lonely old age. Lopez was tied to England, but the bonds had ossified and their wasting fibres exposed a dilemma: to renew those bonds of service, like a prisoner making his cell more comfortable, or to struggle free from the impossible Marrano life, and escape to the warmth and religious liberty of Constantinople? Either way, he had to free himself of debt. He had to shake off the burden of Don Antonio, who lay across Lopez's shoulders like Sir Robert Cecil's hump.

Antonio had failed to break the financial bond by fleeing from England, but he had sawed obliquely at the diplomatic one. Enforced leisure had given him time to identify Lopez's strong and weak points. In London, the Privy Council's judgement had given Lopez the upper hand. In the Low Countries, Lopez was well-connected with the Antwerp merchants. By contrast, Lopez's authority in Constantinople rested on the Doctor's cousin Alvaro Mendes; and he had never been strong in Paris, which had its own faction of Antonio partisans. Antonio had worked on these weak points: he had sent his eldest son Don Emanuel to Paris, to raise funds from the Huguenots, and he had tried to break the Lopez–Mendes axis.

Antonio had fallen out with Mendes around the time of their mutual departure from Paris in 1585. The cause was money: Antonio had none; Mendes was fantastically wealthy and Antonio was jealous. He had blamed Mendes for not providing a French army to invade Portugal, just as he later blamed Lopez even as the Doctor raised an English army. A feud had developed. Mendes had dissuaded Sultan Murad III from assisting Don Antonio in any scheme independent of England. So Antonio had circulated lies in Paris and London that Mendes was a fraudster. These charges were investigated by the Spanish, who saw them as a pretext for impounding Mendes's goods when they passed through Spanish ports; Antonio's claims were found to be unsubstantiated.

Antonio had tried another course. Mendes and Lopez made each other influential by exchanging intelligence: Lopez had sent Mendes the news that the Spanish Armada had been defeated, much to Sultan Murad's astonishment. Antonio had tried to cut the link between the two. In February 1591, Antonio had appointed as his agent in Constantinople another Portuguese Jew, David Passi. On this credential Passi had gained audiences with the English ambassador, Edward Barton, and the Sultan, at which he had repeated Antonio's slander against Mendes. Barton had described the story in a letter to Burghley, bringing the allegation back to its origin in England. Mendes had been furious at Barton, and the baffled ambassador had been drawn into a diplomatic spat.

At the end of 1591, Mendes had sent an emissary, Solomon Cormano, to London to clear his name. His mission had succeeded completely. In March 1592, Elizabeth had written to Murad testifying to Mendes's 'virtue, honesty and industry', and Burghley had despatched a rebuke to Ambassador Barton. Apologising to the Lord Treasurer, Barton had claimed that he had found plenty of industry, but little virtue in Mendes's emissary. The English ambassador was piously scandalised that Cormano had been boasting 'in every tavern' in Constantinople how 'he and all his train used publicly the Jews' rites in praying, accompanied with diverse secret Jews resident in London'.

Cormano had liaised with Lopez in London, and the Doctor had been among the congregation. The London Marranos had broken cover en masse to join Cormano, whose diplomatic status made him immune. It was a sign of confidence in their shady English niche, but they were never wholly safe. When Cormano left, the Marranos went back into hiding. If their faith was an open secret in political circles, it was a closed secret to the wider public.

This diplomatic chaos was Don Antonio's work. Antonio had intrigued among Lopez's friends, reneged on his financial bonds in London, and slandered Alvaro Mendes. The Anglo-Turkish relationship was a delicate bloom, carefully tended by Lopez and Mendes. A personal embassy from Turkey had saved it; another personal embassy in the other direction might strengthen it. Burghley was worried about the Passi–Mendes struggle. He did not want relations with Turkey to be controlled by Don Antonio. Doctor Lopez would have been an ideal emissary, and it appears that he made the journey to Constantinople. Only one image survives from the trip.

A Florentine diplomat reported that Lopez was spotted in Venice with 'his brothers and wife'; the observer thought that Lopez had a 'friendly and agreeable' character. It was a dangerous voyage for an old man. There were two routes: an odyssey across the Channel to Antwerp and then Hamburg, up the Rhine and around the Alps to northern Italy; or directly by sea. In the second case, Lopez may have sailed on a ship belonging to London merchants licensed to import from Venice, whose Letters Patent referred to them as 'Mercatoribus Venetiae', or 'Merchants of Venice'.

The prayers at Solomon Cormano's lodgings had been Lopez's first taste of normal Jewish devotions beyond the Marrano partition, a late vision of the life that had been denied. Some parts of it may have been more novel than others. In Venice, Jews moved freely by day and traded openly among the merchants of the Rialto. But they wore identifying yellow badges on their clothes and at night they were locked behind the walls of a cramped, dirty district, called the 'Ghetto' because it once had been the site of an iron foundry.

Medieval Christianity had deliberately avoided contact with Jews

Venice in the sixteenth century, engraved by Juan Andrés Vavassore. The ghetto, or 'Iudeca', is in the bottom left corner.

and Judaism, but the Renaissance's re-examination of the Hebrew language and Bible brought Judaism and Christianity into intellectual proximity, and their exponents into social company. This had a paradoxical result and a predictable reaction. Instead of bringing enlightenment, it brought out latent competition over the ownership of the sources. Erasmus, the prophet of Humanism, considered Judaism and Christianity to be philosophically antithetical. There was, he wrote, 'nothing more adverse or more inimical to Christ' than the 'plague' of Judaism. In Erasmus's crude conception, later shared by Luther, Judaism was a religion of the law, while Christianity was a religion of the spirit. Even to debate with Jews was to risk the subversion of Christian faith by Talmudic nitpicking.

Meanwhile, the papacy fought back against the reformers. Pope Paul IV was ecumenical in his bigotry: he detested both Protestants and Jews. He banned the Talmud, ordered the burning of Hebrew books throughout Italy and assisted the hunt for Marranos. In 1555, he ordered that the model of the Venetian ghetto be extended to the papal cities. Ironically, the Popes of the Counter-Reformation shared with Erasmus and Luther the conviction that Jewish scholarship was not a valid adjunct to Christianity and the fear that Judaism, rather than being the dead limb of medieval cliché, might be alive enough to regain lost Marranos and plant doubt in Christian minds. Protestant or Catholic, the sixteenth century offered new ideologies for why it was Christian to hate the Jews.

These theological debates between Jews and Christians, and Christians and Christians, were the backdrop to Lopez's life. They also resound through the trial scene of *The Merchant of Venice*. 'By our holy Sabbath have I sworn to have the due and forfeit of my bond,' Shylock tells the Doge of Venice.

Bassanio tries to reason with Shylock, but Antonio warns Bassanio not to waste his words:

> I pray you, think you question with the Jew – you may as well go stand upon the beach, and bid the main flood bate his usual height. You may as well use question with the wolf, why he hath made the ewe bleat for the lamb. You may as well forbid the mountain pines to wag their high tops, and to make no noise when they are fretten with the gusts of heaven. You may as well seek to do any thing most hard, as seek to soften that – than which what's harder? – his Jewish heart!'

Even Antonio's friend Gratiano, who hurls insults at Shylock from the gallery – 'Harsh Jew!' 'Inexecrable dog!' – is made uncomfortable, like Ambassador Barton in Constantinople. 'Thou almost mak'st me waver in my faith,' he admits.

If Gratiano's admission locates the root of hatred in fear, and Antonio has illustrated Erasmus's fear of Judaism, then Portia expounds eloquently the other half of Erasmus's argument. 'The quality of mercy is not strain'd,' she says, 'it droppeth as the gentle rain from heaven upon the place beneath. It is twice blest: it blesseth him that gives, and him that takes. 'Tis mightiest in the mightiest, it becomes the throned monarch better than his crown.' In Portia's reading, compassion, not legal obduracy, is the true 'attribute to God'.

Shylock is not listening. 'My deeds upon my head!' he cries

like Lopez after the Counter-Armada, 'I crave the law!'

Shylock does not care for Portia's argument, or the consequences of following what he admits is 'a losing suit'. Like a real Venetian Jew, he knows he is caught in a legal-theological snare: Jewish law versus Christian mercy; the 'barren metal' of a usurer's gold versus love given without interest; the Jew in his ghetto versus the Doge in his palace. The proscriptions of Erasmus and Pope Paul IV alike have loaded the dice. His case is treated as a theological dispute. As it will be judged in Christian terms, he is condemned in advance, and he knows it.

Although Shylock works on the Rialto, he dwells in another world. The ghetto walls, which protect Christian Venice from doubt and usury, also have an interior face, like the walls of Mountjoy's Inn. The ghetto is a hard Jewish heart in the body of Venice, sustained by its own faith and theology. Inside the shell, the vicious usurer is a loving father, the detested parasite is a pillar of the synagogue, and the law is Jewish law. Only when Shylock leaves the heart of the city for the Rialto and the Doge's Court is he judged to be lacking. Even as Shakespeare indulges theological clichés medieval and modern, he identifies the psychological paradoxes in Shylock and in the Marrano mentality. Inside the ghetto, Shylock is a full human being; outside, he is a theological abstraction. This is the great struggle of Shylock's life, and the great struggle of the lives of Lopez and the thousands of other nameless, invisible Marranos. The speech that is Shylock's claim to grandeur begins with a justification for his hatred of Antonio, but develops into an exposition of a tragic historical plight.

He hath disgraced me, and hinder'd me half a million, laugh'd at my losses, mock'd at my gains, scorned my nation, thwarted my bargains, cooled my friends, heated mine enemies, – and what's his reason? I am a Jew. Hath not a Jew eyes? Hath not a Jew hands, organs, dimensions, senses, affections, passions? Fed with the same food, hurt with the same weapons, subject to the same diseases, healed by the same means, warmed and cooled by the same winter and summer as a Christian is? If you prick us, do we not bleed? If you tickle us, do we not laugh? If you poison us, do we not die? And if you wrong us shall we not revenge? If we are like you in the rest, we will resemble you in that. If a Jew wrong a Christian, what is his humility? Revenge! If a Christian wrong a Jew, what should his sufferance be by Christian example? Why, revenge! The villainy you teach me I will execute, and it shall go hard, but I will better the instruction.

This speech touches the root of the modern discomfort with *The Merchant*. Here, Shylock is rendered as tragically human, but elsewhere he is comically inhuman. His Jewish tragedy is cradled in a hostile plot, and he is the butt of a comedy whose joke is his destruction. Even when he becomes a fully human character, the theological trapdoor in the floor of the courtroom waits for him like the trapdoor in the floor of a stage, ready to drop him into the depths of theological Jew hatred. Like Lopez glimpsed in the throng of the ghetto, or Dekker's lost *Jew*, he rises into focus and then blurs back into the generality.

In the late summer of 1592, Lopez realised that Don Antonio was trying to destroy him, unpicking his network, thread by thread. If Antonio's son Emanuel gained support in Paris, then Lopez lost his Low Countries stranglehold on Antonio's funding. If David Passi replaced Alvaro Mendes as Sultan Murad's adviser, then Lopez lost his Turkish partner. Lopez had everything to lose. He knew he had to stop Antonio, but without stepping beyond the safety of Lord Burghley's patronage, and without contradicting his policy.

Lopez hit upon a way to combine his agenda with that of Lord Burghley. The idea that Don Antonio might be passed to Spain as the opening act of peace negotiations had floated around for nearly a decade. Lopez knew that it would be the ideal way to disburden himself of Antonio. Of course, if Don Antonio left England, Lopez would lose any hope of recouping his money from Antonio, but if Lopez organised the deal, he would receive a Spanish commission that would make up for the loss. This plan would not be against the Cecil policy of exploring a rapprochement with Spain. In fact, it would accord exactly with their policy, and might lead to a ceasefire in the Low Countries, or even a general treaty between England and Spain. To intrigue in the Cecils' interest was what they paid him for.

Don Antonio had failed to organise his own escape from England, and Lopez saw that he might help him achieve that desire. The reception committee on the Continent did not have to be composed of cousin Diego Lopez and a colloquy of Antwerp merchants, or Monsieur de la Chastres and his Huguenots. They could just as easily be the Count of Fuentes, Spanish vizier of the Low Countries, and an armed guard who could escort Don Antonio to some island. The Knights Hospitaller were resident at Malta. Might Antonio, Grand Prior of their Portuguese wing, be shunted there as a permanent guest of the order?

But Lopez knew that to contact the Spanish at all was dangerous. To discuss any deal, whether it concerned Don Antonio or peace treaties, could leave him fatally compromised. The only safe way to work was to take a leaf from Walsingham's book, to operate at one remove from his Spanish correspondents, and to hide his tracks. Although setting up such an arrangement would be complex, Lopez had most of the necessary infrastructure in place. He already used the house in St Katharine Creechurch as a safe house and hostel, and in Manuel d'Andrada he had a field agent who could carry mails back and forth from the Low Countries on a Privy Council

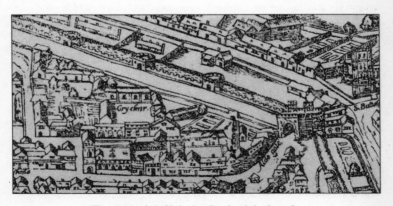

The parish of St Katharine Creechurch in the 1560s.

passport. But he knew that it would be dangerous to exchange letters with the Queen's enemies. Only a fool would put his signature on a letter which, if taken out of context, might seem treasonable. Lopez needed a loyal proxy who was prepared to take that risk, a 'cut-out' who would follow his orders and act as his intermediary. That way, if everything went wrong, the letters would not be in Lopez's handwriting. And as well as a safe house, a mail network and a multilingual courier, Lopez also knew the man for this job.

Among the permanent residents berthed in St Katharine Creechurch was a broken-down Portuguese knight called Estevan Ferreira da Gama. Disillusioned by age and poverty, Ferreira da Gama shared Lopez's perception that Don Antonio had changed from an asset to the Portuguese cause to a liability, and had already developed a little aristocratic intrigue of his own. The Counter-Armada had been Antonio's last chance to raise a foreign army for a Portuguese expedition. After that fiasco, the only way Ferreira da Gama and the other exiles might return to Portugal was via a negotiated surrender. But Don Antonio would never surrender to Philip II: he was the crowned King of Portugal and could not imagine renouncing his claim.

Ferreira da Gama and several other old Antonio retainers had decided that the time had come to replace Antonio with a younger, more credible contender. Antonio's second son, Don Cristovão, was held hostage in Fez by Ahmed IV of Morocco, a human surety against another of Antonio's irredeemable loans. But Antonio's first son and heir, Don Emanuel, was moving between Paris and the Low Countries, winning verbal support for his father's cause, but nothing more. Don Emanuel was ambitious and pragmatic. He had grown up in borrowed homes, surrounded by half-packed cases, and he understood the reality of exile politics. Ferreira da Gama believed that Don Emanuel was prepared to usurp his father's claim to the Portuguese crown and cut a deal with the Spanish. If Lopez had not already detected what his tenant was up to, Ferreira brought him into the scheme in December 1592.

Lopez realised that Ferreira da Gama's plan might be expanded upon. By combining Ferreira da Gama's groundwork with his own connections, the Portuguese coup might be parlayed into diplomatic and financial gains. A team had already taken shape. Andrada and Ferreira da Gama knew each other. Andrada stayed at St Katharine Creechurch when he came to London. Ferreira da Gama had seen Lopez's and Andrada's furtive dance of spymaster and spy, how Lopez hurried into the house just after Andrada's arrival, how the two of them muttered to each other in the back garden, and how Lopez hurried away. Andrada, multiply compromised by profession, was an old hand at truffling for indiscretions at supper when his fellow guests became casual through the intimacies of Lopez's wine and their native tongue. They were already bound to Lopez by unspoken complicity. When the time was right, Lopez would roll them up in his grand scheme. Together they would form a perfect espionage trio: controller, cut-out and courier. Like a reflection on pewter, Lopez's plan took blurred shape.

The plague surged back into London that winter. In the next two years the epidemic was to kill a tenth of the city's population. The mood among those daring or poor enough to stay was apocalyptic. Puritan preachers declared the plague to be a divine punishment; in *Christ's Tears Over Jerusalem*, the usually comical Thomas Nashe warned the sinning citizenry to repent or face worse. The Mayor ordered that all cats and dogs be killed. The theatres, haunts of feigning and transvestism, were closed and prayers were offered in St Paul's. Nothing worked; God was as invisible as the disease. The air stank with the twin smells of tar burnt against the unseen miasma of infection, and an undertone of decayed flesh from shuttered houses. Body pits were dug in the open fields south of the silent theatres of Bankside. The corpses were stacked in tumbrils and carted through the deserted streets like Smithfield carcasses, purpled faces frozen open-mouthed in asphyxiant surprise.

Lopez locked himself up with his family, Mrs Allington and the other tenants of Mountjoy's Inn. If the Doctor ventured out, he went armed with a prophylaxis of prayers and posies, the herbs swinging in sachets from his thick cloak, or stuffed into a metal beak worn over the nose and mouth. He looked like a phantasm from a

Venetian carnival, a crow-like predator on misery, feral companion of looters and undertakers, stray dogs and dog killers. Even on the fringes of the City, the plague consumed the populace. The sextons of nearby St Andrew's, Holborn dragged in corpses from the fields behind Mountjoy's Inn and the streets south of Gray's Inn. 'A maid out of the fields . . . a poor woman out of the street . . . a child out of Fetter Lane . . . a man out of the fields.'

On 20 January 1593, the Doctor left Mountjoy's Inn, crossed the City to St Katharine Creechurch and met with Manuel d'Andrada. The spy had returned from Calais, bearing news for Lord Burghley. Exactly one month later, Lopez returned to St Katharine Creechurch for a second meeting with Andrada. This meeting took place on the day following the start of the new term. Lopez would have seen Lord Burghley after the Lord Treasurer had returned to London in the days before Parliament's first sitting, then passed his instructions on to Andrada. Burghley's main concern was to pre-empt plots against the Queen's life emanating from the mixed bag of Jesuit priests and exiled English Catholics in the Low Countries. He made sure that no evidence survived of his instructions to Lopez regarding Andrada, but the Doctor's intelligence must have pleased the Lord Treasurer.

Just after Lopez became involved with Ferreira da Gama's plot for the Portuguese succession, and just before Andrada came to London, the frozen springs of patronage suddenly flowed forth. Lopez was granted another ten-year aniseed and sumach monopoly. In the machinery of state, the engine of patronage was driven by the cog of service. Lopez had earned the monopoly. In recent months he had performed three essential services for Burghley: interpreting for the Solomon Cormano embassy, clearing up the crisis in Constantinople, and supplying vital intelligence from the Low Countries. His new role as agent for the peace party was paying off.

In the first weeks of 1593, the imminent return of Parliament and the start of the legal term drew the political class back to London. In early February, Essex's intelligence chief Anthony Bacon came to London and took up residence in the Bacon brothers' chambers at Gray's Inn. This was their London base, a legal office, a mailbox for Essex intelligence, and a hostel for their friends. The Inn was the ideal launch pad for a political career, and the Bacons had a stake in it. Francis was a Pensioner, a senior member of the Inn, charged with collecting rents from its members, and would later oversee the construction of ornamental gardens on the wasteland behind the Inn, overlooked from the rear of Lopez's house.

The brothers took their seats in the new Parliament of Monday, 19 February 1593. After the ceremonial, back at his desk in Gray's Inn and feeling himself warm up after the chilly journey from Westminster, Anthony Bacon reported the opening of Parliament to his friend, the spy Anthony Standen, who was waiting at Calais for a passport to return to England.

Apart from Bacon's hope that the coming year would see the triumph of the Essex faction, the greater part of his letter was Court gossip, the mortar of intelligence, most of it sniping at Essex's rival Sir Walter Raleigh. But its final snippet suggested that Bacon had been investigating one of his neighbours: 'Dr Lopez, a physician, is lodged in a fair house in Holborn, lately built by an old gentlewoman called Mrs Allington, hard by Gray's Inn on the Fields side, where he is well entertained and used by her, for physic, as they say.'

Bacon had been in France for over a decade, but some servant or porter had filled him in. The backstairs gossip of Gray's Inn had it that Mrs Allington's 'entertainment' of Lopez extended to more than 'physic'. Confined to Mountjoy's Inn by the plague, the old Doctor and the merry widow had allegedly conducted an affair. It was like a scene from a bawdy comedy. A relationship between the gentlewoman and her lodger was always a pretext for sniggering and, as Ben Jonson would show in *The Alchemist*, popular belief held that romancing a patient was the best way of securing a good fee. The comedy had taken an unforeseen turn in its penultimate act. To the delight of the local scandalmongers, Mrs Allington had fallen pregnant. 'There was very lately a young child laid before the door,' Bacon reported, adding the motto that had been attached to the child.

Señor Lopez, here I come,
Open the gate and take in thy son.
Thy Spanish creed I will not disgrace,
Behold the image of thy face.

Whoever had left the baby on Lopez's doorstep knew him well enough to know about his 'Spanish creed'. The parish records suggest that the gossips of the Inn were right. Henry Allington had been buried on 2 August 1591. Over a year later, 'Richard Allington, son of Widow Allington' was baptised on 20 September 1592. New babies were baptised as quickly as possible, in case their earthly transit was shortened by infant mortality and the plague, so unless Mrs Allington's pregnancy was a medical miracle of twelve months' duration, she had become pregnant just after Christmas 1591, three months after her husband's death. For 'a gentlewoman' from a family prominent in the parish, it was a disgrace to bear an illegitimate child. If her son did not have his father's surname, he would be disinherited. She left him on his father's doorstep and his father's conscience.

Preoccupied with avoiding the plague and designing a new balance of European power, Lopez reacted in the habit of a professional intelligencer: he denied everything, and refused to acknowledge the parcel that had arrived on his doorstep. It was not the response of a physician who had consoled a grieving widow, but then Lopez had not restricted himself to a bedside manner.

Mrs Allington was left to her shame. When she baptised her baby at St Andrew's, Holborn, she had to endure the disapproval of Dr Bancroft the vicar alone. It was highly unusual: most gentlewomen in her position gave the child away, although the previous year, Dr Bancroft had baptised 'Tobias, a bastard', a foundling who had been found on the church steps. Little Richard Allington was the only baby that year whose mother announced her disgrace in Dr Bancroft's church.

By then, the Lopez family were probably out of England. In September 1592, they were away on their mysterious expedition to the ghetto at Venice and the palace at Constantinople. With the

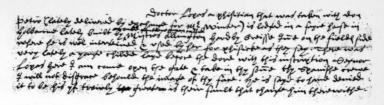

'Señor Lopez, here I come': Anthony Bacon's report to Anthony Standen, February 1592.

plague in London, it was a good time to leave the city, and Doctor Lopez had more personal motives for taking his wife on the holiday of a lifetime. Sara Lopez may not have noticed her husband's trysts with Mrs Allington. Consequently she may have believed his denials of paternity. On the other hand, Lopez might have been a compulsive adulterer and his wife might have been surprised only that he had fathered a bastard at the age of nearly seventy. Or was it that apart from being a gentlewoman, Mrs Allington was also a gentile woman? If Lopez acknowledged his paternity of Richard Allington, he disgraced his wife and also opened to public discussion the precise composition of her husband's blood. Whoever left the baby on her doorstep had known all about the Lopez family's 'Spanish creed'. Given the recent controversy over Solomon Cormano's ostentatious Judaism, perhaps Sara Lopez preferred her humilations to remain as private as her religion.

Roderigo Lopez, royal physician, international diplomat and unfaithful husband known to his English friends as 'Roger' or even 'Roderick', did not realise that he had been followed when he had gone to St Katharine Creechurch the day after the opening of Parliament. His private life was not quite private, and the safe house was not as safe as he thought. As he edged into the limelight he did not see the shadow he cast, or the waiting trapdoor, centre stage.

9

The Prop and the Burden

'Ere I ope his letter,
I pray you tell me how my good friend doth.
Bassanio to Salerio, *The Merchant of Venice*

When Anthony Bacon reported Lopez's indiscretion with Mrs Allington, he came flushed with his entry into Parliament, bearing a full 'cup of news' from Westminster. The recipient of his letter was Anthony Standen, the Essex intelligencer at Calais, and everything he described was of interest to an Essex follower. Bacon did not investigate Lopez solely because the Doctor was reputed to have had an affair with Mrs Allington. Other faults had been charged to Lopez.

Before February 1593, Bacon knew nothing about Lopez: in his letter to Standen, he described Lopez as 'a physician that was taken with Don Pedro'. Bacon thought that Lopez was a recent prisoner, washed up on an English beach in 1588 with Don Pedro de Valdes, commander of the Andalusian component of the Spanish Armada. He did not know that Lopez also worked for Essex. So why did Bacon send his report of Lopez's amorous adventures to Standen?

A tall blond from a family of Surrey Catholics, Standen had begun in the service of Mary, Queen of Scots, but had branched out into numerous other commissions, English, French and Spanish. Based at Florence, he had used an informer in Lisbon to supply Walsingham with detailed information of the Spanish preparations for the Armada. Just before the Armada sailed, he had successfully entered and left Spain. Walsingham's death had left him without a patron. After twenty-eight years in exile, several of them spent in prison, he had decided to return to England. Leaving Spain, he had travelled from Bordeaux to Calais in disguise, but had been held up on 'the other side'. Lord Burghley suspected that Standen had become contaminated by the low company he had kept on the Continent, and saw no reason to assist Walsingham's poacher to turn into Essex's gamekeeper.

Standen's dual loyalty had made his disguise of little use. A Spanish agent had tracked him all the way across France. Another agent was watching him in Calais: Manuel d'Andrada, picking up Spanish commissions on the side of his work for Lopez and Burghley. While Standen had waited at Calais for his passport, he had made contact with the fellow Essex agent and Anthony Bacon correspondent, Anthony Rolston. The Continental ports were bottlenecks for goods, mail and intelligencers. Like Andrada and Standen, Rolston was also a double agent. In the compartmentalised manner of Spanish intelligence, none of the three agents had known that the other two were traitors, but wintering together at Calais, the three double agents had soon sniffed each other out. The upshot of their encounter was that Rolston and Standen had discovered that Andrada was in Calais as an English agent, reporting to Doctor Lopez and Lord Burghley. Although Lopez did not realise it, his cover had been blown.

In January 1593, Standen sent this information to Anthony Bacon in a letter from Calais. When Bacon returned to Gray's Inn, Standen's work waited for him on his desk: intelligence from France and 'bills' from Standen's 'merchants' – Standen's invoices for the espionage he had supplied. Bacon's response was to request more information from Anthony Rolston at Calais, and to tail Lopez. The spark for Bacon's interest in Lopez had been in Standen's mails from Calais.

Signature of Anthony Standen.

Standen's tip-off came just as the Essex faction was gearing for its first assault on the bastion of Burghley's authority. Essex had to convince the Queen that he could mature from flirt to politician. He had to show political acumen, and he had to produce good intelligence; on Essex's first day as a Privy Councillor, the Queen set him the task of writing 'a draft of an instruction for a matter of intelligence' to a hypothetical agent in France. The perfect bridgehead for Essex's assault on the government had just presented itself. The Master of the Rolls, Sir Gilbert Gerrard, was ailing. It was assumed that Gerrard's successor would be the Attorney-General, Sir Thomas Egerton. This would leave the Attorney-Generalship vacant. The Cecils' preferred candidate for the post was the Solicitor-General, Sir Edward Coke. But Essex, with a pack of supporters in the new Parliament and Anthony Bacon's intelligencers hard at work, decided to secure this plum appointment for his protégé, Francis Bacon.

A week later, Parliament debated the 'subsidy', Parliament's gift to the penniless Queen. Sir Robert Cecil proposed an amount; his cousin Francis Bacon backed it and the House of Lords suggested patriotically that the amount be increased. The Queen was about to receive her money when Bacon stalled the process on a technical point: to protect the privileges of the Commons, the Lords' suggestion should be ignored. This procedural objection was a cover for an ambush of the Cecils, and it turned the subsidy into a factional dispute. The debate was passed to a committee. After sessions enlivened by a shouting match between the Burghley adherent Sir Thomas Heneage and Bacon cousin's Sir Edward Hoby, the committee arrived at a compromise elaborate enough to flatter both sides. In his enthusiasm, Bacon had tripped himself up. Uncle Burghley was furious with his unrepentant nephew. The Queen had formed the impression that Francis Bacon, however intelligent, was too clever to be trusted. Instead of proving his legal brilliance, he had marked himself as a disloyal troublemaker.

Standen's hint about Lopez coincided with the outbreak of open hostility between the Essex and Cecil factions. If Anthony Bacon repeated Standen's allegation to Essex, the Earl would have known that Doctor Lopez was playing a double game and was also supplying the Cecils with Low Countries intelligence. This would have explained to Essex a recurring, frustrating problem in his spy service. To be valuable, intelligence had to be timely. It was only topical if it outpaced the progress of events. In 1587, Philip II's well-run spy service had reported that Francis Drake had sailed for Cadiz, but the intelligence had reached Madrid when Drake was already in Cadiz harbour. If intelligence came late, it was irrelevant. And if it had already become known through a rival source, it was worthless. 'An apple in time is better than an apple of gold out of season,' said the Queen.

Whenever Essex arranged an audience with Elizabeth to announce his latest espionage triumph, his news was no surprise to Elizabeth. Anthony Bacon's carefully prepared summaries had already been 'wholly read to Her Majesty'. There was nothing in them that had not been 'hither advertised many months past'. After making a dramatic entrance, Essex had been a clarion for stale news. The combination of self-regard and ineptitude made him ridiculous. 'The Queen, knowing it before, did but laugh at the Earl of Essex,' recollected Sir Henry Savile, one of the Earl's cronies, 'whereby the Earl saw himself utterly disappointed.'

Anthony Bacon had suspected that the problem might be logistical, 'the long stay and late return' of the ships that carried Anthony Standen's correspondence to England. He was wrong. The architect of Essex's embarrassment was Doctor Lopez. When Andrada brought information from Calais, the Doctor made sure to pass it to Lord Burghley before he passed it to the Earl of Essex. Lopez played one patron off against the other and collected commissions from both. To the Earl's friend and secretary Henry Savile, it seemed later that although Essex had 'gotten an intelligencer' in Lopez, the Doctor had proved 'not to be *his* intelligencer'. This 'bred very ill blood between the Earl and Dr Lopez'. In revenge, Essex 'set blocks in the way' of Lopez's suits to the Privy Council, and punished the Doctor with financial pressure.

Now, Essex had two possible reasons for suspecting that Lopez was betraying him. The Doctor had promised his fealty to Essex, and had given the impression that, faced with realignment after the failure of the Counter-Armada and the death of Walsingham, he had opted for Essex's war party. But all the time he still worked for Burghley. Lopez ran agents and mail from the Low Countries via Calais for Burghley, and he did the same for Essex. The ambiguity of using the same agents to serve two masters with such different agendas was obvious. With the Essex–Cecil battle lines drawn, it was an unsustainable contradiction: every word that went to Burghley was a loss for Essex, and vice versa. Essex did not know what Lopez was doing for Burghley in the Low Countries, but he had to find out. Essex feared that Lopez might be spying on him for Burghley, keeping the Lord Treasurer informed of the progress of Essex's schemes, setting up Essex's agents in a projection designed to discredit the Earl and his policies.

Lopez did not know that some inkling of his double game had been detected by Essex's intelligencers, as his attention was fixed on developing Ferreira da Gama's plot for the Portuguese succession. Lopez had proposed that he and Ferreira pool their assets. He said that if Ferreira provided the credibility, he would provide the means by which they would rework the Portuguese succession and make peace with Spain. Lopez laid out the steps of their plan. First, he wanted Ferreira to secure a 'letter of submission' from Don Emanuel: a written statement in which Emanuel claimed the Avis inheritance and expressed a desire to make peace with Philip II. In the meantime they would need to back up Emanuel's claim, so Ferreira would have to secure a critical mass of support among the exiled Portuguese aristocracy in London and Paris.

Desperate and enchanted, Ferreira was drawn into Lopez's web. The Doctor told him the second step of their scheme: to offer Don Emanuel's letter to the Spanish as a basis for negotiation. In this delicate part of the process, Ferreira would provide Don Emanuel, and Lopez would provide political cover and communications. This was where Manuel d'Andrada would be useful. He worked for Lopez as a courier and spy, and his Privy Council passport meant that he could pass through the Channel ports without being searched. In the third stage the plot would go public. At this point Lopez promised that his connections would open the path to riches. As Lopez ran Andrada as Burghley's agent, and the Lord Treasurer was no less interested in peace than Ferreira, when the third step came, and Don Emanuel's letter became a bargaining chip in negotiations, Lopez would be able to add the weight of Lord Burghley to the Portuguese team. In the meantime, this bold, risky scheme would be Lopez's and Ferreira's secret.

By early April, Ferreira da Gama had prepared the ground. In Paris, Don Emanuel had committed to the plan and waited for a signal from Ferreira to put his ambitions into ink. On 4 April 1593, Ferreira da Gama went to Mountjoy's Inn for a meeting at which Lopez informed him of Manuel d'Andrada's imminent arrival in London. Everything was in place. It was time to put their plan into action, and to bring Andrada into the plot.

Lopez had given Ferreira a whispered vision of restoration, and Ferreira now became nervous, torn between hope and dread. He longed to exchange bare lodgings in London for his lost estates in Portugal, yet he was an amateur and feared Andrada as a professional intelligencer with a reputation for treachery. Lopez managed to talk Ferreira round, playing on his hopes and promising that he held Andrada in his palm. Lopez told Ferreira how he had saved Andrada from a traitor's death 'in the time of Secretary Walsingham', and that since that day, Andrada had had no choice but 'to trust him with his life', regardless of his treacherous nature. Andrada, Lopez assured Ferreira, had to follow Lopez's orders. If he did not, the Doctor would feed him to Don Antonio. To Ferreira, a paddler in the Portuguese shallows who had been sucked by the tide into deep and murky waters, this brutal calculation smacked of trustworthy professionalism. Ferreira relented, and Andrada was on board.

Lopez issued Ferreira with money for Andrada's commission and, a few days later, Manuel d'Andrada drifted into St Katharine Creechurch bearing intelligence for Burghley. Lopez paid him for his service, leaving Andrada with idle hours to fill before Lopez returned with Burghley's new instructions. Should Andrada have felt like risking the plague, the theatres had just reopened. There was Barabas in *The Jew of Malta*, or Hieronimo in *The Spanish Tragedy*, set in the Portugal of 1580, but they might have reminded him of work. On 16 April 1593, Ferreira approached Andrada in the safe house. The two had 'a treaty and discourse', each surmising that the other was bound to the Doctor and could consequently be trusted to hold his secrets. Immediately afterwards, Andrada left for Paris to collect Don Emanuel's letter of submission.

As Andrada crossed London Bridge with Lopez's crowns in his pocket, Richard Field the printer finished a production run in his Wood Street workshop. The heavy lead squares embossed with a raised letter were cleaned of ink and stored for their next use. The screw of the press had crushed black footprints of pressed letters across the rippling crenellations of the soft paper. When the ink had dried into matt permanence, the paper was folded and torn, folded and torn again, until the original sheet had been reduced to eight equal sections, octavo pages. A lone word stood at the bottom and top of each page, the stragglers or scouts of the narrative. By tracing these words, the pages were ordered into sequence, then fixed by stitching. On 18 April, Field took a copy to Whitehall. After examination by the censors, it was written into the Stationers' Register. Thus licensed, Field despatched copies to his shop, 'at the sign of the White Greyhound in St Paul's Churchyard', where the fresh words of the living were hawked over the old bones of the dead, Secretary Walsingham among them.

Of the making of books, there is no end, Ecclesiastes had said, sympathetic to writer, printer and reader. A debut was a great occasion for the author, but another day's work for the printer, wrestling with the thick arm of the press, guessing the right load of ink, and fiddling black-fingered at his letters as he improvised the spelling. This time, though, Field shared in the excitement. He had just printed the debut of an old Stratford friend. It was a poem, a small volume whose lightness in the palm matched the ease of its borrowings from Ovid. Light as a hunter's tread, too, in its dedication to the Earl of Southampton.

Right Honourable, I know not how I shall offend in dedicating my unpolished lines to your Lordship, nor how the world will censure me for choosing so strong a prop to support so weak a burden. Only if your

Honour seem but pleased, I account myself highly praised, and vow to take advantage of all idle hours, till I have honoured you with some grave labour. But if the first heir of my invention prove deformed, I shall be sorry it had so noble a godfather, and never after ear so barren a land, for fear it will yield me still so bad a harvest. I leave it to your honourable survey, and your Honour to your heart's content, which I wish may always answer your own wish, and the world's hopeful expectation.

Your Honour's in all duty,

William Shakespeare

Venus and Adonis was William Shakespeare's first published work. By comparison with the raucous *Taming of the Shrew*, which originated in the same period, *Venus and Adonis* was decorous and classical. Its eroticism lay not in the beery romping of Warwickshire rustics, but in the refined, pedigree myths of Ovid's *Metamorphoses*. In a setting half Ancient Greece, half Forest of Arden, Venus, an ageing woman, falls in love with the young man, Adonis. He prefers hunting wild boar. In revenge, Venus arranges for Adonis to be gored in the groin by his prey. His dying blood makes the land fertile. Shakespeare had returned to the recurring theme of his Southampton period, of men and marriage. George Chapman had cast Southampton as Narcissus. Now Shakespeare cast the Earl as Adonis. He implied that, like Adonis rejecting Venus, Southampton risked ruin by rejecting women and marriage. The balance of flattery and warning required a courtier's poise. The poem was hugely successful among the fashionable set. Some of the cultured young men of the Inns of Court were rumoured to sleep with it under their pillows.

While Gray's Inn thrilled to the poetic emasculation of Adonis, over the garden wall at Mountjoy's Inn the political emasculation of Don Antonio gave private delight to a select audience of two. On 24 April, Manuel d'Andrada returned to St Katharine Creechurch with a letter for Ferreira da Gama. The two of them beetled urgently up Holborn to Lopez's house. At Mountjoy's Inn, the Doctor took them into the garden, out of the hearing of his servants. Lopez opened the letter and read the words of Don Emanuel. Addressing his letter to Philip II, Emanuel claimed his father's title and described 'to the King of Spain how he would go for his kingdom' if Philip allowed him to. Attached was a list of 150 names, a roll-call of the Portuguese aristocracy in exile, all prepared to renounce Don Antonio for a pardon from Philip.

Lopez stood in his garden, the paper in his hand. Young Don Emanuel had taken the bait. He had been unable to resist Lopez, an emissary from the cloisters of Crato and the lost kingdom of his dreams, and would be malleable in the Doctor's hands as the older man guided him towards an act of figurative regicide and patricide. Lopez had sought revenge upon Don Antonio in law and had failed, but now he possessed a licence for Antonio's annihilation. His humbling before the Privy Council, his losses, and the dashing of his hopes on the walls of Lisbon would all be repaired.

The first step of Lopez's plot had succeeded. Quickly he instructed Ferreira how to proceed with the second step. The next move was to wave Don Emanuel's letter of submission under the noses of the Spanish. This meant writing to Philip II, sending a letter to him secretly, and receiving a reply in secret. Lopez described how he would provide the means. One of his contacts in the Antwerp underworld was a Portuguese trader called Manuel Palatios, whose counting house also handled mails and money for Spanish intelligence. Manuel d'Andrada could deliver letters to Palatios's mail drop in Antwerp, and from there Palatios could forward them to Madrid. The Spanish reply could be sent via Brussels, where the Count of Fuentes headed the Spanish government of occupation in the Low Countries. From there, mail would be forwarded to Calais, where Andrada would be waiting.

The three conspirators went back into the house and Lopez sat Ferreira down at his desk. The Doctor produced two letters, written in his own elegant hand. He told Ferreira that this moment was his 'fit opportunity' to obtain a pardon and recover his estates in Portugal. Under Lopez's and Andrada's supervision, Ferreira copied the letters verbatim. One letter was to Philip II's Portuguese adviser, Don Cristovão da Moura, and the other was to the King's secretary, Don Juan d'Idiaques. They described Don Emanuel's letter of submission, and offered Ferreira's 'service' as an intermediary in

Don Cristovão da Moura.

negotiations to be conducted via Lopez. The script was Ferreira's and so was the signature, but every word was Lopez's. Some of the terms were obscure to Ferreira, and the other two dictated 'certain hidden words' in cipher to him that he did not understand, but he copied everything just as they instructed. As soon as Ferreira was finished, Andrada took the letters and left post haste for Dover.

Stage two was in motion. Lopez had initiated contact with the Spanish with the minimum of risk. Although his name was cited in the letters as the channel for communications, he had made sure that the real risks had all been taken by Ferreira and Andrada. If something went wrong, Lopez could deny everything and point to the letter writer and the courier. The blame would fall on the weak shoulders of the cut-out, a silhouette in the shape of an earnest Portuguese aristocrat, Andrada would shift for himself, as he always had, and the controller would be safely distanced, free of suspicion.

Lopez had learnt from a lifetime in espionage to protect himself. In 1590, Walsingham had interposed Lopez between himself and Andrada. In 1591, Burghley had interposed Lopez between himself and Andrada. Now Lopez the cut-out turned spymaster, and used the naive Ferreira da Gama as a shield against Manuel d'Andrada.

Lopez was driven by greed, political ambition and a desire for revenge upon Don Antonio. This did not mean that his aims conflicted with the English national interest, only that his motivations were ignoble and his means devious. The aim of the Queen and the Cecils was a treaty with Spain. After three decades of fruitless hostility, the mere suggestion of negotiations would assure a Cecil supremacy over English foreign policy. Lopez was a Cecil intelligencer, and his use of Don Emanuel's letter of submission accorded with the drift of Cecil policy and the purpose of his engagement by the Cecils. Yet to contact the Spanish was treason. Lopez committed this treason in Lord Burghley's name. To what degree did Burghley know what Lopez did in his name in April 1593?

Burghley had known Lopez personally for half a lifetime. He knew of the Doctor's service to Leicester and Walsingham, and he received intelligence from the Doctor. In a time of constant anxiety about the Queen's safety, when rumours of Spanish plots to assassinate her drifted across the Channel like spring fog, Burghley trusted Lopez to be the Queen's physician. Any suspicion of Lopez would have resulted in immediate isolation from his most important client.

Burghley also knew Andrada, Lopez's double-edged instrument. Burghley had used Lopez to keep Andrada at arm's length, but by April 1593, Andrada had been supplying Burghley with Low Countries intelligence for nearly two years. Andrada was a liar, but a useful liar in the Queen's service. If his prior service to Walsingham was counted, Andrada had been an English spy for three years. He was not a rogue agent, but a known double agent.

Burghley knew about Lopez's and Andrada's work for the Privy Council in 1590, when they had offered Don Antonio as a deposit on peace talks. That time, Walsingham had used Lopez and Andrada to gather espionage from inside the Spanish camp. After August 1591, Burghley had continued this arrangement, and had used Lopez and

Andrada to tease out hostile plots in the Netherlands. Was he now using them to tease out a dialogue with Madrid?

There were two components to Lopez's plan: to replace Don Antonio with Don Emanuel, and to use Don Emanuel's letter of submission to open negotiations with Spain. Burghley had explored this kind of deal for years. In the mid-1580s, when England and Spain were already at war in the Netherlands and the Armada was in preparation, Burghley's inclination towards peace had led him to extend peace feelers via Hector Nuñez's network. And in 1590, he had supported a scheme which envisaged the sacrifice of Don Antonio as a taster to negotiations, with Lopez as his intermediary with the Spanish. So there was nothing in Lopez's 1593 plan that Burghley had not already attempted. In 1593, the pressure was on the Cecils. The Earl of Essex was attacking their political power base, flirting his way past their place in the Queen's affections, and trumpeting military adventure as the best course. Burghley needed a diplomatic coup more than ever. His career was almost over and if he failed now, his son's career might never begin.

So if Burghley did not give Lopez explicit sanction, the terms of Lopez's service, the precedent of Burghley's practice and the factional struggle with Essex all gave implicit sanction. And if Burghley did give explicit sanction, that would account for the renewal of the aniseed and sumach monopoly at the exact moment when Lopez had begun reshaping Ferreira's plan, dovetailing personal ambition to the Cecils' political agenda.

Lopez was in technical breach of the treason laws, but he was doubly insulated against the charge. He was running an agent in the Low Countries on behalf of Lord Burghley and he was pursuing the stated policy interest of the Cecils. In the worst-case scenario, Lopez's plan might be prematurely revealed, the paper trail of correspondence would be followed to Mountjoy's Inn, and he risked being gored by his own prey in a no man's land between the Queen and her enemies. But Lopez knew he possessed an ace, a trump to beat the hand of any accuser. This was a dangerous business, so he was cautious and used proxies, but he despatched Andrada confident in the patronage and protection of Lord Burghley. As a fellow seeker after patronage had recently put it in a modish poem, how could the world censure him for choosing 'so strong a prop to support so weak a burden'?

Burghley probably knew what Lopez was doing in his name, but neither of them could know what Andrada did in both their names. Andrada's value was his duplicity: he could enter the enemy camp and report back. This attribute was equally dangerous to both sides, as Andrada was also paid by the Spanish to enter the English camp and report back. In running a double agent there was a balance between reward and risk, between information gained and lost. But Lopez was confident that Andrada could be controlled by compartmentalisation, intimidation and bribery. If Lopez denounced Andrada to Burghley, then the death sentence that had hung over Andrada since 1590 would swiftly be implemented. The Doctor believed he had Andrada in his palm. The Doctor was wrong. Like Hieronimo in *The Spanish Tragedy*, Andrada would only be voluntarily silent when he had cut out his own tongue.

When Andrada stepped off the boat at Calais, he passed beyond Lopez's control. He went on to Brussels, where he reported to the Count of Fuentes and his secretary, Stephen d'Ibarra. Fuentes and Ibarra knew of Lopez's tricky reputation as an intelligencer. Philip II's policy was not dissimilar from Elizabeth's: an openness towards negotiation, combined with a determination not to be fooled. Fuentes and Ibarra decided to play Lopez at his own game.

Back in London, it was impossible for Burghley to know what Andrada was doing in his name. How much did Burghley know about what Lopez was doing in Essex's name? From Essex's humiliation before the Queen, Burghley knew that Lopez was feeding Essex stale intelligence in order to handicap Essex against the Cecils. But over the horizon, the Doctor was enmeshed in the intelligence underworld of the Low Countries. That was his job. He trawled for information and tried to insert himself into a chain of couriers in order to pillage a correspondence. This cast Burghley's diligent, ambitious and vengeful servant into the most compromising of company. If Lopez the courtier was bound by the Hippocratic oath and his oath of service to the Queen, then Lopez the intelligencer was a liar

The Count of Fuentes at war in the Low Countries.

by trade, habitually posing as a traitor, and corresponding with hunted men, heretics and murderers.

In late April 1593, while Lopez and Andrada guided Ferreira da Gama's nervous hand across the page in Mountjoy's Inn, an Essex courier called Robert Draper was on his way to Antwerp. Like Burghley, Essex had seen that there was political capital to be won from detecting hostile plots in the Low Countries. Travelling under the guise of a merchant – and, judging from his eponymous surname, a cloth merchant – Draper was heading for an assignation with an exiled Catholic double agent called Charles Paget. Draper worked for an experienced intelligencer called Roger Walton, a specialist at penetrating Catholic conspiracies against the Queen. In 1586, Walsingham had used Walton to penetrate exiled English Catholic circles in Paris. The playwright Christopher Marlowe may also have attempted a similar task for Walsingham at this time, sniffing around the English embassy for traitors.

Draper was less expert. On his return journey, he fell into the company of two fellow merchants, one thin and one fat. The senior member of the pair was a wealthy Spaniard, a 'fierce, lean, black man with long moustachioes', who rode with 'ten horses in his company'. The other was a portly Portuguese, 'a fat, gruff man'. By nightfall the three travellers were at Ghent. They found an inn, and the two men asked Draper 'to sup' with them. Settling on French as a common tongue, the three merchants shared dinner. Relaxing by the fire after a day on the road, their talk turned to business.

After Draper had volunteered that he had lived in England for many years, the two men became 'inquisitive of him'. One of them asked Draper 'whether he knew Doctor Lopez', and whether Lopez had good 'credit' with the Queen. The two strangers were 'desirous to come on into England as merchants', but first they wanted to 'send a letter to Doctor Lopez, that he might be a means for their safe coming'. Draper replied that he did not know Doctor Lopez. Lulled by the fire, the food and the strong Flemish beer, Draper rambled on with his companions, and then went to bed.

The next morning, Draper and his new friends travelled together to Gravelines, where their paths parted. When the two men discovered that Draper was going on to Calais, they asked him to deliver some letters to a merchant there. Draper took the letters to Calais and found the merchant's house. The Calais merchant took Draper's letters and bundled them into 'a packet' with several others. On the packet, the merchant wrote the name that had come up the previous night at dinner: 'Doctor Lopez'. Then the merchant pressed the packet into Draper's hands, saying, 'You should have the carriage of them, because you brought the first letters.'

The merchant seemed to have mistaken Draper for the designated courier of the packet. Draper realised that he had been duped into carrying letters of unknown content. He had pretended to be a merchant, but so had everyone else. The whole episode suddenly reeked of conspiracy. The Calais merchant was very insistent, threatening even. As soon as Draper crossed the Channel, he gave the packet to Roger Walton, who assured Draper he would pass it on to the Earl of Essex.

Draper thought he had washed his hands of the letters, but their stain returned. Shortly afterwards, Draper accompanied 'Mr Walton' to a clandestine meeting 'in the highway near Kingston', a Thameside village discreetly close to Richmond Palace. Draper saw Walton talk 'familiarly and privately' with an old man 'by the space of a quarter of an hour'. They made sure to keep Draper out of earshot, so he could not tell 'what their speech was'. As Draper trotted after Walton on the way back into London, he asked Walton about the old man with whom he had shared so private a conversation on a country road.

Mr Walton took pity on simple Robert Draper. 'This same man was Doctor Lopez, to whom the packet of letters were sent unto,' he explained.

Draper was baffled. On his next courier run to the Low Countries he conducted a small investigation. To his alarm, he discovered that the tall, moustachioed Spaniard whom he had dined with at Ghent was not a merchant, but 'a Secretary of Spain'. The links in the chain fell into place: from the 'Secretary of Spain' to the Calais merchant, from the Calais merchant to Doctor Lopez, from Doctor Lopez to Mr Walton, and from Mr Walton to the Earl of Essex. Draper realised that he had been drawn into deep waters. His master Essex was dealing in secret contacts with the enemy. Were they secret because they were treasonable, or because they were a projection? Draper became very frightened and decided not to tell anybody in England what had happened.

Although he did not realise it, Draper had stumbled on to one of Lopez's secret correspondences and the route by which it reached London. The merchant of Calais was Estevan Nuñez. A relative of the late Doctor Hector, Nuñez was an old associate of the Lopez family. In Antwerp, Nuñez had handled mails for Sir Francis Walsingham. Back in 1572, he and Doctor Lopez had speculated together on the pepper trade in a cartel that had included Bernaldo Luis, Jeronimo Lopez Soeiro, Luis Lopez and Bernaldo Nuñez: the cream of the Marrano intelligence network.

Estevan had been displaced from Antwerp by the war in the Netherlands, which had wrought havoc upon the Antwerp market. Pirates loyal to the rebel States waited at the end of the Scheldt estuary, preying on any ship that passed, until it had become impossible to do business. The old Portuguese nation of Antwerp was breaking up. Some Marrano merchants had moved their operations north to the small port of Amsterdam and others had gone to Hamburg. Estevan had moved down to Calais in the late 1580s. His counting house still turned an illicit profit as the mail drop for Andrada's correspondence from the Low Countries. Now he was handling another sensitive correspondence for the Doctor.

Draper's source in Ghent had been correct in calling the Spaniard a 'Secretary of Spain', but only in the past tense. In the present tense, the Spaniard was an envoy of King Henri IV of France. In the future tense, he was to be another of Essex's causes. He was Antonio Perez, last and most lurid star in the Lopez story's constellation of Antonios and Anthonies.

10

The Monster of Fortune

If your friend is a doctor, send him to the house of your enemy.

Portuguese proverb

On the morning of 2 November 1591, Antonio Perez, Philip II's erstwhile Secretary, escaped from the Inquisition and fled Spain disguised as a shepherd. The accusations in Perez's wake included charges of heresy, sodomy and, despite being the son of a priest, Jewish origins, but he had not limited his misdemeanours to the merely personal. There were also political charges of murder, torture, treason, raising a rebellion in Aragon against Philip II and seducing the King's mistress. Philip II put a bounty on the fugitive, and Perez was dogged by Spanish agents and assassination plots. He found asylum in Paris at the Court of Henri IV, where he cultivated a megalomaniac vision of a grand anti-Spanish alliance involving Henri IV of France, Elizabeth I of England, Murad III of Turkey and Ahmed IV of Morocco. None of them wanted his plan, but all of them wanted his information about Philip's Court.

As a young man, Perez had been nicknamed 'Pimpollo', or 'Rosebud'. In old age, he was obsessed with his declining looks, convinced that his emaciated body was too fat and that his head was too big for his body. He found a dysmorphic self-image in the Minotaur, a bull-man trapped in the labyrinth, and dramatised the improbable course of his life by nicknaming himself the 'Monster of Fortune' and embellishing his letters with a Minotaur design. An aggressive hypochondriac, he travelled everywhere with a small chest of potions and insisted on medicating anyone within dosing distance. He was especially fond of opiates and Bezoar stones; compacted gravel which, after agglomerating in the stomach of the wild Persian goat, had been picked out from faeces and sold as possessing magical powers against poison and illness. Perez began the day with a glass of sugared asses' milk mixed with musk and amber, and he ended it with an opiate. He slept with a Bezoar stone under his tongue, his flushed face cooled with strawberry water.

Antonio Perez's monstrous motifs, from the 1598 Paris edition of his autobiographical Relations.

In April 1593, when he met Robert Draper on the roads of Flanders, the Monster was on his way to England as an unofficial emissary of Henri IV of France. He travelled with the official emissary, thirty-three-year-old Prégent de la Fin, Vidame of Chartres, the son of the French ambassador in London, Jean de la Fin. Their mission was doubly complex. The first problem was political. Henri IV was a Calvinist, but the majority of his subjects were Catholic. To avoid further civil war, it seemed he would have to convert to Catholicism; five days after Perez arrived in London on 24 April, a conference convened at Suresnes and recommended that Henri convert for the sake of national unity. England and France were allies against Spain, and Elizabeth and her ministers were worried that if

Henri adopted Philip II's religion, he might also adopt his policies. Henri sent Perez and the Vidame to assure Elizabeth that his conversion was only *politique*, and that the alliance would survive.

The second problem was gaining access to the Court. Elizabeth and Burghley wanted nothing to do with Perez: he had already betrayed his own monarch, so why should he not betray England's? Like many others rejected by Burghley, Perez was promptly snapped up by Essex. This was the point of the letter that Robert Draper had delivered to London: via Lopez and Roger Walton, Perez had notified Essex of his imminent arrival in London.

In the next weeks, Essex became Perez's exclusive patron in England, and his exclusive financial supporter. He installed Perez at Gaynes Park in Epping, near his own country retreat at Wanstead. He supplied Perez with money, and attempted to secure him an interview with the Queen. The Vidame of Chartres rented a house at Hackney in order to be closer to Wanstead. Essex lavished banquets and flattery upon the envoys, spending nearly £200 on 'entertainment' in the last week of May alone. Swilling back the Earl's fine wines and viands, Perez beguiled Essex with his delusional plan for an anti-Spanish internationale, and Essex beguiled Perez with the equally delusional idea that the Queen might support it.

Perez's combination of intrigue, narcissism and anti-Spanish mania made him popular among the Essex set. The decadent English aristocrats were fascinated by Perez's drugs and prescriptions. Paternally, Perez presented the Earl with one of his medical treasure boxes, although he asked for it back when the plague broke out. The physic-swigging Anthony Bacon considered Perez to be an expert to rival any professional physician, and Essex's sister, Lady Penelope Rich, recommended Perez's Bezoar stones to her friends. The chemical experimentation nearly ended in tragedy after Perez's home-brewed concoction of sugar, musk and amber almost killed Essex's secretary, Thomas Smith. Apart from its use in perfumery, musk – extracted from the scent glands of the male musk ox – was a stimulant and anti-spasmodic. Smith did not have Perez's addict constitution, and when he took Perez's habitual dose, he collapsed.

A scholar who had translated the *Odyssey* into Spanish, Perez fitted into the atmosphere of literary pretension around the war party. Between doses, Perez did not write letters, but epistles. He was prolific, and patented a grotesquely precious style, mixing masochistic self-abasement with the sadistic overworking of innocent metaphors. When he sent Lady Penelope Rich a pair of dog skin gloves, his covering note read, 'I have been so troubled not to have at hand the dog's skin gloves your Ladyship desires that, pending the time when they shall arrive, I have resolved to sacrifice myself to your service and flay a piece of my own skin from the most tender part of my body, if such an uncouth carcass as mine can have any tender skin.'

Perez became a mentor to the Bacon brothers, who shared his tastes in classical literature, political ambition and sodomy. Anthony Bacon was now a semi-invalid, restricted to the ground floor of his lodgings and prone to crippling cramps in his arms and legs. His relationship with Perez was concentrated in the only sphere in which he still had free movement, the intellectual. He consulted Perez on intelligence, copied out Perez's aphorisms for his friends and commissioned Arthur Atey to assemble an English translation of Perez's *Relations*, his account of how he had betrayed Philip II. Perez's friendship with Francis Bacon was more intimate. In a letter to Anthony Bacon, he described a letter from Francis in terms that hinted bluntly at Francis's sexual tastes.

> Your brother invited me to dinner. He has wounded me in writing – his pen being the most rabid and biting of teeth. As if he himself were above blame – some kind of chaste vestal virgin. You can tell immediately what this imagined modesty of his is all about. For I am just the same. Those who claim to love modesty are in fact the most bold of men, and submit to force, and enjoy the excuse of being taken by force, like the Roman matron in Tacitus who consented to be raped by her lover.

All of which greatly distressed their mother. Anne Cooke Bacon bombarded her sons with stern Puritan letters that told them to stop 'committing foul sins' with 'cormorant seducers' like Perez and 'instruments of Satan' like Anthony Standen. She considered 'that Bloody

Perez' to be 'a proud, profane, costly fellow', and she knew that Francis was his 'coach-companion and bed-companion'. 'I would you were well rid of that old, doted, polling Papist,' she begged Anthony, 'He will use discourses out of season to hinder your health.'

The Bacons did not listen to their mother. Perez was a fellow guest at Essex's table, and Essex would be their route to power.

As the Minotaur settled into his English labyrinth, the Count of Fuentes and his secretary, Stephen d'Ibarra, plotted his destruction. Perez had escaped Spanish assassins at Bearn in France. Philip II had ordered Fuentes and Ibarra to finish the job. In April, Perez had shaken them off on the roads of Flanders, but they had found him again in early May, when Manuel d'Andrada appeared in Brussels. Andrada reported that on the day he had left England, Perez had arrived there. Fuentes and Ibarra wanted to send an agent to London to locate Perez and lay the ground for his murder by a team of assassins. In Brussels, the Count of Fuentes had billeted Andrada with another Portuguese agent, Emanuel Luis Tinoco. The Count decided that if Andrada could provide the thread that would lead him in and out of the labyrinth, Tinoco would be their Theseus.

Like most Portuguese exiles, Tinoco was a nominal follower of Don Antonio who had turned into a follower of his own fortune. He had travelled to Fez with Antonio's second son Don Cristovão and had abandoned Cristovão in Morocco when Ahmed IV had held him hostage against his father's debts. Returning to England, Tinoco had become a courier for Don Antonio and had drifted into the pay of the Spanish at Brussels. In his transits through Calais, he had passed through the same bottleneck as Manuel d'Andrada and Anthony Standen. On these credentials alone, Tinoco might easily have discovered the nascent Lopez plot before he roomed with Andrada at Brussels. In the last week of May, he was summoned to the Count of Fuentes's study.

The Count and his secretary told Tinoco that he was to go to London and make contact with Francis Caldera, a Portuguese in the Vidame of Chartres's household, who doubled as a Spanish informer. Caldera would be able to tell him where Antonio Perez had gone to ground. 'Manuel Andrada doth bind himself to do a certain

The palace at Brussels where Andrada and Tinoco met with the Count of Fuentes and Secretary d'Ibarra.

matter, very important,' they alluded to the Perez mission, 'but we know not if he hath spirit enough for such a work.'

Tinoco was reckless and penniless, and deception was his habit. 'I want no wit,' he said.

Sworn to secrecy, Tinoco returned to his lodgings to wait for the delivery of the mails he was to carry to London. At ten o'clock that night, as he and Andrada shared a late supper, a page from Secretary d'Ibarra appeared and ordered Andrada to attend upon his master. Andrada returned after midnight, visibly pleased, saying that Secretary d'Ibarra had given him mails to take to Paris, whose delivery would make him much money. As Tinoco was about to go to Calais, he asked Andrada to defer his departure by one day. Andrada agreed. The next morning, Tinoco collected letters from the Count of Fuentes and Secretary d'Ibarra to their English contacts, and then he and Andrada set off for France.

(*Left*) The fortress-monastery of the Knights Hospitaller at Crato, scene of Lopez and Don Antonio's childhoods.

(*Left*) Adventures in the spice trade: *Departure from Lisbon for Brazil, the East Indies and America*, engraved by Theodore de Bry in 1592.

(*Below*) The geography of a new life: the streets around St Bartholomew's Hospital, from a survey of 1617.

Spymaster and soldier:
(*Above left*) Sir Francis Walsingham casts a cold eye on his portraitist,
John de Critz the Elder. (*Above right*) A debauched and dapper Robert Dudley,
Earl of Leicester, squints at an unnamed painter, *c*.1575.

(*Below*) A panorama of Lopez's London, including Burghley House (1); St. Paul's (2);
Guildhall (3); the southern gatehouse of London Bridge (4); and the Tower (5). By the
time Cornelius de Visscher drew this in 1616, the Globe Theatre (6) had been built.

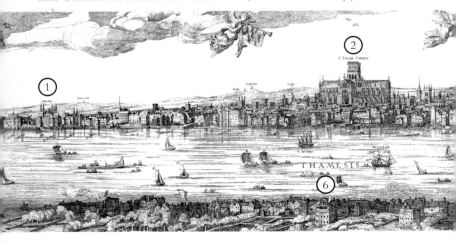

Sero sed serio: Late but in earnest.
(*Above left*) The Lord Treasurer, William Cecil, 1st Baron Burghley, in the regalia
of a Knight of the Garter. (*Above right*) His son, Sir Robert Cecil, with an unopened
letter on the table and the family motto hovering on his shoulder.

The Queen as intelligencer: in *The Rainbow Portrait* by Isaac Oliver, Elizabeth I's dress is patterned with the eyes and ears of the watchful State.

The King Catholic: Philip II taking a break from the paperwork of global dominion, *c.*1580.

(*Below*) *The Ancient Port of Antwerp* by Sebastian Vrancx. Antwerp was the warehouse of northern Europe, but the Low Countries were a religious flashpoint.

Patron and suitor (1)
(*Above left*) Robert Devereux, 2nd Earl of Essex, in martial breastplate, *c.*1596;
(*above right*) Francis Bacon in the robes of high office, *c.* 1618.

(*Below*) Map of Lisbon and Cascais, by Georg Braun and Frans Hogenberg, *c.*1572,
engraving by Joris Hoefnagel.

Patron and suitor (2)
(*Above left*) A flamboyant Henry Wriothesley, 3rd Earl of Southampton, with the
fashionably long hair of the 1590s; (*above right*) a modest William Shakespeare
in the early 1600s, probably by John Taylor.

(*Below*) The Tower of London, 1597, by Haiward and Gascoyne.

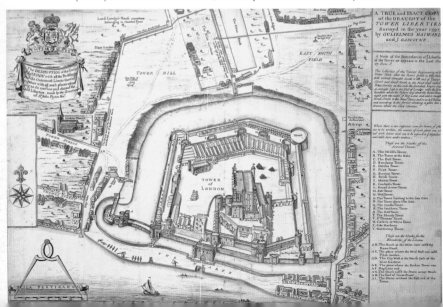

(*Above left*) Antonio Perez, political projector, amateur apothecary and Monster of Fortune, by Alonso Sanchez Coello. (*Above right*) *A Gentleman, presumed to be Anthony Bacon*, possibly by Nicholas Hilliard, and perhaps depicting Essex's chief intelligencer.

(*Below*) Guildhall, scene of Lopez's trial.

(*Above left*) Charles, Lord Admiral Howard, conqueror of the Armada and interrogator of Manuel Luis Tinoco, in 1602. (*Above right*) Sir Edward Coke, Solicitor-General for the Crown, robed as James I's Lord Chief Justice.

(*Below*) *Lopez compounding to poison the Queen*, first published in *Popish Plots and Treasons* (1606), a collection of Elizabethan conspiracies. This engraving is from a similar collection of 1627, *A Thankful Remembrance*. Lopez's speech bubble reads, 'Quid dabitis?': 'What will you give?'

Tinoco and Andrada were of a piece, like the *commedia dell'arte* device of the pair of servants whose masters are friends. Competitors for the same petty spoils, intimates in desperation, each knowing that the other carried secret letters, they both knew that sooner or later they would have to talk, but professional discretion meant that neither gave anything away to the other as they rattled across the flat Flanders terrain. At nightfall they stopped at Ghent, just as Robert Draper and Antonio Perez had done, but they managed to avoid the obvious topic. In the morning they set off without a word. At Lille, one hundred miles from Brussels, their paths forked: Tinoco was eighty miles west of Calais, Andrada was 200 miles north of Paris. They could not resist parting without sharing their unmentionable bond. Having been professional in their silence, they were professional in finding a spot in which to break it.

The two men slipped into the damp, incense-heavy air of the church of St Stephen at Lille. They knelt, crossed themselves and found a quiet pew. Whispering, Andrada told Tinoco a fantastical, lurid tale. Fuentes and Ibarra had given him 'a great commission to have Antonio Perez slain', but first Andrada was on his way to Paris on a greater mission. He had to tell Don Emanuel how the Lopez–Ferreira plot was developing. He had to deliver Spanish mails from Fuentes and Ibarra at Brussels to Ibarra's brother Diego, a secretary in Paris. And, 'under the shadow of Don Emanuel', he planned to carry out 'a great piece of work': the murder of Henri IV. He would make 'a nosegay of flowers or roses'. Posing as a servant – Andrada's speciality – he would gain access to the palace of St Denis, where he would contrive to place the nosegay under the royal nostrils. 'I shall give him such a scent and smell as shall send him packing to another world,' Andrada promised. He opened his palm and Tinoco saw a wrap of powder, the steel-grey filings of arsenic. Andrada produced other powders from his pockets. 'To dye my beard red and black, as often as I shall have occasion,' he explained.

Tinoco was impressed. Andrada confided in him further. As Andrada would be engaged in Paris, the Spanish needed another agent to organise the murder of Antonio Perez. Secretary d'Ibarra had 'greatly recommended' Tinoco to Andrada. Would Tinoco take

Henri IV of France.

on the job? Tinoco accepted. He believed Andrada's 'secret designs', and he needed the money.

Two hardened intelligencers, whispering in an empty church over wraps of poison and hair dye. An implausible, absurd scenario, but wholly credible to Tinoco. Attempts against the lives of Philip II's enemies emanated regularly from Jesuit seminaries and Spanish embassies. In 1582, the Prince of Orange, leader of the rebels in the Low Countries, had been shot and killed by one of Bernadino de Mendoza's agents. In 1586, Mendoza had been expelled from England after planning Elizabeth I's murder with an English Catholic, Anthony Babington. In 1589, Henri IV's predecessor, Henri III, had been assassinated by no less theatrical a personage that a homicidal monk. Within six months of this meeting, Henri IV was to survive an assassination attempt; he escaped with a stab wound to the face after being attacked by a Jesuit-trained teenager, the son of 'a draper living in the palace'.

That the Spanish should plan to kill the King of France, or hunt down Antonio Perez, would not have surprised Tinoco, but Andrada's method might have raised his suspicions. Arsenic was a standard poison, but the idea of a toxic nosegay was a double cliché. It was an image of Machiavellian invention from the Courts of Renaissance Italy, so common that Marlowe had featured it in his *Jew of Malta*, which had been playing at the Rose when Andrada had last visited London. When Andrada went to Paris, he did not get so far as to assemble his bouquet. The story of the nosegay was a trick, used by Andrada to convince Tinoco that he was a real, murderous Renaissance intelligencer, dyed beard and all. If Tinoco was worried by the prospect of murdering Antonio Perez, he could take comfort from the knowledge that at least he did not have Andrada's virtually suicidal commission to kill Henri IV. The two spies left St Stephen's, and outside Lille they parted: Andrada for Paris, Tinoco for London.

On the last day of May 1593, the Earl of Essex hosted a party for his faction at Wanstead, his rural retreat a few miles east of London. Antonio Perez and the Vidame of Chartres were the guests of honour, and Don Antonio came down from Eton for the day. Doctor Lopez, the grease on the wheel of Portuguese intelligence, was invited too. While London woke to the news that Christopher Marlowe had been murdered the previous afternoon in brawl at a Deptford lodging house, Lopez had travelled out of the city, past the flower-blooming fields of Hackney and on to Wanstead, sweating in his black doctor's robes and tight ruff.

There was much to talk about at the party. Apart from acting as spontaneous translator between Spanish, Portuguese, English and French guests, and checking the state of Don Antonio's digestion, Lopez could have analysed the contents of Antonio Perez's medicine chest. In the middle of the jollity, an uninvited guest appeared at the edge of Lopez's vision: the dignified but anxious outline of Estevan Ferreira da Gama, trying to get his attention. Lopez drifted away from the party and into the garden, and when they were sure that no one was watching, Ferreira gave Lopez a letter. The Doctor read it with delight.

That morning, Ferreira had received a knock at the door of St Katharine Creechurch. His surprise visitor was Emanuel Luis Tinoco. 'I have a message to deliver to Doctor Lopez from the Count of Fuentes,' Tinoco had said.

Ferreira and Lopez both knew Tinoco as a small-time intelligencer on the fringes of the Portuguese Court. Ferreira had hustled Tinoco away from his lodgings and sent him to Mountjoy's Inn, but when Tinoco had got there, he found that the Doctor had gone to Wanstead. So Tinoco had written down his message for Lopez and given it to Ferreira, who had then taken it out to Wanstead.

The Count of Fuentes's message came in two parts. One was an *abrasjo*, a chivalric 'embracing' that was a great personal compliment to the Doctor. The second was Fuentes's word. The Count was 'glad that the Doctor was a good servant to the King of Spain', and he wanted to assure Lopez that 'he should be very well compensated' for his services. Philip II was 'desirous' to 'renew the treaty of peace' between England and Spain. Accordingly, the Count of Fuentes requested that Lopez 'procure some thing under my Treasurer's hand': a letter from Lord Burghley to confirm that Lopez was his chosen intermediary and that England wanted peace. After that, Philip wanted Elizabeth to send 'men of quality' to begin negotiations.

Philip II might have taken the bait, but he had chewed it over thoroughly. The King would accept Don Emanuel's 'letter of submission' and would come to an accommodation with the exiled Portuguese Court. He would also accept that the English were prepared to drop the Portuguese cause as proof of their pacific intentions. He had noted Lopez's role and, if all this was true, Lopez would be rewarded. But Philip needed to be certain that Lopez's offer was genuine. The last time Lopez had made an offer like this, Philip had given him a jewel and had received nothing in return. He suspected that Ferreira's letters might be another Lopez projection, designed to gather intelligence under the cover of peace talks, or to draw out Spanish agents in the Low Countries, or to scam another jewel from Philip's coffers. For twenty years, Philip and his secretaries had watched Lopez perpetrate multiple villainies. The Doctor had plundered Bernadino de Mendoza's correspondence, had raised funds for the pirates who stole Spanish treasure ships, and had even organised the invasion of Philip's new kingdom of Portugal. If Lopez was to be the channel for talks, Philip wanted Lord Burghley's word.

Lopez was delighted and relieved: his plan had reached its third stage without the slightest hitch. At this advanced point, obtaining a 'letter of credence' from Lord Burghley did not seem impossible, but the next logical step. Lopez had already assembled a plot and its actors, and had succeeded in contacting and negotiating with the Spanish. He was only one move away from lucrative success. If he could convince Lord Burghley to lend the Privy Council's imprimatur to the plan, it would turn from an unofficial to an official contact. As the creator of peace between England and Spain, Lopez would collect commissions from both sides. His moment of glory was near. It was time to stake out his financial demands.

The Doctor still had the promissory note for 50,000 crowns that Don Antonio had given him before the Counter-Armada. He had carried this worthless piece of paper for four years. It was the licence for his financial hold over Antonio, and also for the Privy Council's hold over them both. At the present rate of recovery, with Lopez one in a queue of creditors, he would never gain a fraction of the money from the dribbling 5 per cent he skimmed from the Guinea trade. There was a better way to deploy Don Antonio's 'assignation'. It could be used to convince Philip II that Lopez was not up to his old projecting habits.

Lopez showed Don Antonio's assignation to Ferreira de Gama. When the English and Spanish 'men of quality' began peace talks, the Doctor promised, the facilitators of their summit would become wealthy men. Their financial worries would be solved for ever, and they would be restored to the comforts from which bad luck and Don Antonio had reduced them. This piece of paper showed that Lopez was owed 50,000 crowns by the Portuguese crown. That amount would be the price of his and Ferreira's diplomatic freelancing. Lopez told Ferreira to send it to the Spanish. In return, Ferreira was to give Lopez a receipt, as if Lopez had lodged it with him for safe keeping. Gently prodded by Lopez, Ferreira edged further out into the quicksand, dazzled by the amber light of reflected gold. Don Antonio's assignation and the Count of Fuentes's letter were folded away and tucked into the Doctor's robes, and Lopez and Ferreira strolled back out of the garden to rejoin Essex's house party, traitors in the Earl's camp.

Everything was going according to plan. Lopez had tried to keep his plot as secret as possible and himself as safe as possible. He had used proxies in his dealings with the Spanish – Ferreira da Gama the ghost writer and Manuel d'Andrada the messenger. When he met his agents, he had used private homes and had taken them into the garden so that they could not be overheard. He believed that his subterfuge had succeeded. He could not have known that, back in January, Andrada had betrayed him to Anthony Standen, that Anthony Bacon was watching Mountjoy's Inn, or that Essex had his own suspicions about his doctor. From what Lopez could see from the appearance of the eye, Andrada had completed his part in the plot and the Count of Fuentes had taken Lopez's proposal seriously enough to employ a trusted courier – Tinoco – to carry his response.

Lopez knew that it was risky to change couriers – it increased the number of conspirators – but Tinoco came with good credentials: the Count of Fuentes' *abrasjo* and a 'little ticket' from Andrada, in which Andrada recommended Tinoco as a trustworthy courier for the advanced negotiations. Anyway, Lopez had no choice but to agree. Tinoco knew about Andrada's work for Lopez and Burghley, he knew about Don Emanuel's letter of submission, and there was no reason to believe he had not heard the whispers of peace talks. If Lopez turned Tinoco away, he would cast Tinoco back out into the mercenary intelligence world as a free agent, loaded with lethal information. A menace had to be turned into an asset. The safest way to deal with Tinoco was to tie him into the plot with bonds of complicity and hope that, as with Andrada, threats might succeed where bribery failed.

A week after Essex's party, Ferreira da Gama reported to Mountjoy's Inn for another dictation. This time, Ferreira wrote to the Count of Fuentes. The letter was intended to rectify Lopez's great disadvantage. For his plan to work, the Spanish had to believe his offers, but they knew Lopez was an English intelligencer and they distrusted him. He had to establish credibility with the Spanish. Lopez sketched a credible self-portrait of an embittered suitor. Ferreira reported that Lopez had served Don Antonio with 'great zeal and expense', but 'little recompense'. Ferreira had seen this and 'had won the Doctor'. Directed by Ferreira, Lopez had advised the Privy Council not to help Don Antonio 'in anything'. Lopez's hatred of Antonio fed a 'great desire and lust' to serve Philip II, and he was willing to 'advertise by word of mouth all he could learn of this kingdom'. If the Count wished to check Lopez's sincerity, he should ask Manuel Andrada, whom Lopez had sprung from prison 'with great art'.

This was close enough to the truth to be convincing. Lopez really had served Don Antonio with 'great zeal and expense', he really had received 'little recompense' and he certainly bore the pretender deep malice. Attached to this litany of personal and financial grievance was Don Antonio's 'assignation' for 50,000 crowns; in this context the assignation would appear not only as Lopez's commission, but as a symbol of transferred allegiance. The impression would be cemented by Lopez's offer to spy for Spain. This made for an appealing package, but its wrapping was more substantial than its contents.

Lopez's offer of espionage, and his suggestion that Manuel d'Andrada might vouch for it, were a verbatim repeat of Walsingham's projection of 1590. He was careful only to offer intelligence 'by word of mouth', not in writing. Lopez's offer was more ambiguous than it seemed. It was the work of an intelligencer stepping to the lip of treason, but no further. His sole purpose was to develop the Count of Fuentes's trust in him, to build a solid platform for negotiations, so that when he obtained Lord Burghley's letter and the diplomats took over, the transition would be smooth and lucrative.

But a platform could become a scaffold and so Lopez organised a petty subterfuge to cover Tinoco's tracks. Ferreira had an old passport that he had used in the service of Don Antonio. He took it to one 'Monox, a forger', and for the price of 20s. had the name and date altered. Ferreira then gave it to Tinoco along with his latest letter. So Tinoco went back to Brussels accredited to Don Antonio, the intended victim of the plot. For Lopez, this was a gratifying irony: Don Antonio's credentials would assist in his usurpation.

In his week in London, Tinoco had not forgotten his other commission. Before Tinoco left, he and Lopez had another conference in Lopez's garden. Tinoco pointed out that now he was working for the Doctor by carrying his letters to Brussels, he expected to be paid for his service. He suggested that as they shared a common interest, it might be resolved to mutual satisfaction. The Spanish felt that there was a second stumbling block to an accommodation: Antonio Perez. It was hardly possible to make peace between England and Spain while a defector from Philip II's secretariat was hosted in England as the honoured guest of the Queen's champion, Essex. Don Antonio and the Portuguese succession were a thorn in Philip II's side, but at least their dispute was between royalty. Antonio Perez was a traitor to Spain and a fugitive from the Inquisition. His presence in England was a personal insult to Philip II. The Spanish wanted him back in their hands, or at the very least expelled to France, where it would be easier to kill him.

In Brussels, the Count of Fuentes had developed a plan to deal with Perez. Through the English exile Sir William Stanley, the Count had penetrated the Catholic underworld in Antwerp. Stanley and Fuentes were working on several schemes – a plan to use fireships against English merchantmen in the harbour at Flushing, and a similar plan to use home-made grenades of 'gunpowder, brimstone and saltpetre' in the harbour at Dieppe – but the most advanced was the most simple: the killing of Antonio Perez. Through Stanley, Fuentes had found an assassination team. The hit man was to be an Irish Catholic called Patrick Collen, who had agreed to shoot Perez with a pistol for £30. His accomplice was another Catholic, John Annias, who would trick his way into the Earl of Essex's household by giving him a jewel, and then set up the assassination. When they reached England, Tinoco would guide them to their target.

Lopez did not know the details of Fuentes's murder plot, but he understood that Antonio Perez was also a threat to his own plans. As a high-ranking defector, Perez was an an intelligence asset to the Earl of Essex, and a pretext for the dispute with Spain that the war party sought. The peace party did not want Perez in England, and Burghley was doing his best to deny Perez access to the Queen. Lopez decided to complement Burghley's tactics by giving the Spanish access to Perez. If Perez was expelled from England, kidnapped by Spanish agents, or simply murdered, Essex would be weakened and the Cecils would be strengthened. Lopez saw that if he assisted the Spanish in their hunt for Perez, his service would help establish his credentials as a trust-worthy negotiator. In policy terms, Perez was Lopez's enemy. If Lopez demonstrated to the Spanish that Perez was his enemy, then he also would be demonstrating that Perez's other enemies – the Spanish – were his friends. So Lopez agreed with Tinoco to target Perez. They would need a cipher code for Perez, to use in their correspondence, and Lopez suggested a private joke, a play on Perez's pretensions towards medical expertise: Perez would be called 'musk and amber', after his favourite concoction. The solution that bolstered Perez's health would be the means of his death.

Lopez found that Tinoco's plan was already at an advanced stage, and that Tinoco had prepared the means by which he might gather intelligence on Perez: Francis Caldera, the Spanish spy in the retinue of the Vidame of Chartres. So Lopez sent the pliable Ferreira da Gama to see Caldera. Promisingly, Ferreira found Caldera 'in extremity of sickness, and destitute'. Ferreira gave him a few coins, but despite his poverty, Caldera wanted nothing to do with Lopez, who was 'a Jew, and his enemy'. Apparently, two years earlier, Caldera had fallen out with Andrada, at which Lopez 'had conceived displeasure against him'. Caldera suspected that Lopez was now trying to set him up, projecting in order to expose Caldera as a Spanish agent.

Ferreira assured Caldera that he should not doubt his or Lopez's sincerity. The Doctor 'had set his foot upon his throat' and he would set his other foot upon Caldera's throat if Caldera did not co-operate. Caldera changed his mind, and agreed to pass Ferreira intelligence about Antonio Perez and anything else he might pick up in the French embassy.

Caldera excelled himself in his efforts to keep Lopez's foot off his throat. He did not just provide Lopez with information, but with verbatim copies of Antonio Perez's correspondence. The Doctor passed the correspondence straight to Lord Burghley and Sir Robert Cecil, and to help the Cecils translate Perez's wordy letters, Lopez provided a translator, Vincent Fonseca, a Portuguese sailor. Through Lopez, the Cecils had acquired a source inside the French embassy at a vital moment in Anglo-French relations. Via his source in the French embassy, Burghley could discover the resolutions of Jean and Prégent de la Fin faster than Henri IV. Lopez's mole could also tell Lord Burghley what Antonio Perez was planning. Abroad and at home, the Cecils would have the informational edge on Essex.

There was, of course, a price. The bill came to Lopez, and he did not tell the Cecils that he paid it. The same intelligence that he supplied to Burghley would be replicated for Tinoco and the Count of Fuentes, and they would use it to assist the murder of Antonio Perez, a guest of the Crown of England. If Lopez already stood on the lip of treason, he now looked over the abyss. His masters the Cecils were engaged in a brutal struggle with Essex, and they needed every possible weapon. Combined with Lord Burghley's age and Sir Robert Cecil's youth, this pressure meant that they did not pay close attention to the source of their rich intelligence. They did not realise that Doctor Lopez, their trusted agent, was spinning out of control.

Each step that Lopez made towards the 50,000 crowns required a trade-off. Promising rewards to Ferreira da Gama and Andrada cost him nothing. But as Lopez edged closer to the prize, the price rose. To secure the trust of the Spanish and the services of Tinoco, Lopez had passed beyond the frail moral boundaries of the cunning intelligencer into a morass so sticky that only the complete success of his scheme could allow him to wriggle free. Passport forgery and projecting were mere incidentals. The Queen's physician was co-operating with the Spanish in a mutual exchange that implicated the Cecils in a plot to murder Antonio Perez, a guest of the Queen. Lopez was also spying on Essex, a Privy Councillor, on behalf of Burghley, another Councillor, and was running a mole in the French embassy, in the knowledge that his mole was also a Spanish agent.

These compromises could only be justified by total success. Anything less, and he would be sucked into the quicksand, pulling everyone else with him, from Privy Councillors to petty couriers.

All eyes converged upon Antonio Perez, the Monster of Fortune, monarch and prisoner of the dark labyrinth. Burghley wanted Perez out of England, but Essex wanted to elevate him as a foreign policy adviser. Tinoco wanted to sell him to the Count of Fuentes, and Fuentes wanted to kill him as a traitor to Spain. Lopez was prepared to sacrifice Perez to his plot, to remove another obstacle between himself and those 50,000 crowns. When Perez lorded it at the Vidame's table, larding the conversation with leering wit, casting epigrams and horoscopes, discussing the therapeutic value of musk and amber, distributing drugs and mocking little Robert Cecil as Monsieur de Bossu – 'Mr Hunchback' – he sat under Francis Caldera's watchful eye as Theseus unwound his thread, unseen in the opiate haze.

II

The Projector

Your mind is tossing upon the ocean;
There, where your argosies with portly sail
Like signors and rich burghers on the flood,
Or, as it were, the pageants of the sea,
Do overpeer the petty traffickers
That court'sy to them, do them reverence,
As they fly by them with their woven wings.

Salerio to Antonio, *The Merchant of Venice*

Suspended midway between Dover and Calais on the face of the waters, the gentleman soldier and scrabbler for small change sometimes known as Emanuel Luis Tinoco – and sometimes known as Manuel Lewis – was in a perfect state of informational equilibrium. By serving all, he knew all, and more than any master, yet he could not use his full intelligence. He was preserved not by the fullness of his knowledge, but only by its sporadic release. He subsisted on short rations of trust, wages paid from his masters' appetite for the complete knowledge they could not be allowed to attain. On a forged passport in the disputed, crooked arm of sea between England and France, a border thicker than the mark of any cartographer's pencil, Tinoco suspended the gravitational laws of patronage like a temporary amphibian.

Tinoco's signature.

Tinoco emerged from the espionage murk and appeared on the doorstep of St Katharine Creechurch bolstered by the appearance of the eye, but even to an operator of Lopez's experience the evidence was complex. Tinoco was a courier accredited to the Count of Fuentes, so Lopez knew that Tinoco was a Spanish agent. Tinoco had been and still pretended to be a retainer of Don Antonio's, so Lopez knew that he was a freelancer, a lost Portingall out for himself. Tinoco left England bearing letters from Lopez, letters written in the nominal service of Lord Burghley, so Lopez considered Tinoco to have added Burghley's commission to his collection. They shared a common enemy in Antonio Perez, and a smirking pun about 'musk and amber'. This much Lopez knew about Tinoco. It added up, and it seemed to Lopez that it balanced out in his favour.

However, there was one final fact about Tinoco that Lopez did not know, a fact that he could not be allowed to know. Tinoco had also left England in the service of the Earl of Essex. Lopez did not realise that after a lifetime's projecting, he had been tricked by a projector.

Tinoco had projected his way into Essex's service with promises of Portingall intelligence from the Low Countries. As a pretext for piracy and war upon Spain, the Portuguese cause was integral to the Earl of Essex's play for control of English foreign policy. The war party needed the idea of a free Portugal but, as Essex could testify from his personal experience of the Counter-Armada, Don Antonio was no longer a credible figurehead. Like Doctor Lopez, Essex understood that the Portuguese cause needed refreshment. But Lopez and Essex differed on their choice of candidate.

Lopez had chosen to persevere with the run-down House of Avis, and to support a direct succession to the imaginary throne. Unlike Lopez, Essex did not approach the question burdened by Portingall nostalgia and legends of the lost Order of Crato. To Essex, Don Antonio and his sons bore the taint of failure, and the fingerprints of their long and grubby handling by Lord Burghley. The best alternative candidature to the House of Avis was the rival House of Braganza, the most powerful noble family in Portugal. João, the sixth Duke, was an Avis descendant and had married one of Don Antonio's

Avis cousins. The Braganza name guaranteed respect, and Duke João was not dogged by salacious rumours of illegitimacy and Jewish blood. Essex backed the claim of his fellow aristocrat.

Unfortunately, Duke João preferred the security of a Spanish pension in the Low Countries to the risk of rebelling against Philip II. Tempting Braganza out of the Spanish fold would be difficult for Essex's nascent intelligence service. Anthony Bacon and the secretaries of Essex House were strong on Spanish and French connections, but they were weak in the Low Countries. This was a serious problem: the Low Countries were the fulcrum of Europe's religious and national struggles, and every deficiency of intelligence had its political price in lost leverage at Court. Low Countries intelligence was the province of the London Portuguese, especially Doctor Lopez and his shady cousin Jeronimo. The obvious path was to follow tradition and engage Doctor Lopez and his Antwerp cousins, but the Earl had good reasons not to do this.

Lopez may have hated Don Antonio, but he was a lifelong Avis follower and would do his best to undermine a Braganza candidacy. Essex also had private reasons to suspect that Lopez, for all his professions of service, was working against him. The secrets with which Lopez supplied Essex were not secret – the Cecils and the Queen knew them before Essex did – and the implication of Anthony Standen's report from Calais was that Lopez was well advanced upon a Portuguese scheme of his own.

If Essex tried to turn the Duke of Braganza into an instrument of English militarism, he would be going against the Cecil policy of peace with Spain. Although the Duke had fallen into the Spanish orbit more through weakness than loyalty, he was technically as much of an enemy of the Queen as any of Philip II's followers. If Essex's contact with Braganza was revealed before it came to fruition, the Earl would be exposed as having set himself against the Cecils, intrigued with the Queen's enemies, and lost. This was not a risk that could be entrusted to tricky Roger Lopus. Parity with the Cecils meant breaking their intelligence monopoly in the Low Countries, and that meant circumventing Lopez.

This was why Essex engaged Tinoco. In May 1593, he entered

England down on his luck, a known double agent, yet he left as Essex's emissary on the Braganza mission. Essex must have had good cause to trust Tinoco, and Tinoco must have had good cause for his luck to turn so suddenly. The most obvious explanation lies in the typical recourse for an intelligencer in Tinoco's plight. The Essex network needed two kinds of intelligence most of all: news from the Low Countries and information that would give Essex an advantage over the Cecils. Tinoco offered both.

At Gray's Inn, Anthony Bacon had Lopez under surveillance, but all he had turned up was the goatish old Doctor's affair with Mrs Allington. In Calais, Anthony Standen had detected that Lopez was a Burghley agent, but could only infer that some unknown Portingall scheme was afoot. At Westminster, Lopez was colluding with the Cecils and making a fool of Essex before the Queen. Essex knew that there was a pattern in the carpet, but he lacked the key piece of information that would unlock its secret.

Tinoco thought he knew everything. Through Andrada, he knew the precise nature of Lopez's work for Burghley. He knew about the plot to replace Don Antonio with Don Emanuel, and that peace talks had been suggested as its outcome. He knew how valuable this information would be to Burghley's and Lopez's enemies. So he sold some of it to Essex, offering himself as a mole in Lopez's and Burghley's service. But Tinoco weighted his intelligence to Essex perfectly, supplying just enough information to make him a source worth his salary, without giving away so much that he condemned himself. Tinoco could not mention to Essex that he was also gathering intelligence on the Earl's guest Antonio Perez, and that while he and Lopez were collaborating on the Don Emanuel plot, they were also setting up Perez for assassination. After all, if Tinoco denounced Lopez to Essex, then Lopez would do the same, and in a competition between the Queen's physician and a Portingall spy, Lopez's words would carry more weight.

So long as Tinoco did not refer to Perez or Lopez, he could sell information to Essex without endangering himself. The best price could be obtained for information relating to the Portuguese succession, the subject of his commission from Essex. Lopez's plan to supplant Don Antonio with Don Emanuel was in direct competition with Essex's plan to supplant Don Antonio with the Duke of Braganza. Tinoco could tell Essex that a rival Portuguese scheme was afoot, and that he had penetrated it. If he named Lopez's intermediary Ferreira da Gama as the inventor of the scheme, he reduced his risk of self-incrimination.

But even Tinoco was not infallible or omniscient. He could not have known that Essex had other intelligence which, though puzzling on its own, assumed a narrative logic when combined with Tinoco's ration of fact. Just after Tinoco left London, Anthony Standen came back to England. Standen had been the source of the tip-off that had led Anthony Bacon to investigate Lopez; immediately upon his return, Standen began working closely with the Earl. Taken in isolation, Essex's intelligence embarrassments before the Queen, the Standen–Bacon inquiry, and Tinoco's hint of a Portingall conspiracy appeared unrelated. But taken in combination, these strands formed a pattern: the stooped, bearded, black-robed outline of Doctor Lopez.

Essex knew that a rival Portuguese plan had been plotted at Mountjoy's Inn. Doctor Lopez had organised a diplomatic thunderclap, apparently with Lord Burghley's approval. If Lopez's strike succeeded, the Portugal question would be settled and the path to peace talks would be open. If England and Spain settled their differences by negotiation, Essex's political future would be destroyed and Sir Robert Cecil would inherit Burghley's role unopposed. It was now obvious to Essex that Doctor Lopez, his personal physician, had tried to set him up. While Lopez had been supplying Essex with physic and intelligence, he had been secretly developing a Portuguese scheme whose success would ruin Essex and profit the Cecils. Essex had to stop Lopez, but at the right moment, just before the fullness of his plan, when Lopez's guilt and his complicity with Burghley were undeniable. That way, the hunter would be led into his own trap and snared helpless in its jaws.

Lopez and Essex each thought they had acquired Tinoco for their own ends, but the greatest satisfaction was Tinoco's. This small-time spy had placed himself at the heart of the espionage game, and now held the balance between Burghley, Lopez, Essex and Fuentes. His masters might be rich, but Tinoco had informational power. Burghley and Lopez – and Essex, too – could not know what Tinoco said in Brussels, and Fuentes and Ibarra could not know what he said in London. Even when Tinoco had sold out Burghley and Lopez to Essex, he had held back a salient fact. He had claimed to be entering Essex's service as a defector from the Burghley network. He had not mentioned that the Spanish had engaged him to track down Essex's guest, Antonio Perez. Compulsively partitioning his loyalties, Tinoco kept every option open. From here, he might kill Perez or save him, boost the House of Braganza or ruin it, turn Don Emanuel into a king or a fugitive, all as coolly and as credibly as Manuel d'Andrada choosing between a red hair day and a black hair day.

Tinoco worked for everybody, but nobody could know for whom he might also work and what, if any, were his final intentions. Tinoco was not concerned with the future map of Europe. He was a caster

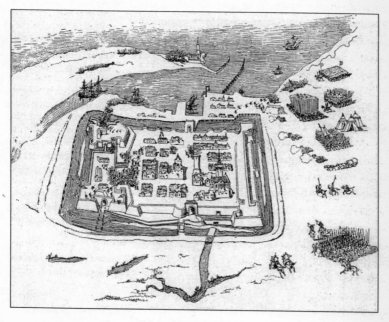

Calais under Spanish attack.

of shapes in a hall of mirrors, a projector selling visions of informational satiety to the highest bidder. Providing he was well paid, he did not care who won, Burghley or Essex, Lopez or Fuentes, Elizabeth I or Philip II, Murad III or Ahmed IV. What mattered was creating informational hypotheses and getting paid for them. Like the Italian acrobat who had celebrated Elizabeth's accession by walking up a tightrope to the steeple of St Paul's, Tinoco did not have to worry about which way he fell, only that he landed on his feet.

On 24 July 1593, Tinoco returned to Mountjoy's Inn after an absence of just over six weeks, bearing a reply from the Count of Fuentes. It seemed that Lopez's efforts to convince the Spanish he could be trusted had succeeded. A deal had taken shape. Lopez was to give Don Emanuel's 'letter of submission' to the Spanish, and he was to persuade Lord Burghley to issue a 'letter of credence' that committed England to peace talks. Meanwhile, the Count of Fuentes would arrange for Lopez's 50,000-crown commission to be lodged in the Antwerp bank of Manuel Palatios. The money would be released when peace negotiations began.

Lopez dictated another set of mails to Ferreira da Gama, confirming the deal. Within forty-eight hours, Tinoco had passed Dover and was on the road to Brussels, with Don Emanuel's 'letter of submission', a promise from Lopez that he was about to obtain Lord Burghley's 'letter of credence', and a personal commission from Lopez: information on the whereabouts of Antonio Perez.

When Tinoco left Mountjoy's Inn on 26 July bearing Don Emanuel's submission, it is difficult to imagine that, somewhere along the road between Holborn and Dover, he did not show them to an Essex agent, or even to the Earl himself.

Lopez's plan had now developed to such corrupt and fabulous dimensions that retreat was impossible. The point of no return was a distant speck over his shoulder, the last sight of land before a mariner turned to the great ocean. Lopez had cast off into a sea of political ambition and personal mania, and there was no way back. He had engineered Don Antonio's deposition by his own son, and had surrendered the House of Avis to Spain as if it were a disputed cargo, impounded and auctioned on the dock at Plymouth. Almost in afterthought, he was assisting the Spanish in arranging the assassination of Antonio Perez, and was spying on Perez and his hosts in the French embassy. He had struck a Faustian deal with Tinoco: the lives of Don Antonio and Antonio Perez for the security of a Cecil supremacy and 50,000 crowns. If he succeeded, the Earl of Essex would not forgive him, and his life would be in danger. If he failed, he would have to flee England: he would have offered himself to Philip II, but failed to provide the political gains that justified the offer. And there were numerous further justifications for his recent conduct that might be even harder to explain. Where would he go?

The Doctor and his wife were old and their children were almost all adults. His English odyssey and the Tudor dynasty were both running to an end. As the childless Queen aged, the obvious question was who would succeed her, but to talk of it was treason. The Elizabethan ship of State creaked worryingly, its timbers threatening to cave in upon themselves like the whalebones of the Queen's corsetry. There was little part for an aged Tudor servant in the unknown English future. In victory or defeat, Lopez knew he would be happier elsewhere. The 50,000 crowns meant liberty and a fresh start. There was always Antwerp, but his generation had fragmented. The tight family of Marrano merchant-spies who had speculated on the pepper trade as young men had dispersed into individual futures. His brother Luis was dead, his cousins Jeronimo and Diego Lopez Soeiro had settled as the twin axes of the London–Antwerp trade, and Estevan Nuñez was in Calais. As Antwerp declined because of the war in the Low Countries, the Marranos were moving north to Amsterdam, where a new generation of merchants had risen to supplant the old. Lopez knew that just as there was no return to Portugal, there was no way back to Antwerp. He had to find somewhere else.

As the Doctor wanted to shake the rheumy northern damp from his old bones, so he wanted to leave the intelligence game, and slip the accumulated bonds of loyalty and deceit, bonds that threatened to truss him. On his secretive trip across Europe he had glimpsed the two alternatives to the Marrano life: the ghetto at Venice, or religious liberty under the Ottomans. He settled upon Constantinople.

He might see out his days as a free Jew, a companion to his cousin Alvaro Mendes, advising Sultan Murad III on English affairs. If the past was finished, he might yet redeem his future.

Constantinople, seat of the Ottomans and haven for Jews.

With the clarity of desperation, Lopez saw that to succeed, he must follow his plan to every end, however brutal. Antonio Perez was incidental, Don Antonio was a straw man, and the Queen wanted little to do with either of them. The real obstacle – and the real threat to Lopez's survival – was the Earl of Essex, who would exert every effort to prevent peace talks. Lopez realised that when his plan became public knowledge, and he was fêted in London, Madrid and Antwerp as the man who had brought back peace and prosperity to Europe, the Earl would blame Lopez as the architect of his fall. Lopez had to ensure that the Cecils' victory over Essex was conclusive and swift. So, having stitched a noose for the Earl's political career, Lopez assembled a scaffold for the Earl's honour.

In the summer vacation, when Lopez 'might very well be spared in regard of his patients', he went to Eton, where the ex-priest Antonio Perez was lodged in the ex-monastery of the ex-King Don Antonio. Both Antonios were seasoned debauchees, and Lopez joined in, 'making merry' with his intended victims. With malice and drunken bravado, the Doctor spilled the secrets of his casebook and began 'bitterly to inveigh against the Earl of Essex'. He told them 'some secrecies' about the Earl's medical history, and 'how he had cured him' and of what diseases, with some other things which did disparage his honour'.

If Essex's 'diseases' were worth gossiping about, they must have been personally embarrassing: common afflictions were the stuff of small talk. The Elizabethans were fascinated and confused by the obscure workings of the body, and they developed a casual attitude to the sharing of symptoms. Anthony Bacon's correspondence interpolated secrets with a running narrative of his struggle with gout. The native cuisine prized brains, offal, asparagus and rhubarb, very little water and a great deal of alcohol; kidney stones were endemic among those who could afford the diet. In the political class, 'the stone' was a topic of polite, obsessed conversation. Detailed accounts were made of the size of the voided crystals and the duration of their transit. Ignorance and desperation gave the search for relief an optimistic recklessness. Lord Burghley allowed his urine to be 'weighed and assayed' by the popular German charlatan Valentine Russwurin; in 1574, Russwurin was charged with the murder of twenty-three patients. In his trial, it transpired that his remedy for the cataracts of one Mr Castleton of Cambridge had been to 'put out his eyes clean'.

If Essex's 'diseases' reflected upon his 'honour', they must have been more intimate. Two conditions would have been suitably shaming. In the first scenario, Essex suffered from the rich diet and erratic digestion of his class, and developed a royal case of haemorrhoids. Consequently, he required the assistance of Doctor Lopez, provider of enemas to the gentry. There is a Chaucerian relish to the scene, but its comic potential might have been lost on Lopez's foreign audience at the party in Windsor. In the second scenario, the dashing Earl's disease was no laughing matter. Its revelation was not comic, but deeply shameful. The 'diseases' that reflected most upon Elizabethan 'honour' were venereal, especially the new and terrible death sentence of *Spirochaeta pallida*: syphilis.

Syphilis was endemic to Renaissance society, both in brothels and at Courts. One of the gossiped charges against Elizabeth I was that she was sterile due to inheriting the disease from her father Henry VIII, who had caught the disease in the battlefield brothels of France. Essex may well have transacted his infection in the same manner; in 1591 he had fought with his tangerine and cream cavalrymen in northern France. The disease gained its name and nickname from a poem published in 1530 by the Veronese physician and humanist Girolamo Fracastoro, *Syphilis, or, the French Disease*. In the poem, a shepherd named Syphilus has insulted Apollo. The god's revenge is to afflict him with a 'pestilence unknown', whose 'foul sores' can only be cleansed with quicksilver. When the disease first 'arose in the generative organs', it would 'eat away the groin' and then spread through the body. Severe pain in the bones follows, 'unsightly scabs break forth, and foully defile the face and breast'. Fracastoro's poetic diagnosis was accurate. After initial visibility in the form of genital sores, syphilis dropped into a latent period. It re-emerged in its tertiary stage, commonly attacking the nervous system. The patient lost physical co-ordination and behaviour became erratic. Eventually, the sufferer became insane.

In the primary and secondary stages of syphilis, the prescribed treatments were a brutal variation on Hippocrates's idea that desperate diseases needed desperate cures. If he could afford it, the patient was isolated for up to a month. After an obligatory bleeding and the scraping out of the urethra, *unguentum Saracenium*, a mercury-based ointment, used to treat scabies and leprosy, was applied to the sores. The patient underwent an intensive course of mercury treatments, aided in his perspiration by fires, blankets and 'rubbing and tubbing' – slowly baking in a specially heated barrel. Mercury was known to induce heavy salivation and sweating, and to make the sores fall away. According to the Theory of Humours, this was proof of efficacy: if the pox produced an excess of phlegm, then the mercury was driving it out. This was illusory. The mercury had only removed the symptoms, without curing them. As the mercury dosage rose in the tertiary stage, affliction and treatment became indistinguishable in a terrible duet of bone damage, tooth loss and gum ulceration.

'A night with Venus, a lifetime with Mercury' ran the popular gag. Public knowledge of tertiary syphilis, and the mental damage it would cause, effectively disqualified the sufferer from public office. If Lopez wished to discredit Essex before the two Antonios, this was the ideal allegation. It suggested that their sponsor would never be able to deliver on his promises. Essex would be overtaken by his disease, marginalised at Court as his behaviour became ever more bizarre, then shunted to some discreet country retreat for mercury rubs and dribbling madness. It would have been credible, too. Essex was exactly the kind of swaggerer most likely to succumb. He had a reputation as a gallant to maintain. Court gossip rumoured him to be regularly 'grateful to ladies', and he certainly exhibited the characteristics of secondary syphilis. There were no visible sores on his face, yet his behaviour was explosive and erratic, disturbing to those around him. The only evidence to doubt Lopez was that Essex had always been prone to irrationality and fury. But that hardly recommended his political prospects, either.

The Doctor thought that this was a cunning stroke against Essex, but he underestimated his audience. Don Antonio and Antonio Perez were no more sincere than Lopez himself. When Lopez had left, the two Antonios 'went instantly to the Earl of Essex'. To 'ingratiate themselves' in the Earl's favour, they acquainted him with 'all the several passages' of Lopez's betrayal. Essex already had an animus against Lopez. He knew the Doctor had played him for a fool in the disbursement of intelligence. Through Tinoco, he knew that Lopez was advancing Burghley's foreign policy. Lopez had used Essex's commission to lay a plot that was entirely against the Earl's interests and against the intelligence service that Lopez purported to assist. To this political cozening was added the ultimate personal insult. A cheaper comedy, and a more humiliating betrayal, could hardly be imagined. The trust between doctor and patient, between patron and patronised, aristocrat and commoner, had been abused for the most naked of personal and political antagonisms.

Lopez expected that Essex would become his enemy, but he did not realise that he already had made Essex his enemy. As the Doctor's plot reached its climax, it obtained unstoppable momentum. Too many people knew about it for it to be abandoned. As the wheels turned faster and faster, Tinoco's next trip to London was a flying visit. He arrived on the last day of August, to find that Lopez was out of town, attending to Essex at Wanstead. The Doctor hurried back to Mountjoy's Inn the next morning, dictated a hurried reply to Ferreira da Gama, and despatched Tinoco back on to the Dover road. Tinoco had passed in and out of England within twenty-four hours.

In their hurried letter writing and whispering in the garden, Tinoco had advised Lopez of his plan for the closing stage of the plot. After delivering Lopez's reply to Brussels, Tinoco would station himself at Calais, so that when Philip II's approval reached Brussels, Tinoco would bring it over to London. In the meantime, Lopez would obtain a 'letter of credence' from Lord Burghley to prove that the English were genuinely interested in peace talks. Both sides would thus have exchanged written undertakings prior to negotiations.

Surrounded by the ripe scents of late summer in his walled city garden, Lopez examined the two letters in his hands. They supported everything Tinoco had told him. One was from Don Cristovão da Moura, Philip II's Portuguese adviser in Madrid. The other was from the Count of Fuentes at Brussels, in which Fuentes sent his best regards and asked in cipher for 'peace'. Like a jeweller crafting a gemstone, Lopez was one stroke of the hammer from perfection. All he required was an exchange of two 'letters of credence', one from Philip II, the other from Lord Burghley. Judging from the two letters from Brussels, Philip II was ready to commit himself. And everything that Lopez knew about Lord Burghley, the hard-won knowledge of more than two decades of service, told him that the Lord Treasurer badly needed an opportunity like this, to settle the long war with Spain and secure the futures of England and Sir Robert Cecil at a single stroke. Lopez had created a masterpiece, and the next time a courier came from Brussels he would carry Lopez's destiny. The Doctor was hurtling towards riches, and his 'musk and amber' were about to turn to gold. All he had to do now was choose the moment when he presented the perfect jewel of his plan to Lord Burghley.

But Lopez had been so dedicated to his own double games that he had not noticed that Emanuel Luis Tinoco was playing a double game of his own. Just as Lopez had taken on Essex's commission in the sure knowledge that some day his service to Essex would result in a conflict of loyalties, so Tinoco had sold himself to Essex in the knowledge that his work for the Earl would clash with his other work for Fuentes and Lopez. And now, with Essex secretly courting the Duke of Braganza while Lopez hawked Don Emanuel's letter of submission in Brussels, and with Lopez bringing his plot to its climax while Essex waited to pounce, Tinoco knew his moment of crisis was imminent. Whom would he save, whom would he ruin, and how would he extract himself from his multiplicity of allegiances and betrayals?

Tinoco improvised a plan. He had already betrayed Lopez to Essex. When Essex revealed the Lopez plot, Tinoco would be safely distant at Calais. From there, he could watch developments in Brussels and London, and make his next decision: to continue releasing selective information to Essex, or to change sides and help Lopez and the Cecils. They would pay him for his help and their trust might advance his other commission from the Count of Fuentes, the surveillance of Antonio Perez. One way or another, Tinoco planned to come out richer.

With Essex primed to reveal the plot at its moment of fruition, Tinoco knew that the next courier run would be the last. When arrests were made, the courier would be picked up and, like Andrada in the hands of Burghley's 'Mr Mills', he might be tortured to see what else he knew. Tinoco was already disqualified from another courier run between Brussels and London: the last stage of Lopez's plot required him to wait at Calais for a letter from Philip II. The task would be devolved on to someone else, a convenient cut-out.

A week after Tinoco's departure, Lopez and Ferreira da Gama

met to discuss Tinoco's replacement as courier. Lopez did not suspect Tinoco of any trickery, as the fulfilment of Lopez's plan obliged Tinoco to wait at Calais. A week after this meeting, their man came to the safe house in St Katharine Creechurch. Gomez d'Avila was a Marrano follower of Don Antonio, a neighbour of Lopez's who lived 'hard by' Mountjoy's Inn. He was probably suggested for the courier job by Tinoco, who needed someone to serve as the vehicle for the last stage of his projection, and as the human evidence that would lead Essex to Lopez.

To Lopez, Gomez was the innocent, ignorant bearer of momentous news. Just as Lopez had with his other couriers Andrada and Tinoco, he used Ferreira da Gama as his proxy in dealing with Gomez d'Avila, and told him as little as possible. Only Ferreira da Gama was at St Katharine Creechurch to despatch Gomez, and he spoke in vague, incomplete terms. As far as Gomez understood, his mission was to collect 50,000 crowns not for Doctor Lopez, but for Don Antonio. Gomez knew nothing about the plot against Antonio Perez, about any prospective peace talks, or that the money was really intended for Lopez. From what Ferreira da Gama could tell, Gomez's interest was more mercenary than political. He would not leave until Ferreira had given him £20 for his journey. As Lopez was with Essex at Wanstead, Ferreira had to travel out to Wanstead, collect an indenture from Lopez, take it into the City, cash it with a Marrano merchant called Alvaro de Lima, and then pay Gomez in cash. On 18 September, Gomez d'Avila took his money and set out for 'the other side'.

Lopez expected him to return with a letter of credence from the Spanish, and instructions for how the Doctor was to pick up his 50,000 crowns. Now, only one letter and an interview with Lord Burghley stood between Lopez and a rich retirement in Constantinople. In April, Manuel d'Andrada had made the journey to Paris and back in only eight days. With good autumn weather and a quick turnaround on the other side, Gomez d'Avila could be back in the same time. Lopez sensed that he was on the cusp of greatness.

This was an illusion. Lopez thought he knew Tinoco, that Tinoco was a finite quantity to be weighed and assayed like a mineral on an apothecary's scale. From his first dealings with Tinoco, Lopez had known Tinoco was a double agent for the Spanish. He had believed that his knowledge of Tinoco's deviousness would be the leash with which he could control Tinoco, just as he had controlled Manuel d'Andrada. But Tinoco had played Lopez at his own game. Tinoco had reserved for himself the single fact that would give him the advantage, and he had played the role of earnest traitor while reporting everything back to the betrayed. Like an alchemist fooling his investors with pyrotechnics and incantations, Tinoco had fooled Lopez with illusions of sincerity and reward. And like an alchemist's 'gull', Lopez had allowed himself to be drawn in by distractions and promises of untold wealth. Dazzled by Tinoco's projections of riches, Lopez had failed to discriminate between the glimmer of amber and that of real gold. It had taken a projector to catch a projector. The Doctor of all people should have distrusted the appearance of the eye.

Lopez counted the hours as the last of September filed past in agonising sequence: three days, a week, eight days and then nine, the slow creep of panic attending the wasting of the calendar. The tenth day came and went without any sign of Gomez d'Avila, and Lopez became itchy. Gomez should have returned by now. Lopez knew that something must have gone wrong, but could not identify the mis-stitch in the tapestry. On the twelfth day, the Doctor broke cover and went to St Katharine Creechurch to ask Ferreira if he had heard anything. Ferreira had not heard from the courier either, and was no less anxious. October came, two weeks and then three, as the dark afternoons of early winter settled over the fields behind Mountjoy's Inn. In his physic garden the herbs shrivelled in the first frosts and the dead leaves rustled beneath his feet. Lopez checked with Ferreira again, with no result. He asked his cousin Jeronimo to keep an eye on the ordinary post, in case the Spanish reply came through the merchants' mail. Where was Gomez d'Avila? The fourth week passed. Lopez had devoted his life to intrigue, had sent and received a thousand mails. His intelligencer's imagination had carried him across Europe and back, given flight by a phrase or a ciphered name. And now he needed only one, single piece of paper, the final piece of the puzzle of his life.

Early in the morning of Thursday 18 October 1593 Ferreira da Gama heard someone knocking at the door of the house in St Katharine Creechurch. Hurrying down to open it, he expected to find Gomez d'Avila on his doorstep, cold and hungry from the Dover road, quietly triumphant in a traveller's beard. To his surprise, Ferreira opened the door not to a lone figure, but to a huddle of armed men.

They came on the orders of the Earl of Essex, and they took Ferreira da Gama away.

III

Now we come in the next place to declare the fowle practise of Doctor *Lopez.* A thing hatefull and detestable to thinke on. Wherein, in the judgment of an honest man, the King of *Spain* lost more honour then if in a set battell he had lost the field. For the *losse of a field* may be *recovered*; but the *losse of reputation* by practising or procuring villany can never be *repaired.* The matter was thus discovered.

12

The Huddler Underhand

He that sinneth against his Maker
Will behave himself proudly against a physician.
The Wisdom of Ben-Sira, 1st century CE

After the dawn raid at St Katharine Creechurch, Ferreira da Gama was handed over to his sovereign Don Antonio, and imprisoned in Antonio's monastery at Eton, watched by Portuguese jailers. Ferreira's papers were taken from St Katharine Creechurch for examination by the Earl of Essex and his secretaries. This was Essex's triumph, ill-defined as it was. He had obtained from the Queen a 'straight and direct order' that placed him in exclusive control of the investigation. Any Portingall attempting to enter England by the Channel ports was to be arrested, and all ordinary post 'directed to Portingall merchants, and others of that Nation' in London were to be intercepted for dissection at Essex House.

Essex aimed to deliver an espionage coup that would damage the Cecils. He suspected that Doctor Lopez had abused his commission and had secretly advanced the Cecil agenda – and his own obscure ambitions – under the cover of his service. Revealing a plot would confirm Essex's intelligence credentials, and trapping Lopez would be personally gratifying, but the real prize lay in trumping the Cecils. To do this, Essex had first to detect a plot that threatened the national interest, and then to trace its threads to their root. He had to connect the house in St Katharine Creechurch with Mountjoy's Inn, and Mountjoy's Inn with Burghley House.

This intelligence campaign would form one arm of Essex's pincer assault on power. The other arm was factional advancement by placing his supporters in governmental office. The Attorney-Generalship was still vacant, and Essex still intended to secure the post for Francis Bacon, despite Bacon's hobbling of his chances in the subsidy debate of the previous February, and despite Lord Burghley's preference for Sir Edward Coke, the incumbent Solicitor-General, over his Bacon nephew. After the end of the legal term in June, Essex had laid the ground for an assault on the summit. In mid-July he had promised Anthony Bacon that he would expend his 'whole rest of favour and credit' on Francis's case. At an audience with the Queen on 21 August, Essex had secured a begrudging 'amnestia' for Bacon's behaviour in the subsidy debate. Meanwhile, Lady Bacon had written her own appeal to her brother-in-law Lord Burghley. Essex was confident that the next legal term, Michaelmas, would see his protégé installed as Attorney-General.

At the beginning of the new term, the Cecils had pushed back. On 27 September, they had gently deflected the pressure with synchronised letters to Francis Bacon. Sir Robert Cecil had given his Bacon cousin friendly advice that he might improve his chances by more regular Court attendance; Lord Burghley had explained that, although he had advanced Bacon's suit to the Queen, she had requested the Lord Keeper, Sir John Puckering, to provide a list of candidates from which she might choose. This had bought the Cecils a little time, but they knew Essex had not been fooled and would not be deterred.

By early October Essex's campaign was in full swing, with Francis Bacon busily flattering Sir John Puckering, and the Earl securing royal audiences for both Anthony Bacon and Anthony Standen. Unfortunately, Anthony Bacon's advancement had been sabotaged by his kidney stones. On 9 October, he had been on the point of setting out for Windsor when 'a long fit of ague' and 'a shrewd pang of the stone' had struck him down. On 13 October, he had tried again and had been only miles from Windsor when his shrewd pang turned to an 'extreme fit', forcing a withdrawal to the house of his friend Doctor Pamant at Eton.

That Saturday night, Essex had apologised to the Queen for

Anthony Bacon's absence, and had used the audience to advance Francis Bacon's case before her. She had suggested that although Bacon was older than Coke by four years, Coke was the more experienced candidate. Even Bacon's uncle Burghley seemed to consider him the second-best candidate. But Essex had left the audience sure that his artful 'mingling of arguments of merit with arguments of affection' had 'moved somewhat' the Queen's opinion. He was certain that further gentle shaking of the tree would cause the plum to drop into Francis Bacon's hands.[5]

This had been the state of factional play at the point of Ferreira da Gama's arrest: mounting pressure from the Essex faction, finely balanced responses from Burghley and the Queen, Essex still confident that his attritional flattery would pay off. The timing of Ferreira da Gama's arrest may not have been dictated solely by Essex's pursuit of the Attorney-Generalship for Francis Bacon, but a success for his covert intelligence operation was the perfect complement of his very overt factional campaign.

Essex needed to find the links in a chain of evidence that might be entwined around both the Doctor and the Cecils. He knew it would not be easy to link Ferreira da Gama, Lopez and Lord Burghley. The relationships between Burghley and Lopez, and Lopez and Ferreira were imbalanced. Biased towards the more powerful partner, they were designed to pass information up the hierarchy, while responsibility for the dubious circumstances of its gathering was passed downwards. By lifting the lid from Portingall affairs, Essex had exposed a bubbling conspiracy. Essex's first challenge was to anatomise his findings. He faced two difficulties. Tinoco's tip-off had been incomplete – it was Ferreira da Gama who had been arrested, not Doctor Lopez – and Gomez d'Avila's transit through the plot had been compartmentalised so successfully that Gomez had not been able to discover what Lopez had planned.

Essex's dragnet landed a haul of letters. 'I have made a great draught,' he crowed. 'And I doubt not that some good fish will be taken among the fry.'

Among the mercantile mails intercepted in the ordinary post from Antwerp was an obscure letter 'written in the Portingall language, in style of merchants, and in a disguised hand'. A Francisco de Torres had written to a Domingo Fernandes in terminology that seemed to be a cipher for greater matters. Torres reported that 'the merchants on the other side' were delighted with their English wares, which they found 'special good, rare, well-coloured, and in great request'. The 'musk and amber was highly esteemed', and other references were made to 'cloth, scarlet threads, of pearls, a diamond, and sundry kinds of merchandise so sorted'. The merchants had never had 'any factor that sent so'. Assuring Fernandes of 'good account and return' on his next shipment, Torres asked him that 'the jewels be sent'.

But the letters complicated Essex's task without clarifying it. Essex's enquiries produced no 'Domingo Fernandes' in London, and no 'Francisco de Torres' who worked for him. The cipher remained uncracked for two weeks, until 4 November, when the lost courier Gomez d'Avila stepped off a ship from Calais. If Gomez had not been inserted into the plot by Tinoco as an Essex infomer, he showed remarkable alacrity in assisting the Earl's enquiries. When Gomez landed at Dover and was picked up by Essex's arrest party, he immediately handed over the Torres–Fernandes letter and announced that it had been issued to him by Tinoco. Essex now knew that 'Torres' was Tinoco and, as he also knew that Tinoco was involved in a plot with Ferreira da Gama, this indicated that Ferreira was 'Fernandes'. But because Gomez did not know on whose orders Ferreira had been acting, his evidence petered out just short of Lopez. For the moment, the Doctor's careful distance from the actors in his plot kept him free from accusation, but lines of communication ran in two directions and, under surveillance by Essex, the channel through which Lopez had issued his orders now became the trail that led Essex to Mountjoy's Inn.

The second step in the anatomising of the plot was accidentally provided by Ferreira da Gama. Ferreira was an amateur intelligencer, and his resolve had weakened while he had sweated in his cell for two weeks, hoping that Doctor Lopez would use some of his vaunted influence with the Queen. When, instead of hearing an order for his release, he heard that Gomez d'Avila had been arrested and was assisting Essex's inquiry, Ferreira panicked. What worried him most was not Don Emanuel and his 'letter of submission', or Lopez's contact with the Count of Fuentes – those were at least semi-official ventures – but the surveillance of Antonio Perez. Essex's reaction to discovering that Lopez and Ferreira had been party to an assassination plot directed at his guest would be lethal.

Ferreira attempted to contact Lopez. He asked his jailer, a Portuguese named Pedro Ferrera, to take a walk from Don Antonio's monastery to the Vidame of Chartres's lodgings at nearby Eton College. There, he was to ask Francis Caldera, the Spanish agent who had spied on Perez, to 'pass along under the window of the chamber' where Ferreira da Gama was imprisoned, so that they might speak 'two or three words'.

When he was approached by Pedro the jailer, Caldera refused. But Pedro's service had convinced Ferreira da Gama that he could trust his jailer, so he wrote a letter to Caldera and asked Pedro to deliver it. It was a risk, but Ferreira was very frightened by 'what diligence they make here'. The letter told Lopez to 'prevent the coming over' of him 'who brings all things' – Tinoco – 'for if he should be taken, the Doctor were utterly undone, without remedy'. The Doctor must send a messenger from the London Marranos to Brussels to tell the Spanish that the plot had been rumbled. If the messenger met a courier heading for London, he should intercept any letters addressed to 'Domingo Fernandes' or Jeronimo Lopez. 'Consider there be not matters to leave to adventure,' he begged, 'not so much as one paper doth 'scape them.'

Francis Caldera replied coolly. 'Tell Ferreira I have already done that which he requireth,' he said. 'That is, I have spoken to Doctor Lopez, who hath thrice written to Antwerp that they should not send any letters here by the ordinary post.'

As soon as he had heard of Ferreira's arrest, Lopez had plugged the source of the letters and had advised Tinoco not to come back into England. The trail would have gone entirely cold had Ferreira da Gama not persisted in sending letters from his cell. One was delivered to Mountjoy's Inn by Brother Diego Carlos, Don Antonio's cousin and confessor.

Ferreira had led the inquisitors straight to Lopez. To wriggle out of suspicion, Lopez took the letter back to the monastery at Eton and showed it to Don Antonio. The Doctor could see that Ferreira da Gama was about to crack. He had to exculpate himself in advance and denounce Ferreira before Ferreira could denounce him. From the very beginning he had set up Ferreira as the 'cut-out', the one to bear the blame if everything went wrong. This way, Ferreira would sink faster, and without dragging Lopez down with him.

The immediate consequence of Lopez's visit was to focus attention not on the letter, but on Pedro the jailer. Upon interrogation, Pedro produced Ferreira's letter to Caldera. This gave Essex's intelligencers written evidence of the links between Ferreira and Lopez, and Lopez and the Spanish at Brussels. The vague pattern of a closing net could be discerned in the murky Portingall waters, and Essex's men sent the good news to their master. On 10 November, the Earl of Essex received a letter from Francis Bacon. Bacon wrote in cipher and requested that Essex destroy it upon reading it: 'I pray, Sir, let not my jargon privilege my letter from burning, because it is not such but the light showeth through.'

Essex's intelligencer Anthony Standen watched as the Earl read the letter 'with more length and attention than infinite others I have seen him read before, and immediately committed the same to the candle'. The information in Francis Bacon's letter, so secret that it merited encryption and burning, was a single, obscure sentence: 'The late recovered man that is so much at your Lordship's devotion worketh for the Huddler underhand.'

Francis Bacon may have considered this basic cipher so simple that 'the light showeth through', but it has kept Baconographers in the dark for four centuries. Candidates for the identity for 'late recovered man' have included Lord Burghley, Sir Robert Cecil, Lord Keeper Sir John Puckering and the intelligencer Anthony Standen. Jostling in the crowd of potential Huddlers are Solicitor-General Sir Edward Coke, the spy Anthony Rolston and, doubling for the other side, Sir Robert Cecil again. To add to the confusion, the etymology is not as clear as it appears, as the senses of 'recover' and 'huddler' have shifted slightly over the last four centuries.

The Elizabethan sense of 'to recover' was broader than the

modern. It meant not only to regain physical strength after an illness, or to take an item back into one's possession, but also 'to bring, draw, or win back a person to friendship or willing obedience' (1576), and 'to bring back a weapon to a certain position' (1594). In all the senses of 'recovery', nobody fits the role of 'late recovered man' better than Gomez d'Avila. He had 'lately' been taken back into the Earl's possession after his return from the Continent. He was, as Francis Bacon told Essex, 'much at your Lordship's devotion'. As Ferreira da Gama warned Lopez in his smuggled letter, Gomez was suspiciously zealous in his assistance of Essex's inquiry: 'Gomez d'Avila . . . doth offer to help them to those letters in which he sayeth all the declarations come at large, and they speak of him in all matters.' Now, like a cocked crossbow Gomez was 'a weapon drawn back to a certain position', ready to be fired off again in Essex's service.

If the identity of 'late recovered man' fits Gomez snugly, that of 'Huddler' is even closer to Lopez's skin. Again, the Elizabethan meaning differs slightly from the modern. 'Huddler' is from the noun 'hud', the husk, pod or shell of a fruit. 'Hud' is long obsolete, but the related 'hide' has survived. 'Hide' retains a general sense of concealment and a couple of its secondary uses – 'animal hide' or 'a bird-spotter's hide' – have retained some of their ancestral 'hud'.

To an Elizabethan, 'huddle' had two senses. One was identical to the modern, a 'mass of things crowded together in hurried confusion' (1586), like Antonio's losses in *The Merchant of Venice*, 'that have of late so huddled on his back'. The modern implications of such a gathering are mixed. If what is going on in the huddle is unclear, it may be conspiratorial, but it may just as easily be an accidental consequence of the confused nature of a 'huddle'. The Elizabethans were less equivocal about a huddler's motives. He was deliberately clandestine, invariably with some underhand motive; the compound 'hudder-mudder' (1583) meant 'concealment'. A group of related terms emphasised this sense. 'To hugger' was 'to lie concealed', or 'to conceal' (1600). As far back as 1526, to keep things 'hugger-mugger' was 'to hush them up', 'to keep them secret', or 'to proceed clandestinely'. In *Hamlet*, when King Claudius rues the secret burial of Polonius, 'hugger-mugger' is used as a direct homonym for corrupt secrecy:

> . . . we have done but greenly
> In hugger-mugger to inter him.

To merit the codename 'Huddler', a man had to be suspected of secret, devious practices. Just what Essex and his intelligencers suspected of Doctor Lopez. Only one interpretation of Francis Bacon's supposedly indecipherable message makes sense. Bacon was telling Essex that the inquiry possessed clear evidence that Gomez d'Avila, the 'late recovered man', had been engaged by Lopez, 'the Huddler', but 'underhand', in a secret fashion that had remained undetected until the interception of Ferreira's smuggled letter from prison.

The next morning at Eton, Ferreira da Gama was 'narrowly examined'. He had nowhere to hide. His inquisitors knew that Tinoco was 'Torres', that more mails were expected from 'the other side' and that 50,000 crowns were at stake. They knew he was in league with Lopez. From the inside information they rubbed in Ferreira's face, it was clear to him that both Gomez d'Avila and Doctor Lopez had denounced him. Ferreira, a gentleman fallen among scoundrels, confessed that he was 'Domingo Fernandes'. Straight away, he was 'drawn to set down a large declaration under his own hand'.

In case the target of the inquiry was not clear, Ferreira's confession was headed 'That which passed with the Doctor Roger Lopez'. Ferreira described the obtaining of Don Emanuel's letter of submission, the plan to use it to buy peace between Philip II and the Portuguese exiles, Ferreira's offer of service to the Spanish and, running through the narrative like a golden thread, Lopez's guiding role. But Ferreira did not mention that this Portuguese settlement had been an element in a wider plan aimed at starting Anglo-Spanish peace talks, nor did he mention the plot against Antonio Perez. When he was pressed about the 50,000 crowns, he stuck to the line he had given to Gomez d'Avila: the money had been for Don Antonio. With no evidence to the contrary, his examiners accepted his account. He had given them enough: a signed confession that Doctor Lopez had offered himself to Philip II as a spy.

Essex had linked Ferreira to Lopez. Next, he tried to link Lopez to Burghley. Yet he did not take the obvious route of showing Ferreira's confession to the Queen. More than two months were to pass before this document and its allegations were made public. In that time Essex, the Queen's purported champion, would keep private a document containing the explosive allegation that the Queen's physician was a Spanish agent. Essex had lifted the stone that covered Portingall affairs, and had disclosed the habitual writhings beneath, but so far his discoveries had little significance outside the sphere of Portuguese exile politics. He had to wait, to draw out the full story and trace back the skein of conspiracy to Lord Burghley. For the moment, Essex restricted himself to a merely verbal denouncement.

At one of his regular emotional private audiences with the Queen, Essex told her 'how far Doctor Lopez was touched' in the Portingall mystery. Elizabeth already knew that Lopez had been in touch with the Spanish: at the time of his engagement by Essex, the Doctor had told her that Essex had asked him to contact Spanish agents as a projector. Yet Essex affected outrage at Lopez for doing what he had paid him to do. Elizabeth identified this announcement as an unsubtle stroke in Essex's factional struggle with the Cecils. She was openly sceptical about the significance of the intercepted mails, an 'interpretation' which may have been prompted by Lord Burghley. Still, Essex was relentless.

This placed Elizabeth in a dilemma. If she accepted Essex's interpretation, she licensed him to confront the Cecils. If she denied it entirely, Essex would react with his usual petulance and she would be involved in a further variety of confrontation. She did not want to get drawn into a dispute between her favourite and her chief minister, and her response was an implicit rejection of Essex's claim. She ordered that Ferriera's papers should be examined on her behalf. As the papers were in Portuguese, a Portuguese speaker should do the job. She nominated Lopez. By royal command, the accused would assist in his own investigation. She had given Essex what he had asked, but in a way that would prevent him from getting what he wanted.

Doctor Lopez went from the Court at Windsor to the monastery at Eton. Watched by Essex's men, he unfolded the 'Torres–Fernandes' letter that Tinoco had given to Gomez d'Avila. In the unlikeliest of circumstances, Lopez read of the progress of his plot while his reactions were monitored by one of its targets.

Sir,

The Bearer will tell your Worship the price in which your Pearls are held. I will advise your Worship presently of the uttermost penny that will be given for them, and will crave what order you have set down for the conveyance of the money, and wherein you would have it employed. Also, this bearer shall tell you in what resolution we rest about a little Musk and Amber, the which I am determined to buy. But before I resolve myself, I will be well advised of the price thereof. And if it shall so please your Worship to be my partner, I am persuaded we shall make good profit.

As the delivery of Lopez's 'pearls' was linked to payment, 'pearls' was most probably a cipher for 'peace'. 'Musk and Amber' were ciphers for the doomed Antonio Perez, and the price which had yet to be agreed was Lopez's fee for assisting in abduction or murder. The next part of the letter confirmed to Lopez that Essex had discovered his use of the ordinary post as an alternative route for correspondence, and that the Earl knew that his cousins Jeronimo and Diego Lopez Soeiro had been intermediaries.

The order to send hither your Letters which you recommend unto me, I have found out very convenient, and with the first commodity I will send them. But it is very necessary to advise the merchant to whom they go directed beforehand, that he presently deliver them, and mingle them not with his own. I think this bearer knows, and will tell you his name.

. . . I sent not by way of Diego Lopez Soeiro any packet, because he complains that all things which come from there come into Extreme peril.

Worse, there was a detailed report that Lopez's money had arrived, and a description of the arrangements for payment. The first of two instalments would be lodged with Manuel Palatios in Antwerp prior to Lopez collecting it.

> The money that I expected (as I understand) is come. . . . These gentlemen are desirous to gain the half for you, and therefore Your Worship must advise me how your accounts go with him; and it were good to finish them and, paying him, to have no more to do with him. This Bearer [Gomez d'Avila] is a good witness, both by Ear and Eye, and therefore to him I refer you. Moreover, this bearer will tell you of a Flemish merchant, a right honest man and rich; if Your Worship will deal with him, I am of opinion he will discharge himself, and assist you with present money . . .
>
> . . . I kiss your Worship's hands.
>
> Francisco de Torres'

With all eyes on his response, Lopez remained outwardly composed. Although Essex had uncovered the Portingall connection and Lopez had been placed at its heart, its furthest ramifications still remained hidden. Lopez hoped that if the damage was limited, his plot might yet move forward. His channel to the Spanish, and the offers it had generated, still stood, and if the Cecils supported his plan, peace talks might yet take place. And by appointing Lopez as her investigator, the Queen had signalled her scepticism at the Earl's claims of treason. When Lopez reported back to Burghley and the Queen, his analysis of Ferreira's papers agreed with their 'interpretation'. That brought the royal inquiry to an end. The Doctor had escaped the Earl's net.

Essex had been thwarted, but he would not give up. The cavalry commander had tried a frontal charge, but had foundered on the defences of the Queen and Burghley. A more subtle tactic was required to draw out Lopez and outflank the Cecils. In Essex's chambers at Windsor Castle, the Earl and his intelligencers plotted an entrapment. Gomez d'Avila, 'recovered' like a reloaded weapon, would be the bait. In the story later circulated by Essex, Gomez was brought from his cell to Essex's chambers. When he got there, 'by chance' he bumped into an 'honest gentleman' who 'understood the Spanish Tongue'. So Gomez had 'intreated' the honest gentleman to let Doctor Lopez know that he had been arrested, and the 'honest gentleman' had searched the castle precincts to inform Lopez.

This account is not supported by the chronology. Lopez already knew that Gomez d'Avila had been arrested and was assisting Essex's inquiry: he had been warned of this in Ferreira da Gama's smuggled letter. Lopez had even seen proof of this: when Lopez had examined the correspondence for the Queen, Essex's prime exhibit had been the 'Torres–Fernandes' letter handed over by Gomez d'Avila after his arrest at Dover on 4 November. Therefore, the Essex version of Gomez's interview in his chambers cannot be true. It has all the markings of a cover story, an attempt to mask a deliberate entrapment, a projection carried out in the Queen's own palace.

Neither of the two 'gentlemen' in Essex's camp who were most fluent in Spanish could be described as 'honest'. The 'honest gentleman' was either the 'cormorant seducer' Anthony Standen, or the 'instrument of Satan', the 'old, doted, polling Papist' Antonio Perez. Given that Lopez's targeting of Antonio Perez had not yet come to light, the Monster of Fortune can be discounted. Standen, on the other hand, had been a constant shadow over Lopez. It was Standen who had crossed paths in Calais with Manuel d'Andrada, and Standen who had alerted Anthony Bacon to the Doctor's double game. Standen was a veteran projector, a lifelong dissembler. Entrapment and deception were his specialities. Gomez d'Avila was Lopez's weakest point, and that was where the pressure would be applied.

The 'honest gentleman' found Lopez 'in the ball court at Windsor' and told him that Gomez d'Avila was in Essex's custody. This caused a 'sudden' and satisfying 'alteration in Lopez's countenance'. Lopez's panic cannot have been caused by this information alone – he had known it for weeks – but what would have 'altered' his countenance was the realisation that with both Gomez and Ferreira in Essex's custody, the Earl could manufacture further evidence at will. As Lopez digested this news, Gomez d'Avila's wife appeared at the court, begging the Doctor to arrange her husband's release.

Lopez was caught on the horns of a classic projection, where two seemingly unrelated encounters corroborated each other: the same technique that Lopez and Bernaldo Luis had used in 1590 to entrap Manuel d'Andrada for Walsingham. Even if Lopez recognised the tactic, he had little choice but to respond. Obliging testimonies from Gomez d'Avila would be used to pressure Ferriera da Gama, Ferreira would crack, and the real, damaging core of the plot would leak out: peace talks and the murder of Antonio Perez. If that happened, the Doctor was a dead man. Like Andrada in 1590, Lopez did not have the option of doing nothing. It was imperative to separate Gomez d'Avila from Essex, even if that was what Essex wanted Lopez to attempt. The Doctor had to allow himself to be played in the projection, in the hope that he could regain control of his actions in the new circumstances it created.

Lopez appealed to Burghley for Gomez to be released and succeeded, because Burghley saw that Essex was using Gomez against Lopez and, by extension, the Cecil family. The order was issued in Lopez's name; another similarity to Andrada's release from prison in 1590, when Walsingham had used Lopez to cover his hand. Lopez might have reduced the chances of further confession by Ferreira, but at a price: by linking himself to Gomez d'Avila, Lopez gave confirmation of his links with Ferreira da Gama, which in turn confirmed Ferreira da Gama's confession about his work for Lopez. By exculpating himself, Lopez had closed the circle of evidence and given more ammunition to his pursuers.

Gomez d'Avila was free. He promptly disappeared into the Portingall undergrowth, but did not attempt to leave England. Although the ripples of the Lopez affair were to widen alarmingly in the coming weeks, Gomez was never rearrested and was never asked to make a witness statement. Despite having left and entered England under a false passport, with a potentially treasonous correspondence hidden in his person, he was never charged with any offence. He had been a cat's paw, a means for Essex to penetrate the Lopez plot. Through Gomez d'Avila, Essex had obtained the 'Torres–Fernandes' letter and Ferreira da Gama's confession, in which Ferreira had condemned himself and incriminated Lopez.

Gomez had entered Lopez's plot on a hidden mission for Essex, and he left it in the same way.

The Doctor knew that Essex was hunting him, setting traps on his path. For the moment, Lopez could count on the support of Lord Burghley and the trust of the Queen, but for how long? Essex had pushed against Lopez, and Burghley had pushed back, protecting Lopez in order to protect his own position. This could not continue indefinitely. Ferreira da Gama might be bullied into making a full confession or wild allegations, either of which would destroy Lopez. More letters might turn up from 'the other side', feeding Essex's fascination. The plot against Antonio Perez might be discovered. If Essex raised the stakes against the Cecils, the cost of supporting Lopez would rise.

Lopez had to act immediately if he was to limit the damage and erase his tracks. The accumulated deceptions, projections and counter-projections had reached such complexity that only one option was left: to tell the truth, or a close approximation to it. The drama of Essex's accusations derived from the secrecy they claimed to unmask, as secrecy implied bad conscience and guilt. It would only be a matter of time before Essex discovered that the real aim of Lopez's negotiation with the Spanish had been to initiate peace talks. If Lopez confessed this in advance, he removed the taint of subterfuge and turned Essex's next firework into a damp squib. The truth would be Lopez's shield, a Bezoar stone against lying tongues. Of course, there were some things which the Doctor could not afford to confess, such as his complicity in the plot to murder Antonio Perez.

Lopez met with the Queen and 'other honourable persons about Her Majesty' – Lord Burghley and Sir Robert Cecil. The Doctor bitterly criticised Essex's behaviour and made 'very lewd suggestions' against him. Lopez also gave 'hard informations' against Don Antonio, saying he had earned betrayal by his own son. Lopez said that he and Ferreira had laid 'a good foundation to work upon' for peace negotiations with Spain. Ferreira had lost everything in Antonio's cause, said Lopez, and in return had received nothing but poverty. If the Queen would release Ferreira from prison, there was no 'fitter instrument in the world to work a peace between the two kingdoms'.

This was no longer the time for such initiatives. Essex was fanatically opposed to the idea and was using Lopez as a stalking horse against the Cecils. Spanish intentions would have to be taken on the basis of obscurely worded mails. The Queen and Lord Burghley turned down Lopez's offer. The 50,000 crowns waiting in Manuel Palatios's Antwerp counting house suddenly seemed less solid. Realising this, Lopez offered a contingency plan. He propounded to the Queen first in the abstract and then in the concrete, whether 'a deceiver might be deceived': if Elizabeth could not obtain peace from Philip, she might still trick 50,000 crowns from him. 'What a good deed it were to cozen the King of Spain,' Lopez mused.

This candour was in breach of all protocol, an offence to the 'princely disposition' of the Queen. Philip II was an anointed monarch. If he was to be subverted, it must be done discreetly and without acknowledging the Queen's acquiescence. English privateers had 'cozened' Philip's shipping for decades, but always under a fig leaf of legality that had allowed Elizabeth to claim innocence of their crimes. Lopez's public reference to Elizabeth's complicity in piracy and his frank suggestion that she join in his 'cozening' of a fellow monarch embarrassed her. She 'did both greatly mislike, and sharply reprehend' her impudent physician.

Under pressure, the Doctor was losing his assured touch. The 50,000 crowns had turned to fool's gold, an amber illusion. Lopez withdrew from the audience humbled and poorer, yet safer. He had protected himself against Essex's pursuit. The Queen and the Cecils were fully aware of his contacts with Spanish agents, and that large sums of money had been discussed. They knew of the intentions behind his freelance diplomacy, whether carried out in the name of Essex or Burghley. Although they did not want to follow up on Lopez's manoeuvrings, they knew that his purpose had accorded with their own. The mark of suspicion that Essex had striven so strenuously to lay upon Lopez had been scrubbed from his name. Essex might have put the Cecils on the defensive, but when they drew up the drawbridge, Lopez was inside the castle.

He was safe, but his safety was the claustrophobic comfort of the besieged. Defensive walls could still turn into prison walls. He was under the closest surveillance, and Essex had not abandoned his campaign. To Essex and his intelligencers, the Lopez defence was proof of the Doctor's wicked sophistication. To Francis Bacon, Lopez, 'though a man (in semblance) of a heavy wit', was 'yet indeed subtle of himself, as one trained in practice, and besides as wily as fear and covetousness could make him'. He was trying to cover himself by pre-emptively laying 'as many starting-holes and evasions as he could devise, if any of these matters should come to light'. Essex was determined to catch Lopez, but for the moment the wily Doctor was once again impervious to his machinations.

The battle plan with which Essex had begun Michaelmas term had run off course. In the chess game of factional war, Essex had played a typically flamboyant opening, but Burghley had checked his advance with stolid defence, and Essex's twin assaults on the Attorney-Generalship and Doctor Lopez had both been rebuffed. In the last weeks of the term, a frustrated Essex reverted to his usual erratic behaviour. On 22 November, he vanished from Windsor without any explanation. Three days later, he reappeared at six in the morning. These 'starts of his in stealing manner much trouble his followers and well-willers', admitted Anthony Standen to a stone-stricken Anthony Bacon. 'He came so late to town, as he will be in bed until noon, and so no speaking to him until dinner time.'

With Michaelmas term over and winter deepening, the Court moved from Windsor to Hampton Court. This provided a new back-drop for Essex's melodramatics. Two weeks after his last disappear-ance, he bolted again, this time for four days. According to Anthony Standen, this was the most extended aristocratic vanishing act in living memory. It was widely believed that Essex had fled in pique at another defeat by the Cecils in his efforts for Francis Bacon. 'The court doth murmur of great disgust between both parties; for that other, ever since the Earl's going, hath been in great agitation, and none can guess about what. But my thought is that Mr Francis' matter may be the cause.'

Essex's enemies in the Cecil faction took the opportunity of his disappearance to spread a 'lewd and false bruit' that he had ridden for Dover. The Queen was so 'altered' by this that by the time of his reappearance on the fourth day she was on the point of sending out a search party. This circus of petulance was hardly the behaviour of a Privy Councillor, and it did not recommend Essex's hostile judgement of Lopez. Neither was it likely to help Francis Bacon in his own 'great matter'. Yet Essex remained committed to his pursuit of Lopez, and he assured Francis Bacon that he was committed to renewing his suit 'until Easter term'.

Essex had hoped for a cavalryman's quick victory over the Cecils, but he was prepared to fight a long campaign if necessary. Honour and ambition demanded that he fight on. The Earl approached the delicate, dirty game of Court politics like a courtyard tilt, a game of chivalry. He did not notice that he was being drawn on to Burghley's terrain, where tangerine and cream cavalry might founder in the heavy bogs of patronage, and the will to fight could be sapped by the endless struggle for the Queen's favour. A cavalry charge was a chaotic affair. If it worked, a battle became a rout, but if it did not, the initiative passed to the enemy. As disordered horsemen attempted to regroup, they were vulnerable to counter-attack.

The Christmas hiatus brought an uneasy calm. No more suspicious letters appeared from hypothetical merchants. Don Antonio, terrified of assassination, appalled at his son Don Emanuel's treachery, and embarrassed that the conspiracy had centred upon his Court, packed for France. Antonio left England with all hope of restoration to Portugal dashed, forced to seek shelter from his usurping son, but his long English sojourn ended on a note of bitter gratification. On the day he left, Antonio sent a letter to Elizabeth, denouncing Lopez as a traitor. As Shylock was to say, 'The villainy you teach me I will execute, and it shall go hard, but I shall better the instruction.' Antonio had his revenge upon Lopez, the childhood associate turned in-law, the physician turned creditor, the friend turned enemy. He made sure that as Lopez's royal burden slipped from his shoulders, it was replaced by a further, fatal weight, the suspicion of treason. All Essex's influence and ambition would now press that weight on to the Doctor, until he collapsed.

As the ebullient lawyers of Gray's Inn prepared their riotous Christmas theatricals, over the wall at Mountjoy's Inn a more sombre atmosphere prevailed. Doctor Lopez would not be emigrating to Constantinople, collecting 50,000 crowns on the way. Burghley and the Queen had rejected his peace plan, and his freelance diplomacy had degenerated into a feud with Essex. The great flourish of his retirement had turned out to be the ruin of his career. But at the darkest point of the year, he could console himself that he was alive, had withstood Essex's onslaught, and would soon be free of Don Antonio.

He might have got away with it, had Emanuel Luis Tinoco not turned up.

13

The Treasurer's Defence

TUBAL: One of them showed me a ring that he has of your
daughter for a monkey.
SHYLOCK: Out upon her! – thou torturest me Tubal – it was
my turquoise, I had it of Leah when I was a bachelor: I would
not have given it for a wilderness of monkeys.

The Merchant of Venice

Emanuel Luis Tinoco, sincerest of deceivers, passed Christmas
in a lodging house at Calais, where the winter wind whipped
through the streets of the town. Hidden near at hand were
two letters for Doctor Lopez, from the Count of Fuentes and
Secretary d'Ibarra. Tinoco had been on the point of taking ship for
England when he had received Lopez's desperate message that
Ferreira da Gama had been arrested. That this had happened was
no surprise to Tinoco – he had set up Ferreira for Essex – but it
meant he had to proceed cautiously. One of the complications in
serving every master was remembering which lie had been told to
whom. Tinoco hovered in Calais, waiting to see which way the wind
blew before he left his draughty nest.

Calais was an informational crossroads, and Tinoco had stayed
well informed while Essex sallied forth and Lopez huddled beneath
Burghley's robe, writing letters that warned of 'shadows' over the
peace plan. Tinoco had not expected Essex's inquiry into Ferreira
da Gama to be so ferocious. He had not realised that Essex hated
Doctor Lopez quite so much, or that Essex had long suspected Lopez,
and he had not foreseen that Essex would use Ferreira da Gama to
dig into Lopez's affairs. If Essex continued the excavation, the danger
was that he would unearth the plot against Antonio Perez. This
would be fatal for both Tinoco and Lopez. It was now impossible

for Tinoco to return to England in Essex's service: the Earl would have some very uncomfortable questions for Tinoco. Fortunately, Tinoco had another option. He recalculated the algorithms of service and jumped towards the Cecils.

Just after Christmas, Lord Burghley received a long letter from Tinoco, written in Portuguese. The agent offered to 'discover matters of great importance concerning highly Her Majesty and the State', and recommended he should come in secret, so that neither the Earl of Essex nor Doctor Lopez should know of his arrival.

Instead of keeping the letter from Lopez, Burghley gave it to the Doctor for translation. A copy of Lopez's work survives in the Public Record Office, endorsed in Sir Robert Cecil's hand as 'The memorials of E. de L., translated out of Portuguese'. Tinoco's letter covered five densely written pages, a bravura assembly of confession, self-exculpation, intelligence and ingratiation. Adopting the familiar posture of repentant sinner, Tinoco admitted that he had spied for the Spanish, but sought to redeem himself by turning back into an English agent. He bought Lord Burghley's trust like a medieval sinner purchasing a papal indulgence, quantifying his serial betrayals in the currency of information. Tinoco knew the price, and he paid it. He reported that the Count of Fuentes had engaged a priestly assassin to kill the Queen; in fact, the target was Antonio Perez, but Tinoco could not admit this. However, he did admit that Fuentes had used him to gather intelligence on the English navy and the defences of the south coast. In addition he admitted that, while carrying out his missions for Lopez, he had also contacted Duke João of Braganza. In other words, Tinoco, while party to a plot against the Queen's life and spying for the next Armada, had also been an intelligencer for the Earl of Essex.

Tinoco's timing was excellent. Like Tinoco, Burghley had been surprised at the vehemence of Essex's assault on Lopez. The skill of Essex's intelligencers had been another unpleasant surprise. The Earl's service had performed brilliantly in their first real test, and Essex had forced the Cecils on to the back foot. The closest Burghley came to a cavalry charge was trotting about on his pardoner's donkey, but he possessed the strategic vision of a general. He had built the

Elizabethan State carefully and mercilessly, and was determined to bequeath its curateship to Sir Robert Cecil. Essex had attacked the Cecils with the twin clubs of the Attorney-Generalship and Doctor Lopez. He had not succeeded, but he would try again.

After a chastening Michaelmas, the Cecils used the Christmas break to plan their counter-attack upon Essex. By some black art of espionage, they obtained a copy of Ferreira da Gama's confession of 11 November 1593. This document was Essex's ace, held back as the clincher in his case against Lopez. Essex had withheld it from the Queen, despite the security implications of Ferreira's claim that Lopez was a Spanish spy. When the Cecils read their copy, they also decided to withhold it from the Queen's attention. The Cecils wanted to use it against Essex more than they wanted to use it for the Queen. Now, both factions were concealing evidence relating to Elizabeth's personal safety.

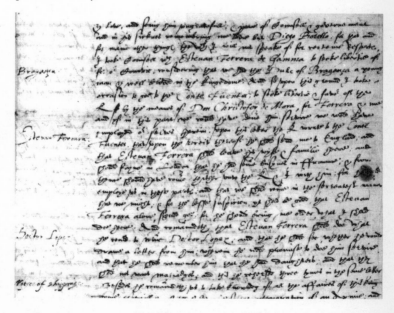

Excerpt from the translation of Tinoco's letter to Lord Burghley from Calais, just after Christmas 1593. The margin indexes read: 'Braganza . . . Steven Ferreira [da Gama] . . . Doctor Lopez . . . Notice of Shipping'.

Tinoco's admission that he had contacted the Duke of Braganza gave Burghley the weapon he needed. In Michaelmas term, Essex had tried to discredit Burghley by linking him to a plot to change the Portuguese succession, and showing that his intermediaries Ferreira and Lopez were Spanish agents. Now, Burghley had evidence that Essex had cultivated his own scheme for the Portuguese succession and that his chosen intermediary – Tinoco – had been a Spanish agent. In Easter term, the Cecils could turn Essex's scheme back on to its creator. Immediately, Burghley despatched a passport to Thomas Jeffries, the English consul at Calais.

Doctor Lopez had worked closely with Burghley in the analysis of Tinoco's letter. Burghley ordered his son Sir Robert Cecil to take over the Tinoco case; in effect, the Lord Treasurer was using his own son as a 'cut-out' in handling Tinoco. So Lopez conferred with Sir Robert Cecil, too. Sir Robert had had few if any dealings with Lopez before this, but the Doctor came with Lord Burghley's imprimatur. He was the Cecils' man, and father and son both knew that Essex's campaign against Lopez was a stalking horse for his real agenda, the supplanting of their niche in the Queen's trust. To defend Lopez was to defend themselves, and if Lopez was besmirched by his links with Tinoco, that was an occupational hazard of intelligence gathering and precisely why they used people like Lopez as intermediaries. They did not doubt Lopez's loyalty. Neither did they know everything about him.

Lopez had given the Cecils intelligence on Antonio Perez, but the Cecils had no idea that Lopez had passed the same information to the Spanish. The assassination plot against Perez was the terrible secret that none of the conspirators wanted to admit. It was why Lopez had denounced Ferreira da Gama. It was why Tinoco had asked Burghley to keep his arrival in England secret from Lopez, and why Tinoco had described Fuentes's plans for an assassination as being aimed at the Queen. As Lopez and the Cecils plotted their counter-strike against Essex, the Doctor kept this secret locked in the dark repository of his conscience. The catastrophic collapse of his plot had turned him from spymaster to fugitive, from actor to acted upon. His only hope was to fasten himself to his patrons. As he washed back and forth on the tides of the Cecil–Essex conflict, the most important aim was to stay afloat.

In Calais, Tinoco was hustled aboard a ship so quickly that he had no time to pack. Half-prisoner, half-guest, he sailed escorted by a guard from the English consulate. 'I embarked with a servant of Thomas Jeffries, with one shirt only on my body,' he recalled. 'And when I embarked myself, with what secrecy and brevity!'

On his previous missions, Tinoco had relied upon Doctor Lopez's hospitality, but this time he travelled incognito. It was late in the evening by the time Tinoco and his guard reached Windsor, and they had trouble finding somewhere to sleep. They tried the home of Don Antonio's aide, Captain Edward Perrin, but in this dangerous time of arrests and 'shadows', Perrin closed his door in Tinoco's face. The two travellers were forced on a midnight tour of Windsor doss-houses, Tinoco shivering in his single shirt. 'Thomas Jeffries's servant and I ran all about the town before we could find a lodging,' he moaned. 'And I and Thomas Jeffries's man lay both together, for lack of beds.'

In the morning, a tired, cold and crumpled Tinoco was collected by one of Lopez's Marrano in-laws and taken to Sir Robert Cecil's chambers at Court. Misled by his megalomaniac tendencies, Tinoco expected a private audience and was taken aback when Sir Robert Cecil's assistants entered the room. In walked Doctor Lopez and Captain Perrin. The Doctor, said Sir Robert, had translated Tinoco's 'memorial'. Tinoco had specified that Lopez should be kept ignorant of his coming to England – the Doctor might denounce him as the instigator of the plot to murder Antonio Perez – and Tinoco now became convinced that he had walked into a trap. He still had mails from the Count of Fuentes and Secretary d'Ibarra hidden on his person, but he felt it was too dangerous to deliver them.

Sir Robert Cecil passed him Ferreira da Gama's confession of 11 November 1593, secretly copied from Essex's original. Tinoco read it and noted with relief that Ferreira had not mentioned the word 'peace' or the dread name 'Antonio Perez'. He offered his professional opinion, using a metaphor from usury: 'The confession is very good, but the principal wanteth therein.'

Tinoco would not describe this missing 'principal' of 'peace' and 'Perez'. He only offered Cecil the intriguing but indeterminate promise that its discovery might be 'resulting to the good of all Christendom'. With Doctor Lopez clearly assisting the Cecils, Tinoco did not feel safe enough to discuss the proposed peace talks, or to show Cecil the mails from Fuentes and Ibarra. As he later rued in a prison cell, 'I dilated the giving my letters.'

Like everybody who talked with Tinoco, Sir Robert Cecil came away from their meeting with a portion of truth and a great deal of wishful supposition. On that incomplete basis, he decided that he and his father could use Tinoco against Essex without endangering themselves. Tinoco had implied this, and Doctor Lopez had confirmed it. Cecil did not realise that Tinoco and Lopez had a conspiracy of silence: it was imperative to both of them that no one mentioned the worm in the apple: Antonio Perez. The need to keep this hidden, and to seek the protection of the Cecils as Essex stormed after them, meant that they lied to Sir Robert Cecil, sending him out into the field with faulty and incomplete intelligence.

After tucking away his copy of Tinoco's 'memorials', off went Sir Robert Cecil to see the Queen. He imparted Tinoco's allegations to her before an infuriated Essex. 'This party is a principal actor in conveyance of these Portingall practices!' protested Essex. Essex produced his collection of intercepted mails and pointed to Tinoco's handwriting as evidence that Cecil's new witness was neck-deep in treasonable dealings with the Spanish. How, Essex asked, could the Queen trust the word of a suspect? As the official investigator of Portingall malpractice, Essex insisted that she grant him a chance to interrogate Tinoco personally.

Once again, Elizabeth interpreted the latest twist of the Portingall plot as an aspect of the Essex–Cecil struggle, and once again she took Lord Burghley's advice. She gave Essex permission to interrogate Tinoco, but she appointed his bitter enemy Sir Robert Cecil as his co-inquisitor.

Doctor Lopez was still at Windsor. One of Essex's men, perhaps the same 'honest gentleman' who had tormented him in December, gloatingly told him that Tinoco was about to be handed to Essex.

Lopez was physically stunned, beginning 'suddenly to sink down'. In the interview in Sir Robert Cecil's study, Lopez had seen how compliant and shifty Tinoco could be. There was no reason to believe that he would be any less self-preservative when Essex got hold of him. Essex knew that the fragments of some grand scheme lay in his pile of disparate gleanings. Lopez feared that when Tinoco was afraid for his life, the Antonio Perez plot would be shaken from him. Lopez would be destroyed and the Cecils discredited. Lopez went straight to his chamber at Court and burnt every piece of paper he found.

Meanwhile, Tinoco was taken to 'the Lodge in the park at Hampton Court' for examination by Cecil and Essex. In front of witnesses, and with a straight face, Tinoco explained that he had come into England merely from 'zeal, and affection to do Her Majesty service'. Specifically, he had come 'to advance a matter which by his privity had been broken before to the Earl of Essex'. Less specifically, Tinoco would not go into details about Essex's 'matter'. For more information, and to give his account 'credit', they should check with Doctor Lopez.

This was the giddy work of a true maniac. The reference to Doctor Lopez was inspired. Tinoco desperately needed to talk with Lopez, as they had to work out how they were going to hide their plot against Antonio Perez. And Lopez would have to corroborate Tinoco's allegations to save his own neck.

Just as brazenly, Tinoco had admitted that he had shared a secret 'matter' with Essex. He had not described it, alluding only to its existence, and this vague menace called Essex's bluff. The Earl did not know to which 'matter' Tinoco was referring. Was it the Braganza initiative, or was it the Earl's entrapment of Lopez? Everybody had something to hide, and Essex was no exception. Through Tinoco, he had penetrated the Cecil spy service and set up Lopez in order to harm the Cecils. He could not allow this to become public.

Essex knew that Tinoco was threatening him, and the threat was clear – if Essex persisted, Tinoco would spill the whole story: that Essex's intelligencers had been watching Lopez for months before Ferreira da Gama was arrested; that Tinoco had been paid by Essex to aid in Lopez's entrapment; that Gómez d'Avila had been planted in the Lopez plot by Tinoco and the budding Machiavellis of Essex House; that Essex and his intelligencers had allowed Lopez's plan to ripen before striking, in the hope that they could maximise the damage to the Cecils; and that while they were waiting for the rotten apple to drop from the tree, Tinoco had burrowed further into Lopez's service, gnawing at the root of the Cecils' intelligence apparatus on their behalf.

Tinoco could now change sides seamlessly. Instead of destroying Lopez to hurt the Cecils, he might help them ensnare Essex in the very allegations the Earl had concocted against them. When he had been presented with Tinoco's mails, Essex had crowed, 'I have made a great draught, and I doubt not that some good fish will be taken among the fry.' If Essex pressed Tinoco too far, he would continue to help the Cecils. Then the biggest fish landed by the investigation might not be Lopez, but Essex. The Earl abandoned the interrogation.

Having survived Essex's onslaught, Tinoco trusted Sir Robert Cecil a little more and produced the letters he had been carrying for the last week. This gave the Cecils a further advantage, as they now knew exactly how far Lopez's negotiations had advanced. In their letters, the Count of Fuentes and Secretary d'Ibarra requested Lopez to obtain Lord Burghley's 'letter of credence', so that talks might begin. The Cecils showed these letters to the Queen, as proof of Lopez's innocence and proof that Essex was engaged in a vendetta against her physician. Given the close co-ordination between the Cecils and Lopez in their handling of Tinoco, it is highly likely that Lopez saw these letters too and sensed vindication.

Meanwhile, Essex still insisted on his right to examine Tinoco on the 'meaning and secret sense of those letters', as if they had an occult meaning that only he understood. Sir Robert Cecil produced his prisoner, and Tinoco delivered another virtuoso performance. In the face of Essex's 'diligence', Tinoco 'held his mouth so close, and had his lesson so well conned, as a man might easier pluck out his teeth than the truth'. This dental recourse was not yet available to Essex. Tinoco was in the hands of the Cecils and he was singing their tune. He insisted that the most able expounder of the letters was Doctor Lopez, and he offered to continue working as an English agent. Neither of these outcomes was desirable for Essex, as both would incriminate him.

With the interview finished, the Cecils removed Tinoco from Hampton Court and tucked him away at 'the gate house in Westminster'. There, the Cecils' servants recovered further letters from Tinoco. When Tinoco was undressed and 'laid in the bed', his jailers searched his dirty clothes and found two credit notes issued by the Spanish at Brussels. In the case that the Cecils were building against Essex, these notes would be further evidence.

The curved surface of a pewter cup was covered in a myriad random scratches, but if the light of a single candle was held to it, the scratches assumed a rippling, concentric pattern that appeared to emanate from a single point of reflection. Tinoco was a repository of numinous intelligence gleaned from all sources. Under the hard light of the Cecils, his assemblage assumed a narrative shape. Impassive Lord Burghley and his flush-cheeked cripple son had used this narrative to bounce Essex's imputation of treason straight back at him. The Treasurer's defence threatened to turn the focus of the investigation into Essex himself.

If a swashbuckler was not to be pushed back, he had to press forward. Essex made another of his crabwise assaults, swapping his hunt for Lopez with his pursuit of the attorney-generalship for Francis Bacon. But Lord Burghley had prepared a response to that move, too. On 20 January, there was 'some long arguing this afternoon betwixt the Queen and my Lord Treasurer' in which Burghley advocated his supporter Sir Edward Coke for the Attorney-Generalship. That would leave the lesser position of Solicitor-General vacant for Francis Bacon. The Queen summoned old Sir Gilbert Gerrard, the outgoing Master of the Rolls, and asked his opinion. A decision was imminent.

If Burghley got his way, Francis Bacon would get a place in office, but it would not give Essex the political supremacy he sought. Instead, Bacon would be neutralised with flattery, and Essex would have no cause to complain. As the Queen reflected on Sir Gilbert Gerrard's advice, Essex swung back on to the Lopez tack and played a wild card. He had been sitting on Ferreira da Gama's confession for two months. The confession named Doctor Lopez as a servant of Philip II. On 20 January, Essex showed it to the Queen.

The inquiry into Doctor Lopez had begun as a complementary scenario to the struggle over the Attorney-Generalship, but it had displaced the matter of Francis Bacon's prospects and become the locus of factional struggle. The long preliminary dance of feint and insinuation was over. Essex had made the battle public. Even if the Queen detected a crude political agenda in Essex's timing, she could not ignore this latest and most sensational revelation about her physician. She gave an order that Lopez be interrogated.

The Cecils were one jump ahead. Someone had tipped off Lopez about Essex's accusation and he had fled from Hampton Court. As the Queen ordered his interrogation, Lopez was on the road to Mountjoy's Inn. He burst into the house and frantically burnt 'all his letters and papers', gathering up every scrap of evidence and forcing it into the flames. At Court, Burghley and Sir Robert Cecil played for time, haggling out the terms of the inquiry with Essex. It was late in the evening before the Queen appointed all three as examiners. The next morning, when Lopez reported to Burghley House on the Strand, Mountjoy's Inn was turned over by Essex's men. They found a grate clogged with warm ash. Essex's evidence had gone up the chimney and into the night sky.

The Earl was on ferocious form that morning. He had moved Ferreira da Gama down from Eton for the occasion, and the sick, sallow prisoner was produced by Essex's oafish steward Gelly Meyrick, who forced Ferreira to repeat before Lopez's face that the Doctor was a Spanish agent.

Lopez was outraged. With the secret exception of the Antonio Perez surveillance, he was the Queen's loyal servant. Confident in the protection of the Cecils and the destruction of his papers, he 'did utterly with great oaths and declarations deny all the points, articles and particularities of the accusations'. 'It is pity of my life if any of them were true,' he said, expertly balancing truth and melodrama.

When the search party returned from Mountjoy's Inn empty-handed, Essex knew he had been stymied once again, 'opposed in his enquiry by the other two'. The interrogation was over, but instead of being released, Lopez was committed to the custody of Gelly Meyrick at Essex House. When the Cecils allowed Essex to lock up Lopez, the Earl thought they had made a telling error. He would have Lopez in his grasp and, by playing him off against Ferreira da Gama, he could force a confession from the impudent, cunning Doctor.

This was what the Cecils wanted Essex to think. While the Earl smacked his lips and planned Lopez's next interrogation, Sir Robert Cecil raced back to the Queen at Hampton Court. 'There is no matter of malice,' Sir Robert told Elizabeth. 'For in the poor man's house were found no kind of writings of intelligences, or otherwise, that hold might be taken of him.'

Cecil added that Lopez, despite his palpable innocence, was now installed in a dungeon at Essex House. It seemed as if Essex, not content with slandering the 'poor man', now wished to torment him.

The next morning, Cecil returned to Essex House to assist in the Earl's interrogation of Ferreira da Gama. Essex had no idea that Cecil had already outflanked him with the Queen. Relishing his chance to grill Lopez, he charged forward like an undisciplined caval-ryman, oblivious to his exposed flank. He knew the Cecils had outsmarted him with Tinoco and that Burghley was about to shunt Francis Bacon into the Solicitor-Generalship, but in his anger, he did not see that the Cecils were still running dainty rings round him, pre-empting every move and turning every attack to a counter-attack.

Essex's morning with Ferreira da Gama was a further study in frustration. A long 'commission' with subverting Sir Robert Cecil produced nothing of any value. All that emerged was that Ferreira had been used by Lopez, and that the two had tried to scam money from Philip II. Infuriated, the Earl ordered that his prime exhibit be brought up from the cells.

Unfazed by a night in the cold bowels of Essex House, Doctor Lopez appeared before Essex and Cecil with 'composed countenance and demeanour'. He knew that Essex had little evidence against him. Lopez's best defence would have been neither to deny everything, nor to tell the entire truth, but to settle somewhere in between: to admit to his peace initiative and avoid any mention of Antonio Perez.

This would have placed him securely under the Cecil wing. But he did not take this course. As he was sure that, sooner or later, Essex would link him to Perez, Lopez decided to deny everything.

When Ferreira's new confession was shown to him, Lopez responded with more virtuoso outrage. Abusing Ferreira with 'execrable oaths', he damned himself 'to the lowest pit of hell' if any part of Ferreira's confession was true. This was a mistake. Ferreira's confession was a substantially accurate account of how he and Lopez had obtained Don Emanuel's 'letter of submission'. It was difficult to contradict under examination.

Essex was determined to extract a confession from Lopez. As if decanting a fine sherry, Essex drew the truth 'by degrees, being drawn from him as wine is drawn by force, first through a single hole, and then through a larger and larger' by the use of 'drawing irons'. Gradually, Lopez's secrets dripped out on to the page.

Asked about Don Emanuel's letter of submission, he equivocated, 'It might be such a thing was shown to me, but I did not regard it.'

Then, 'being better urged' by Essex, Lopez came 'a degree further', like a man fording a fast-flowing torrent, jumping from stone to slippery stone. 'I think I saw such a thing, if that answer would be allowed.'

This constructive ambiguity spurred on the Earl. Lopez hopped on to the next stone and teetered uneasily: 'I remember I saw the submission.'

Essex flexed his 'drawing irons'.

'I read it' – Lopez tipped into the water and then surfaced – 'but being a matter that did not concern Her Majesty, I thought it was no offence to Her Highness.'

Now Essex had him. Lopez 'was led by steps' to confess 'the sight and reading' of letters from the Spanish. At this confirmation, a paper was produced and Lopez had to sign it.

Doctor Lopez, being again this morning examined, doth confess that Ferreira did shew him the letter he did receive from Cristovão da Moura and that he did read it.

He did further confess that he saw also the letter of Don Emanuel to

the King of Spain, and he also doth confess that Ferreira did tell him
he had sent Gomez d'Avila to the Count of Fuentes.

He doth likewise confess that he would have drawn any money from
the King of Spain, but he sayeth he would, when he had it, have told
the Queen of it.'

Essex considered this sufficient: Lopez had confessed to contact with
the Spanish and that 'amounted to no less than treason'. He added
Lopez's confession to his bundle of papers, and prepared for a
triumphal announcement before the Queen.

Sir Robert Cecil had not opposed Essex's masterly examination.
Rather than block the Earl, he had adopted the subtler strategy: to
divert Essex's thrust and turn its energy back on him. Essex did not
realise it, but his examination of Lopez had confirmed the Cecils'
insistence that Lopez was innocent of any real wrongdoing.
Everything to which Lopez had 'confessed' had been known to the
Queen and the Cecils for months, if not years. It was the job of an
intelligencer to draw out the enemy's agents and to gull the enemy's
money, and that Lopez had done so did not justify sacking his home
and accusing him of treason. And Lopez's loyal refusal to admit to
Essex that he had been sketching out peace talks in the service of the
Cecils' foreign policy proved that he was still their honourable servant.

Just in case, the next morning Sir Robert Cecil privately interviewed Tinoco, obtaining a confession that corroborated Lopez's and
Ferreira's accounts. Tinoco admitted that he had delivered Don
Emanuel's submission to Brussels. He also gave a brief precis of
Andrada's dealings with Lopez, including the gift of the ruby ring
from Philip II, and ended with the suggestion that 'good heed be
taken to the letters of Jeronimo Lopez, . . . he is a great friend of
the Doctor, and hath intelligence with some in Antwerp'. This could
not have been news to the Cecils: Jeronimo Lopez had served them
for years. Everything added up. If Lopez had been keeping lower
company than usual, it was only to remove the Portuguese obstacle
to peace talks with Spain. And while that outcome would have spelled
the end of Don Antonio, it would have been a boon to the Cecils.

'In Lopez's folly,' Burghley told his son, 'I see no point of treason intended to the Queen, but a willingness to make some gain to the hurt of Don Antonio.'

The Cecils had set up Essex again. As Sir Robert Cecil had already primed the Queen without Essex's knowledge, the confessions with which Essex would attempt to condemn Lopez would be the means of his vindication. Like Sir Edward Norris at Coruña, Essex would trip up and impale himself on his own pike. That night, when Anthony Standen sought to speak with Lord Burghley to further Francis Bacon's suit, he was refused an audience. The Lord Treasurer was 'indisposed, and could not be spoken with for eight days to come'. The Cecils drew in their defences and waited.

Oblivious, Essex prepared for his moment of triumph. On Friday, 25 January 1594, he went to the Queen and announced that Lopez was a traitor.

Elizabeth trusted Lopez as her physician and she had the word of the Cecils that he was innocent. Essex had soured Court life for months with his Lopez obsession. His latest accusation against the Doctor was an affront not just to the Queen's advisers, but to her honour. Her patience snapped: 'Rash and temarious youth, to enter into a matter against the poor man which you cannot prove, and whose innocence I know well enough!'

As Essex reeled, Elizabeth told him that she knew he was driven not by patriotism, but 'malice' against Lopez. Essex's cruelty was obnoxious and an insult to her 'honour'.

Essex was humiliated and surprised. He had not thought that someone might have 'prepossessed Her Majesty'. He responded to his shaming after his habit, storming off to his chambers and retreating to his 'cabinet' with a slamming of doors. He stayed there for two days, sulking behind the oak as the Cecils' ally Lord Admiral Howard tried to find out what the Earl was plotting on the other side of the door, while pretending he had come to negotiate Essex's 'atonement'.

On Sunday morning the Earl ventured out and apologised to the Queen. He was still bitterly angry, though. The Cecils had parried his every thrust, had tricked him and humiliated him before the Queen. Essex was gripped by 'a canker', a malevolent, metastising obsession that mixed rivalry with the Cecils and loathing of Lopez. He saw huddlers underhand behind all his troubles. That night, he hurried back to London, all fatigue and hunger overridden by his galloping 'canker'. The next morning he wrote to Francis Bacon 'in haste'.

> I have kept both these two days together in my [chamber], having been so tired with examinations, and I had scarce leisure to eat. I have discovered a most dangerous and desperate treason. The point of conspiracy was Her Majesty's death. The executioner should have been Doctor Lopez; the manner, poison. This I have so followed, as I will make it appear as clear as the noon-day.

The first sentence was untrue. Essex had spent 'two days together' in his room, but not in order to recuperate from the rigours of cross-examining Lopez, as he claimed to Francis Bacon. He had sulked there after a showdown with the Queen that could only have harmed Bacon's candidacy.

The rest of the accusation was the bitter fruit of Essex's two days of paranoid gestation in his cabinet. The Cecils had protected Lopez and had vouched for him to the Queen. With monomaniac clarity, Essex saw that such closeness might be used against them. If Lopez had conspired to murder the Queen, what did that say about the judgement of the ageing Lord Treasurer and his novice son? The Cecils would have cultivated and shielded an assassin.

In repeating his wild claim to the Queen, Essex spared no imagination. 'Lopez is a very villain, and had poisoned others,' he announced, absurdly naming the late Sir Francis Walsingham as one of the Doctor's purported victims. Essex promised further unrevealed 'proofs' against Lopez: 'I do not doubt but that he played the villain on both sides, and did intend to poison the Queen!'

With this flash of destructive inspiration, Essex turned the tables on the Cecils. The Queen's sanctity was the supreme value of the English State, and her safety was its guarantee. The Cecils' counter-attack crumbled before the gravity of Essex's allegation. 'On Tuesday at noon,' a gleeful Anthony Standen reported, 'Lopez, for all the favourers he had, was committed to the Tower.'

It was a fight to the death, and not just for the Doctor.

14

The Jew of Malta

'Were you the doctor, and I knew you not?'
Bassanio to Portia, *The Merchant of Venice*

There once lived a Jew of Malta named Barabas. He was an international businessman and banker, a potentate more powerful than any prince. He cared only for his precious daughter Abigail, and the accumulation of gold and jewels. Locked in his counting house, he gloried over 'bags of fiery opals, sapphires, amethysts, jacinths, hard topaz, grass-green emeralds, beauteous rubies, sparkling diamonds'. He called this wealth 'infinite riches in a little room', but his real power lay in the invisible bonds of trade, commerce and influence which he manipulated across Europe through the 'scattered nation' of his fellow Jews, including his friend 'Nuñez of Portugal'.

When the Sultan of Turkey demanded that tiny Malta pay tribute to his empire, Ferneze, the Governor of Malta, followed custom and ordered that the local Jews should pay off the Turk by surrendering half their estates. Barabas resisted the order. Apart from not wanting to lose a lifetime's profits, he did not see why his wealth should be abrogated in a gentile dispute. As a punishment, Governor Ferneze ordered that all of Barabas's money and jewels be impounded.

Barabas's daughter Abigail cried for her father, but he told her not to despair. Hidden under the floorboards of their house were 'ten thousand Portagues, besides great pearls, rich costly jewels, and stones infinite'. Unfortunately, he had not realised that Governor

Ferneze had taken Barabas' house, too. To add a theological sting to their poverty, Ferneze had turned the house into a nunnery.

Barabas thought up a plan to recover the money and jewels. He persuaded Abigail to feign conversion to Christianity so that she might enter the nunnery as a sister. 'Religion hides many mischiefs from suspicion,' he explained.

Abigail joined the nuns. Later that night, she lifted up the floorboards and dropped the gold and jewels off a balcony to her waiting father. He had his loot, but he had lost his daughter. Abigail's temporary dissembling among the nuns had convinced her to stay as a Christian. Barabas was distraught, and consumed with a desire for revenge upon the Christians. When the Turks besieged Malta, he got his chance.

Barabas betrayed the Maltese to the Turks. In reward, the occupiers appointed him Governor. He plotted a terrible rampage of slaughter. First, he poisoned his daughter's Christian suitor. Next, he poisoned the well that supplied his old house, killing the entire nunnery, including his own daughter. Then he and an accomplice strangled and beat to death two monks. He even offered his debtors a poisoned nosegay, and plucked his lute for them as they choked to death. Finally, as Barabas was no more loyal to the Muslims than he had been to the Christians, he offered to betray the Turks to the Christians. Taking ex-Governor Ferneze into his confidence as an accomplice, he plotted the murder of the Turkish commander and his men.

Barabas invited the Turks to a banquet. When they arrived, he and Ferneze welcomed them from the minstrel gallery. As the Turks sat down, they did not realise that their chairs rested on a collapsible floor. But the betrayer was betrayed. Instead of cutting the cord that would send the Turks tumbling through the floor of the banquet hall, Count Ferneze released a trapdoor in the floor of the gallery. Barabas shot down through the floor and landed in a giant cauldron. The Jew boiled to death, the Turks left Malta and Ferneze restored Christian rule to the island for ever.

This is the plot of Christopher Marlowe's *The Jew of Malta*, probably first performed in 1592 at the Rose Theatre by Lord Strange's

Men. Barabas is the final element in the fictive compound that is Shakespeare's Shylock. But while Shylock is an uneasy blend of theological polemic and naturalistic characterisation, Barabas is a cruder blend. He is a parody constructed from two abstractions, one modern, the other medieval. Marlowe clad Machiavellian *politique* in the weeds of a medieval ghost from the earliest days of European theatre. He revitalised the satanic spectre of the Jew as fraudulent doctor, poisoner of wells, sadistic usurer and starter of wars. Barabas was a comic figure, as exaggerated and inhuman as the bulbous false nose worn by his actor. Yet this did not mean he bore no relation to the world-view of an Elizabethan audience. For Barabas to be comic at all, there first had to be a serious belief that he was capable of such subversion and depravity.

With the exception of the hidden Marranos, an Elizabethan audience had no Jews with which the stereotype might be compared. The great weight of medieval Christianity supported Marlowe's characterisation, as did the contemporary references that littered the play. Apart from 'Nuñez of Portugal', Marlowe invoked the Continental wars of religion – naturally, started by Barabas – and the Turkish conquest of Malta in 1522. If Barabas's medievalism was antique, his Machiavellianism was scrupulously modern. Disharmony in Christendom, the power of Islam in the Mediterranean and the growth of international trade networks had all freed him from the medieval straitjacket. He was a freethinking cynic, whose only belief was a form of unbelief: self-interest unrestrained by religious conscience or social respect. He gained further purchase upon reality because his creator was notoriously associated with such attitudes; just before his murder, Christopher Marlowe had been investigated by the Privy Council on charges of sedition and atheism.

On 1 February 1594, three days after Doctor Lopez was transferred to the Tower, *The Jew of Malta* was revived at the recently reopened Rose Theatre. As London thrilled to rumours of poisoning and betrayal at Court, theatregoers were reacquainted with their old friend Barabas the conspirator, poisoner and traitor. On 4 February, Philip Henslowe's counting house recorded receipts of fifty shillings. Two days later, the Rose debuted a revised version of Shakespeare's

Titus Andronicus, an ugly bloodbath involving rape, murder, mutilation, cannibalism and a hoard of hidden gold. Despite possessing all the attractions of revenge tragedy at its crudest, *Titus* took only forty shillings. Marlowe's *Jew* was a bigger draw than Shakespeare's Roman. In its 1592 run at the Rose, *The Jew of Malta* had been played twelve times in twelve months. Its 1594 revival would see twelve performances in only six months; it would become the Rose's most popular play of the year.

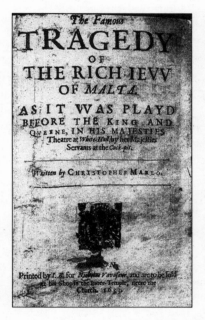

Frontispiece of The Jew of Malta, *not published until 1633.*

In the Tower of London, the Jew of Mountjoy's Inn begged for the Queen's mercy in a manner that would have appalled both Barabas and Shylock. Elizabeth's response was supportive but qualified. Her Doctor should 'suffer no loss' for matters that he already had revealed to her, but if further charges were raised, 'it was fit for the honour and justice of the State that he should make his defence'. Elizabeth had taken care to preside over the Essex–Cecil conflict without joining in. If Essex insisted on inflating a treason case against Lopez and dragging her in as evidence, it was better that he be thwarted by judicial process than royal command. The Earl's rage, a force as incandescent and unpredictable as a festal firework, would be diffused away from her and the Cecils.

At dawn on Lopez's first morning in the Tower, he was interrogated by Essex and Sir Robert Cecil. When Essex accused him of attempted regicide, the Doctor raged at the Earl with 'irreligious swearing', 'protestations' and 'profane speeches'. 'I love Her Majesty better than God!' Lopez averred.

Lopez blustered and swore his innocence with the self-righteous outrage of a defendant innocent of one charge, but guilty of another. Nothing hid a secret better than the truth. Once again, selective honesty allowed Lopez to deny everything. Apart from the grandeur of the charge, Essex had no new evidence bar the meagre gleanings of the raid on Mountjoy's Inn. His last question was about the ruby ring from Philip II.

'My wife did sell it about half a year ago, for fifty pounds to a goldsmith,' Lopez replied.

This was a lie, and both Essex and Sir Robert Cecil knew it: the ring had been found in Lopez's home. To Cecil, this hinted that Lopez was trying to cover up some aspect of his dealings. To Essex, it was an opportunity. The Earl tried to build on it by hauling up Ferreira da Gama, but Ferreira confessed to nothing more heinous than forging a passport for Tinoco. Ferreira had now confessed to almost everything he knew, but Lopez had only confessed to most of what he had been asked about. Whole swathes of secrecy remained undetected and, with Sir Robert Cecil on his side, they were likely to remain obscure. The Cecils did not want the link between Lopez and Antonio Perez to emerge. The truth was dangerous: through Lopez, the Cecils had spied on the French ambassador and his son, had intercepted Perez's correspondence and had subverted the Earl of Essex. They did not know, and Lopez was determined not to let them know, that a far more explosive secret underlaid the Lopez–Perez link: a murder plot involving Spanish agents.

Essex was convinced that Lopez's lie about the ring hid a greater secret, and he could see that the Cecils were determined not to allow him to discover it. Apart from Lopez's aggressive denials and consistent caginess, the Jew had no reason to lie about the ring unless he had something to hide. And if the Cecils were sure that Lopez was completely innocent, they would not have defended him so doggedly, as if they too had something to hide.

Essex and Sir Robert Cecil left the Tower as rivalrous, uncomfortable companions. Essex was exhausted, sure that his 'enemies' intended his ruin, and frayed from another fruitless examination. Cecil, who only the day before had had the upper hand over Essex, had been forced back on the defensive. The Earl had been a constant source of unpleasant surprises. His ambition to supplant the Cecils was blatant, but his strategies had been disconcerting. Lord Burghley was a rational strategist, and Sir Robert Cecil was similar in his lawyerly, calm logic. Essex played by different rules. Unable or unwilling to moderate his ambition with *politique*, and enchanted by the strange music of paranoia, Essex threatened the solidity of the State even as he sought to take control over it.

The tactical struggles of the previous weeks had stripped the pretence of shared loyalty to the Queen, baring the hostility between Sir Robert Cecil and the Earl of Essex. In the jarring, cell-like confines of a shared coach rattling over unmade winter roads, Cecil chose to raise the most sensitive topic of all. He began with an intelligence that suggested he was closer to the Queen than Essex: 'My Lord, the Queen has resolved, ere five days pass, without any further delay to make an Attorney-General. I pray Your Lordship to let me know whom you will favour.'

Essex rose to the provocation. 'I wonder that you should ask me that question,' he replied, 'seeing it could not be unknown to you that, resolutely against all whosoever, for Francis Bacon I stand.'

'Good Lord,' Sir Robert affected equal surprise. 'I wonder Your Lordship should go about to waste your strength in so unlikely or so impossible a matter.'

Essex's efforts on Bacon's behalf were well known but, asked Cecil, was there a single precedent for the elevation of 'so raw a youth' to a 'place of such moment' as the Attorney-Generalship?

In 1594, Francis Bacon was thirty-three years old. Raw, perhaps, but not youthful by any other standards than those of senior office. Essex admitted that he could not think of a precedent for a young Attorney-General, and then repaid Cecil in his own snide coinage. 'A younger than Francis Bacon, of lesser learning and no greater experience, sueth and shoveth with all force for an office of far greater importance, greater charge, and greater weight than the Attorneyship.' If Cecil so desired, Essex could name this upstart for him.

Robert Cecil felt the sting of this sharp, accurate barb. Thirty years old, he knew he was even rawer than his cousin Francis Bacon. How could Cecil deny that his speedy rise had been propelled by his father Burghley's influence? His candidacy for a seat on the Privy Council, and his grooming as inheritor of his father's role, were palpable proofs. Having been favoured over his Bacon cousins and at their expense, Cecil now sought to deny them similar benefits of patronage. Offended, he could only invoke the privilege for which Essex had mocked him: 'I well know Your Lordship means myself. Although my years and experience are small, yet weighing the school I studied in, and the great wisdom and learning of my schoolmaster, and the pains and observations I daily passed in that school, I think my forces and wisdom to be sufficient.'

Cecil knew they were not and was impelled to add the paternal seal to his claim. 'My father's deserts in these his long and painful travails of so long an administration', said Cecil, merited 'a mark of gratitude in the person of his son'. In the face of this claim, perhaps Essex was overreaching himself in the matter of 'Mr Francis'. Patronisingly, Cecil suggested that Essex should settle for placing the junior cousin in a junior office. 'I pray your Lordship to consider, if at least your Lordship had spoken of the Solicitorship, that might be of easier digestion to her Majesty.'

This had the desired effect. 'Digest me no digestions!' Essex erupted. 'For the Attorneyship for Francis is that I must have, and in that I will spend all my power, might, authority and amity, and with tooth and nail defend and procure the same for him against whomsoever getteth this office out of my hands for any other! Before he have it, it shall cost him the coming by, and this be you assured of, Sir Robert, for now I do fully declare myself.'

'For your own part, Sir Robert,' Essex frothed on, 'I think strange both of my Lord Treasurer and you, that can have the mind to seek the preferment of a stranger before so near a kinsman.'

Cecil did not reply to this personal insult. His aim had been to provoke Essex, and he had more than succeeded. Essex had now passed the point of no return on both aspects of his assault on the Cecils; if the Cecils did not demonstrate Essex's manifest unsuitability for high office, the Earl would do the job for them. The rest of their journey passed in bitter silence.

Rather than realising he had fallen into Cecil's trap, Essex decided that their exchange constituted some kind of verbal victory. Having re-enacted every thrust and parry of the argument for his intelligencer Anthony Standen, Essex went to Francis Bacon's chambers at Gray's Inn for a further 'long half-hour' of self-congratulation. Bacon was 'most joyful and consolate' that his patron had 'so stoutly stuck unto him, and so far declared himself for him against Monsieur de Bossu'. The political implications of Essex's intemperate rudeness seemed lost on Bacon.

Two days later, on 2 February, lawyer Bacon lost some of his rawness. He argued his first case before the Queen's Bench, a property dispute in which he acted for Essex's brother-in-law Sir Thomas Perrot. At eleven o'clock that night, Essex summoned Anthony Standen. He had good news about Francis Bacon's performance, but harsh if unsurprising news from the Court. Essex came 'at that instant' from the Queen. She had told him that, influenced by 'you woot whom' – Elizabethan for 'you know who' – she had finally decided on her new Attorney-General.

'You woot whom' was Lord Burghley. Elizabeth had settled on Burghley's candidate Sir Edward Coke as Attorney-General. She had also agreed to the nomination of a new Privy Councillor: Sir Robert Cecil. The nominations were to come into effect within days. The news had galvanised the Court. So sudden and complete was the Cecil victory that, wrote Standen, 'all stand gasping for it with open mouth', including 'the old maid and the son', a mocking cipher for the Cecils.

Essex's long efforts on behalf of Francis Bacon had come to naught, and his harsh agitations against the Cecils had only pushed the Queen to confirm their supremacy. As if in confirmation of Essex's exclusion from power, Burghley imposed strict security around the Queen's person. Access to the royal person was forbidden to all but her 'ladies of nearest attendance' and four advisers, two of whom were Burghley and Sir Robert Cecil. The reason for the clampdown was unclear, and rumour filled the gap. It was whispered that a Spanish 'pensioner' lurked undetected in the Court. Essex's followers aped their master in their determination to interpret everything through the distorting prism of his Lopez obsession. 'It appeareth all are not discovered,' reported Anthony Standen. As with Essex's suspicion of Lopez, they were right, but they did not know why. A fanatical concentration upon the Doctor had blinkered them to the broader intelligence picture.

In late January and early February, Sir Robert Cecil's inquisitorial efforts were no less rigorous than Essex's. Apart from examining Lopez, Cecil also oversaw a second series of enquiries, without Essex's knowledge. Both Essex and the Cecils knew that there was another aspect to the Lopez affair, a hinterland of unknown depth like the bulk of an iceberg. It was Sir Robert Cecil's detection of this aspect that had caused Burghley's sudden clampdown at Court. While Essex stormed and schemed, Sir Robert Cecil gradually mapped out Lopez's secret.

The trail led back to that compulsive beater of paths through the information jungle, Emanuel Luis Tinoco. In mid-January, after arriving in England on a passport issued secretly by Lord Burghley, Tinoco had composed his 'Advertisements to be made known to Her Majesty for the safeguard of her person'. Among the items was his warning that the Count of Fuentes was about to send an assassin into England. The real target was Antonio Perez, but to avoid incriminating himself, Tinoco had named the Queen as the target.

Following Tinoco's 'advertisment', in late January, the Irish assassin Patrick Collen and his sidekick John Annias had been intercepted by the Cecils as they entered England. Over a week of preliminary interrogations by Sir Robert Cecil and Lord Admiral Howard, the details of the assassination plot emerged. The Count of Fuentes had given John Annias a jewel, which he was to have presented to the Earl of Essex in order 'to have become his man'. This would have allowed Annias and Collen access to Antonio Perez. At a suitable moment, Patrick Collen was to have shot Antonio Perez with a pistol, killing with one bullet the prospect of the anti-Spanish alliance that Perez was hawking in London and Paris.

This discovery should have been a triumph for the Cecils: it was just the kind of intelligence success that Essex had failed to find. Instead, the further Sir Robert Cecil dug into the Lopez affair and the Collen plot, the more he saw that they were related, as he unearthed a tangle of subterranean roots between the two plots.

Like Doctor Lopez's initiatives for peace and a Portuguese settlement, the Collen plotters had passed through the Count of Fuentes's office in Brussels. The passport that Doctor Lopez was to have used to travel to Antwerp to collect his 50,000 crowns turned out to have been arranged by Patrick Collen's jewel-bearing assistant John Annias. A third link came on 5 February. Robert Draper, the Essex courier who had been duped by Antonio Perez into carrying mails to Doctor Lopez, had hidden this embarrassing episode for the previous nine months. The hue and cry following Lopez's arrest had confirmed Draper's worst fear: he had been a courier for the Queen's enemies. Draper did not want to be accused as a party to treason for having hidden evidence, so he confessed the story of his embarrassments at the inn in Ghent and the counting house in Calais to Justice Richard Young. Young told Sir Robert Cecil.

For the first time, one of Lopez's English clients saw the full lineaments of the Doctor's double life. Like Marlowe's Barabas, Lopez was loyal to no one but himself. While Lopez had been working for the Cecils, he had worked with the Spanish to kill Antonio Perez, the Queen's guest and Essex's friend. Therefore, through the person of Doctor Lopez, into whose defence they had so publicly leapt, the Cecils were linked to the murder plot against Perez. Sir Robert Cecil had to act at once, to find out exactly how far the Cecils were compromised. The truth about Doctor Lopez that he had winkled out so diligently threatened to destroy him and his father.

With Robert Draper's confession in front of him, Cecil drew up a list of questions for Patrick Collen and John Annias. Hurriedly he rigged together an impromptu commission of Cecil loyalists for a cross-examination. Within hours, Collen and Annias were brought before Sir Robert Cecil, Solicitor-General Sir Edward Coke, Justice Young and William Wade, Clerk of the Privy Council and specialist Catholic hunter. The first question on Cecil's list was whether John Annias knew Emanuel Luis Tinoco.

Annias cracked before the judicial battery. The first words he said turned Sir Robert Cecil's bad day into a nightmare. 'I was late acquainted with a Portugal. I think his name was Manuel Luis. I know him not very well.' Annias went on to name Tinoco as having organised the Perez assassination plot on behalf on the Count of Fuentes.

For Sir Robert Cecil, Annias's confession, and its explicit naming of Tinoco, were harbingers of catastrophe. Through Doctor Lopez, the Cecils had bought intelligence from Tinoco about Antonio Perez. In mid-January, the Cecils had smuggled Tinoco into England on a passport bearing Lord Burghley's signature. They had coveted him, had isolated him from the Earl of Essex, and had collaborated with him in preparing their counter-attack against the Earl. Even as Annias spoke these words, Tinoco was publicly identifiable as Cecil property, held in the gatehouse at Westminster so that only they could use him. After tying themselves to Tinoco, the Cecils now

Sir Robert Cecil's notes for the interrogation of John Annias, 5 February 1594, annotated by Lord Admiral Howard. Cecil asks, 'Patrick Collen was come into England to do a great service, which was to kill a Spaniard in England. Who was this Spaniard?' To which Howard adds, 'By what means should the Spaniard by killed? Do you know a Portingall called Emanuel Luis [Tinoco]?'

discovered that their cherished implement of revenge upon Essex was, like their Doctor Lopez, embedded in the plot to murder Antonio Perez. If this became public knowledge, it would be impossible to disentangle the Cecils' plot to monitor Perez from the Spanish plot to kill him. The two strands were plaited together, because they had been carried out by the same operatives: Lopez and Tinoco.

The twin tracks of Lopez's and Tinoco's double dealings led straight to Lord Burghley and Sir Robert Cecil. There was written proof: one of the letters from Philip II's adviser Don Cristovão da Moura had referred to Burghley by his title of Lord Treasurer. The agents that Doctor Lopez had controlled had run out of control. Like the Turkish knights at Barabas's banquet, Lord Burghley and Sir Robert Cecil had allowed themselves to be flattered and cajoled by Doctor Lopez, while all the time their chairs rested on a false floor. Worse, the Cecils had responded to the Earl of Essex's assault on their political influence by linking arms with first Doctor Lopez and then Tinoco, and had used the two intelligencers to retaliate against Essex. By doing so, they had unwittingly fulfilled Essex's intemperate, paranoid prophecy.

Essex had tried to frame Doctor Lopez as a secret negotiator with Spain, and the Cecils as the patrons of his treason. When that had failed, Essex had made unfounded, hysterical allegations of a murder plot. Yet all the time Doctor Lopez really had been a Spanish agent and the Cecils had protected him. They had encouraged the Queen to receive Lopez in private audiences. For months, Lord Burghley had supported Lopez's protestations of innocence. Little more than a week earlier, Sir Robert Cecil had sneaked behind Essex's back to tell the Queen that Lopez was completely innocent. When the Cecils had given Lopez their unambiguous support, they had vouched for a traitor and a party to murder.

Before Sir Robert Cecil's interrogation of John Annias, Doctor Lopez had been too valuable to the Cecils for him to be surrendered to the Earl of Essex. Now that Cecil had finally prised the lid off the seething corruption of Portingall matters, the Doctor was too dangerous to keep. If the Earl of Essex heard any report of these examinations, the Cecils were finished. The Earl had assembled a template for a treason trial and Sir Robert Cecil held the evidence that would fit Essex's template as snugly as a trapdoor fitted the floor of Barabas's minstrel gallery. When the lever was pulled, somebody would have to fall into the cauldron. Over the next two days the Cecils devised a three-step plan to exculpate themselves.

The first step was to divert the inquiry away from Antonio Perez and the French embassy. Although John Annias and Patrick Collen had provided detailed and matching accounts that the Count of Fuentes had hired them to kill Antonio Perez, they were pressured to change their story. They were forced to 'confess' that when they had referred to 'the Spaniard', they had meant 'the Queen'. This was politically acute. To invoke the Queen's safety gave almost unlimited licence to the inquisitors. Essex had used this tactic against Lopez. Sir Robert Cecil would use it to co-opt Essex's attack. As soon as satisfactory confessions had been extracted from Collen and Annias, preparations were made for their trial.

The second step for the Cecils was to sever all contact with Doctor Lopez. If the Cecils aligned themselves with Lopez, they would fall through the trapdoor with him. This would be problematic. If they dropped Lopez, they removed his incentive to stay silent and abandoned him to the Earl of Essex. If Essex had a free hand against Lopez and Ferreira da Gama, the prisoners might become a fount of unwanted confessions; if Lopez told Essex anything approaching the truth, the Cecils would be ruined. A treason inquiry always

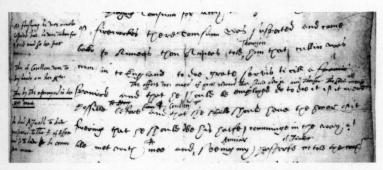

The cover-up begins: Lord Howard annotates a confession about 'killing a Spaniard' with 'This, by "the Spaniard", is Her Majesty meant.'

produced evidence, and often by the threat or use of torture. Therefore, while the Cecils had to drop Lopez, they could not drop their role in the inquiry.

This led to the third step. To control the outcome, they would have to control the interrogations. On the morning of 8 February, William Wade, Clerk of the Privy Council, took over the investigation into Doctor Lopez.

15

The Spanish Prisoner

'My deeds upon my head!'
Shylock in *The Merchant of Venice*

William Wade was a hothoused secretarial bloom. His father Armagil Wade had been Clerk of the Privy Council at the time of Elizabeth's accession, when Lord Burghley was still Sir William Cecil. William Wade had been planted in the soil of Cecil patronage and raised to inherit this scribal post. Strict, diligent and above all loyal to the Cecils, he was habituated to the procedural prose of legal form, and skilful at its subversion in the service of the State and the Cecils. In the early 1580s, Wade had been a regular diplomatic emissary for Lord Burghley, until he was badly beaten up on a French road under suspicion of spying. After that, Burghley had kept him in England and used him as a detective in the most sensitive cases. In 1594 he was forty-eight, a humourless Puritan with three decades' experience at carrying out Lord Burghley's dirty work.

In 1586, Wade had assisted in the entrapment of Mary, Queen of Scots by pillaging her papers and then rearranging them so carefully that his piracy went undetected. If there was a Catholic to be interrogated or a Jesuit to be tormented, Wade was the specialist. His detestation of Catholics exceeded patriotism, and his methods were remorseless. He was to be involved – or incriminated – in the detection of all the major treason conspiracies of the late Elizabethan and early Jacobean years. 'That villain Wade' was the opinion of one of his victims, Lord Cobham, who claimed that Wade had tricked him into signing a blank sheet of paper, and then forged his confession. When Wade was given the job of dealing with Lopez, his finest and basest hour lay eleven years away. In 1605, Sir Robert Cecil would use Wade to anatomise the Gunpowder Plot. Wade would produce his body of evidence with fanatical enthusiasm, leaving visible traces of torture, and fainter traces of forgery. In 1608, he would erect in the Tower a monument to his life as detective of conscience, quoting in Hebrew from the Book of Job, 'He discovereth deep things out of darkness, and bringeth out to light the shadow of death.'

William Wade, Clerk of the Privy Council.

In a discussion on religious policy, Wade's late father Armagil had once advised Elizabeth with a metaphor from water torture: 'Glasses with small necks, if you pour into them any liquor suddenly or violently, will not be so filled, but refuse to receive the same that you would pour into them. Howbeit, if you instill water into them by little and little, they are soon replenished.' When the Cecils sent William Wade into the investigation, they set him the opposite task. He was to stopper the overflowing, unstable glass of the Lopez affair, to allow a few, controlled drops of information to drip on to the pages of the narrative he would assemble, damming and channelling them to his ends.

Wade's task was simple: to disconnect the Cecils from the scandal, and to frame Lopez. He was to take Essex's claim that Lopez was a poisoner, and stitch it together with the Cecils' order that he frame Lopez as a traitor. This would limit the damage that both Lopez and Essex could cause to the Cecils: if Lopez was condemned as a traitor, then the force of Essex's attack on the Cecils would divert on to the Doctor. Wade's conclusion was already clear: the merciful hand of Protestant divinity had interceded to save the Queen's life, thwarting the Jew Lopez and his Catholic co-plotters. Therefore, his task was to work backwards, from end to means, and to construct a narrative retrospectively. He would cut clear paths through the dense under-brush of the case, expunging entirely any knotty roots that might entangle the Cecils, so that the very noticeable figure of Doctor Lopez would be left standing alone on a bleak heath of treason.

As soon as Wade had finished assisting Sir Robert Cecil in extracting confessions from Patrick Collen and John Annias, he fell to severing the Cecils from the Lopez plotters, and fitting Lopez's neck for the noose. Wade began with Tinoco, the only prisoner against whom he had conclusive evidence. Collen and Annias had named Tinoco as their collaborator and controller in the plot to kill Antonio Perez. So Wade transferred Tinoco from the gatehouse at Westminster to the Counter prison, a few doors along from Wade's home in Wood Street. In preparation for his interview, the prisoner was 'pinched': denied all food and drink, apart from the moisture on the damp roof of his cell.

As Wade set to work on him, Tinoco had little room for manoeuvre. An experienced intelligencer, he knew that his only hope was to collaborate, and sign whatever was placed before him in the hope that his life might be spared. Denouncing Lopez was Tinoco's last chance.

On Friday 8 February, Wade emerged from the Counter bearing a seven-line note. Its sixty-eight words were a complete revision of Tinoco's original story, and completely at odds with his previous confessions, as well as those of Ferreira da Gama and Doctor Lopez. After his 'pinched' enlightenment by Wade, Tinoco now claimed that:

> The letter which I left written in the hands of Stephen Ferreira da Gama was altogether directed by Manuel d'Andrada. And as I understand, under 'the peace' was understood 'the death of the Queen's Majesty'. And 'the letter which was required of the Lord Treasurer' was meant to have [been] a letter from the said Doctor wherein he should assure them that he stood firm in his promise.
>
> Emanuel Luis Tinoco.

This text is the only extant copy, kept in the Public Record Office. It is in English, not Portuguese, and there is no Portuguese original

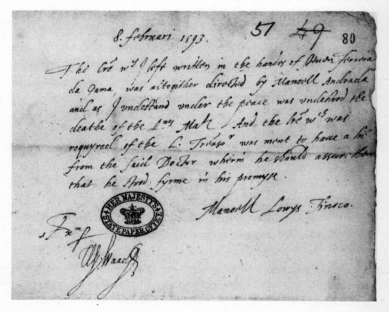

Tinoco's 'clarification' accuses Lopez: a copy in Wade's handwriting, 8 February 1594.

with which it might be compared. Tinoco's name is at the bottom of the confession, but the note is written and signed by William Wade. The letter to which Tinoco had referred was among those he had delivered to St Katharine Creechurch on his flying visit to London at the end of August 1593. Despite its centrality to the case – or perhaps because of its centrality – it does not survive.

According to Wade's and Tinoco's new interpretation of the evidence, the words 'peace' and 'Lord Treasurer' were ciphers. Just as the Collen plotters had used the words 'the Spaniard' not in reference to Antonio Perez, but as a cipher for 'the Queen of England', so Doctor Lopez and the Count of Fuentes had used the words 'the peace' and 'the Lord Treasurer' as ciphers for 'the death of the Queen' and 'Lopez'.

Ironically, Lopez's correspondence was already littered with obvious ciphers, such as the references to 'Musk and Amber', 'merchandise' and 'pearls and diamonds'. The Wade interpretation held that this cipher system coexisted with a second set of ciphers. This detached the correspondence from reality and turned every word into a cipher for something else. The meaning of the ciphers became subject to Wade's whim. This was the object of his exercise, to break down fact and reassemble it in safer, more pleasing shapes. This was bizarre and illogical from any perspective other than those of Wade, the Cecils and Tinoco, but viewed from Burghley House or a cell in the Counter, it was a sensible act of survival. Wade returned to his house on Wood Street, just along from Lopez's old home, and pondered how best to interrogate his old neighbour when they met the next morning.

In the Tower, Roderigo Lopez had been waiting to see what would happen next. When Lopez's cell door opened to reveal William Wade, he knew he had to be careful. Lopez and Wade had known each other for over a decade, if not longer, with mixed results. In 1581, Wade had gone to Paris with letters from Lopez to Don Antonio. When Wade had met Antonio he had been publicly derided by Antonio's courtiers, and his letters had been ignored because of Lopez's low standing among Antonio's Paris adherents. If this had affected Wade's estimation of

Lopez, it may have been counterbalanced by their shared shadowy service to the Cecils. When Lopez saw his inquisitor, he knew that the Cecils still steered the inquiry. He also knew that if they had entrusted the tiller to Wade, they had a definite course in mind. So Wade could not be trusted. The Doctor did not know where Wade's course might lead, so he had to set his own, one which ran away from Antonio Perez.

Lopez decided to use the truth to mask his lie. He confirmed everything to which he had confessed at Essex House. Yes, he admitted to Wade, he had exchanged mails with the Spanish via Ferreira da Gama and discussed his payment, but he had done so only 'to abuse' Philip II of his money. He added a further truth, which he hoped would satisfy Wade. 'I did offer, if the King of Spain did mislike the remaining of the King Don Antonio here in the realm, that I would find the means that he would be sent out of the realm.'

Wade was aware that Lopez's loquacity was a false lead and he already knew the path he wished to follow. He probed Lopez about Antonio Perez.

At the mention of that name, Lopez realised that all his efforts to conceal the Perez plot had been fruitless. Someone had confessed. 'For Antonio Perez, I know nothing,' the Doctor blustered.

Wade knew that Lopez was hiding something, but he did not persist. His immediate priority was to sound out the precise depths of the plot to kill Antonio Perez. Any weak points that he detected now could be pressured later, when the Cecils had been safely disconnected from the plot, and the target had been changed from Perez to the Queen. Wade passed along the line to his next suspect. The Doctor could wait.

Back at the Counter in Wood Street, Wade worked 'very diligently' on Francis Caldera, the Spanish spy in the French embassy. Caldera's first allegation was that Lopez was a Jew; an accusation of heresy, not treason. This was not what Wade wanted. It took Wade several examinations to draw out the full story from Caldera and to shape it to his purpose.

The common element between the Lopez and Collen plots had been their shared interest in Antonio Perez. Lopez had spied on

Perez for the Cecils, and Collen had planned to kill Perez for the Spanish. Although their intentions had differed, the two plots had overlapped: Lopez, Tinoco, Ferreira da Gama and Francis Caldera had all served both the Cecils and the Count of Fuentes. As Sir Robert Cecil had just discovered to his belated horror, this meant that Doctor Lopez's double game had connected the Cecils with the assassin Patrick Collen. Wade produced a narrative which made Lopez the instigator of the French embassy plot, and whitewashed any connection between Caldera and the Cecils.

Originally, Caldera's intelligence contact with Tinoco had pre-dated any link between Caldera and Doctor Lopez or Ferreira da Gama. Yet in the new Wade account, Caldera had only become a Spanish agent when he had been blackmailed by Ferreira da Gama's warning that Lopez 'had his foot upon his throat'. Wade's account ascribed the cause of Caldera's treachery to Lopez and Ferreira, not the Count of Fuentes and Tinoco.

In the summer of 1593, after Lopez and Ferreira had muscled into the Caldera–Tinoco connection in the French embassy, Caldera's intelligence had passed to Ferreira and then divided into two tracks. One had led via Tinoco to the Count of Fuentes at Brussels. The other had led via Lopez to Lord Burghley. Yet Wade now covered this second track entirely. No mention was made of Vincent Fonseca, the translator supplied by Lopez so that Lord Burghley might have speedy translations of Antonio Perez's corre-spondence. Instead, Wade limited Caldera's confession to 'Tinoco was the ledger to make and send away the dispatches'. Only one track had led from Ferreira da Gama, the track leading to Brussels.

Wade had worked from end to means, reversing the natural order. The seven-line confession that he had forced from Tinoco had supplied Lopez's motive: to kill the Queen. The examination of Caldera had provided the means: through Tinoco, Lopez had access to Patrick Collen and his pistol. And as it had already been estab-lished, Collen's target was not Antonio Perez, but the Queen. Wade had set up Lopez as the fall guy. With his narrative established, all that Wade needed now was the evidence.

* * *

While Wade bullied his prisoners, the Essex camp were left in perplexity. For months the Cecils had resisted Essex's assault on Lopez, but now it appeared that they had suddenly caved in. Yet Essex and his intelligencers knew this appearance was deceptive. The Cecils had given the impression that they agreed with Essex's charge, but this was a smokescreen. With the Queen isolated by Lord Burghley's security clampdown, the Cecils had deployed William Wade, whom Essex's men knew to be 'especially in credit' with the Cecils, and 'trusted in these services of weight'. Wade's findings would match his masters' will. It was clear that the Cecils had only concurred with Essex's claims in order to co-opt them and frustrate the strategy behind them. To find out what Wade was up to, Anthony Bacon sent Nicholas Faunt to pay a personal visit to Wade.

Like Wade, Faunt was a veteran. He and Lopez had first crossed paths in the Paris embassy in 1572. They had both worked for Sir Francis Walsingham, and had both gravitated into the Earl of Essex's pay after Walsingham's death, Faunt with rather more sincerity. On the night of 10 February, Faunt found William Wade at home in Wood Street, warming himself after a day in the damp cells. Wade knew what Faunt wanted, but he made him wait. At first their talk rested on nothing more significant than the relative size of Wade's kidney stones versus Anthony Bacon's. 'I find it very good against the growing of the stone to drink every morning a good draught of beer that is not over strong nor too stale,' Wade recommended. Drinking beer at breakfast would not have ameliorated a condition made worse by dehydration, although the anaesthetic effect may have been welcome.

After politely enduring a guided tour of Wade's gravel-strewn kidneys, Faunt turned to the real reason for his visit: their 'common friend' Anthony Bacon wanted 'some account of the situation of things'.

Wade obliged at once and laid a false trail for Faunt. 'The subject is yet a secret to most of the greatest men,' he teased, but he offered to tell Faunt everything. 'I have discovered a most dangerous and desperate practise, concerted with great art, and coming directly from the King of Spain, the Count of Fuentes having been for a long time a principal instrument of it.'

Slowly, Wade fed Faunt each morsel of the Cecil version. The Spanish had sent Patrick Collen to kill Antonio Perez but, Wade titillated Faunt, 'another circumstance reached farther'. 'One of the prisoners apprehended hath twice been near Her Majesty as she went to the chapel,' he confided, referring to Collen.

Wade told Faunt that Doctor Lopez had provided 'assistance' in these plots and had already confessed to corresponding with the Spanish. 'To be short,' Wade promised, 'this will prove a most resolute attempt, and most deeply advised of in the Court of Spain, if Lopez be well sifted, who is a most vile person, and void of all shame in common humanity.'

In case Essex doubted these words from a Cecil loyalist, Wade assured Faunt that he had been professionally impressed by Essex's 'great sufficiency, both in the searching out of this secret plot, and in all other public services'. 'He is the hope of our age!' Wade announced improbably. 'I am opposed to all that shall not honour his Lordship!'

Leaving Wade to his aching kidneys, Faunt hurried off into the night and wrote to Anthony Bacon. The news brought joy in the Essex camp. Everything that Essex had claimed in his outburst of 25 January had turned out to be true. There really had been a plot against the Queen's life, Doctor Lopez really had been involved, and Wade's inquiry had vindicated the Earl's histrionic behaviour. The Lopez case might yet turn into an Essex victory. This news arrived almost simultaneously with another hopeful report regarding the Earl's other obsession, Francis Bacon's suit for the attorney-generalship.

The legal term had ended in the afternoon before Wade's fireside confessional to Nicholas Faunt. As the Queen had not yet confirmed Sir Edward Coke as her Attorney-General, any announcement would be delayed for weeks. In the dying moments of the term, Francis Bacon had won a case before the Queen's Bench. It had been a chance to prove his worth, 'and a choke pear to praters that say he never yet entered into a place of battle'. Although Bacon's showy performance had made him more memorable than likeable, his victory had ended the term on a hopeful note. With Doctor Lopez ruined and the Attorneyship still vacant, the pendulum of factional favour might yet swing back for the Earl of Essex. Henry Gosnold, one of the Bacon brothers' waggish Gray's Inn friends, wrapped up the term with a joke as desperate as the faded hope on which it punned. 'If it please Her Majesty to add deeds, the Bacon may be too hard for the Cook.'

The Cecils had no intention of ceding the field to Essex. William Wade had confided in Faunt and eulogised Essex as 'the hope of our age' only to keep Essex out of the inquiry. Doctor Lopez would be found guilty, just as Essex desired, but the Cecils would ensure that Essex's victory would be as hollow as one of Henry Gosnold's jokes.

William Wade had constructed Doctor Lopez's motive: to kill the Queen for Spanish gold. By rewriting Patrick Collen's mission to kill Antonio Perez as a plot against the Queen, Wade had constructed the method. Now he needed to find the murder weapon.

Wade used the tactic known to torturers and game theorists as the 'Spanish Prisoner'. In this scenario, prisoners are held in isolation and interrogated in turn. The interrogator presents the second prisoner with the purported testimony of his fellow suspect, who has accused the prisoner of some further offence. The second prisoner cannot know if the interrogator is lying in order to entrap him, or whether he has been betrayed by his fellow suspect. If he denies the charge, the interrogator can return to the first prisoner and use the same technique to collect more information. If he confesses to the charge, he merely makes the interrogation of the first prisoner easier. The interrogator works between the two cells, chipping at the mutual trust between the prisoners. As the confessions and accusations pile up, each prisoner tries to save himself by denouncing the other. Eventually, a Spanish Prisoner has no option but to condemn himself.

Wade began with Ferreira da Gama, psychologically the weakest of the three Spanish Prisoners. Ferreira had been imprisoned for longest, he had less experience than Tinoco or Lopez and, from the beginning, they had both marked him as the scapegoat if everything went wrong. Ferreira was the one who had written and signed the treasonable correspondence with Brussels and Madrid.

To crack Ferreira da Gama, Wade produced Pedro Ferrera, the corrupt jailer from Eton. Pedro offered this inventive account of how Ferriera da Gama had confided in him during his imprisonment at Eton: 'Ferreira and Doctor Lopez wrote into Spain, and made offer to give to the Queen a syrup,' parroted Pedro.

By his own word, Pedro the jailer had been sitting on this vital information for over three months. He had known that Doctor Lopez was a potential assassin, but had told nobody, even while the Doctor continued to minister to the Queen. To keep secret a threat to the Queen's life was treason. Yet Pedro Ferrera was never prosecuted. He produced the magic word 'syrup', and disappeared without leaving its recipe. Like Gomez d'Avila, or the messenger in a play, Pedro delivered a few functional lines to drive forward the narrative, then vanished.

Ferreira da Gama collapsed. Coaxed by Wade, he provided a confession to match Pedro's accusation.

He doth believe that if the King had sent him money, that the Doctor had poisoned the Queen, and further sayeth that the Doctor said to him every day that he was ready to do the service, but that he had no answer from thence.

He remembreth that he said to Peter Ferrera that if the King of Spain would sent the money, without doubt Doctor Lopez would poison the Queen.

He sayeth that Manuel Andrada, about a month before he went out of England, did declare unto him that if the King of Spain would, that Doctor Lopez would poison the Queen of England, and the King Don Antonio also.

This speech, used by Andrada, Estevan Ferreira da Gama afterwards did communicate to Doctor Lopez near unto the door of his garden, whereunto the Doctor answered, 'As for the King, he shall die with the first sickness that shall happen to him; but for the Queen, we have no answer as yet from the other side.'

*Signatures of Ferreira and his interrogators at the end of his confession,
18 February 1594: Ferreira da Gama, Peter Bales the cryptologist, the Earl of Essex,
Thomas Wilkes, and William Wade.*

Wade tested Ferreira's confession on the Doctor, but Lopez denied
everything and would not play the Spanish Prisoner. So Wade went
back to Ferreira da Gama and squeezed him for more 'evidence'.

A believer in the false promises of his inquisitor, Ferreira hoped
that his last confession had saved him. Instead, it had caused Wade
to press him further. As much as Ferreira tried to buck the charges,
Wade kept his grip. At one point Ferreira went down on his knees
before Essex, offering his 'hand and promise' in return for the Earl's
protection. Essex spurned the genuflector 'like an experienced
general' and would not 'cove or condition with him at all'. For four
days Wade relentlessly bullied and tormented Ferreira, pressing him
'like a resty jade, loath to go forward but as he was spurred', until
Ferreira was completely broken, willing to say anything or sign
anything. Wade put the words in Ferreira's mouth, and Ferreira let
them fall into the chill air of the interrogation cell.

'The Doctor said, if he might have 50,000 crowns given him, he
was content, and would poison the Queen of England,' Ferreira said.
Pressed, he went further: 'The Doctor said unto me very often that
he wondered that the money and the answer came not. And that he
was ready, if the answer and the money come, to poison the Queen.
And that he would go and live in Constantinople.' Wade extracted
another useful admission: 'No Englishman, nor anybody else, knew
of the letters but the Doctor and I.'

Ferreira was left to his straw pallet, and the inquisition moved on

to Tinoco, emaciated and thirsty after days of starvation. Tinoco
had willingly endorsed Ferreira's earlier claim that Lopez was a
Spanish agent, but he balked at the new charge of regicide. Plotting
to assassinate the Queen of England was not a charge to be wriggled out of with vague promises of 'service'. Tinoco was stronger
and more devious than Ferreira da Gama. He had used Ferreira as
a proxy, and he had the further defensive advantage that most of
his dealings had been in Brussels and Calais, where there were no
witnesses. When Wade and Essex presented Tinoco with the spectacle of a broken, blabbering Ferreira da Gama, Tinoco refused to
endorse a single word. So they threatened him with torture.

'There is no law to warrant torture in this land,' boasted Sir
Edward Coke that year, comparing English liberty to the tyranny of
Spain. It was true that torture had been outlawed since Magna Carta,
but the practice was integral to Elizabethan treason inquiries and
was used routinely against Catholic suspects. There were two varieties: the manacles and the rack.

There was only one rack in England, in the Tower of London.
It was 'much spoken of' by Londoners, who considered it 'odious',
as though unsporting. The rack was an oak frame not unlike a bed.
The prisoner was laid on top, with his wrists and ankles roped to
rollers at each end. The rollers were turned by degrees as he was
exhorted to confess. In Burghley's investigation of the Duke of
Norfolk in 1572, 'rackmaster' Thomas Norton claimed to have
stretched Alexander Bryant, one of Norfolk's servants, 'one good
foot longer than ever God made him'. Even a mild racking caused
dislocation and permanent damage. The mere sight of the apparatus was often enough to induce florid confession. 'Ay, but I fear
you speak upon the rack, where men enforced do speak any thing,'
Portia tells Bassanio in *The Merchant of Venice*.

The manacles were considered a milder torture. The suspect was
suspended by the wrists against a wall with adjustable manacles that
could be tightened over time. A wooden support was beneath his
feet. This was taken away for extended periods, so that the full body
weight pulled at the manacles, causing cramp, rupture and dislocation. An alternative form of manacling was constriction, chaining

the wrists and neck to the ankles in a metal brace; this doubled the body in two and caused agonising muscle cramps. Either method could result in permanent disability. 'It will be as though he were dancing a trick or figure,' promised Richard Topcliffe MP, when he manacled the Jesuit Edward Campion.

Exhausted, hungry and thirsty, Tinoco was 'brought to the manacles'. The torments were common knowledge, especially in Tinoco's circles. He preferred the alternative. Turning to Wade, he announced he had changed his mind.

'When Luis saw we were in good earnest, he offered to confess,' noted a satisfied Wade.

Tinoco matched Ferreira word for word. The two were now so compromised that 'they did contend who should most readily and voluntarily confess their most uttermost knowledge'. Anything they could remember, and anything they were asked, was thrown up for Wade's dissection. Their stories matched so well because they were mostly true: the meetings, conversations, courier runs, proposals and assignations they described had all taken place. Only one element was added, and that cast a different light on everything, like a flaw in the gemstone: for 'peace', read 'poison'.

'This business was like a round circle,' Wade wrote, 'and when anything was gotten of them, the rest were presently dealt withall upon these points, and did sometimes confess the same, sometimes enlarge and give more matters to work upon.'

Wade moved between the cells with his papers and his clerk until he had assembled a watertight narrative, a web of confessions proving that Doctor Lopez was a long-time traitor. Any hint of official sponsorship by Essex or the Cecils was avoided. Wade was ready for his third Spanish Prisoner.

On the morning of Monday 25 February 1594, Doctor Lopez was brought up from his cell. If his interrogation was anything like Tinoco's, he would have been 'brought to the manacles' beforehand. The Doctor would have been confronted with the instruments of that other, informally trained anatomist, the torturer. He knew what precise agonies, what extremities of rupture and cramp, could be inflicted upon the bones of a septuagenarian whose muscles were stiffened by a month of confinement in the rheumatic depths of the Tower.

Waiting for him were Lord Burghley, Sir Robert Cecil, the Earl of Essex and the Cecil ally Charles, Lord Admiral Howard. With 'very grave and mild persuasion' they warned him not to aggravate his 'foul offences' with 'impudent and fruitless denials'. In unconscious revelation of the workings of a treason inquiry, whose legal process ran back to front, they told Lopez that his co-conspirators had already 'condemned and accused' themselves. The 'whole course of his treason' had already been revealed by Ferreira and Tinoco. He could save himself a great deal of pain, and perhaps some punishment too, if he confessed.

Lopez fell to his knees on the stone floor. Covering his eyes with his hands, he raised his face to the invisible heavens beyond the chamber, beyond the Tower, beyond the City, and swore to God that he had commissioned no such treachery.

The interrogators watched his face as the confessions of Ferreira da Gama and Tinoco were read out to the 'faithless renegade' before them. Lopez could only beg for pity as he heard that he was a poisoner, a spy and a regicide. These were not his words, not his acts. 'I cannot tell what to say,' he said, 'unless I might, being drunk, use such speeches.'

'You were not overshot, but that you could, when you came to yourself, remember what had passed in a matter of that quality.'

'But I never meant any such thing.'

He had meant that only a helpless inebriate would have spoken of such a crime, and not that he might have forgotten saying it because he was drunk.

'That is not the question,' they insisted, 'but whether you had any speech or conference of any such matter. Whether Ferreira did write in such sort, to make that offer.'

Lopez saw he was trapped. His patrons had allied against him. The Cecils and Essex were working in open concert, and were determined that he should confess. The more Lopez told the truth about his conspiracy with Ferreira, the more he would confirm the poisoning allegation. He tried to step between the two points, but fell: 'Ferreira might write so, and I did let him write what he list.'

What Ferreira had written, Lopez had allowed him to write. This was 'the matter', and its 'quality' had already been proven. Like the others, Lopez had been led to condemn himself out of his own mouth. Delicately, the inquisitors suggested that he 'discharge his conscience', and Lopez, trapped and knowing it, allowed Wade to lead him through the charade. Lopez's confession was a mirror of Ferreira's, and he accused Ferreira in the same terms as Ferreira had accused him. The last act of the Spanish Prisoner. 'I never meant to do it, but Ferreira meant verily her Majesty should have been destroyed with poison,' the Doctor dictated. 'I told Ferreira that I would minister the poison in a syrup.' He had edged to the lip of the pit, but then sprang back like a dancer: 'Which I said because I knew Her Majesty never doth use to take any syrup.'

Lopez had detected the unforeseen flaw in the testimonies, the single mis-stitch in the traitor's garment: the method of poisoning. The Queen was always wary of poison and she never took medicine in the dilute form, because the thick, sugary liquid of a syrup might hide the bitter taste of toxins. When Wade had assembled the confessions of Pedro the jailer, Ferreira da Gama and Tinoco, he could not have known this. It was the Queen's last defence against her enemies, pragmatic and superstitious. The fewer of her intimates who knew about it, the more effective it would be. Wade was only the Clerk of her Council, a glorified secretary, but Lopez was her body physician, one of the trusted few.

Lopez gave the prosecutors their confession, while simultaneously sidestepping their charge. Glibly, he admitted his alleged speech with Ferreira da Gama about a 'syrup', but used the story against its inventor. Yes, he said, he had known that Ferreira had written to Spain with an offer to assassinate the Queen. Of course the King of Spain was aware of this: who else was to provide the payment? And yes, there was a promise of a reward, which had now assumed the glamorous shape of 'fifty thousand crowns in Rubies and Diamonds'. But all this had been a trick, a projection predicated upon a syrup which he had known would never have reached the Queen's lips. 'I first did break this matter to Andrada,' he explained, 'to abuse the King of Spain. When the money was come, I meant to bring it to Her Majesty, and to have told her that the King of Spain had sent me to poison Her Majesty.'

Lopez hoped that when the Queen heard the 'evidence' against him, she would know that the syrup was a logical impossibility and that therefore he was innocent. The Doctor had used the confession of his guilt as the evidence of his innocence. Of course, this was a highly dangerous strategy, because he had confessed to something he had not done. If his hidden message to the Queen did not have the desired effect of inspiring a royal intervention, he would be executed like a traitor, hung, drawn and quartered for the mob. But he had no choice. In this small room in the Tower, Lopez was oppressed by the full weight of the 'honour and justice of the State'. With or without torture, his confession was assured. If he was to be saved, it would not be by law, as the same 'justice of the State' was the weapon now aimed at him. Innocent or not, he could only be saved by the Queen, the final judge. She had told him, 'For such things as you have revealed, you should suffer no loss.' She never took medicine in a syrup. If she confirmed this, she proved Lopez's innocence. Beneath a codicil that his confession contained 'the very truth', he signed himself, 'Roger Loppez'.

Unaware of Lopez's feint, Wade thought his work was complete. He had 'discovered deep things out of darkness, and brought out to light the shadow of death'. Once Lopez's signed confession had been obtained, the Cecils held a 'great consultation' at Burghley House. Afterwards, Wade again used Nicholas Faunt as a mouthpiece to pass their resolution to the Earl of Essex.

'Meeting with Mr Wade,' wrote Faunt, 'he telleth me that now all appeareth manifest, as well by the confessions of those here taken, as by the letters found of the other parties beyond seas. Whereby it appeareth that the practice hath continued long, and Lopez is no new Traitor.'

The Cecils were in 'exceeding great haste' to obtain a conviction. Although William Wade did not believe he could assemble the raw material of the Crown's case before the following weekend, the Cecils gave him seventy-two hours to complete the job. While Wade ploughed through his papers and passed the evidence to the prose-cutor, Solicitor-General Sir Edward Coke, the Cecils accelerated the legal process. The legal term would not begin for several weeks, so a Queen's Bench trial was impossible. Instead, they persuaded the Queen to order a Special Commission of 'Oyer and Terminer'. This was a medieval relic among trial processes: it minimised the defen-dant's right to speak and maximised the judges' discretion. It was perfect for sensitive cases where the Crown had weak evidence, such as treason trials based on forced confessions. The Cecils intended it to fulfil its traditional function as an exercise in foregone conclusion.

Lopez had confessed on Monday morning. On Tuesday, the fifteen judges who would form the Grand Jury received their summons, and a writ of habeas corpus was sent to Sir Michael Blount, Lord-Lieutenant of the Tower, ordering him to 'bring up the body of Lopez' for trial on Thursday morning. The terminology is revealing. Lopez had been reduced from a person to an object; a 'body' was to be tried, not a character. That night, Sir Robert Cecil and the Earl of Essex had a long conference; the enemies were now united in a common purpose. On Wednesday, the charges against Lopez were read to the jurors at the Guildhall. This being an Oyer and Terminer trial, the prisoner was not present at his indictment.

The case against Lopez was assembled so frantically that its pivot – the poisoned 'syrup' – remained undefined. Like the case itself, the vessel was filled, but speculatively, as a receptacle of the pros-ecution's imagination.

'In Lopez's folly, I see no point of treason to the Queen,' Lord Burghley had confided to Sir Robert Cecil four weeks earlier, 'but a readiness to make some gain to the hurt of Don Antonio.'

When Sir Robert Cecil had read the name of Lopez's real target on Lord Burghley's letter, he had scratched from the page the names of both Lopez and Don Antonio. Lord Burghley and Sir Robert Cecil both knew that Lopez had not plotted the Queen's death. Somebody else had been the Doctor's mark, and the Cecils both knew who it was. Lopez had a list of targets whose names could have been written on Burghley's letter. Any or all of Don Antonio, Antonio Perez, the Earl of Essex, or Philip II could have been tricked, flattered and

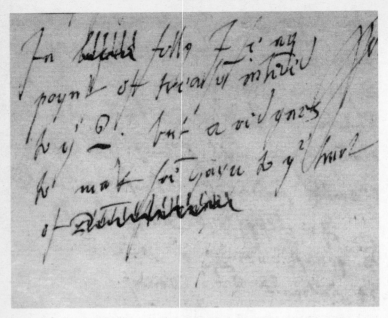

The Cecils cover their tracks: Lord Burghley's letter to Sir Robert Cecil, with the names of Lopez and his victim scratched out.

cajoled into standing on the trapdoor, but in the scandal of the Doctor's double life, the Cecils too had lined up as potential victims. They could not allow this to happen. Where the name of Lopez's intended victim had been written, Sir Robert Cecil left a block of blank ink like a trapdoor in the page.

16

The Queen's Pawn

DUKE: Go one and call the Jew into the court.
SALERIO: He is ready at the door – he comes, my Lord.

The Merchant of Venice

Just after dawn on Thursday 28 February, Doctor Lopez was taken from his cell. Sir Michael Blount and his guards manacled the Doctor to a cart and rolled him through the streets of the City to the Guildhall, like a bale of spices freshly unloaded on to the wharves by the Tower. For thirty-eight days, Lopez had been deprived of fresh air and daylight, divorced from the world in a bizarre mortal drama. He emerged from the dark tunnel of imprisonment into the waking City on a workaday Thursday, sailing through the streets like a ghostly mariner. On the way he stopped the traffic, Barabas made flesh, squinting in the grey half-light of a February morning. An object of fascination, a body in evidence.

They unloaded him by the west door. He could hear the noise of voices from inside, a dense crowd shouting, joking and laughing as it waited for him. Entering Guildhall, Lopez emerged from beneath the low ceiling of the musicians' gallery into an expanse of colour, light and air vaulted by the church-like roof. After the darkness of his cell, the weak February light was golden, pouring through the stained glass of the great Gothic window at his back, falling on pale flags bearing the escutcheons of the City livery companies, and catching intimations of medieval glory in the gold-embossed shields ranked along the cornice, the Arms of England, the Arms of the City, and the Arms of the twelve Great Livery Companies of London.

Reflected by Gothic vaults and rippled arches, the sunlight sought out dark crevices in the cracked gilding and paint of the stonework, suffused the dust suspended in its rays, and fell sixty feet through the rising smoke of candelabra to land on the luminous flagstones amid long flickering shadows.

Everything was now silent, expectant. He saw that Guildhall was crowded, packed with politicians and courtiers, merchants and poets, like a medieval tableau, and that everyone had turned to stare. The knot of dandy, proud Essex supporters saw their prey. Anthony Standen and Nicholas Faunt, lifelong intelligencers watching the conclusion of another mission, Faunt as if he had never known Lopez, had never worked with him for Walsingham; Francis Bacon, wishing he were one of the jury and still hoping for the attorney-generalship; Antonio Perez and Thomas Smith, the poisoner and his victim come to hear other tales of musk and amber; Essex's secretaries Henry Cuff and Henry Savile, ready to report to Anthony Bacon, the absent friend; and near them, the Earl of Southampton and his retainers, perhaps his tutor John Florio and his poet William Shakespeare, too. And somewhere in the flock of craning heads another poet, Thomas Nashe, the gossip correspondent of the great City come to secure his exclusive.

A long aisle stretched ahead of Lopez. At its end was a stage, and on it there waited his fellow actors in this brief, scripted perform-ance. Twenty-one of the most important political figures in England had assembled, their offices reflecting their patronage, and the supremacy of the Cecils. The prosecutor was Solicitor-General Sir Edward Coke, the Cecil candidate for the Attorney-Generalship. Sir John Puckering, Keeper of the Great Seal, through whose waxy imprint the Queen would attend the trial in image, was also a Cecil appointee. The trial would be dominated by the triumvirate of Lord Burghley, Sir Robert Cecil and their ally Charles Howard, Lord Admiral of England, the conqueror of the Armada, now the defender of England against a further Spanish conspiracy. The Earl of Essex was outnumbered and outgunned, backed only by his brother-in-law Robert, Lord Rich, and his supporter Lord Buckhurst. Tall, fair and exquisitely dressed, a courtier and champion, the Shepherd of

England's Arcadia waited for Doctor Lopez, the most errant of sheep. On the fringes of the jury William Wade, waiting to hear his confessions trip from the sharp tongue of Sir Edward Coke, and Cuthbert Buckle, the Mayor of London, the City's token juror, outnumbered and out of his depth.

Lopez began the most notorious walk in England: 150 paces in the steps of Archbishop Cranmer and Lady Jane Grey. After this walk, the accused were never acquitted, but always guilty. His only hope was a pardon after conviction.

The official record condenses the trial into five short sentences. It grants Lopez only two words, the reply to which is unanimous and capitalised in brutal emphasis.

> Lopez, being brought to the bar, is arraigned, and pleads Not Guilty. Venire awarded instanter. Verdict: GUILTY. Judgement: as is usual in cases of High Treason. Execution to be had at Tyburn.

This is not what transpired on the stage.

Sir Edward Coke's arraignment was an elaborate assault; its elaboration lay not in its inclusiveness, but in its multiple exclusions. 'He did conspire, imagine and fantasise the death and destruction of the Queen's Majesty, and to stir Rebellion and War within the Realm, and to overthrow that State of whole common weal of this Realm,' charged Coke. These words, a formula of treason trials, were familiar to Coke. Only a week earlier he had read the indictment of Patrick Collen before another Special Commission of Oyer and Terminer, many of whose members now sat in judgement of Lopez. Then, Coke had accused Collen of having 'conspired, imagined and compassed the deposition and death of the Queen'.

Lopez fell within the same legal ambit as Collen, and within the same narrative ambit. The jury was directed away from the details of the plot and its connection to the Cecils, and towards the imperatives of national security and nebulous Catholic threat. Coke recited a list of Lopez's meetings with Andrada and Ferreira da Gama. He described how the Doctor had dictated letters to Ferreira and had received a jewel from Philip II. All these events had occurred, but their original purpose was replaced with another aim: 'the death and destruction of the Queen's Majesty', as a prelude to the fall of Protestant England to Philip II.

In his relentless, hectoring manner, Coke announced that after having 'conspired to depose and kill the Queen', Lopez had planned to 'raise insurrection and rebellion, and overturn the established religion and government'. He had gathered intelligence for the Spanish as they prepared the next Armada, so that 'Philip II and his ministers' might prepare their forces, and order and direct their armies' against England and its Queen.

Lopez was accused of attempting to overthrow not just Elizabeth I, but also the entire nexus of spiritual and legal authority which held the State together. Not just the Settlement of 1559, but the whole apparatus of Englishness: social, political and religious. From the whispered exchanges in Lopez's garden, Coke raised terrible blooms, prophesying the ruin of the Tudor dynasty, the strangulation of its nationalistic religion, and a return to chaos, civil war and Continental interference.

The prosecution had deliberately mixed Lopez's case with the Collen Plot and conspiracy theories about Philip II's desire to destroy England. These were extravagant, insupportable claims, but they possessed a cock-eyed logic. Elizabeth I was old and childless, and her succession was an obvious but taboo issue. There were many precedents for Catholic conspiracy in Elizabeth's reign, all of them had links with Philip II, champion of the Church of Rome, and they had often involved Jesuit graduates like Patrick Collen. There was also a masochistic terror of a second Armada, an anxiety confirmed by rumours of shipbuilding in the ports of Spain. And Lopez was a foreigner with a secret religion. Coke's case was credible and volatile. Lopez's image overlapped with other monsters of the popular imagination, from Barabas to Philip II, unmoored from particulars of fact, floating freely in the frightened imagination like a plague virus.

To sustain such an interpretation, the evidence had to be heavily edited. Doctor Lopez's past was annihilated. No mention was made that he had been a trusted intimate of the Privy Council for over two decades, that he had supplied intelligence and physic to the Earl of Leicester and Sir Francis Walsingham, that he had helped organise the Counter-Armada against Philip II, that the Queen had continued to admit him to her presence despite Essex's calumnies, or that the circumstances that Coke described had developed while Lopez had been an intelligencer for Lord Burghley.

The recent past was also whitewashed. Manuel d'Andrada was referred to in passing as 'an alien enemy', not a double agent who, after serving Walsingham and Lopez, had been paid by Burghley to gather 'such news as he found in the streets' of Calais and to 'run with the Count of Fuentes'. No explanation was offered for why Gomez d'Avila, by Coke's account as deeply involved as any other player in the plot, had not been charged and had not provided any written statement. At no point did Sir Edward Coke mention the crucial, ambiguous figure of Emanuel Luis Tinoco and the inevitable multiplication of questions about his work for Essex, his work for the Cecils, his work for the Count of Fuentes, and the Privy Council passports on which he had travelled.

Similarly, none of Lopez's dealings between April and September 1593 were reported. This created an erroneous impression that nothing of note had happened in those five months. The truth was the opposite. Those five months had been crucial to the conspiracy, or the overlapping conspiracies, now being tried. In April 1593, Lopez had obtained Don Emanuel's 'letter of submission'. In June 1593, Tinoco had joined Lopez's conspiracy. In July 1593, the 'letter of submission' had been sent to Brussels. By then, Lopez had become an active agent in a Spanish plot to kill Antonio Perez, the Queen's guest, and had been in regular contact with Spanish agents. All the while, Lopez had attended upon the Queen, Lord Burghley and the Earl of Essex. This catalogue of deception and greed contained enough evidence for a treason trial, yet none of it was mentioned.

To discuss the Doctor's dealings between April and September 1593 would not only have dropped Lopez into the cauldron. Each answer would have raised a question. If Manuel d'Andrada had conspired the Queen's death, as Coke claimed, why had Lord Burghley paid him to spy in the Low Countries? If Ferreira da Gama had written to Philip II's adviser Cristovão da Moura offering Lopez's service as a poisoner, why had da Moura's reply requested 'a letter from the Lord Treasurer'? What was the relationship between Lopez and Lord Burghley, why had Lopez spied on Antonio Perez and how had Burghley not noticed that his spymaster had turned traitor? And for that matter, why had Lopez's other master, Essex, also failed to notice?

Curiously, having leapfrogged the most intense period of the conspiracy, Coke's account of Lopez's elaborate treason stopped in October 1593. The Solicitor-General did not mention that Lopez and Tinoco had penetrated the French embassy and plotted the murder of Antonio Perez. Although this was a genuinely treasonable act, it was expunged from the record because while setting up Antonio Perez, Lopez had passed Perez's stolen correspondence to Lord Burghley and Sir Robert Cecil.

Coke also omitted any connection between Lopez and any Privy Councillors. He did not relate how the Earl of Essex had sat on Ferreira da Gama's first confession for two months before telling the Queen of its existence – an ambiguous, if not treasonous, withholding of evidence – or that Sir Robert Cecil had repeated the offence by not showing his own, stolen copy of the confession to the Queen. Neither did Coke relate how, from the very beginning, the Earl's hunt of Lopez had been blocked by Lord Burghley and opposed by the Queen. Nor did he describe how Lord Burghley and Sir Robert Cecil had defended Lopez against Essex, and that only a month earlier Sir Robert Cecil had vouched Lopez's innocence to the Queen.

Coke's prosecution showed a scrupulous lack of interest in the rest of Lopez's intelligencing. There was a whole continent of dubious dealings and outright malice to be explored. Lopez was manifestly culpable on several accounts. He had plotted the betrayal of Don Antonio into the receptive clasp of Philip II, and had incited Don Emanuel to usurp his father. He had plotted to murder Antonio Perez, and had spied on the French ambassador. These acts had all been committed against the Queen's personal guests, and consequently they were treasonable. He had also slandered the Earl of

Essex, lied to Lord Burghley and Sir Robert Cecil, and bankrupted Don Antonio. By way of character reference, he had humiliated Mrs Allington, disowned his bastard son, lent money at high interest and conducted heretical rites in secret. To round off the list of charges, his contingency plan had been secretly to defraud the King of Spain and to skip the country.

Yet all of this remained as unknown as Australia. Lopez was charged in a vacuum. The prosecution showed no interest in his actual crimes, because the evidence of those crimes led back to their commissioners. Those commissioners were now judges, and they all had something to hide. The only common ground between Essex and the Cecils was the need to dispose of Lopez. A charge of regicide could not be ignored, and was all the more accommodating for being unsubstantiated. The subtle grounds and washes of the intimacies between patron and servant were overpainted with one primary colour, a blood-red stroke of treason. Lopez would be condemned not for what he had done, but for what he might safely be accused of.

A skeletal frame of narrative remained, gutted of all context. The twin spectres of Catholic rebellion and Spanish conspiracy were summoned to fill it. For proof, Coke had only to point to Lopez's signed confession.

After Coke's tirade, Lopez had his chance. He repeated the defence that he had used in the Tower, that all had been 'to cozen the King of Spain'. This distinction had no effect on the commissioners. Under the treason laws, Coke had only to prove that Lopez had thought or talked of poisoning the Queen, not that he had attempted it. Also, the accused had not tried to rebut the charges of inciting revolution, rebellion and civil war. Lopez may not have understood his legal position. He had not been told his rights, because a treason suspect did not have any.

Lopez changed course. He referred to his examination by Lord Burghley, Sir Robert Cecil, the Earl of Essex and Lord Admiral Howard, and his signed confession to treason. 'I did confess indeed to them that I had talk of it,' he said, 'but now I must tell truth.' Before the packed hall, Lopez claimed that his confession had been forced from him at the threat of torture. 'I lied only to save myself from racking.'

Amid uproar from the audience, Sir Robert Cecil protested indignantly at Lopez, swearing 'by our Souls' witness' that the 'vile Jew' was lying.

As the format of the trial prevented Lopez from cross-examining anyone, this exchange brought his defence to a sensational but fruitless end. Solicitor-General Coke called the commissioners to a vote. They found Lopez unanimously 'guilty in the most highest degree of all Treasons'. The Guildhall echoed to 'the applause of all the world', the audience's pleasure echoing in the ears of Lopez, the Cecils and Essex alike. The formalities of his own deposition and destruction having been observed, and with proceedings having been only slightly marred by Doctor Lopez's intemperate interruption, the condemned man was whisked back to the Tower to await his death or his pardon.

There was no hiatus for the Cecils and William Wade. The next morning they were among the commissioners in the trial of Patrick Collen, who received a swift death sentence. Immediately afterwards, Lord Burghley directed the dogged, overworked Wade to draw up 'a short narration of the Treasons of Doctor Lopez', to fix the narrative of treason before its clay had dried. Meanwhile, Sir Robert Cecil asked his father-in-law Lord Cobham to send a servant to Calais, 'to receive such bags, papers and portmanteaux' as Tinoco had left there with Mr Jeffries the consul, to pre-empt any unpleasant revelations at the trial of Lopez's co-conspirators.

William Wade had been exhausted by his triple performance as interrogator, detective and juror, and he felt the clammy fingers of influenza on his bones, but the Cecils deluged him with orders for further bureaucratic exploits. Shivering beneath 'an inclination towards an Ague', Wade locked himself into his house for three days, compiling a 'short narration' of the Lopez affair for Lord Burghley. Just as he finished, Tinoco's papers appeared from Calais. Wade dived back into his labours for another five days, wrestling with the evasions of Tinoco and Ferreira da Gama, extracting further brief confessions to clarify the Crown's case, translating prolix and obscure mails to Lopez from Alvaro Mendes at Constantinople. If sickness and paperwork were not enough of a burden, Wade also suffered the pestering of a penurious neighbour. Bartholomew Quiney, a fellow resident in Wood Street, needed to find a guardian for his third daughter. He kept appearing at Wade's door, asking if Wade had remembered his promise to put in a word with Lord Burghley.

'I am busied still about these Portugal causes,' Wade understated on Saturday, 9 February, 'and in truth, I have not been well.'

In Wade's long career of disinformation and entrapment, the case against Tinoco was his greatest challenge. Although Doctor Lopez was the public focus of the scandal, Tinoco was the real fulcrum, the pivot upon which the interlocking wheels of the conspiracy had turned. He had played a double game of pathological brilliance, as if personality were like the mercury on the back of a mirror, a reflective surface separated from the world by glass. In England, Tinoco had talked peace with Lopez, but had spied on the English navy and coastal defences. In the Low Countries, Tinoco had plotted with the Spanish, but had spied on Catholic exiles for Lopez and Lord Burghley. He had tricked his way in and out of the studies of both the Count of Fuentes and Sir Robert Cecil. He had taken commissions from both Lord Burghley and Secretary d'Ibarra. He had acted in both the intelligence and murder plots against Antonio Perez, as if the plot, not its end, were the reward. He had sworn himself to Don Antonio, Philip II and Elizabeth I with equal sincerity and equal futility. Tinoco had the fractionated genius of cracked glass. To trap him would be like nailing down mercury.

Wade's only hope was to bypass Tinoco. Like Perseus evading the eye of Medusa, for ten days Wade considered his enemy in image only. Wade stayed at his desk and worked on a narrative, lopping the snake heads from Medusa's scalp one by one, not daring to venture down Wood Street to Tinoco's cell in the Counter prison until Tinoco's wildness had been contained. On 10 March, Wade's narrative was solid enough to risk eye contact with Tinoco, and he went to the Counter. Tinoco wriggled and shifted frantically, but Wade kept his eye on the reflection, not the object. Tinoco was too late; by then Lord Burghley was annotating a complete chronology of the plot, to be used at Tinoco's trial.

There were two other human inconsistencies that Wade had to iron out. He saw the suspicious absurdity of not extending the proceedings to include the one courier who had not been interrogated, and he knew that the Earl of Essex wanted it that way. 'It were not amiss Gomez d'Avila should be removed to Bride Well,' Wade suggested to Essex. 'Your Lordship knoweth him to be a most impudent, lewd person, and it will fall out he is as deep in this practise as the rest.'

Essex had been a prolific angler for evidence before Lopez's trial, but he ignored Wade's suggestion. If Gomez d'Avila was 'deep in this practise', it was in much the same way as the Earl himself. Essex had inserted Gomez into the Lopez plot as a stooge, a disposable means of entrapping the Doctor as his scheme came to fulfilment. After that function, Essex expected Gomez to take his fee and melt away into the Portingall undergrowth. If Gomez were 'brought to the manacles' and spilt this story, he would set Wade on a track that Essex wanted to keep hidden, its footsteps leading to Essex's ambiguous connection to Tinoco.

While Essex blocked one path of enquiry, Wade and Sir Robert Cecil blocked another. Wade had held the Doctor's cousin Jeronimo Lopez Soeiro in the Counter for a month. Jeronimo was clearly implicated in the Doctor's plot: cipher mails from Tinoco and the Spanish had been hidden in his 'ordinary post'. When Sir Robert Cecil had interviewed Tinoco on 16 January, Jeronimo had attended their meeting. Subsequently, Tinoco had named him in his confessions. Like Gomez d'Avila, Jeronimo was an accessory to treason. Yet instead of interrogating and charging him, Sir Robert Cecil paid him 'twenty pound in gold' and hustled him out of England. On 12 March, as the indictments against Tinoco and Ferreira da Gama were read to the Special Commissioners in the Guildhall, Jeronimo Lopez was escorted to Gravesend under guard and put upon a boat for the Low Countries. The gold was not for his information, but for his silence: Jeronimo had assisted in the Cecils' surveillance of Antonio Perez.

As fast as the case was prepared, new problems arose. Sir John

Popham, Chief Justice of the Queen's Bench, had been designated to preside over the trial of Tinoco and Ferreira da Gama, but he was ill. Only one other Queen's Bench judge was scheduled to be in London before Easter, and he would not arrive in London for another week.

Meanwhile, Doctor Lopez's jailers reported an alarming deterioration in their charge. He appeared to have lost the will to live. 'Doctor Lopez hath kept his bed for the most part since the trial,' Sir John Puckering reported. 'Whether he practises anything by slow poison to prevent his execution may be doubted.'

If Lopez's health continued on its downward trajectory, he would die in a cell, not on a scaffold. This would open the Cecils to suspicions of victimisation, torture and discreet murder: all the imputations they had sought to avoid by using a public trial. Sir Robert Cecil conferred with Attorney-General Sir Thomas Egerton, the Cecil candidate for the still vacant Mastership of the Rolls.

Attorney-General Sir Thomas Egerton.

'If Lopez should die before execution, great dishonour and scandal might ensue,' advised Sir Thomas. He thought that a delay would be 'more dangerous to Her Majesty, and more dishonourable in the opinion of the world' than forcing through an unorthodox trial in the absence of a Queen's Bench judge. Egerton nominated a minor member of the Lopez jury, William Daniel. 'I hath acquainted him with the state of the cause, and doubt not his sufficiency to direct in form of law, and manage the proceedings. A judge's name gives countenance, but adds nothing to learning.'

Hinting that there was no alternative, Egerton asked if the Cecils had any 'directions concerning Lopez, in regard to the inconvenience should he die before execution.' William Daniel was to make his debut as a judge in a case in which he had previously served as juror. The 'form of law' would be observed, and nothing more.

With Wade and the Cecils editing the evidence that reached the Solicitor-General's office, Sir Edward Coke had an easier task. He understood that the Cecils were under attack from Essex. As he did not know about the Cecils' compromising links with Tinoco, Coke could follow the Cecils' orders with a clear conscience. They had even supplied him with a memorandum suggesting how he should assemble the Crown's case against Tinoco and Ferreira da Gama. The verdict against Lopez should be used to condemn his co-conspirators, with heavy emphasis on the Doctor as national and religious alien.

Lopez hath divers kinsmen naturalized. And that to one of them Lopez hath written and received Letters of Answers from them. Lopez himself confessed that he is a Jew, but the said Lopez was Christened, though he now be by proof . . . a false Christian.

Heretofore might be added to shew the abundance of God's favour to Her Majesty and contrariwise, the abundance of the Malice of Her Majesty's Enemies; that even about the time of the Conspiracy [of] this most horrible Treason, there were found persons, some English, some Irish, that were corrupted with money, and all were by certain English Jesuits in a kind of shrift animated with promise of Salvation to enterprise the Queen's Death.

Guided by this advice from the Cecils, Coke sketched his opening salvo in his densely knotted script. 'This island flourishing with unbound peace, by the goodness of God, under Her Highness's most happy and politique government above all the kingdoms and states of Christendom' – he surrendered to the temptation of Latin tags and then resurfaced – 'hath been to the great and perpetual honour of Her Majesty a Sanctuary to distressed states, and a Bulwark against the tyranny of mighty usurping princes.'

The platitudes dispatched, Coke struck the bedrock of the case. If England was Christendom's only resort against tyranny, then its enemies were aliens. The going became heavier as Coke sought to embody this thesis. Sentences were begun and abandoned, scored out and written over. Stuck, he mined a suitable illustration of the dangers of being a 'Sanctuary and a Bulwark' from Herodotus's *Histories*.

Zopyrus was a Persian nobleman who had fought in Darius's army of Persians in their siege of Babylon. After 'a year and seven months' of siege, and greedy for the prizes that would be his reward, Zopyrus developed a desperate scheme to gain entry to Babylon: he would pose as a Persian defector. To make himself convincing, 'he cut off his own nose and ears', so that he could claim to have been mutilated by Darius. When they saw 'a Persian of such exalted rank in so grievous a plight, his nose and ears cut off, his body red with the marks of scourging and with blood', the Babylonians believed Zopyrus's story and welcomed him into their city. Shortly afterwards, he betrayed them to Darius. After the city had been stormed Darius, who was not unimpressed by Zopyrus's sacrifice of his nose and ears, made Zopyrus governor of Babylon.

On 14 March, Coke informed the jury at the Guildhall that the moral of this slab of Grecian apocrypha was that they should distrust the appearance of the eye. By blindly accepting Zopyrus into their city, the Babylonians had condemned themselves to 'the miserable word of a foreign prince'. Like Zopyrus at Babylon, smooth Doctor Lopez, from whose lips Christian liturgy slipped as easily as a courtier's compliment, had another allegiance. Just as he had entered the Church only to disguise and further his real loyalty to the Synagogue, so he had entered the Queen's Court only to serve Philip II. Distracting his patients with smoke and mirrors, Lopez came not to cure the Queen, but to kill her. His helpers were the same. Ferreira da Gama had come to England as a refugee, yet he had attempted to open the gates of the city to the Queen's enemies. Emanuel Luis Tinoco had entered the country professing to serve the Queen, but had actually been 'employed by the King of Spain and his ministers for the better effecting of the horrible treasons' they had plotted.

The Portuguese were like Zopyrus, a fifth column who ostentatiously exhibited their losses in order to distract the generous English. The 'Portugall Jew' and 'his traitors' were 'enemies both to Almighty God' and to the Queen, whose trust and coffers had been so abused. They were a guerrilla army of earless, noseless Zopyruses, soldiers of the diabolical 'Roger Lopez, a Portugall Jew', and behind them there tiptoed a foreign horde, the heretical army of a foreign prince. 'For Doctor Lopez, the perjuring murdering Jewish traitor, you have his treasons plainly and previously proved,' Coke alliterated.

By emphasising the prior conviction of Doctor Lopez, Coke avoided discussing Tinoco's and Ferreira's actual conduct, and turned their case into a judgement of whether the jury had done its patriotic duty in Lopez's trial. If further evidence was needed, he illustrated the treasons of the 'Portugall traitors' Tinoco and Ferreira da Gama by 'three several oppositions and antitheses'. While 'poor Protestants flighteth into this Realm for religion', 'Popish Portugals' came only for treason. Ergo, the Lopez plot, despite being the work of a 'perjured, murdering Jewish traitor' was a 'papisticus' plot. 'These Popish Portugalls!' he marvelled. 'There is no discoursing between treason and religion, and there is no treason that the Pope shall not defend.'

Coke thus completed the rhetorical somersault of ascribing the Lopez Plot as both Jewish and Catholic in its motivations. It was an alien irruption into the Protestant civility of Elizabeth's England, wrought by Papists and Jews. It had been generated overseas, not at Burghley House, Wanstead or in the shadows of the Court, and it had nothing at all to do with the government.

Tinoco had the sense to agree with this theological illogic, and pleaded 'Guilty'. Reading his fate in the distorted lens of a treason trial, he hoped that complicity in his conviction might be read as proof of willingness to serve. Ferreira da Gama, always naive enough to believe in his own innocence, pleaded 'Not Guilty'. The verdicts were unanimous, and they joined Doctor Lopez in the Tower, the ante-room of violent death.

Like Lopez's trial, the proceedings against Tinoco and Ferreira da Gama were full of inconsistencies and false evidence. Gomez d'Avila, who had been accorded a single fleeting mention in Lopez's trial, was not mentioned at all, despite the fact that Ferreira da Gama had hired him. Tinoco was described as having come to London on 16 January 1594, not to meet Sir Robert Cecil, but to meet Ferreira da Gama at the house in St Katharine Creechurch. This was impossible: by 16 January 1594, Ferreira da Gama had been a prisoner at Eton for two months.

Any connection between Tinoco and the Cecils had been expunged. Tinoco was not a Cecil double agent run amok, but solely a Spanish spy. The 'memorials' that Tinoco had written for the Cecils when he came to England were not referred to: they remained hidden in Sir Robert Cecil's study, along with the contents of Tinoco's trunk, brought from Calais in haste and secrecy. It was not mentioned that Tinoco had entered England on a passport issued by Lord Burghley, or that he had spent ten days as the Cecils' guest. The Cecils did not disclose that they had obtained a stolen copy of Ferreira's confession before it was brought to the Queen's attention by Essex, and that they too had hidden it from her.

The Cecils had achieved their objective. A court assembled by royal fiat had judged that the Lopez affair was a foreign matter. They had done so in a manner subtle enough to grant Essex his purported objective – the patriotic discovery of treason plots – while thwarting his covert plan to dominate the government. They had two good reasons for doing this. Essex had tried to use Doctor Lopez as the stalking horse that would draw the Cecils into a factional battle over foreign policy. When they had discovered that Lopez and Tinoco were implicated in the plot to kill Antonio Perez, they had known that they could no longer afford to protect the Doctor. But they could not throw him to Essex. Instead, they diverted Essex's attack from the explosive issue of foreign policy on to the common good of the Queen's safety, the supreme value of the State. For 'peace', they had read 'poison'.

The price was the lives of Doctor Lopez, Ferreira da Gama and Emanuel Luis Tinoco, and an implicit agreement not to wander from the narrative track of conspiracy. A series of trade-offs sustained the prosecution's claim that Lopez had planned to poison the Queen. The Cecils did not mention that Essex had used Tinoco to contact Duke João of Braganza. Essex did not mention that he had used Tinoco to infiltrate the intelligence network that Doctor Lopez ran for the Cecils. Neither faction mentioned Antonio Perez. The Cecils had to hide the truth that their intelligencers had set up Perez's murder by Patrick Collen, and they had made sure to deprive Essex of any grounds on which to drag Perez into the inquiry. When Patrick Collen and John Annias had confessed that they had come to kill 'the Spaniard', William Wade and Sir Robert Cecil had forced them to admit that they had meant 'the Queen'. None of the searchers in the labyrinth acknowledged the Monster of Fortune as they felt their way past him in the dark.

Essex's self-advancement versus the Cecils' self-preservation: their motives diverged, but the effect was the same. The official record covered the tracks of both factions. The Cecils had obscured, rewritten and falsified the evidence to protect themselves, and grant Essex a victory big enough to gratify him, but small enough to frustrate him. A false account had been presented by the Queen's most trusted servants, and had been endorsed by her commissioners. At the end of the proceedings, Sir John Puckering produced the Great Seal and pressed it into the puddle of unformed hot wax. It dried in a red pool, imprinted with the image of the enthroned Queen.

The Great Seal.

17

The Pound of Flesh

But is it true, Salerio?
Hath all his ventures fail'd? What, not one hit?
From Tripolis, from Mexico and England,
From Lisbon, Barbary and India,
And not one vessel 'scape the dreadful touch
Of merchant-marring rocks?
    Bassanio to Salerio, *The Merchant of Venice*

In the Tower, Doctor Lopez grew weak and desperate. He petitioned the Queen 'more than ever', begging her to intercede, casting himself on her 'knowledge and goodness'. He knew he had not let her down at his trial, had not described that she had known of his intelligencing for the Cecils and Essex. Instead, he had endured the slurs of Solicitor-General Coke, the contempt of the commissioners, the mockery of the mob and the applause of the world. After the judgement, his home had been confiscated in law, attaindered to the Crown. Lopez's creditors wanted their money and his debtors had defaulted, but Essex's man Thomas Phelippes would not release his goods from the Customs House. Meanwhile, Sara and his children were penniless, pawning their possessions for food, and Sara's father Dunstan Añes had died from worry and shame. Lopez knew that only the Queen could save him.

Each letter received the same reply: 'Not a hair on your head should perish.' Lopez must 'be content' and 'have patience'. The terrible process in which he had been snared must be allowed to play itself out: 'all things must be done with the honour of the State'. His misery in the Tower would be 'but a short imprisonment, and a little loss of practice in his profession'. If he sacrificed his dignity and 'credit' to the State, he would prove his loyalty to the Queen, and that would secure his liberty. There was no argument that he could offer; he had no other hope. Exhausted, Lopez ailed broken in his cell, as his jailers searched for evidence of 'slow poison'.

Tinoco had not despaired. Like a gardener trapped in his own maze, he spent his last days frantically scribbling letters and voluntary 'confessions' to the Cecils, trying to find the path that would free him, the iota of information that would bring him back to life by making him valuable again. He offered to betray everyone, to inform upon everything, to spy upon anyone. The only reply he received was a visit from William Wade, prompted by a reference Tinoco had made in one of his appeals to Lord Burghley having paid a hundred *cruzados* to Manuel d'Andrada. Wade reminded Tinoco that this was unmentionable and Tinoco obliged with another letter, identical but for an absence of references to the Cecils.

Ferreira da Gama had abandoned any hope of earthly salvation. He realised that Lopez had set him up when he had dictated their letters to the Spanish. Although all three – Lopez, Tinoco and Ferreira – were condemned by each other's testimony, only Ferreira was incriminated by his own hand. Rather than petition the Queen, he recommended his soul to the Almighty and wrote his will. It was a straight-faced testament, earnest and hopeless. 'I choose my name-sake St Stephen for my advocate and guard, to defend me from Devils in his voyage to Heaven,' he wrote. He apologised to Don Antonio for his betrayal, forgave the pretender his debts and advised God that the various Portuguese with whom he had conspired were innocent of treason. Offering his daughter a choice between marriage or a nun's wimple, Ferreira passed his lost estates to his son Francisco, and prayed that the Almighty would keep little Francisco 'from Princes' affairs, and from the shame of the world'. Having settled his spiritual estate, Ferreira composed himself for death.

It did not come. This was a torment for the prisoners, and a dilemma for their persecutors. Every day that passed without an execution increased the risk of embarrassment for the Cecils.

Diplomatic gossip had carried the sensational allegations about the Queen's physician from Whitehall to the palaces of Europe. 'There is news from London that a conspiracy to poison the Queen has been brought to light; so her Doctor confessed under torture. He is said to have kept up secret relations with Spain for the last ten years,' Tomaso Contarini, Venetian ambassador at Prague, told the Doge and Senators of Venice. If Contarini's next letter reported that the Doctor had died in suspicious circumstances, the Queen of England and her ministers would appear to have ordered an extra-judicial murder in the manner of the Medici.

The news had also reached the Court of Murad III at Constantinople, probably via the Doctor's Antwerp cousin Diego Lopez Soeiro. For Alvaro Mendes, losing Doctor Lopez meant the severing of his connection to the Privy Council and a loss of influence over Murad III. This had been a danger prior to the Lopez scandal: for the last four years Mendes and Lopez had fought Don Antonio and his Turkish agent David Passi for influence over England's Turkey policy. In late 1593, Mendes had despatched an emissary to London named Judah Serfatim, whose task was to convince the Privy Council that the slanders circulated by Don Antonio and David Passi were untrue.

Serfatim arrived in London a week after Lopez's conviction. He appealed in writing to both Burghley and Lord Admiral Howard, but was denied an audience. Instead, Burghley directed Serfatim to William Wade.

'The chiefest thing this messenger doth extremely labour', Wade reported to Burghley, 'is to have the Execution stayed of Doctor Lopez, as he hath told Your Lordship and my Lord Admiral (as he sayeth), for besides the dishonour, as he sayeth, that will come to his master, he feareth it may be a way to his utter overthrow, being already sought underhand.'

Wade refused to contemplate a reprieve for Lopez. Although the Doctor's fall might stem the flow of intelligence to London from Alvaro Mendes, the Cecils felt that domestic priorities overrode diplomacy. 'I told him that the fact was so odious, importing Her Majesty so highly, and the discontentment of the people so great, as I assured myself he should find none of Your Lordships that would once make that motion, and the Execution was in the hands of those that were Commissioners.'

Serfatim did not know that Wade had been among 'those that were Commissioners'. Even if he had, it would have made no difference. Wade was absolutely determined to stonewall Serfatim, to the point of implying that Serfatim was involved in Lopez's treasons. Somehow, Serfatim found that his mission to rescue Alvaro Mendes's reputation had turned into a defence of Doctor Lopez, and of his own motives for coming to England. It seemed that the Privy Council preferred damaging the Turkish alliance to contemplating a reprieve for Doctor Lopez. After several wasted, humiliating weeks in London, a defeated Serfatim took ship for Constantinople, leaving the deep currents of Court politics to drag the Doctor on to the rocks like a storm-racked argosy.

While they beat off the Turkish embassy, the Cecils fought a propaganda battle on the domestic front. The 'discontentment of the people' would be gratified, but it would be done strategically. After the sentencing of Tinoco and Ferreira, Lord Burghley spent several days editing William Wade's 'short narration' of the Lopez affair. To Burghley, directing the blame for the Lopez Plot away from England towards Philip II was also an opportunity to warn the newly Catholic Henri IV of France against an alliance with Spain. If there was not to be peace with Spain, Burghley wanted to retain the balance that had preserved England for thirty years: keeping France locked in dispute with Spain in the Low Countries. At some point this manuscript passed through Sir Robert Cecil's office, where it acquired a frontispiece design for possible future publication.

Meanwhile, the Essex camp prepared their own interpretation of the divine will, also based on Wade's 'short narration', but with another purpose. William Temple, one of Essex's junior secretaries, had copied Wade's document, inserted further material from the Essex files, and passed this expanded account to Francis Bacon. Retreating to Twickenham during the legal recess, Bacon assembled the Essex version, *A True Report of the Detestable Treason Intended by Dr. Roderigo Lopez, A Physician Attending Upon the Queen's Majesty*.

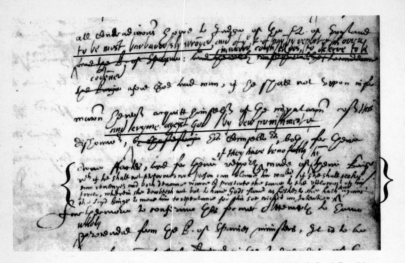

*An early draft of the Cecil version of events, with annotations by both Lord Burghley
(underlined) and Sir Robert Cecil (bracketed), March 1594.*

Bacon used the Cecils' argument to draw a different conclusion.
His characterisation of Lopez was consistent with Coke's prosecu-
tion, with added overtones of the frustrated doctor-courtier Gabriel
Harvey's bitterness at Lopez's sprightly ascent of the winding stair.

> This Lopez, of nation a Portuguese, and suspected of sect to be secretly
> a Jew (though here he conformed himself to the rites of Christian reli-
> gion), for a long time professed physic in this land. Being withall a man
> very observant and officious, and of a pleasing and appliable behaviour,
> in that regard, rather than for any great learning in his faculty, he grew
> known and favoured in Court, and was some years since sworn physi-
> cian of Her Majesty's household; and by Her Majesty's bounty, of whom
> he had received divers gifts of good commodity, was grown to good estate
> of wealth.

If Burghley wanted to deflect blame for the Lopez affair on to
Philip II, the Essex camp wanted to use it as a pretext for war.
Bacon's summary mixed flattery, divine intervention, jingoism and

anti-Catholic invective into an unsteady brew. He alleged that by treacherously engaging Lopez the poisoner, Philip II had forfeited his royal immunity from civil law. By implication, the charges should move from the courtroom to the battlefield.

> And surely, if a man do consider, it is hard to say whether God hath done greater things by Her Majesty or for her; if you observe on the one side how God hath ordained her government to break and cross the unjust ambition of the two mighty potentates, the King of Spain and the Bishop of Rome, never so straitly between themselves combined: and on the other side, how mightily God hath protected her, both against foreign invasion and inward troubles, and singularly against the many secret conspiracies that have been made against her life; thereby declaring to the world that he will indeed preserve that instrument which he hath magnified. But the corruptions of these times are wonderful, when that wars, which are the highest trials of right between princes (that acknowledge no superior jurisdiction), and ought to be prosecuted with all honour, shall be stained and infamed with such foul and unhuman practices. Wherein, if so great a king hath been named, the rule of civil law (which is the rule of common reason) must be remembered: *Frustra legis auxilium implorat, qui in legem committit*: he that hath sought to violate the Majesty Royal in the highest degree, cannot claim the pre-eminence thereof to be exempted from just imputation.

Bacon was distorting the law for factional ends, and faction was the root of the 'corruption of the times': the channelling of opportunity through patronage. His paper was the authentic voice of the Essex campaign against the Cecils, hiding malice behind law and ambition behind patriotism. Yet, as ever, Bacon's unscrupulous oratory went unrewarded. On 27 March, the Queen brought thirteen months of factional bitterness to an end by promoting her Attorney-General, Sir Thomas Egerton, to Master of the Rolls. It was now a formality that Sir Edward Coke, fresh from his triumphs in the Lopez affair, would in turn rise from Solicitor-General to Attorney-General. The Cecils had won again.

To kill off Essex's and Bacon's hopes with kindness, Sir Robert

Cecil wrote to Sir Thomas Egerton recommending 'my cousin Bacon, above which I have no kinsman living (my brother excepted) whom I hold so dear' for the consolation prize of the solicitorship. In Cecil's backhanded compliment, no one apart from Francis Bacon was 'likelier for his own worth to deserve it'.

Essex enacted his disappointment in another 'passionate' theatrical before the Queen, but she had had enough. 'Go to bed, if you will talk of nothing else,' she ordered.

That brought Francis Bacon's campaign for high office to its shaming close. All his efforts and those of Essex, the flattery, bullying and bribery, had come to nothing. Having failed to make an impression on public life, Bacon announced a dramatic retirement. 'I cannot but conclude with myself, that no man ever received a more exquisite disgrace,' he wrote to Essex. 'I will, by God's assistance, with this disgrace of my fortune, and yet with that comfort of that good opinion of so many honourable and worthy persons, retire myself with a couple of men to Cambridge, and there spend my life in my studies and contemplations, without looking back.'

The Cecils had successfully blocked Essex's assault on the Attorney-Generalship. Only one loose end remained – Doctor Lopez – and with Judah Serfatim despatched, only one obstacle blocked Lopez's path to Tyburn: the Queen. The Special Commission of Oyer and Terminer had been assembled under her Great Seal, and had been empowered to carry out its sentence, yet precedent indicated that to presume too confidently upon this royal licence was dangerous. The Queen was evidently unconvinced as to Lopez's guilt. She demurred from signing the royal warrant that would set his execution in train.

The Cecils and their servants edged forwards and backwards, trying to push Lopez on to the scaffold without their hand prints being too visible on his back. Eight times in eight weeks they made preparations for Lopez's execution. The procedure was that the warrant had to be read and endorsed by the Queen's Bench, but each time the case appeared, there was no royal warrant to be read and the session was adjourned. Neither the Cecils nor Essex could persuade Elizabeth to put her signature to the warrant.

When the chance arose, the Cecils used anxiety as a cover for their ambition. On 16 April, Ferdinando, Lord Strange died. Strange was the nephew of the exiled traitor Sir William Stanley and had been a focus of the Catholic conspirators in Antwerp. After complaining of a chill following a hunt, Strange had taken to his bed and never left it. For sixteen days he had vomited blood while his doctors deployed a battery of 'clister drinks, fomentations, oils, poultices, plasters and stirrings'. They had dosed him with 'Bezoar Stone and Unicorn's Horn'; they had administered a total of twenty-nine enemas; and one of them had even inserted a catheter into his urethra and sucked it, but nothing had worked. Apart from witch-craft, indigestion and overexertion, poisoning was suspected. Six months previously, Strange had been approached by Catholic exiles and asked if he would be their figurehead in a revolt against the Queen. The plotters had been arrested, but it was rumoured that their accomplices had murdered Lord Strange before he could give evidence against them.

It appears that Lord Strange's death frightened Elizabeth into signing Lopez's death warrant. It reminded her that, regardless of the factional exaggerations and manipulations of the previous months, her physical safety rested solely on the diligence of her servants. The day after Lord Strange's death, Sir Robert Cecil sensed the anxious shift in the royal mood, obtained a signature and imme-diately sent an order to Sir Michael Blount at the Tower: Doctor Lopez and his co-conspirators were to be presented for execution on 19 April, and the Queen's warrant was on its way.

Sir Michael Blount was the Earl of Essex's father-in-law. He knew that by office and marriage, he would be the Cecils' preferred candi-date to take the blame should there be a judicial mishap resulting in the accidental execution of her body physician. Blount had no intention of turning from jailer to prisoner, and he refused to release his prisoners without the warrant. He intuited that although Elizabeth had just given Sir Robert Cecil a signed warrant, she had not ordered its release. 'Since Your Honour doth signify that Her Majesty will have the executions stayed till I hear further of Her Highness' pleasure therein,' Blount replied, 'I will stay the prisoners accordingly.'

Blount was wise to be cautious. Elizabeth's distress about Lord Strange, and the pressure she was under from the Cecils, had only partially shifted her judgement of Lopez. She was still adamant that Lopez should not be executed, and was wary of the Cecils' haste. She ordered Sir Robert Cecil to tell Sir Michael Blount that even if 'any warrant to deliver Doctor Lopez' reached the Tower, Blount was not to carry it out. Blount, still suspicious of the Cecils' motives, asked for clarification. Cecil had ordered that Lopez, Tinoco and Ferreira should be 'delivered'; the Queen's stay of execution had only referred to Lopez; did this mean that Blount should proceed with despatching Tinoco and Ferreira?

Sir Robert Cecil was forced to admit that it did not. Four days later, on 29 April, the Queen's Bench held its last session of the legal term. Doctor Lopez would not be executed until after the new term began on 4 June. The royal warrant remained in Cecil's hands, vital and powerless. Elizabeth had delayed a final judgement on Lopez, but now she was under pressure from both the Cecils and Essex to despatch the Doctor. One by one, Essex and the Cecils had realised that Lopez was a double-edged asset and that he was too dangerous to keep. Elizabeth also realised that he was expendable, but she deferred the moment of decision, perhaps hoping that the pause between legal terms would throw up a new focus for the factions.

For five more weeks, Doctor Lopez waited in the Tower, suspended between life and death. In Wood Street, Burghley House, Twickenham Park and the Tower, the quills scratched at paper as the competing narratives took shape, each story a noose for his neck. Across the Thames, within sight of the Tower's battlements, *The Jew of Malta* continued its run at the Rose, Barabas's story entwining with the gossip of the Lopez case, of hidden jewels and daughters' dowries, betrayal and callous poisoning.

While Lopez's case was in suspension, William Shakespeare made another light upward step on the winding stair. If Shakespeare had left London in the Earl of Southampton's retinue to avoid the plague, he was back in the City by early summer. He was probably still living at Southampton House in Holborn. He had passed the plague season working on two or even three stage comedies, an extended poem on a classical theme and more sonnets for private circulation. One of the comedies was *Love's Labour's Lost*, which bears all the marks of a private entertainment, full of allusion to the inmates of Southampton House and the potroom world of literary backbiting. There was more than a pinch of Antonio Perez in Shakespeare's pompous, bragging Spaniard, Don Armado; something of Southampton's tutor John Florio in the pedant Holofernes; and a cartoon of Thomas Nashe in Moth, from whom words fly as light as flies. As Doctor Lopez waited for death, Shylock's creator played the salon comedian.

On 9 May, Richard Field the printer entered a second Shakespeare poem on the Stationers' Register, *The Rape of Lucrece*. Once again, it was a Classical story – this time from Livy – dedicated to the Earl of Southampton. This time, apart from writing a longer and better poem, Shakespeare's allegories of sexual dilemma included a political subtext. In the poem Sextus, son of the tyrannical King Tarquin of Rome, was besotted with Lucrece, a Roman matron. Sextus satisfied himself by threats and force. Ashamed, Lucrece committed suicide. The combination of Sextus's outrage and his father's cruelty led to the expulsion of the Tarquinian family from Rome, and the introduction of a republican government.

Like Francis Bacon's narrative of the Lopez affair, Shakespeare's poem implied a limit to monarchic absolutism. Like Bacon's Philip II, or like Elizabeth I in the logic of Catholic rebellion, Tarquin and Sextus had forfeited both royal authority and legal immunity. Hidden in the foliage of verse and allusion was the most dangerous Renaissance idea of all: that subjects might modify their legal relationship with the monarch, even to the point of suspending the monarchy and declaring a republic. In less than fifty years, England would fall into a civil war over this issue, and Puritan parliamentarians would execute their monarch. The legal-political authority that Lord Burghley had built up as a bulwark against disorder would become the foundation of republicanism.

The legal bureaucracy was also the agent of Lopez's end. Within hours of the start of the legal term, Sir John Puckering, Keeper of the Great Seal, received a letter from the Court, which had followed the Queen out of London on a summer progress. After staying at Lambeth and Wimbledon, she had reached Osterley, west of London, where he had been prevailed upon to issue an order for the closure of the Lopez affair. Written by the Earl of Essex, and signed by Essex and Lord Howard, the letter informed Sir John Puckering that, 'Her Majesty hath resolved that the late conveyed traitors Doctor Lopez and the two other Portugals that remain in the Tower of London, Ferreira and Manuel Luis [Tinoco], shall no longer keep from their deferred executions.'

Something had happened at Osterley in the days before the new legal term. From the signatures on the letter, it was clear that the Cecils and Essex, though rivals for power, had dovetailed their mutual need to dispose of Lopez. In the face of this pressure, the Queen had apparently abandoned her physician.

'We have therefore to sway your good Lordships to confer with the Judges,' Essex told Puckering, 'in what sort the same may most conveniently be done, and to write of such.'

But the process was not as straightforward as these words implied. After Puckering had replied with his suggestions, a second Essex–Howard letter showed that the Cecils and Essex were taking great care to avoid responsibility for Lopez's execution. The Privy Councillors wished only to initiate a legal process: final responsibility of the order for execution should devolve upwards to the Queen, or downwards to the judiciary. In their evasions, they even claimed an implausible ignorance of the law.

'We do like very well of either of these courses which your Lordships have propounded for the occasion,' they wrote, 'and refer the choice of them to the judgements of your Lordships and the Judges, who understand these courses better than ourselves.'

Hours later at the Tower, Sir Michael Blount received an order to produce Lopez and his co-conspirators at the Queen's Bench in Westminster on Saturday 7 June. Remembering Sir Robert Cecil's recent failure to persuade Blount to release the prisoners without a royal warrant, Essex and Howard instructed Sir John Puckering how to circumvent Blount's caution.

'For the freeing of the Lord-Lieutenant of the Tower from his

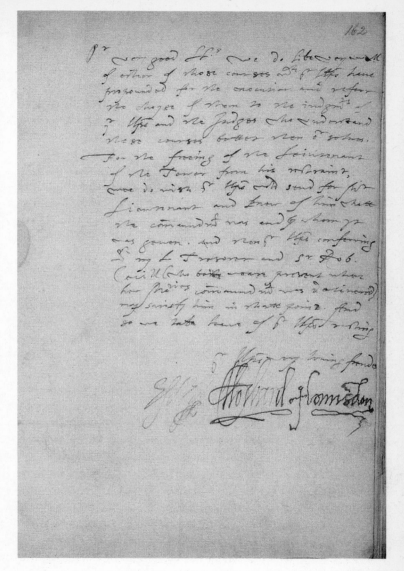

'My Lord Treasurer and Sir Robert Cecil, (who both were present when Her Majesty's commandment was delivered), may satisfy him in that point.': Essex and Howard's second letter to Sir John Puckering, 4 June 1594.

restraint, we do wish your Lordships would send for Sir Lieutenant and know of him what the commandment was, and by whom it was given, and then, your Lordships conferring with my Lord Treasurer and Sir Robert Cecil, (who both were present when Her Majesty's commandment was delivered), may satisfy him in that point.'

This was what Essex and Howard were trying to hide: the Queen had only issued a verbal order at Osterley, and still refused to release the royal warrant. So if the pieces still did not quite fit, they would have to be forced into place: when Blount cavilled and insisted on seeing a royal warrant, Puckering was to refer him to the Cecils. And they would confirm what they had heard from the Queen at Osterley: Lopez was to be executed. Just as the Cecils had acted in the Queen's name when they had first ordered Blount to release Lopez for trial on 17 April, and had then passed on her verbal countermanding of that order, so now they were passing on another verbal command from the Queen. Despite the unorthodox procedure, Blount could deliver Lopez to the Queen's Bench without a royal warrant, but with the personal assurances of Lord Burghley, the Queen's most trusted and senior Councillor.

'And so we take leave of your Lordships', wrote Essex and Howard, passing the buck to the judges.

They came for Doctor Lopez on Saturday 7 June. Early in the morning, the Tower guards took Lopez, Tinoco and Ferreira da Gama from their cells, conveyed them down to the water stairs by the Old Swan public house and ferried them upriver to Westminster, where Sir John Popham, the Chief Justice, waited for them.

While Lopez bobbed on the Thames, the Queen awoke to the fresh country air of Osterley. In the afternoon she would travel north to Highgate, and from there to Theobalds, the Cecils' Hertfordshire seat. By then, her physician would be dead. In her absence, and the absence of her warrant, the Cecils had found a way to get rid of Lopez.

If the Queen would not release the warrant that had resulted from the original Oyer and Terminer trial, then a new warrant could be obtained by trying the prisoners a second time before the Queen's Bench, which also had the power to pass a death sentence. That way, if the Queen wanted a scapegoat for Lopez's execution, the blame would fall on the legal system, not her advisers. The Cecils would be nowhere near the scene of the judicial crime. They were out of town at Theobalds, preparing for the honour of a royal visit.

Before Chief Justice Popham, Sir Edward Coke recited the 'particular proofs of the treasons as the same were set forth in evidence to the Jury'. Coke had prepared an elaboration of the original indictment from the Oyer and Terminer trial, pin-sharp in its attack on Lopez's character.

> For the poisoning of Her Highness, this miscreant, perjured, murdering traitor and Jewish doctor hath been provided a dearer Traitor than Judas himself.
>
> This plot and practise, more wicked, dangerous and detestable than all the former.
>
> He was Her Majesty's servant sworn, graced and advanced with many seemly and great favours and rewards, used in special place of credit and trust, permitted to have often access to Her Highness' person, and so not feared nor suspected, specially by Her Majesty, whose gracious nature and princely magnanimity is such as her heart was never touched with the fear of her most potent and capital enemies, much less with suspicion or doubt of any of her own servants.

After Coke had recited his catalogue of regicidal conspiracy, the prisoners had their chance to speak. Although the Queen's Bench allowed the accused far greater rights than an Oyer and Terminer trial, Coke did his utmost to prevent the prisoners from making their defence. Apart from the embarrassing details that might leak from the lips of desperate men, the government's case had already been endorsed by the Commision of Oyer and Terminer. To dispute it was to challenge the authority of the Great Seal and the monarch whose image it bore. John Stow, the tailor and historian under whose windows the accused had passed on their way from the docks to St Katharine Creechurch, recorded the scene as Ferreira da Gama attempted to writhe out of the charges: 'One of the Portingales began in his language to tell a long tale, but was willed to be short; which he answered could not be done without circumstance, et cetera, whereupon he was willed to hold his peace.'

Tinoco attempted an explanation, too. Seeing that Ferreira had been silenced, Tinoco began to write frantically an account in Portuguese. He passed it to an interpreter, who started to read it in English, but Coke cut him off and ordered him to stop, saying, 'It is not true.'

Last came 'Roderick Lopez', as Stow knew him. The Doctor spoke in English. 'I never thought harm to Her Majesty,' he pleaded in futile sincerity.

Chief Justice Popham endorsed the Oyer and Terminer verdict, and issued 'a writ' for execution. The prisoners were carried from the Queen's Bench and ferried back across the river to Marshalsea prison in Southwark, hard by the Rose Theatre. With the small ceremonial of bureaucratic process, they passed from Sir Michael Blount's custody to the Sheriff of London. The hurdles were ready, the weak prisoners were forced down and strapped on to them, and the procession began. To the west, the Queen and her ladies in waiting prepared to set out for Highgate.

On his back, Lopez saw the thatched roofs and idly smoking chimneys of the slums of the south bank, the silent citadel of the Rose and the great sky above. He crossed London Bridge as if crossing the Styx, the current sluicing through the arches, the Tower of London appearing over his left shoulder. The crowds gathered along their route through the City, his home for more than thirty years. St Katharine Creechurch, Wood Street, Guildhall, St Bartholomew's, the personal geography of half a lifetime, then the midden vapours of the City ditch and the scented June fields behind Mountjoy's Inn.

At Tyburn before the roaring crowd, three naked men stood on the scaffold. At their centre, an old, white-bearded Jew, weak from imprisonment, stripped by his executioners of the dignity of a doctor, the appurtenances of a courtier, the artifice of an intelligencer. He pleaded his loyalty to the Queen and God, but his words were carried away on the gusting laughter of the mob. When he regained consciousness after the hanging, he struggled with the Sheriff's men as they pinned him down for castration and disembowelling. The anatomised offal went into the cauldron, a pound of flesh for the Cecils, a pound of flesh for Essex, a pound for the mob and all for the Queen.

The second man gave no resistance and cheated the crowd. Ferreira da Gama died with the grim despair in which he had lived. But the third fought off the Sheriff's men and, for a moment, it seemed as if he might escape. The crowd surged forward, calling the odds for and against the brawl on the stage as though betting on a Southwark bout between Sackerson the chained bear and a pack of dogs. The dogs won, and Emanuel Luis Tinoco went wriggling into the air, still searching for the final contortion.

That summer, Philip Henslowe did good business with a topical *Jew of Malta*. The audiences streamed across London Bridge to Southwark, and as they passed beneath the gatehouse at the southern end of the bridge, they caught a flicker of shadow from Doctor Lopez's limbs, mounted on spikes above them, flailing and kicking towards the sun and the City. From August onwards, Henslowe rotated *The Jew of Malta* with another play, since lost, called *The Venetian Comedy*. The *Venetian* was to last just under a year in the repertoire of the Admiral's Men; the last reference to it in Henslowe's diary is dated '8th May 1595, received . . . 30 shillings'. But a theatrical Venice was to reappear at the Rose the following year. In January 1596 Henslowe, always looking to turn a few entrepreneurial shillings, sold a costume to one of his players for an upcoming production.

> Sold unto Steven Magett, the 20th of January 1596, a doublet of fustian plain, and a pair of Venetians of braid cloth, with two laces of Belmont, for 16 shillings, to be paid by 12 pence per week, beginning the 23rd of January 1596, being Saturday.

If Shakespeare's *Merchant of Venice* did not already exist in an earlier, simpler form when actor Steven Magett donned his Venetian costume, then Shylock was only months away; the version of *The Merchant* preserved in the first printing of 1600 refers to events in August 1596. As with most early comedies, the gestation of the play was obscure and probably extended. Shakespeare's *Merchant* is both a composite of influences and a transformation of them. Ser Giovanni's *Il Pecorone*, Marlowe's *Jew of Malta*, Dekker's lost *Jew of Venice*, the even more lost *Venetian Comedy*, Anthony Munday's *Zelauto*, the usury debate, and the trial and execution of Roderigo Lopez can all be traced in Shylock's parentage. If Shylock emerged from this cloud of influences literary and historical, then Lopez disappeared into it.

Through legal process, the Doctor had been turned into a chattel of the Crown; through the official account, in preparation through the summer of 1594 as Barabas bestrode the Rose, he became a posthumous tool of propaganda. After his violent death, Roderigo Lopez passed into another kind of double life. Light falls curving onto the convex mirrors of history and literature, casting the distorted reflections of the Burghley version, the Baconian version and the Shakespearean. There is no anatomist's incision that can lay bare the relationships between the images, no stroke of the jeweller's hammer that will crack the unfinished stone along its hidden fault line to reveal a perfect diamond, hard enough to cut through glassy imitation, a prism to imprison clear light.

Lopez had already metamorphosed from human to literary form before Shakespeare created Shylock; long before 8 October 1594, when Henry Carey, the Lord Chamberlain, wrote to Cuthbert Buckle, Mayor of London, to allow the erstwhile Lord Strange's Men to return to the stage as the Lord Chamberlain's Men, performing at the Cross Key Inn in Gracious Street. A proto-Shylock might have appeared on the stage in the yard of the Cross Key Inn before the end of the year, an opportunist variation on Dekker's *Jew of Venice*. And Shakespeare might have been among the great crowd that had gathered the previous June to see Lopez butchered at Tyburn, watching the Jew hung 'like a wolf for slaughter'.

Equally, Shakespeare may have been in Hampshire, or have stayed behind at Southampton House to work on a sonnet, and Shylock might have emerged fully formed in the summer of 1598, in time for Francis Meres to list *The Merchant* last, and presumably latest, in the catalogue of Shakespeare's comedies. That Lopez and Shakespeare were contemporary travellers on the winding stair, and that their worlds overlapped, cannot be doubted, but to make them best friends is to overshoot the evidence and deny Shakespeare's transformative brilliance. Lopez and Shylock cast a diffracted light upon each other; although Lopez preceded Shylock, Shylockian figures preceded Lopez. The imaginative continuum is hard to discount; only its chronology is obscure.

In November 1594, while the Lord Chamberlain's Men settled in at the Cross Key Inn, a more obvious fictionalisation of Lopez appeared. After painstaking editing by William Wade, Lord Burghley's account of the Lopez affair was published as *A True Report of Sundry Horrible Conspiracies*. It did not bear the Lord Treasurer's name, only that of its publisher, Charles Yetswirt, the Clerk of the Signet Office, who had wrought clerical miracles in preparing digests of the prosecution's case against Lopez. By then, Lopez's plot had become further abstracted into anti-Catholic conspiracy theories. Aware of the ambiguity of the cipher letters and forced confessions on which Lopez had been committed, William Wade had advised Burghley not to reprint most of the correspondence that had been cited in the prosecution. The result was curiously anodyne. The Doctor's plot and its coy references to 'Musk and Amber' were overshadowed by a lurid account of another of Sir William Stanley's schemes, involving Jesuit assassins and the kissing of poisoned Bibles. Lopez made poor fiction: his life had been a richer work.

Sir Edward Coke received a copy of Burghley's untrue *True Report*. He annotated its frontispiece in his ant-like hand, 'The Lord Treasurer thought best to tell personally truths and substances of the cause, against any confusion or dispute; and this book was never answered, to my knowledge; and this is the best kind of publication.'

It is tempting to find an answer to Coke and the Cecils in Shylock's greatest moment, the speech in which he breaks the bonds of medieval cliché and Marlovian cartoon, resisting the weight of social bigotry and legal process which seek to turn him into a cipher for wickedness: 'Hath not a Jew eyes? Hath not a Jew hands, organs, dimensions, senses, affections, passions?' Yet this speech is also the

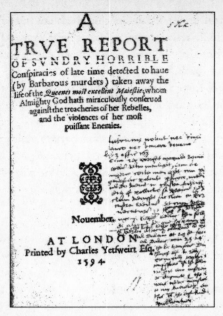

The annotated frontispiece of Sir Edward Coke's copy of A True Report, *November 1594.*

moment at which Shylock not only transcends the ghetto walls of Venice, but also transcends his origins, literary or historical. He becomes as convincingly human as any 'real' historical figure and perhaps more so; who can articulate their dilemmas with Shakespeare's clarity? Shylock outstrips Lopez as Shakespeare's art outstrips life, and life resists condensation into a play.

There are real and fictional jewels in the Doctor's story. Once there was a ruby ring, its stone dug from the mines of the Spanish Empire, from South America, Africa or India. It came to Madrid on a caravel or a galleon, where it was stored in one of the King's many treasure chests. One day, the King needed it, as payment in a diplomatic matter of espionage and intrigue. The lid of the chest was lifted, and light fell again on the stone. It was ferried secretly from Madrid to London by a professional intriguer, who tried to keep it for himself, but was caught out by its intended recipient, a Jewish physician. Hidden in the house of the physician, the ring's significance was as deliberately ambiguous as a Marrano oath. It may have been nothing more than the blood-red fruit of an elaborate fraud. It could have been a bribe for an assassin, a gift for a Queen, or a dowry for a daughter. It might have become the stone upon which peace was built. It was too valuable to publicise and too dangerous to sell, so the Doctor hid it in his home with his other secrets. After his execution, the ruby ring passed to the Queen, one item in the catalogue of his possessions.

The Queen wore the ring at her waist for the rest of her life.

Epilogue

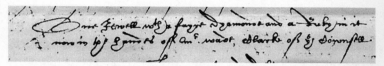

'One jewel with a fair diamond and a ruby in it, now in the hands of Mr. Wade, Clerk of the Council.' From an inventory of Lopez's possessions made after his conviction.

In the late summer of 1594, a destitute **Sara Lopez** petitioned Elizabeth I to lift the attainder against her husband's estate. The 'condemned and poor widow of Doctor Lopez' was 'utterly confounded and dismayed' by 'the heavy ruin' of her family. Her children were starving, her home had been stripped, and still the creditors knocked at her door. She had appealed to Lord Burghley, but he had refused to help. Through the long winter, no answer came. Over the garden wall at Gray's Inn, the lights shone from the hall windows as the lawyers gathered for their Christmas theatricals, the *Gesta Grayorum* – starring Francis Bacon – and an inebriated performance of Shakespeare's *The Comedy of Errors* which was so riotous that the Inn subsequently referred to it as *The Night of Errors*.

In the spring, the Queen showed mercy. Although she would not relinquish the ruby ring, she did grant the Doctor's wife and children 'full right, title and term of years' to 'a tenement called Mountjoy's Inn' and a 'certain other House, . . . being situated in the parish of St Katharine Creechurch, lying in Aldgate of the City of London'. Shortly afterwards, Anthony Lopez resumed his studies at Winchester, after the Queen had restored the £30 stipend she paid towards his fees. By lifting the attainder, the Queen did not imply that she considered the Doctor to have been innocent. It was common practice to return attaindered estates, even modest ones, to a traitor's family after his execution. It removed a pretext for revenge, and reduced the number dependants that had been left unsupported. It was the legal closure of a legal episode.

After the scandal, many of the **London Marranos** disappeared from London. Visiting Constantinople in 1612, the pioneering English tourist Thomas Coryate attended a circumcision in the house of 'a certain English Jew, called Amis, born in Crutched Friars in London, who hath two sisters more of his own Jewish religion . . . who were likewise born in the same place'. The 'Amis' trio were Sara Lopez's siblings, Benjamin, Elizabeth and Rachel Añes, who had fled to Constantinople and joined Alvaro Mendes. Only one of the Añes children, William, stayed on in London with his wife and children. **Jeronimo Lopez** kept him company. After the scandal had died down, Jeronimo came back to London and picked up where he had left off. By 1597, he was an Essex intelligencer, corresponding with Anthony Bacon. Of Roderigo Lopez's children, only Anne Lopez, the Doctor's eldest daughter, stayed in London; she married the Marrano merchant Francisco Pinto de Brito. It is likely that Sara Lopez and her younger children fled with her brother and sisters to Constantinople, or perhaps to her Lopez in-laws in Antwerp.

In the seventeenth century, Amsterdam became what Antwerp had been to the sixteenth century, the greatest port in the world. The Portuguese nation of Antwerp moved north to Amsterdam, where a liberal dispensation allowed freedom of worship. They established a remarkable community of traders and rabbis, the more picturesque among them doubling as models for Rembrandt's biblical portraits. In 1655, Rembrandt's neighbour, Menasseh ben Israel, came to England for the Whitehall Conference, convened by Oliver Cromwell to discuss the resettlement of Jews in England, and the following year saw the establishment of a small overt Jewish community.

Shortly afterwards, it was discovered that a small community of Marranos had been living near the docks in London all the time. They showed no interest in ending their underground existence and promptly disappeared again: for some Marranos, the experience of a double life did not permit a return to the past. Others found themselves pressed forward into the future: the most famous product of the Amsterdam community was Baruch/Benedictus Spinoza, the son of a Marrano who was excommunicated from first synagogue and then church for thinking beyond the intellectual bounds of both. In his ambiguous allegiances, Roderigo Lopez the Marrano was emblematic of a wider confusion, his dilemmas a way station on the road to modernity. Traces of Marranism continued to be discovered into the modern era, in the hill country of Portugal and the most remote corners of the erstwhile Spanish and Portuguese Empires. Even today, evangelising rabbis scour the Amazon basin, searching for residual Marranos who can be reconverted to Judaism.

Doctor Lopez's old flame **Mrs Allington** may have remarried shortly after his execution: on 4 September 1597, Mr Doctor Bancroft married a 'Mary Allington' and Stephen Button in St Andrew's, Holborn. If so, her happiness was brief. On 31 January 1604, the Pensioners of Gray's Inn leased to Sir Thomas Savage, 'for the term of sixty years a parcel of ground belonging to Gray's Inn, and lying within a brick wall lately erected by Mrs Allington, deceased'. This 'parcel of ground' was Doctor Lopez's garden. In 1663 the lease passed to Charles Rich, 4th Earl of Warwick, the great-nephew of the 2nd Earl of Essex who had shown such interest in what had taken place in the garden.

After that, **Mountjoy's Inn** was known as Warwick House. On 9 February 1693, Dame Barbara Allibone paid Gray's Inn £500 for the right to build over its garden 'a street . . . extending north and south to be twenty-four foot wide . . . the houses to be thirty-five foot in depth, and no privies'. Named Warwick Court, the street was decorated with 'a pair of iron gates with a wicket, exceeding the value of £20', and had a turning space for carriages at its southern end. One hundred years later, the name 'Gray's Inn Place' was inscribed on the gates. The Elizabethan physic garden where Doctor Lopez had plotted with Ferreira da Gama and Emanuel Luis Tinoco disappeared beneath the cobbled geography of Georgian London.

Don Antonio, King of Portugal and Prior of Crato, died poor and embittered in Paris on 25 August 1595, aged sixty-four. He was attended by his last courtier, his cousin and confessor Brother Diego Carlos, the monk who had brought Ferreira da Gama's smuggled note and Essex's attention to Lopez's door in November 1593. Among the papers found in Don Antonio's cabinet were his tormented *Psalms Confessionales*. An English translation, *The Royal Penitent*, was printed in London in 1596. In life, Don Antonio had been torn between home and exile, religious office and royal debauch. He was divided in death too, but with a little more decorum. His body was buried in the Gondi chapel of the Grand Convent of the Franciscans in Paris, but his heart was buried in another convent, the Daughters of the Ave Maria, behind a plaque bearing the Portuguese arms and an epitaph composed by Diego Carlos. Like his childhood companion and mortal enemy Roderigo Lopez, Antonio was posthumously dismembered.

The Avis claim passed to the eldest of Antonio's ten children, the traitorous Don Emanuel. He married Emily, daughter of William of Orange, and died in Brussels in 1638; the claim passed to his son Emanuel II, who had four daughters, after which the Avis claim eddied into the variegated bloodstream of Netherlands aristocracy. In 1909, a direct descendant of Don Antonio, Woltera Gerardina Irmgard van Schuylenburch, finally returned to the royal Court of Portugal. She was the wife of the Netherlands ambassador to Lisbon, the more modestly named Excellency Monsieur Willem Isaac Doude van Troostwijk.

Philip II died in 1598. When Portugal regained its independence from Spain in 1640, the new Portuguese King was not from the House of Avis, but the House of Braganza. A persistent strand of Avis nostalgia persisted for decades, the 'Sebastianist heresy', which held that one of Don Antonio's more successful predecessors had been serially reincarnated.

One day in the summer of 1594, wrote **Antonio Perez**, 'I chanced to be walking near the gates of the City, in the neighbourhood of St Paul's' as the severed heads of his would-be assassins Patrick Collen and John Annias were mounted on spikes. Perez left England in August 1595, escorted by a retinue supplied by the Earl of Essex, and carrying £300 in cash borrowed from Jeronimo Lopez. In 1596, he returned to England on a second, equally unsuccessful mission. The forgotten man of the Lopez affair, Perez lapsed into poverty and sickness, and died in Paris in 1611.

In 1596, **Robert Devereux**, 2nd Earl of Essex got his chance to lead an attack on Spain. Improbably paired with the Cecil adherent Lord Admiral Howard, he led a successful raid on Cadiz, but this triumph led to his fall. In the following year, the 'Islands' Voyage' to the Azores was a financial disaster. Combined with his increasingly erratic behaviour – Essex drew his sword in one argument with the Queen – it was clear that his political star was in the descendant. When Elizabeth sent him to Ireland to subdue a rebellion, it appeared that he had plotted with the Irish rebels to overthrow her. On his return, Essex House became a focus for reckless young gentlemen excluded by the Cecil supremacy, and Essex and the Earl of Southampton plotted a rebellion.

On Thursday 5 February 1601, the Earl of Southampton sent a message to the Globe Theatre, ordering the players to revive Shakespeare's *Richard II* on the following Saturday. The play, which depicted the deposition of a king, was performed as ordered. The Privy Council already knew about Essex's plot, and it ordered that he and his supporters be confined to Essex House on the Strand. The next morning, Essex and 200 men broke out of Essex House and stormed through the City, trying to raise a revolt. Nobody joined them. After twelve hours the plotters emerged one by one from Essex House and surrendered. Above them, smoke poured from the window of the Earl's study. In his haste to destroy any evidence, Essex had set fire to a large metal trunk that contained most of his private papers, presumably including many relating to the Lopez affair.

At Essex's trial, the prosecutor was Sir Edward Coke. Francis Bacon testified against his old patron; as Bacon had written, 'The traitor in faction goeth lightly away from it.' On 25 February 1601, Essex was beheaded in the Tower with three strokes of the axe. On 5 March, Essex's secretary, **Henry Cuff**, his steward, **Gelly Meyrick**, and his father-in-law, **Sir Michael Blount**, Lord-Lieutenant of the Tower, were convicted of high treason. On 13 March, Meyrick and Cuff followed the tracks of Lopez's hurdle to Tyburn, where they were hung, drawn and quartered. Five days later Blount, the invigilator of Lopez's imprisonment, was beheaded in the Tower whose Lord-Lieutenant he had been. Essex's failed rebellion was a death throe of the old feudal aristocracy that had been replaced by the new men of the Tudor era, most notably the Cecils.

Too crippled to wave a sword, **Anthony Bacon** died in bed and in debt in May 1601. Two other survivors from Essex's party provided accounts of the Lopez conspiracy. The literary expert **Sir Henry Savile**, Warden of Merton College, Oxford and Provost of Eton College, told the story of the Lopez affair to Bishop Godfrey Goodman for his *The Court of King James*. **William Temple**, the Essex clerk who had copied William Wade's account of the Lopez conspiracy for the Earl, continued to work for Anthony Bacon until Essex's fall, after which he was never heard of again.

Francis Bacon's denunciation of the Earl of Essex did not recommend him to Elizabeth I any more than had his earlier allegiance to the Earl. Under James I, Bacon emerged from premature retirement and finally achieved the political preferments he had sought. In 1613, twenty years after he had lost the battle for the attorney-generalship to Sir Edward Coke, Bacon levered a furious Coke into the office of Lord Chief Justice and replaced Coke as Attorney-General. Two years later Bacon had the further satisfaction of leading a commission to investigate Coke for financial corruption and insulting the King. This time, 'the Bacon was too hard for the Cook'. From there, Bacon rose still further to the office of Lord Chancellor. In 1621, James I appointed him Viscount St Albans.

The inevitable fall came within three months, when Bacon was accused of corruption. Aptly, the investigator into the charges was Sir Edward, now Lord, Coke. Disgraced, Bacon retired – this time permanently – to his private studies. It is a measure of their value that his posthumous reputation as philosopher and scientist has outrun his contemporary reputation for financial corruption, betraying his friends and buggering his servants. There are two theories of Bacon's death, both of which invoke scientific method. Either he caught a chill after stuffing a dead chicken with snow as part of his research into the preservation of food at low temperatures; or he was poisoned by an accumulation of opiates and saltpetre through reckless self-medication with 'physic'.

In 1616, when the Lord Chief Justice, **Sir Edward Coke**, was convicted of corruption and insulting the King, he was probably guilty of little more than vanity, asserting the prerogative of the law over the will of the monarch, and the understandable offence of feuding with Francis Bacon. In 1622, a year after avenging himself on Bacon, Coke was briefly imprisoned in the Tower for his opposition to James I's pro-Spanish policies. In retirement, Coke concentrated on arguing with his young second wife, Lord Burghley's granddaughter Lady Elizabeth Hatton, and on compiling his mammoth *Institutes of the Laws of England*. Completed in 1644, the *Institutes* shaped the legal profession's view of its past and the priorities of its development, including its conviction of its own importance. Despite this legacy no biographer has yet attempted a defence of Coke's rancorous technique as a prosecutor, which seems accurately to have reflected his bitter character. He died in 1634, at the age of eighty-two.

Having already infuriated Elizabeth I by secretly marrying one of her ladies in waiting, Henry Wriothesley, 3rd **Earl of Southampton**, was sentenced to death for his part in the Essex rebellion. Although Southampton had caused uproar in his trial by accusing Sir Robert Cecil of being a Spanish spy, the death sentence was commuted to imprisonment largely through Cecil's agency. In 1603, James VI of Scotland's first action on assuming the English crown was to release Southampton. A lifelong sponsor of literature, he was an ornament to the Court of King James, just as he had been to that of Queen Elizabeth.

Southampton's tutor, **John Florio**, flattered his way to the top of the winding stair. In 1603, Florio was rewarded with a salary of £100 per annum as reader in Italian to Anne of Denmark, wife of James I, and a year later the King appointed him Gentleman-Extraordinary and Groom of the Privy Chamber. Thoughtfully, Florio revised his pioneering Italian dictionary *A World of Words* as *Queen Anna's New World of Words*. He died in 1625 in bucolic Fulham, west of London.

In 1611, **William Shakespeare** retired to Stratford-upon-Avon. A successful businessman, landholder, grain speculator and playwright, he died in 1616, aged fifty-two, after catching a chill, probably from drinking too much with his actor friends at the wedding of his daughter Judith. The poet who had striven to garland his verse in allusions to Ovid was not classical enough for the seventeenth century, but in the eighteenth century he ascended like a Roman emperor to posthumous divinity as the presiding spirit of English literature. The subject of films, biographies and novels, the hanger-on at Southampton House became the most researched commoner of the Elizabethan age. Arguments still rage in the universities and the press about the sources of his plays, the order in which he wrote them, when he wrote them, when he might have rewritten them and what the printers used as the basis of their folios. He towers over his era and ours with uncanny percipience, his greatness renewed as each era finds its reflection in his glass. Like all divinities, he has spawned heretical cults. In December 1885, more than 200 years after Shakespeare's death, a society was founded to propagate the literary antinomianism that if Shakespeare had ever existed, he had not been a playwright, and that the real author of the 'Shakespeare' canon was Francis Bacon.

In 1595, Shakespeare's Stratford associate, **Richard Field** the printer, published the English translation of Antonio Perez's *Relations* that had been prepared by Essex's secretary Arthur Atey and edited by Anthony Bacon. Field became the leading English printer of Spanish literature, operating under the pseudonym 'Ricardo del Campo'. In 1595, Field also printed a fine edition of North's translation of Plutarch's *Lives*, source for much of Shakespeare's Roman material. A liveried member of the Stationers' Company, Field died in 1624.

In December 1594, the playhouse manager, **Philip Henslowe**, and his son-in-law, the actor Ned Alleyn, secured a substantial interest in the Paris Garden, a bear-baiting venue near the Rose Theatre. A speculator in starch, pawnbroking, moneylending and property, Henslowe became a prominent Southwark landlord, the owner of many inns and lodging houses, some of which were rented to brothel keepers. Influential in his parish, and a regular communicant at his local church of St Saviour's, Henslowe died in January 1616. The notebook that he kept between 1592 and 1603, in which ticket receipts are interspersed with IOUs and folk remedies for the common cold, turned out to be a vital document of the Elizabethan theatre.

In August 1605, James I appointed **William Wade** as Lord-Lieutenant of the Tower of London, and two months later Wade entered Parliament. His governorship of the Tower came in time for him to assist in the examination of the Gunpowder Plotters. Wade was involved at all levels of the inquiry, including the production of a tampered confession from the plotter Thomas Winter. He was knighted by James I, and in 1612 was among the investors who bought Bermuda from the Virginia Company. In May 1613 the sixty-seven-year-old Wade was dismissed from the Tower, charged with carelessness in guarding his prisoners and the embezzlement of their jewels. Appropriately, he was wholly innocent of the charges. In August 1613, Wade resigned his Clerkship of the Privy Council and retired after a lifetime of diligent, brutal service. He died two months later. His narration of the Lopez affair survived in a bundle of manuscripts, bound together with a collection of reports on minor Catholic conspiracies.

William Cecil, **Lord Burghley** died on 4 August 1598, after piloting the ship of State for four decades as the Queen's constant companion. He had ruled more in care than inspiration and more in cunning than compassion but – perhaps uniquely among Elizabeth's courtiers – this relentless servant had earned her trust and affection, and not squandered it. Along the way, Burghley grew fantastically wealthy and gained a reputation for greed, but he lived abstemiously, with the moderate hobbies of gardening, reading and trotting around on his little mule. He had lived to see the death of his enemy Philip II, and the establishment of his son Sir Robert Cecil as Elizabeth I's chief adviser. The Queen nursed Burghley personally in his last illness, and when he died she was bereft.

Elizabeth I died in 1603. According to **Sir Robert Cecil**, her last words were, 'I will that a king succeed me, and who but my kinsman, the King of Scots.' Conveniently, this matched the detailed secret preparations that Sir Robert Cecil had already made. He presided over the passing of Elizabeth's kingdom to her cousin James VI of Scotland, who became James I of England, first of the Stuart kings. In 1604, Cecil negotiated a peace treaty with Spain and became James's chief minister. James ennobled Cecil as first Viscount Cranborne and Earl of Salisbury. After Cecil's death in 1612, his descendants became one of Britain's foremost political dynasties. His namesake Robert Cecil, third Marquess of Salisbury, was a three-time Conservative Prime Minister under Queen Victoria and Edward VII. The current Lord Cranborne's negotiations with the Blair government over the modernisation of the House of Lords prompted one disgruntled Tory peer to comment, 'Never trust a Cecil.'

A final image as the curtain falls. A spring night in London in the year 1605. It is the 15th of Nissan, *Pesach*, the night of the Passover. A group of elderly Marranos meet in a house in the shadow of the Tower for the *seder*, the retelling of the Exodus of the ancient Hebrews from bondage in the Egypt of the Pharaohs. As the blackamoor servant hovers and the candles cast flame on the polished pewter, the owner of the house, a white-bearded Jew well into his eighth decade, takes his seat at the head of the table: **Jeronimo Lopez**. Among his guests is a Lisbon-based merchant named Vincent Furtado, passing through London en route for Hamburg. In four years' time, Furtado will be arrested by the Inquisition, and his account of Jeronimo Lopez's *seder* will form part of his confession. Seated with Jeronimo Lopez and Vincent Furtado are five members of the da Moura family; Gabriel Fernandes, the London merchant with whom Furtado is staying; and, next to his English wife, another elderly Portingall: **Gomez d'Avila**.

Jeronimo Lopez and Gomez d'Avila are bound by their Portuguese roots, a lifetime of crypto-Judaism, a parallel career in espionage and an unmentioned taint. Half a lifetime ago, Gomez d'Avila betrayed his fellow Portingall and fellow Jew Roderigo Lopez to the Earl of Essex. A few months after that, Jeronimo Lopez escaped from the resulting scandal, abandoning his cousin Roderigo to the Cecils for £20 in gold. Worse, when Jeronimo returned to England, he became an agent for Essex, his cousin's other persecutor. Jeronimo and Gomez were complicit then – in survival, in betrayal, in opportunism, in fear – and they are complicit now, bonded by guilt and secrecy, seated in the shadow of their absent friend Doctor Lopez. In the candlelit room shuttered against the April night and the eyes of strangers, they read the ancient story of slavery and liberation. The perfect Marrano occasion: a *seder* with overtones of the Last Supper.

The blackamoor servant watches as the service begins.

HEREVNTO
ARE ADDED FOR THE
MORE MANIFEST PROOFE OF
the matters here reported, sundrie letters and
confessions of the offendors, in the same
maner as they are extant vnder the hand-
writing of the offendors, without change
of anie sentence or words.

Picture Credits

we come to the fowle practice, (from Carleton), p.207; The Jew of Malta frontispiece, p.245; Essex and Howard to Sir John Puckering, Harl. Mss. 6996, f.162r), p.303; A True Report frontispiece, p.310; and Hereunto are added, (from Carleton), p.323, by kind permission of the British Library.

Signatures of Alvaro Mendes (p.58), Manuel d'Andrada (p.69), and Emanuel Luis Tinoco (p.190); Lopez to the Privy Council (SP12/225/21r), p.84; Andrada to Lopez (SP12/239/72), p.119; Tinoco to Cecil (SP12/247/12/f.4), p.228; Cecil and Howard's notes (SP12/247/41), p.252; Howard's annotations (SP12/247/38), p.254; Tinoco's confession (SP12/247/51), p.259; signatures upon Ferreira's confession (SP12/247/70/f.3), p.267; the Great Seal, p.291; and Lord Burghley and SÀir Robert Cecil's annotations (SP12/250/10), p.296, by kind permission of the Public Record Office, Kew.

Sir John Norris & Sir Francis Drake, p.73; William Wade, p.257; and Sir Thomas Egerton, p.285: by kind permission of the London Library. 5 November 1575, p.44; and 'This day, Mr. Doctor Lopus', p.46: by kind permission of St Bartholomew's Hospital Archives & Museum. One jewel with a fair diamond, p.313: by kind permission of the Marquess of Salisbury. Anthony Bacon to Anthony Standen, p.155; and Anthony Standen's signature, p.157: by kind permission of Lambeth Palace Library. The Cecils cover their tracks, p.274: by kind permission of Cambridge University Library. Ve·nice, p.145; Calais, p.195; Cristovão da Moura, p.165; and San Lorenzo del Escorial, p.113: by kind permission of Foto Archivo Espasa-Calpe, Spain. The Count of Fuentes, p.169: by kind permission of Foto Labatorio de la Biblioteca Nacional, Spain. The palace at Brussels, p.178: by kind permission of the Museo del Prado, Madrid.

No copyright traceable for: Don Antonio, p.48; Antonio Perez motifs, p.174; Constantinople, p.198; and Henri IV, p.180

Notes

Abbreviations used in footnotes:

BL	British Library
CSPD	Calendar of State Papers, Domestic
CSPF	Calendar of State Papers, Foreign
CSP Venetian	Calendar of State Papers, Venetian
CSP SP	Calendar of Spanish State Papers at Simancas
DNB	Dictionary of National Biography
GL	Guildhall Library
HMC	Historical Manuscripts Commission
(T)JHSE	(Transactions of the) Jewish Historical Society of England
LASP F	List & Analysis of State Papers, Foreign
LPL	Lambeth Palace Library
PRO	Public Record Office
SBHR	St Bartholomew's Hospital Reports

NB: The first number shown refers to the page on which the reference features, the second number refers to the paragraph. 'Q' refers to quotations at the heads of chapters.

Prologue

4:1   Description of Lopez's death: Goodman, p.155; William Camden, *Annales*, London 1625, p.75; and Stow, '. . . laid on hurdles, and conveyed by the Sheriffs of London . . . and so to Tyburn: and there hanged, cut down alive, holden down by strength of men, dismembered, bowelled, headed and quartered, the quarters set on the gates of the City' (*Annales*, pp.768–9).

In *Dr Rodrigo Lopes' last speech from the scaffold at Tyburn*, Edgar Samuel makes a convincing case that Lopez, in typical Marrano fashion, made an ambiguous reference to 'Our Lord' rather than to 'Jesus', as reported by Camden. In this interpretation, a Christian audience would have interpreted 'Our Lord' as referring to Jesus, while a Jewish or Marrano listener would have understood it as a discreet reference to the Jewish God. Samuel's theory would appear to be confirmed by Wade's account of Lopez's protests under interrogation.

4:3   Marlowe, *Doctor Faustus* (the A-Text of 1604), IV.i, 132–4. In a later version, the 'B-Text' of 1616, Lopez is anonymous: 'O, what a cozening doctor was this!' (the B-Text of 1616, IV.iv.27).

6:3   Lopez on stage: In Middleton's *A Game at Chess* (1624), the Black Knight informs the Black King (Philip II of Spain) that there is 'promised also to Doctor Lopez for poisoning the maiden Queen of the White Kingdom, ducats twenty thousand'. In Dekker's *The Whore of Babylon*, Lopez appears as himself, saying, 'What physic can, I dare, only to grow (but as I merit shall) up in your eye.'

6:4   'O, what a cozening doctor was this!': Marlowe, *Doctor Faustus* (the B-Text of 1616), IV.iv.27.

8:1   Stephen Dedalus's reflections on Lopez and Shylock: James Joyce, *Ulysses*, pp.306–7 (Everyman ed., 1992).

8:2   Burning of the Globe, 1613: Sir Henry Wotton to Sir Edmund Bacon, quoted in Logan Pearsall Smith, *The Life and Letters of Sir Henry Wotton* (Oxford: Clarendon Press, 1907), cited in Holden, *Shakespeare*, p.301.

9:1   'Found in the kitchen at Pipe Hall': Contemporary description added to Cecil Papers 331/2, a sixteenth-century copy of a philosophical commentary on Genesis i:I-VI by Judah ben Moses ben Daniel of Rome, also known as Leone Romano (1292–c.1350). For attribution, see the letter of 13 November 1968 from J. Leveen of Cambridge University to Librarian Ms Clare Talbot, preserved at Hatfield House. Bound together with a Portuguese manuscript, this manuscript appears to have been turned up in the investigation of Lopez, after which it passed into the hands of Lord Burghley or Sir Robert Cecil.

1. The Anatomist

15:3   Lopez's early life: *Revista Da Faculdade De Letras*, III Serie, Numero

5, pp.380–1 (Universidade de Lisbon, 1961). See also: the correspondence of Charles Meyers of New York with the Librarian of St Bartholomew's Hospital, 1979.

19:1   Leonardo's anatomy drawings: Porter, *The Greatest Benefit to Mankind*, p.177.

19:3   Vicary on Vesalius's anatomy: *A Profitable Treatise on Anatomy* (1548); cited in Moore, 'The Physicians and Surgeons of St Bartholomew's Hospital Before the Time of Harvey', *SBH Review*, XVIII, pp.335–6.

The *Profitable Treatise* and its expanded version *The Englishman's treasure with the true anatomy of man's body* were accurate pictures of the Hospital's medical practice in the sixteenth century. In their dedication to Sir Robert Hayward, President, in the 1626 edition, the four editors describe themselves as 'we who daily work and practise in Surgery, according to the deepness of the Art, as well as in grevious Wounds, Ulcers and Fistules, as other hid and secret diseases upon the body of Man, daily used in St Bartholomew's Hospital and other places' (Medvei and Thornton, *The Royal Hospital of St Bartholomew, 1123–1973*, p.109).

23:1   'In converting Jews to Christians, you raise the price of pork': Jessica to Lorenzo, *The Merchant*, III.v.32–3.

26:2   Lopez and the Inquisition of Coimbra: Antonio Jose Teixera, *Documentos para a historia dos Jesuitas*, p.247; see *Revista Da Faculdade De Letras III Serie*, Numero 5, 1961 (Universidade de Lisbon), pp.380–1.

27:3   On 29 April 1757, a builder discovered a pamphlet in the roof of the Shakespeares' Henley Street home, which turned out to be a 'spiritual will' whose fourteen articles conformed to Catholic faith, apparently bearing John Shakespeare's mark. Modelled on the 'last testament' of Archbishop Carlo Borromeo of Milan, written during a severe outbreak of plague in his diocese in the 1570s, and subsequently smuggled to Catholics all over Europe. In 1580, the Jesuit Edmund Campion visited Borromeo at Milan and ordered 'three or four thousand' copies of the testament. His return journey brought him to Lapworth, twelve miles from Stratford, where his host was Sir William Catesby, a relative by marriage of Shakespeare's mother Mary Arden, and whose son Robert was to be executed for his part in the Gunpowder Plot; see Holden, pp.24–6.

2. A House in Paradise

31:5   *Merchant* story from the First Story of the Fourth Day of Ser Giovanni's *Il Pecorone*.

32:2   Lopez engaged by St Bartholomew's Hospital: 'Ruye de Lopes physician lately admitted to serve for one year from next Christmas in curing helping and comforting the sick and sore in the House of the Poor, without any salary save his house where Thomas Vickar's [Vicary's] widow now dwelleth' (Corporation of London Records Office, Repertory 15, fo.118v., September 1562).

33:2   Henry VIII to King Ferdinand the Catholic re Dr Hernando Lopez, 20 October 1515: CSPD Henry VIII, ii, p.271, art.233.

       Conviction of 'Ferdinando' Lopus for 'whoredom' in 1550: Wriothesley, *A Chronicle of England*, ii, pp.36–7. His 'naughty lying and devilish practices': *Acts of the Privy Council*, iii pp.28–9 (11 May 1550).

34:1   Alves·Lopes's house: From the confession of Gaspar Lopes, who was picked up by the Inquisition in Milan in 1540 while on a mission for his cousin Diego Mendes: Roth, 'Jews in Tudor England', in *Essays in Jewish History*, pp.76–83.

34:2   Hector Nuñez was made a Fellow of the Royal College of Physicians in 1554. Dunstan Añes became a freeman of the Grocers' Company three years later. No date for Lopez's admission into the Royal College survives, due to the destruction of the College in the Great Fire of 1666. In 1570, Lopez was invited to give the annual Royal College of Physicians anatomy lecture. He refused, possibly because he did not want to handle the bodies of plague victims (a common source of material for anatomy), possibly because he was abroad. He paid a £4 fine and was not invited again. See, Munk, I, p.64.

35:2   West Smithfield, and Newgate Market: *London Encyclopaedia*, pp.561, 773, 812. Plaques on the perimeter wall of St Bartholomew's Hospital record the executions of William Wallace, and the Protestant martyrs John Rogers, John Bradford and John Philpot. Until 1547, the butchers had their own church abutting the abattoirs on Newgate Street, St Nicholas by the Shambles. West Smithfield had changed little by the time of its description by Dickens in *Oliver Twist* (1837–8): 'The ground was covered nearly ankle-deep with filth and mire; a thick steam, perpetually rising from the reeking bodies of the cattle, and mingling with the fog, which seemed to rest upon the chimney-tops, hung heavily above. All the pens in the centre of the large area, and as many of the temporary pens as could be crowded into the vacant space, were filled with sheep; tied up to the posts by the gutter side were long lines of beasts and oxen, three or four deep. Countrymen, butchers, drovers, hawkers, boy thieves, idlers and vagabonds of every low grade, were mingled together in a mass; . . . the hideous and discordant din that resounded from every corner of the market, and the unwashed, unshaven, squalid and dirty figures constantly running to and fro and bursting in and out of the throng, rendered it a stunning and bewildering scene.'

35:4   'poor, sick and impotent people' and 'all manner potecary ware and other things necessary . . .': Moore, p.157. (CSPF January 1581–June 1582, pp. 137–8, art.147)

First mention of soap in *The Journal*, 30 April 1558: Moore, *The History of St Bartholomew's Hospital*, ii, p.277.

36:1   The surveyor's report of 1552: *The Ordre of the Hospital of S. Bartholomewes in West-smythfielde in London*, pp.10–11.

36:2   Thomas Vicary's arsenal as listed in his will, proven 1 February 1562: Moore, ii, p.589.

37:1   Lopez's marriage: no records of the marriage exist, but as their first child Ellen was baptised on 9 January 1564, the latest date for Roderigo and Sara Lopez's marriage would be March/April 1563 (Baptism record in parish records of St Bartholomew the Less, *Baptisms*, p.4).

37:2   'A meal of steam': Ben Jonson, *The Alchemist*, I.i,26.

37:3   Births of 'Ellyn Lopus, d. to Maister Doctor Lopus' and 'Ambrosse Lopas, s. to Mr. Lopas' , and the death of 'John Lopas, s. of Doctor Lopas of this parish' are in the parish records of St Bartholomew the Less: *Baptisms*, p.4 and p.5; *Burials*, p.7.

38:1   Lopez ordered to repay thirty shillings, 8 December 1567: 'Casual receipt: Item received of Mr. Doctor Lopus by order of court on December 8th 1567, and received, the reparation of xxx s' (*The Ledger of the Court of St Bartholomew's Hospital*, vol. II,1562–88, ff.107v–108r). On 28 June 1567, the money was paid to 'Bedon the Surgeon' – William Bedon, who became a salaried employee of the hospital in 1569.

On Lopez's salary, e.g, 'xls paid Doctor Lopus in mony for his livery': see payments made in the year ending 1574 in *The Ledger of St Bartholomew's*

Hospital, ii, 1562-88, f.184; also f.197 and f.209 for years to 1575 – 'The twelfth day of March' – and 1576; f.245, f.258 and f.270 for 1579,1580 and 1581; there are no records of payments to Lopez in 1577, 1578 and 1582.

39:1   Duke of Alba to Philip II, 8 August 1569: CSP SP 1568–75, pp.186–7, art.131.

39:2   The engagement of Walsingham by Cecil: the earliest correspondence between the two is dated September 1568, but there are precedents for private citizens being engaged on a casual basis for intelligence gathering and many cases of missing correspondence, so Walsingham may have begun working for the government earlier; a letter of 1586 by Francis Mylles refers to 'twenty years' in Walsingham's service (Haynes, p.26).

'look well to her food . . .': Salis. I, p.361; advice from Captain Thomas Franchiotti, cited in Read, *Walsingham*, I, p.55.

42:3   Shinbone of Lord Burghley's servant: Royal College of Physicians MSS in *Hist MSS Comm. 8th Report*, p.227a; see Zeman, p.300.

43:1   Walsingham's illness of 1571: see Fénélon, *Correspondance*, iv, p.247.

'My disease grows so dangerously upon me': Walsingham to Burghley, 16 September 1571; see Read, *Mr Secretary Walsingham*, pp.445-6.

Lopez's visit: Walsingham's diary for 'Novembre Anno 1571': *The Journal of Sir Francis Walsingham*, p.12.

43:3   Lopez's hall is boarded, 14 March 1572: *The Journal*, II, f.113.

Lopez in Antwerp, 1572: '*Liste des Portugais établis a Anvers le 3 Novembre 1572, avec le relevé des quantités de 'cervoise' consommées du 11 april au 11 septembre de cette année*', in Goris, pp.614–16. The whole Portuguese Nation imported 640 *aimes* of pepper between April and September 1572; at approximately 6 *aimes* to the ton, this totalled 107 tons. A reduced version of the list of investors, including relevant names:

Name	April–May	June–July	August–September
Jeronimo Lindo	16	-	-
Diego Lopez Alemano	8	-	-
(aka Lopez Soiero/Sapaya)			
Balthazar Nuñez	15	-	4
Salvador Nuñez	3	-	-

Jeronimo Lopez Sapaya/			
Soiero	3	4	-
Estevan Lopez	4	-	-
Estevan Nuñez	12	6	-
Bernaldo Luis	8	-	2
Alvaro Mendes	4	-	-
Antonio Lopez	-	8	1
Luis Lopez	2	2	-
Dr Alvaro Nuñez	12	-	2
Dr Lopez	4	-	-
Bernaldo Nuñez	3	4	-
Francisco Mendes	-	2	-
Henrique Nuñez	-	-	-
Pedro Lopez Soeiro	6	-	2
Antonio Nuñez	-	2	-

44:1   Lopez's home improvements:

19 June 1568: 'This day it is ordered by the courte that Mr. Doctor Lopus Gallo hall shall be borded forthwith with dele borde or other like' (*The Journal*, II, f.40r).

22 January 1575: 'Mr D. Lopus. This day order is taken by the corte that Mr. Doctor Lopus shall have out of the store house one c. of pale borde towards the repayring and amendyng of the payle in his garden, he paying for the workmanship thereof' (*The Journal*, ii, f.113r).

3 October 1578: 'Item, order is taken by this Court that Mr. Doctor Lopus his house shall be amended in tiling where it is needful' (*The Journal*, ii, f.162v–163r).

44:2   Walsingham writes of his illnesses, April 1575 and 21 November 1575: BM Add. Mss 33531, f.151 and Harl. Mss 6992, no.13; cited in Read, *Walsingham*, iii, pp.445–6.

44:3   The Court of the Hospital reprimand Lopez, 5 November 1575: 'This day order is taken by the Court that Mr Doctor Lopus' parlour shall be boarded forthwith in consideration that he shall be the more painful in looking to the poor of the Hospital' (*The Journal*, ii, f.124r).

44:5   Lopez's children, from references to Lopez's family in the parish records of St Bartholomew's the Less, West Smithfield:

The Double Life of Doctor Lopez

Type	Date	Surname	Forename	Comments	Source
Bapt.	Jan 9th 1564	LOPUS	Ellyn	d. to Maister Doctor Lopus	Baptisms p.4
Bapt.	May 6th 1565	LOPAS	Ambrosse	s. to Mr. Lopas	Baptisms p.5
Burial	Dec 12th 1567	LOPAS	John	s. of Doctor Lopas o.t.p.	Burials p.7
Burial	Apr 20th 1573	LOPUS	Jeromme	——	Burials p.8
Bapt.	May 13th 1573	LOPUS	Douglas	s. of Doctor Lopus	Baptisms p.7
Burial	Aug 23rd 1573	LOPAS	Elonr	ch. of Doctor Lopus	Burials p.8
Burial	Mar 24th 1574	LOPUS	——	The Crysome Child of Doctor Lopus	Burials p.9
Bapt.	Mar 26th 1574	LOPUS	Anne	d. of Doctor Lopus	Baptisms p.7
Bapt.	Oct 24th 1577	LOPAS	Willm	s. of Roger Lopas, doctor	Baptisms p.8
Bapt.	Mar 1st 1579	LOPUS	Anne	d. of Doctor Lopus	Baptisms p.9
Burial	Nov 7th 1579	SAGASTIVERRIN		Dominicus Lopus de, Sacristan [?], Gentleman, Secretary to the ambassador	Burials p.9
Burial	July 23rd 1580	SLOWES	Nicholas	Dairyman and door-tender to the Lord Ambassador	Burials p.10

(From *St Bartholomew's The Less, West Smithfield, Transcript of Baptisms 1547–1894* and *St Bartholomew's The Less, West Smithfield, Transcript of Burials 1547–1848*, both transcribed and indexed M. Spearman, taken from the parish register, ref. SBL 10/1.)

There is no record of the birth or christening of Anthony Lopez, youngest son of Dr Lopez. He is not mentioned in these parish records. As he was fourteen or fifteen years of age at the time of his readmission to Winchester College in 1596, he would have been born in 1581 or 1582.

There are also no records of the births of two further daughters; in her petition to the Queen after Dr Lopez's execution, Sara Lopez describes herself as 'the mother of five comfortless children . . . three of them maiden' (Salis. IV, p.601).

45:2   'extremely hated in Wales': *Leicester's Commonwealth*, p.86.

'Murder . . . in secret, committed upon divers occasions as divers times': *Leicester's Commonwealth*, p.192.

Bailey, Culpeper, Dee, Allen, Julio, Lopez, Verneys and Digby: *Leicester's Commonwealth*, pp.279–80.

A later versified version, Leicester's Ghost, described Lopez thus:

> Lopus and Julio were my chief Physicians,
> men that were cunning in the Art to kill,
> Good scholars but of passing ill conditions,
> Such as could rid mens' lives yet no blood spill,
> Yea, and with such dexterity and skill,
> Could give a dram of poison that could slay,
> At end of year, the month, the week or day.
> (Leicester's Ghost, p.6, stanza 27)

45:3   Leicester's impotence and his Italian aphrodisiac: *Leicester's Commonwealth*, p.39.

46:1   'make dead flesh arise . . .': *Leicester's Ghost*, stanza 58, ll. 7–8, p.14.

46:2   Contract to supply the army with wheat, 17 and 20 March 1579: Lopez was given a licence to export 'four hundred quarters of wheat', half to be shipped to the army in Ireland, and half to be sold in Portugal. Two ships were sent, 'the one called the *Golden Noble*, of 100 tons, with twenty men, a master and a boy; the other the barque *Burr*, of the burden of 90 tons, released to carry such wheat as Doctor Lopes was licensed to send into Portugal'. (*Acts of the Privy Council of England*, IX, 1579–80, pp.420 and 424).

Lopez also interceded with the Privy Council on behalf of the Genoese banker Benedict Spinola in a bankruptcy case. On 18 June 1578 he wrote, 'It may please your good L. to remember the humble suit of D. Lopus, in the behalf of Mr. Spinola, for a debt of xx li due by Mr Henry Howard' (SP12/124/38; see CSPD 1547–80, p.592, arts. 35–40). This was not to be the last time that the paths of Howard, a penurious Catholic aristocrat, crossed paths with the London Marranos. Three years later Mendoza, the

The Double Life of Doctor Lopez

Spanish ambassador to London, would describe Howard to Philip II as 'at your Majesty's service' and as being 'of very good parts and understanding, and is friendly with the ladies of the Privy Chamber, who tell him exactly what pases indoors'. (Mendoza to Philip, 25 December 1581, CSP SP 1580–86, pp.245–6, art.186). Two years after that, when Howard was imprisoned in the Fleet for treason, Hector Nuñez was among his creditors.

47:1   'All rising to great place is by a winding stair': Francis Bacon, 'Of Great Place', in *Essays* (1597), pp.92–3.

Lopez's suit to let his house and move into the City, 9 May 1579: *The Journal*, ii, ff.166v–167r.

3. The Lord Ambassador

50:1   'in great want of money' and Antonio's disguise: Don Bernadino de Mendoza to Philip II, 17 January 1581 (CSP SP 1580–86, pp.80–1, art.66). Mendoza sent this letter to Philip on a ship bound for Laredo, and sent a second copy overland via France.

'he was hidden for three days in a tavern' and Antonio's escape from Portugal: Mendoza to Philip II, 17 March 1581 (CSP SP 1580–86, pp.89–90, art.75). Mendoza reported this via one of his informants, who claimed to have read 'the reports sent to the Queen by [Sir Henry Cobham] about Don Antonio'.

50:3   'If King Philip had Portugal in quiet . . .': Richard Topcliffe to the Earl of Shrewsbury, 16 March 1579, in Lodge, ii, pp.164–6. This letter also describes Lopez as 'now chief physician to my Lord of Leicester' and 'a very honest person, and zealous'.

52:1   'as much bronze ordnance' and 'the Antwerp merchants': Mendoza to Philip II, 26 June 1580 (CSP SP 180–86, p.37, art.31).

52:3   'I pray you herein to show yourself a true Portuguese': Lopez to Leicester, 19 August 1580 (CSPF 1579–80, pp. 389–90, art. 402).

The dinner at Leicester House, and 'among the best of them . . .': Mendoza to Philip II, 21 August 1580 (CSP SP 1580–86, pp.49–51, art.41).

53:1   The *White Falcon*: Mendoza to Philip II, 20 December 1580 (CSP SP 1580–86, pp.70–1, art.58).

'the richest Aldermen and merchants of London': Mendoza to Philip II, 27 September 1581 (CSP SP 1580–86, pp.173–4, art.137).

53:3   Antonio 'booted and spurred, after dinner . . .': Mendoza to Philip II, 11 September 1581 (CSP SP 1580–86, p.172, art.135).

'a coach and four Hungarian horses': Mendoza to Philip II, 1 October 1581 (CSP SP 1580–86, pp.177–8, art.135).

54:1   'doubtless Lopez was an Englishman': Edward Prim Correa to Walsingham, 28 April 1581 (CSPF January 1581–June 1582, pp.137–8, art.147).

55:1   Warehousing of impounded goods under Lopez's name, December 1581: Mendoza to Philip II, 4 and 11 December 1581 (CSP SP 1580–86, pp.232–4, arts.177–8).

'Leicester and Walsingham have managed to get the embargo raised': Mendoza to Philip II, 25 December 1581 (CSP SP 1580-86, p.247, art.187). 'By placing the goods in the hands of Lopez, she was actually taking such a decision, as he was the representative of Don Antonio, who was in rebellion against Your Majesty.'

55:4   In late 1581, the London end of the Lopez–Añes operation shipped a boatload of surplus wheat to Portugal; William Añes went with it under the pretext of supervising the delivery and the loading of a cargo of pepper, but also with mails for Marranos and supporters of Don Antonio. When Antonio led a French fleet to the Azores in 1582, Benjamin Añes was on board, sending reports to Walsingham under 'special charge from Doctor Lopez, my brother-in-law' (Benjamin Añes to Walsingham from Angra, 5 March 1583: CSPF, January–June 1583 plus Add., pp.176–9, art.159).

58:2   Alvaro Mendes: See, Wolf, *Jews in Elizabethan England*, pp.24–9; and Roth, *The Duke of Naxos*, pp.205–8.

59:1   'fickle Portuguese': Mendoza to Philip II, 27 December 1579 (CSP SP 1580–86, p.707, art.610). Mendoza had sent an emissary to ask Elizabeth not to receive Don Antonio. Elizabeth had replied that she 'would be glad to receive him in her country, and entertain him and give him what help she could'.

Luis Lopez as courier: Sir Henry Cobham to Walsingham, 12 November 1581 (CSPF January 1581–June 1582, p.365, art.392). 'Doctor Lopez's brother is departing for England.' He was sent via Rouen to avoid the 'scattering soldiers' who already had harassed Walsingham on the roads and had beaten up 'another Englishman in his company, called Skeggs'.

Mendoza's description of William Añes: Mendoza to Philip II, 1 October 1581 (CSP SP 1580–86, p.179, art.139).

59:2   Lopez to Dieppe and Rouen to see Don Antonio, 13–25 March 1583; Lopez to Walsingham (CSPF January–June 1583 plus Add., pp.193–4, art.175); and Antonio to Walsingham (ibid., p.673, art.721).

59:3   'Pardon me if I am tedious to you . . .': Lopez to Walsingham, 15 January 1583, requesting assistance in recovering goods imported from Terceira to London in Don Antonio's name, but impounded following Spanish protests and 'divided among the officials' of the Customs House. 'Tell the customers to take only the ordinary expenses,' wrote Lopez. 'Otherwise, the goods being little, no part will remain for Don Antonio, still less to meet the expenses incurred' (CSPF January–June 1583 plus Add., p.42, art.37).

60:2   Lopez as 'ambassador': See Norris to Walsingham, 2 July 1581 (above); also references in St Bartholomew's the Less register to the burials of 'Dominicus Lopez de Sagastiverrin, Sacristan, Gentleman, Secretary to the Ambassador' on 7 November 1579, and 'Nicholas Slowes, Dairyman and doortender to the Lord Ambassador' on 23 July 1580 (Burials, p.9 and p.10).

61:1   4 March 1580: 'This day Doctor Turner made request to the Governors of the house for the room of Mr. Doctor Lopus, physician. Order is there fore taken by this court that the said Doctor Turner shall have the room of the physician after the death or other departure away of the same Doctor Lopus with the duties thereto belonging, in as ample a manner as the said Doctor Lopus hath the same, so long as he shall do his duty therein, and be found a fit man for the same and not otherwise' (The Journal, ii, f.183).

3 June 1581: 'This day Mr. Doctor Turner, being Physician, asked to be admitted to the house in the tenure of Mr. Doctor Lopus within the Hospital of Little St. Bartholomew's which doth appertain to him, in the right that he is now Physician to this House, and as yet the said Doctor Lopus holdeth the same. Order is therefore taken by this Court, for as much as the said Dr. Lopus is now departed from the service of the poor of this house, that immediately there be warning given to the said Mr. Dr. Lopus to avoid the same house before midsummer or St. James' Tide next coming, at the furthest, and that the same Mr. Dr. Turner in the mean time shall have such fees and duties as to the Physician of this house shall appertain' (The Journal, ii, f.188).

9 September 1581: 'Order to be made to Dr. Lopus: This day order is

taken by the Court that there be a letter made and delivered to Mr. Doctor Lopus, to avoid his house at Michaelmas next without any further delay' (*The Journal*, ii, ff.192–3).

6 December 1581: 'This day Mr. D. Turner made further request to the Master and Governors of this house, for that he is destitute of his house, and can not yet the house that belong to him, in Mr. D. Lopus' tenure. Order is therefore taken by this house that there shall be a letter written to Mr. D. Lopus requiring him to depart at Christmas next, or at New Year's time next, according to his swore and promise made to the Governors of this Court, and that Mr. D. Turner may have the house' (*The Journal*, ii, f.199r).

3 February 1582: 'This day Mr. Doctor Turner came to this Court and made request that two of the Governors of this Court would assess the house late in Mr. Doctor Lopus' tenure. Order is therefore taken that Mr Young and other the assessors shall upon Monday next would assess the same house, and to make report thereof at the next Court in what state Mr D. Lopus left the same in' (*The Journal*, ii, f.202v). The following minutes for the Courts of 10 and 22 February do not record the contents of this report.

61:3   Stephen Gosson's *The School of Abuse*: Introduction to the Arden *Merchant*, p.xxix; see Gross, p.7.

61:5   Lopez appointed physician to the Queen, 3 October 1581: PRO/C66/1208/m.21 (part xi, 23 Eliz.). See *Calendar of the Patent Rolls, Eliz. I, Vol. IX* (1580-1582); and index reference to 'Rogero Lopo' in PRO/C66/1208/m.17 (Part ii, Eliz. xxiiij).

62:2   Ten-year royal grant of a monopoly for aniseed and sumach, 26 June 1584 (reconfirmed 4 January 1593): PRO/C66/1239/m.29 (26 Eliz., part iii, f.220v).

63:1   Elizabeth meets Antonio at Lopez's house: Mendoza to Philip II, 29 November 1585 (CSP SP 1580–86, p.552, art.415 / Paris K.1563.161).

'the Queen caresses and makes much of him, giving him 1000 or 2000 crowns a time', and 'a great quantity of silk and cloth of gold': Mendoza to Philip II, 6 March 1586 (CSP SP 1580–86, p.570, art.428 / K.1564–56).

63:2   'needy and in want of money': Mendoza to Philip II, 6 August 1586 (CSP SP 1580–86, p.599, art.464 / K.1564–142).

Antonio's complaints: Mendoza to Philip II, 8 November 1586 (CSP SP 1580–86, p.648, art.582 / K.1564–218).

64:1   'much grieved', and 'constantly unwell': Sampson (Antonio d'Escobar) to Mendoza, 14 February 1587 (CSP SP 1587–1603, p.17, art.19).

64:2   Antonio's colic: 'On the 13th Don Antonio was attacked with a colic, from which he was in danger for some hours' (Escobar/'Sampson' to Mendoza, 15 August 1587, CSP SP 1587–1603, pp.130–1, art.134/K.1565.35).

Lopez treated Antonio with regular enemas of what Mendoza's described as 'Indian acacia'. This was the tropical shrub, genus cassia, or senna, whose leaves and pods were also brewed as a tea for digestive problems. Varieties of 'Acacia' were known by their exotic origins; Lopez could choose from Alexandrian, Arabian or Indian senna. Despite Lopez's offer, a lethal dose would be virtually impossible to administer.

Drake and Lopez to the Privy Council: The Portuguese spy Antonio da Vega to Mendoza, 17 December 1586, (CSP SP 1580–86 pp.671–2, art.524).

64:3   'overburdened with debt': Sampson (Antonio d'Escobar) to Mendoza, 14 February 1587 (CSP SP 1587–1603, p.17, art.19).

'almost starving': Mendoza to Philip II, 26 March 1587, (CSP SP 1587–1603, pp.47–8, art.48/K.1266.82). Mendoza wrote, 'Don Antonio was very dissatisfied, and Dr Lopez, who is a great friend of my informant [da Vega?] told him . . . that Don Antono was in despair of the Queen ever giving him help to undertake any enterprise himself, and was almost starving. I hear the same from other sources.'

'He [Antonio] had fallen out with the barber who has served him for over twenty-seven years, because he would not clothe the latter any longer': Mendoza to Philip II, 9 June 1587 (CSP SP 1587–1603, pp.99–100, art.101/K.1566.148).

66:2   Da Vega at London to Mendoza at Paris re Drake's destination, 25 April 1587 (CSP SP 1587–1603, p.74, art.75/K.1566.114).

Mendoza at Paris to Philip II at Aranjuez, 30 April 1587 (CSP SP 1587–1603, pp.74–5, art.76/K.1566.117).

66:3   Philip to Mendoza re the arrival of his letter and his sources in London: 13 May 1587 (CSP SP 1587–1603, p.83, art.86/K.1448.118).

4. The Pretender

68:Q   'So may the outward shows be least themselves . . .': Bassanio in *The Merchant*, III.ii.73–4.

68:2   Andrada's background: Andrada to Burghley, 18 August 1591 (PRO/SP12/239/152; see translation in CSPD 1591–4, pp.93–4, art.92).

70:1   Andrada's offer to Mendoza: Mendoza to Philip II, 24 July 1588 (CSP SP 1587–1603, p.417, art.420/K.1568; see also footnote to p.417).

70:2   'Ojo!': written by Philip II in the margin of a report from the Genoese agent in London, Marco Antonio Messia, 5 November 1588 (CSP SP 1587–1603, p.482, it.470/K.1568).

70:3   'With regard to employing David in one place or another, you will use your own discretion, and use him where you think he may be most profitable': Philip II to Mendoza, 27 December 1588 (CSP SP 1587–1603, p.499, art.493/K.1448).

71:3   Burghley's 'Articles of offers from Don Antonio, 20 September 1588: CSPD 1581–90, p.545, art.33; see Hume, *The Year After the Armada*, p.22.

72:2   Terms of English support: 'Plan of an expedition' (CSPD 1581–90, p.545, arts.32 and 33; see also Hume, ibid., pp.19–20).

73:1   Don Antonio's attempted escape, March 1588: He went to Brentford on 10 March 1588 'for a week' (Antonio da Vega to Mendoza, 11 March 1588, CSP SP 1587–1603, p.229, art.237/K.1568). One of his courtiers tipped off the Queen. Meanwhile a 'minute description of the dresses and appearances' of Antonio and Captain Perrin was issued by a Spanish spy in his Court, for his arrest in case he reached the Low Countries (Anonymous Portuguese – probably da Vega – to Mendoza, 22 March 1588, CSP SP 1587–1603, p.240. art.245/K.1567). The dog of which Antonio was 'very fond' was the means of detection at Dover ('Sampson's Advices' to Mendoza, 22 April 1588, CSP SP 1587–1603, pp.271–2, art.273/K.1567). These 'Advices' also described the Queen's 'caressing' and Howard's salute.

Antonio's last diamond was sold to a M. Sancy of Paris, whose name the diamond bore in its subsequent possession by James II of England; it ended up on the imperial crown of Russia.

74:2   'arms and furniture': Norris to Walsingham, 8 April 1589 (CSPD 1581–90, p.590, art. 73).

74:4   'disconsolate', 'dishonour', 'loss': Drake to Burghley, 8 April 1589 (CSPD 1581–90, pp.589–90).

75:1   *'peregrinus'*: *The Roll of the RCP of London*, ed. Munk, I, pp.49 and 64–5.

76:1   Captain Sydenham: Wingfield, p.62. Captain Anthony Wingfield, cousin to the Earl of Shrewsbury, had fought with the Earl of Essex in the Netherlands. His account of the expedition, *A True Copy of A Discourse*, was published later that year.

77:1   'If the Earl of Essex has joined the fleet, they are to send him home instantly': Walsingham to Drake and Norris, 4 May 1589 (CSPD 1581–90, p.595, art.10).

78:3   'the wind was great and the sea was high': Wingfield, p.69.
   'the push of the pike': ibid. p.70.

80:1   Complaints about food on the way from Peniche to Lisbon: The Portuguese diarist of *Relacio de lo subcidido del armada enemiga del reyno de inglaterra a este de Portugal çon la retirada a su tierra, este año de 1589*, MS Gayangos Library, translated in Hume, *The Year After* . . ., p.53.

80:2   'We are in great alarm and have passed a very bad night. God help us!', and 'fishing in troubled waters was profitable to the fishermen': Don Francisco Odonte, Adjudant-General to the army in Lisbon, in CSP Venetian, vol.VIII, pp.448–9, art.844.

80:3   'old folks and beggars . . .': Wingfield, pp.74–5.

81:3   'reduced by the heat', and 'the greatest cowards ever seen': Drake and Norris from 'the camp at Caskales' to the Council, 1 June 1589 (CSPD 1581–90, p.603, art.77).

   'the wind being east and northerly ever since His Lordship's being in these parts': Devereux, I, p.202.

82:1   'the greatest storm we had all the time we were out': Wingfield, p.90.

82:2   Allegations against the Mayor of Plymouth: Norris to Walsingham, 15 July 1589 (CSPD 1581–90, p.610, art.30).

82:3   Don Antonio heckled as a 'dog': Andrada to Mendoza, 21 July 1589 (CSP SP 1587–1603, pp.549–52, art.554/K.1569).

85:1   Lopez apologises to Walsingham and the Queen, 12 July 1588: PRO/SP12/225/21; see CSPD 1581–90, p.609, art.21.

   Lopez requests monopoly renewals, 12 July 1588: PRO/SP12/225/22; see CSPD 1581–90, p.609, art.22.

5. A Kind of Jewish Practice

86:Q   'Which is the merchant . . . ?': Portia, disguised as a lawyer, *The Merchant*, IV.i.170.

89:1   1600 quarto title-page and 1598 Stationers' Register entry from J. R. Brown's introduction to the Arden *Merchant*, p.xi.

90:3   'I should not see the sandy hour-glass run . . .': Salerio, *The Merchant*, I.i.25–7.

91:1   'Thou almost mak'st me waver in my faith . . .': Gratiano, *The Merchant*, IV.i.130–8.

91:2   Bassanio 'upon the rack', and Portia's reply: *The Merchant*, III.ii.25 and 32–3.

93:1   Grant of revenues from Tredington and Blockley to 'Rogeri Lopes, in medicinis doctori' on 28 October 1589: PRO/C66/1307/m.5, (30 Eliz., pt.iv, f.341r). See also 'Shakespeare and Shylock', letter of E. A. B. Barnard to the *Times Literary Supplement*, 12 May 1950.

93:2   'very bad terms': Anonymous 'Advices from London' to Mendoza, 5 March 1590 (CSP SP 1598–1603, p.575, art.583/K.1571).

       'but with a very ill grace': Mendoza to Philip II, 21 February 1589 (CSP SP 1587–1603, p.571, art.579/K.1571).

95:4   'The due and forfeit': *The Merchant*, IV.i.36–7.

97:1   The Privy Council on the Gambia trade and Antonio's debts, 21 December 1589: *Acts of the Privy Councils of England* (NS), vol.XVIII, 1589–90, pp.264–5. See also Andrada to Mendoza, 21 July 1589 (CSP SP 1587–1603, p.551, art.554/K.1569).

97:3   'Revenge is a form of rough justice . . .': Bacon, 'Of Revenge' in *Essays*, p.72.

98:3   *The Merchant*, I.iii.152–5.

98:5   In 1999, Robin Marris, Emeritus Professor of Economics at Birkbeck College, London, used a computer model to worked out that to produce an approximate modern equivalent, Elizabethan figures for income, expenditure and property should be multiplied by a factor of 500. See Holden, p.7.

99:1   Exchange rate for the ducat: the rate, stable since 1586, was noted by Lord Burghley in a list of the early 1590s as '1 Italian ducat: 14s.43/4d' (LASP Foreign, vol.V, July 1593–December 1594, art.163).

100:1   John Shakespeare's usury conviction: Holden, p.146.

100:3   *The Merchant*, I.iii.39–47.

100:4   Background to Usury Act of 1571: Gross, p.36.

102:1   Shakespeare as issuer of credit and litigator: Holden, pp.213–4 and 262.

102:2   'who came ruffling it out hufty-tufty in his suit of velvet': Nashe on Harvey's 'hobby-horse revelling and domineering' when the Queen came to Audley End on her 1578 progress (quoted in Smith, *Gabriel Harvey's Marginalia*, p.19).

103:1   Gabriel Harvey's marginalia to *In Iudaeorum Medicastrorum calumnias, & homicidia: pro Christianis pia exhortatio* (*Calumnies upon Jewish Physicians and their Murders; an Exhortation to Christian Faith*) by Johannis Thomae Fregius (Johann Thomas Fregius), '*continens historiam ecclesiasticam*', printed at Basle, 1583. Harvey's edition was a gift from 'Joachim Strippius, Doctor of Medicine', whose dedication ran, '*Magnifico viro, Iudaicae, & paracelticae Medicinae aduersario communi, Dr. Erasto . . ., amico etsi ignoto: dedit Joacim: Strippius D*' ('To the magnificent Lord Erastus, the opponent alike of Jewish and Paracelsian medicine, a friend although unknown, Joachim Strippius, Doctor, has given [this]') (BL shelfmark C.60.h.18).

6. The Double Bond

107:Q   From the physician and the attorney . . .': *First Fruits*, p.666.

108:1   §'I have always been an Artist in iniquity . . .': *The Royal Penitent, or The Psalmes of Don Antonio*, Psalm 32, p.23.

'O how great hath my misfortune been . . .': *The Royal Penitent . . .*, Psalm 38, p.29.

108:4   'I am environed with a thousand evils': *The Royal Penitent . . .*, Psalm 6, p.9.

M. de la Chastres: Mendoza to Philip, 9 June 1587 (CSP SP 1587–1603, p.100, art.101/K.1566.148); and 'Sampson' (Escobar) to Mendoza, 30 July 1587 (CSP SP 1587–1603, p.130, art.134/K.1565.35).

The interception of Mendoza's mail, October 1589: CSPF Lists & Add., vol.I, p.358, art.614.

The interception of Andrada's ciphered mail: Mendoza to Philip II, 21 February 1590 (CSP SP 1587–1603, pp.570–1, it. 579/K.1571).

Lopez's role in the interception of Andrada's mail: Burghley to Mr Mills, 3 August 1591 (PRO/SP12/239/123; see CSPD 1591–4, pp.82–3).

110:3   Andrada's account of Don Antonio's escape plot, his capture and release by Lopez: Andrada to Mendoza, 5 March 1590 (CSP SP 1587–1603, pp.572–5, art.582/K.1571).

Andrada's feigned illness: '*Et je demeurait encores 15 jours dedans Londres, apres (faisant le malade) iceluy Doctor* [unclear] *visites plusieurs fois, alquel temps je faisoy tout* [unclear] *luy que j'avoys taut du pays, et des affaires de Don Antonio, et peut aussy scavoir plusieurs languages'* (Andrada to Burghley, 18 August 1591, SP12/239/152; see CSPD 1591–4, p.94).

The prosecution in Lopez's trial later dated Lopez's house call as having taken place on 31 January 1590 (PRO/SP12/247/100 and 101; see CSPD 1591–4, p.445).

111:1   Billiards: Richler, *On Snooker*, pp.26–7. Richler notes that in 1846 Pope Puis XI had a table installed in the Vatican.

112:1   Andrada's letter to Mendoza, intercepted and copied for Walsingham, 5 March 1590 (PRO/SP12/238/68, summarised and apparently misdated in CSPD 1591–4, p.16).

112:2   Andrada's opinion of Lopez (in translation of an intercept): Andrada to Mendoza, 5 March 1590 (PRO/SP12/238/68; see: CSPD 1591–4, p.16).

Mendoza on the ciphers: Mendoza to Philip II, 21 February 1590 (CSP SP 1587–1603, p.571 footnote).

See also Roderigo Marques's report on Andrada in London: Mendoza to Philip II, 21 February 1590 (CSP SP 1587–1603, pp.570–1, art.579/K.1571).

112:3   Andrada's message to Lopez before leaving Paris for Spain was later dated to 1 May 1590 (PRO/SP12/247/100 and 101; see CSPD 1591–4, p.445).

Walsingham's burial: Stow, p.761.

113:2   Philip II's gout: Andrada to Burghley, 18 August 1591 (CSPD 1591–4, p.93, art.150).

Andrada's hopes after the meeting: Andrada to Burghley, 1 July 1591 (PRO/SP 12/239/72; see CSPD 1591–4, p.65).

114:2   Philip II's response to Andrada's offer, after 4 April 1591 (Paris Archives Nationales, Fonds Simancas, K.1578.7, reprinted in translation in Hume, Appendix to *The So-Called Conspiracy . . .*, pp.53–5):

It appears that there can be no objection in letting this man [Andrada] return to England; and to give him pretext for doing so, it will be necessary to seize upon the first point of his proposals. He may therefore go to Calais, and write from there to Dr. Lopez, that his coming has been prompted by the common good, begging him to send him a passport.

When he receives the passport, he may proceed withersoever Dr. Lopez may instruct him. On his arrival, he may tell him that he had proposed the peace negotiations here, as Lopez had requested him, and had set forth the Doctor's good services; whereupon all the [Spanish] Ministers had asked him what letters of credence or any other authority he could produce to enable him to deal in the matter. This will lead them to infer that, if he had brought such credentials, he would have been favourably listened to; although, at the same time, he may say that he was told it would be necessary for the peace suggestions to be accompanied by due satisfaction for the offences inflicted upon Spain. Andrada should also be instructed to express hopes of success on some such basis as this, as if of his own motion, in order that he may have an excuse for remaining there safely for some time, and when he thinks best he can return, ostensibly on the same matter.

He must be instructed that, while he remains in England, he may urge Dr. Lopez's brother-in-law to do the secret service proposed. And moreover, since Dr. Lopez himself gave his word to get Don Antonio expelled from England if His Majesty desired, he should be asked to fulfil his promise in this respect, as his offer to do so has been accepted, and his good service in all things will be acknowledged.

Under cover of all this, Manuel de Andrada must inquire and discover everything he can that is going on there, and send us full advices of the same.

It is only reasonable that he should have a grant in aid. He himself proposes a grant secured on some Portuguese revenues. His other demands must remain in abeyance for the present, but he may proceed on his service in the assurance that on his return he shall be very highly considered.

In addition to the grant in aid in Portugal, he will need some money for his voyage, as much as appears necessary. He asks for a jewel to be given to him for the daughter of Dr. Lopez, and he attaches importance to this.

This document was sent to Don Cristovão da Moura, Philip's Portuguese adviser, for assessment:

The opinion of Don Cristobal de Moura, respecting the matter of Manuel de Andrada: He should be given 300 reals as a grant in aid for the expenses of his journey to England with his companion. In addition to this, he may be told that he shall have a grant not exceeding thirty reals [per month], secured on Indian revenues, but other than those that he proposes, as they cannot be allowed. It will be just to give him something for the daughter of Dr. Lopez, and this may be one of the old jewels from His Majesty's caskets. It will also be advisable to give him something for the brother-in-law of Dr. Lopez, who offers to do the service, and also for the other confidant, who gives information. But as at present there is no money to spare, it will perhaps be best to take for this purpose also some of the jewels from the said caskets belonging to His Majesty, as is suggested above, for the other gift.

114:4   Andrada to Lopez from Dieppe: Andrada sent multiple copies of this letter. Two reached Lopez, one through a servant attached to an English gentlewoman sailing to Newhaven, and the other through Andrada's sidekick Roderigo Marques. Andrada wrote on the 1 and 6 July 1591 (PRO/SP12/239/72; see CSPD 1591–4, pp.65 and 69).

117:1   Dates for the knighting of Cecil, and the appointment of Essex and Cecil to the Council: Burghley's chronology, Salis. IV, p.91.

118:3   Mr Mills: See LASP Foreign, vol.I, p.308, art.506. The Queen 'sent Mr. Mills to Calais to find out the truth' of rumours of a reverse suffered by French Protestants at Étaples. While he was there, Mills met with a Walsingham agent named Gourdain. On 30 January 1590, Walsingham ordered Thomas Jeffries, the English consul at Calais, to pay Mills 30 livres. Jeffries was later involved in the Lopez plot.

Burghley's instructions to Mr Mills, 3 August 1591 (PRO/SP12/239/123; see CSPD 1591–4, p.82).

119:1   Andrada to Don Antonio asking that his treachery be 'scruffed off' (Andrada to Antonio, 2 August 1591, PRO/SP12/239/122; see CSPD 1591–4, p.82).

Andrada told Burghley he had been freed 'By the means of Doctor Lopez . . . The said Doctor and Sir Francis Walsingham knew better than any others the cause and procedure of that imprisonment.' He listed reasons why Burghley should trust him: 'Firstly, my conscience. Secondly the parole and service that I had from Sir Francis Walsingham and Doctor Lopez.' Thirdly, that Bernadino de Mendoza had believed him, and fourthly that Lopez would vouch for him (Andrada to Burghley, 18 August 1591 PRO/SP12/239/152; see CSPD 1591–4, p.94).

There was a two-week delay between Burghley's order to Mills and the interrogations; this was to wait for Andrada's effects to arrive from Dieppe, where Monsieur de la Chastres had held them following his arrest of Andrada, who had attempted to enter England posing as a negotiator for the release of Armada prisoners.

120:3   'Golden bullets': Guy, p.338.

121:2   Andrada paid 100 *cruzados* to report from Calais and 'run with' Fuentes: Tinoco to Sir Robert Cecil (PRO/SP12/247/82 and 83; see CSPD 1591–4, p.439).

122:1   Andrada kept the ring to himself, but Lopez found out about it through Roderigo Marques, the London Portuguese who had delivered Andrada's letter to Lopez in July: Harl. Mss 871, f.24r.

7. A World of Words

124:Q   'He who serves two masters . . .': in Mencken, p.770.

125:3   *A Survey and Admeasurement made the Fourth day of June Anno Dio 1587 by Raffe Treswell Citizen of London, of all the Land and tenemente belonginge to St. Bartholmews Hospitall in London lying and being in the Countyes of Essex and Hertforde.*

126:2   The Pembrokeshire woods in Trevelyan, p.167.

127:2   The Court on Hatfield Broadoak, 4 March 1592: SBH Ledger, HA1/3, f.100r.

129:1   The Allingtons: William Allington was admitted to Gray's Inn in 1551 (*The Register of Admissions to Gray's Inn . . .*, I, p.22 (f.484). In 1568, he was a collector of rents for the Inn (*The Pension Book of Gray's Inn . . .*, I, p.467; that year, he also ordered 'one C of lime and a half' for building works' (p.474). On 20 May 1570, he was elected as a Reader of the Inn (p.8); the following year, he was an Assistant Reader (p.9).

Henry Allington was buried 2 August 1591: *Register of Burials, 1558–1623, St Andrew's Holborn*, GL/Ms 6673/4627.

131:2   'want-wit sadness': *The Merchant*, I.i.6.

131:4   *The Merchant,* I.i.130–4.

131:6   *The Merchant,* I.i.138–9.

134:2   Essex's secretaries: 'Mr. [Henry] Wotton a linguist of great experience, Mr. [Henry] Cuff a great philosopher, and Mr. [William] Temple, a man not inferior for a secretary for either; to whom he might add Mr. Jones . . . Mr. Wotton is already secretary for Transylvania, Polonia, Italy and Germany': Mr Edmonds (another secretary) to Essex, 1596, in Birch, *Memoirs,* I, pp.239–40. Thomas Smith and Edward Reynolds also assisted.

137:1   Essex's commissioning of Lopez: related to Geoffrey Goodman by Henry Savile (later Provost of Eton, and 'very great' with Essex in the 1590s), in Goodman, pp.150–1.

8. The Jew of Venice

140:Q   'The marble not yet carved can hold the form / Of every thought the greatest artist has': Michelangelo, *Sonnet,* trans. Elizabeth Jennings and John Folger (Manchester: Carcanet, 1988), opening quotation in Anton Gill, *Il Gigante,* (London: *Review,* 2002).

141:1   Meres on Shakespeare in *Wits' Treasury, Palladis Tamia* (London: P. Short for Cuthbert Burbie, 1598; see *Francis Meres' Treatise 'Poetrie',* ed. D. C. Allen, University of Illinois Press, 1933, p.76); see also the Arden *Merchant,* p.xxii.

141:2   'sundry times acted by the Right Honourable the Earl of Pembroke his Servants': Holden, p.124.

143:2   Mendes to Murad III re the Armada: Giovanni Moro, Venetian ambassador in Constantinople, to the Doge and Senate, 9 October 1588 (CSPV, 1581–91, p.399, art.753). 'The Pashas merely replied, "God grant that it may be so", and showed that they doubted it.'

   Barton to Burghley re Passi's allegations, 10 May 1591 (CSPF, July 1590–May 1591, arts.849–50). Barton calls 'Passo' 'a very knave'.

144:1   'virtue, honesty and industry': Elizabeth to Murad, March 1592 (BL Landsdowne Mss 67/101; in Latin, trans, Wolf, *Jews in Elizabethan England,* p.27). Burghley wrote on 22 March 1592.

   Barton's defence: Barton to Burghley, 19 August 1592 (LASPF, Vol. VI, May 1592-June 1593, p.397, art.684).

144:3   Mercatoribus Venetiae: Draft of Letters Patent in Salis. V, p.15 (October 1594).

144:4   Lopez in Venice: Wolf, *Jews in Elizabethan England*, p.31. Wolf cites Cecil Roth's discovery of a reference to Lopez 'in the State Archives at Florence, dated 16 February 1594' (*Archivio Mediceo dopo il Principato*, filz.4185, f.238b).

At the time this reference was written, Lopez was in prison in London; it must refer to an earlier date. It would have taken at least six weeks to travel to Venice and return to London, and longer for the round trip to Constantinople. There are two gaps in the archives large enough to allow Lopez an extended absence from London: 30 November 1591 to March 1592; and March 1592 to December 1592. The second is more likely; Lopez's appearance in Venice followed Solomon Cormano's embassy to London and would have been part of the English effort to stabilise the Anglo-Turkish entente following Don Antonio's assault upon the Lopez–Mendes link.

145:1   'Nothing more adverse or more inimical to Christ can be found than this plague.': Erasmus on Judaism, in Israel, *European Jewry in the Age of Mercantilism*, pp.11–12.

146:2   'And by our holy Sabbath have I sworn / To have the due and forfeit of my bond,': Shylock to the Doge, *The Merchant*, IV.i.36–7.

146:4   'I pray you think you question with the Jew . . .': Antonio to Bassanio, *The Merchant*, IV.i.70–80.

146:5   'Harsh Jew!' 'Inexecrable dog!' and 'Thou almost mak'st me waver in my faith.': Gratiano to Shylock, *The Merchant*, IV.i.123, 128 and 130.

146:7   'The quality of mercy is not strain'd . . .': Portia (as Balthazar the lawyer) to Shylock, *The Merchant*, IV.i.180–191.

147:2   'a losing suit': Shylock to the Doge, *The Merchant*, IV.i.62.

'My deeds upon my head . . .': Shylock to Portia, *The Merchant*, IV.i.202–3.

'For when did friendship take / A breed of barren metal of his friend?': Antonio to Shylock, *The Merchant*, I.iii.129–30.

147:3   You call me misbeliever, cut-throat dog,
         And spit upon my Jewish gaberdine,
         And all for use of that which is mine own.
         Well then, it now appears you need my help:
         Go to then, you come to me, and you say,
         'Shylock, we would have moneys,' you say so:
         You that did void your rheum upon my beard,

> And foot me as you spurn a stranger cur
> Over your threshold, moneys is your suit.
>
> (Shylock to Antonio, *The Merchant*, I.iii.106–114.)

148:1   'He hath disgraced me . . .': Shylock to Salerio and Salanio, *The Merchant*, III.i.47–66.

150:2   Ferreira da Gama's resolution to seek accommodation with Philip II: Diego Maldonaldo to Philip II, 25 April 1593 (CSP SP 1587–1603, p.579, art.591/k.172).

After fleeing Portugal in the early 1580s, Ferreira da Gama had been stationed by Don Antonio at Lyons where, under the pseudonym Juan Luis, he had distributed anti-Spanish literature. His wife and child came to England with the Counter-Armada in 1589; Antonio wrote to him, 'At Alvelade, I was lodged in your country house, where I found your wife, Doña Maria, although I was previously unaware she was there, as I had been told at Torres Vedras she was in hiding. When the sickness of my soldiers made it impossible for us to enter Lisbon, and had had to retire, it would have been dangerous for her to return to her house, so I decided she had better embark with us . . .' (Don Antonio to Ferreira da Gama, 8 July 1589, CSP SP 1587–1603, p.547, art.550/K.1569).

150:3   Ferreira da Gama and Lopez discuss Ferreira's Portuguese scheme: in Ferreira's confession of 22 February 1594, he dated this to 'thirteen or fourteen months sithence', i.e. December 1592 or January 1593 (Harl. Mss 871, f.41r).

152:1   Unidentified plague deaths: *Register of Burials, St Andrew's, Holborn*, 1591 (GL/Ms 6673/1).

152:3   Lopez–Andrada meeting of 20 January 1593 (PRO/SP12/247/100; see CSPD 1591–4, p.445).

Renewal of aniseed and sumach monopoly: 'A grant made unto Doctor Lopez, one of Her Majesty's physicians, for ten years of the whole trade and traffic of bringing in and selling of Anis seed and Sumack within the Realm of England, assuring to her Majesty all Incomes and Subsidies due for the same. The said grant to begin after the expiration of a former grant made unto the said Dr. Lopez for the like term of years' (*Signet Office Docket Books*, PRO/SO3/1/f.385r).

This grant was entered on the Patent Rolls on 4 January 1593: 'A licence to Roger Lopez, Doctor of ye Physic, to buy and provide Anis Seeds and

Sumack, & the same to utter & sell for ten years' (PRO/C66/1397/f.16r/35 Eliz. I). See also, *Index to the Calendar of the Patent Rolls*, 31–37 Eliz. I (PRO/O12/f.16r).

153:1   Bacon brothers' lease of chambers at Gray's Inn, and their right to build, 21 November 1588: *The Pension Book of Gray's Inn . . .*, I, p.82.

Francis Bacon had been appointed a Reader of the Inn in 1587 (ibid., p.77); he was made Pensioner on 19 November 1590 (p.101); and later, he may have stood in for the Treasurer.

153:3   Anthony Bacon to Anthony Standen, undated in February 1593 and 19 February 1593: LPL Ms 648, it.99 (see Birch, pp.91–2).

154:1   Anthony Bacon to Anthony Standen, 19 February 1593: LPL Ms 648, art.99 (see Birch, pp.91–2).

154:2   'Richard Allington, son of Widow Allington' was baptised on 20 September 1592: *Register of Baptisms, 1558–1623, St Andrew's Holborn*, GL/Ms 6667/1/3331.

154:4   'Tobias, a bastard': *Register of Baptisms, 1558–1623, St Andrew's Holborn*, GL/Ms 6667/1/3071.

In the *Register of Marriages, 1558–1623, St. Andrew's Holborn*, 'Stephen Button and Mary Allington were married the 4th of September' 1594 (GL/Ms 6668/1/1618).

9. The Prop and the Burden

156:Q   'Ere I ope his letter,
I pray you tell me how my good friend doth.
Bassanio to Salerio, *The Merchant*, III.ii.232–3.

156:2   'Doctor Lopes, a physician that was taken with Don Pedro (lately delivered by exchange for Mr Winter) is lodged in a fair house in Holborn . . .': Anthony Bacon to Standen, 19 February 1593 (LPL Ms 648, f.162/film 792).

157:3   Standen's 'bills' and 'merchants': Anthony Bacon to Standen, undated, February 1593: Birch, p.92.

158:1   'a draft of an instruction for a matter of intelligence': Dedijer, p.22.

159:1   Anthony Bacon's surveillance of Lopez, February 1593: Bacon read Standen's mail in early February at the earliest. There is no evidence that Bacon suspected Lopez before Standen's advice. Judging from his description of Lopez as 'a physician that was taken with Don Pedro', he knew nothing about him. The date of Bacon's letter to Standen – 19 February 1593 – suggests that Bacon was informed that Lopez was working for Burghley at a date after the Lopez–Andrada meeting of 20 January 1593, but before the Lopez–Andrada meeting of 20 February 1593. The prosecution in Lopez's trial gave the dates of 20 January and 20 February 1593 for meetings between Lopez and Andrada (PRO/SP12/247/100). No date for a meeting was supplied for the period between 30 November 1590, when Lopez obtained the ruby ring from Andrada, and their meeting on 20 January 1593. No source was provided for these dates; it is likely that they were generated by the Standen–Rolston–Andrada encounter in Calais, and the Standen–Bacon letter of 19 February 1593.

'An apple in time is better than an apple of gold out of season', and Anthony Standen's intelligence being out of date: Anthony Bacon to Standen, 14 March 1593, in Birch, I, p.93.

159:2   Sir Henry Savile on Essex's embarrassment before the Queen: Goodman, I, pp.151–2.

161:2   'in the time of Secretary Walsingham': Harl. Mss 871, ff.17v–18r.

161:3   'to trust him with his life': Ferreira's confession of 22 February 1594, Harl. Mss 871, ff.40v–41r.

162:1   Lopez and Ferreira da Gama's meeting of 4 April 1593, and Ferreira da Gama's 'treaty and discourse' with Andrada on 16 April 1593: *Baga de Secretis*, p.286.

164:1   Andrada's return with Don Emanuel's letter of submission, and Lopez's reading of it: Ferreira's confession of 29 February 1594 (Harl. Mss 871, ff.46v–47r).

165:1   Ferreira's letters to da Moura and Idiaques, 24 April 1593; the use of Manuel de Palatios as an intermediary: Ferreira's confession of 11 November 1593. 'First, I showed him [Lopez] the writing of Don Emanuel, in his own lodging and house, before Manuel d'Andrada, and we did all there agree that, by the means of Manuel de Palatios, I should write to Don Christofero da Moura how, besides myself, who sought to accommodate myself, I did hold Don Emanuel sure; and that the said Andrada should procure answer to Calais, whether he went; and from thence should advertise all that he knew of this business' (Harl. Mss ff.17r–v).

Ferreira's copying of the letters: ' . . .both of them together gave me the draught, and before them I made it, after the order they gave me, in which went certain [f.47r] hidden words, which I could never understand' (Harl. Mss ff.46v–47r).

As part of their general simplification of their case, the prosecution were to claim that all meetings were in St Katharine Creechurch. However, in his confession of 25 February 1594, Ferreira specified that both Mountjoy's Inn and the house in St Katharine Creechurch were used by the conspirators: 'Manuel Andrada . . . did always communicate with Doctor Rui Loppez, in his house, and there he did diet most part of the time he was here [i.e, in St Katharine Creechurch]; and the Doctor Rui Loppez did conceal me, that I should procure pardon from the King of Spain, thereby to benefit myself. And presently, he [Lopez] called the aforenamed Manuel Andrada into his [Lopez's] garden [at Mountjoy's Inn]. And there we talked with him . . . And presently, four or five days after, I did appoint to write a letter, and having made a draught, the Doctor with Manuel Andrada made another in form; and I, coming to the house of D. Ruy Loppez [i.e, to Mountjoy's Inn] to write the said letter to Don Christofero da Moura, both of them together gave me the draught, and before them I made it, after the order they gave me, in which went certain [f.47v] hidden words, which I could never understand. And one month before the departure of the said Manuel Andrada, I went to his [Andrada's] house, and said unto him that he well understood that I was at the service of the King of Spain . . . And with order departed the said Manuel Andrada, . . . and I in his [Lopez's] garden demanded this question of him' (Harl. Mss. ff.46v–48r).

Ferreira said that he *went* to Lopez's 'house and lodging' to write the letters. If he and Andrada were staying at St Katharine Creechurch, then the letter writing must have occurred at Mountjoy's Inn.

172:1   Robert Draper's examination, 5 February 1594 (PRO/SP12/ 247/41; see CSPD 1591–4, p.425).

No mention of Lopez's work for Walton and Essex was made in his prosecution.

10. The Monster of Fortune

173:Q   'If your friend is a doctor, send him to the house of your enemy': *H. L. Mencken's Dictionary of Quotations* (London: Collins, 1982), p.229.

174:1   Perez's morning drink: Ungerer, I, p.324.

Bezoar stone: From the Persian 'pad-zahr', 'counter-poison'. Considered as an antidote to all known poisons and a cure for all diseases; the best and rarest variety was the Persian lapis bezoar orientale. There was also lapis bezoar occidentale, courtesy of Peruvian llamas, and the less valued German Bezoar, from the European chamois goat. As recommended in Nicholas Monardes's *Joyful News Out of the New Found World . . . Whereunto are Added 3 Other Books Treating of the Bezoar Stone* (London: 1580).

Strawberry water: In the *Anatomy of Melancholy*, Thomas Browne recorded that strawberry water was good for cooling the flushed faces of melancholy men; he also recommended that it was 'good overnight to anoint the face with hare's blood, and in the morning to wash it with strawberry and cowslip water' (Everyman's Library, No. 887, pp.251–4). At the French court, strawberry water was used as a mouthwash.

175:3 Essex's support of Perez and the Vidame: The party at Wanstead 'and many days before and after at the entertainment of the Vidame and the French ambassador' cost £193.14s.7d. (Ungerer, *Perez*, I, p.152).

175:4 Perez's gift of medicines to Essex and his accidental poisoning of Thomas Smith: Ungerer, *Perez*, I, p.324.

176:1 Perez and the dog skin gloves for Lady Penelope Rich: Ungerer, *Perez*, I, p.199.

176:3 Perez to Anthony Bacon, undated, probably January 1595: *Epistolarum centuria una* (Paris, 1601), Epistola 73; see Ungerer, *Perez*, I, pp.490–1. Translated in Jardine and Stewart, *Hostage to Fortune*, p.163.

177:1 Anne Cooke Bacon's warnings against Antonio Perez: Anne Cooke Bacon to Anthony Bacon, 27 April 1594 (LPL Ms 653, art.175); apart from 'I would you were well rid of that old, doted, polling Papist,' (undated, probably 1594, LPL Ms 653, art.177).

'Doted' ('dooted') meant 'foolish, in second childhood, decayed (of a tree). 'Polling' meant 'exacting, cheating' (Ungerer, *Perez*, I, p.221).

177:3 Tinoco's origins: the examination of John Annias, 5 February 1594 (PRO/SP12/247/40; see CSPD 1591–4, p.425).

181:1 Tinoco's and Andrada's dealings at Brussels and Lille in May 1593, as described in an undated late confession by Tinoco: 'The Count Fuentes and Stephen de Ibarra had intelligence how Antonio Perez did pass over into France, and as they have order from the King of Spain to cause him to be slain, they did ask of me from Francis Caldera, if he were gone into

France . . . And so we came in company together to the town of Lille. And as I desired greatly to know his secret designs, I did what I could to learn it of him. And he, having charge given him to say nothing unto me, did keep it till the very hour that we were to part one from another . . . "I carry the powder with me, and I carry other powder about me likewise, to dye my beard red and black . . .". And opening his hand, he shewed me the same, and those things he carried, and told me further he carried a great commission to have Antonio Perez slain, and that Stephen Ibarra had greatly recommended this diligence unto him. All these things Manuel Andrada did impart unto me in the church of St. Steven in Lille' (Harl. Mss 781, ff.61v–63r).

Tinoco's reference to this conversation having occurred in September 1593 – presumably to lessen his culpability – was a misdating; all other evidence points to the date for Andrada's ceding of his role to Tinoco as being prior to Tinoco's mission to London of late May 1593.

December 1593 assassination attempt against Henri IV: LASP F, Vol.V, July 1593 – December 1594, pp.350–1, art.429.

182:3   The Count of Fuentes's message to Lopez via Tinoco, given to Lopez by Ferreira on 31 May 1593, as related in Ferreira da Gama's confession of 30 January 1594: 'He confesseth that Manuel Lowys [Tinoco], at his being here before, told this Examinate about six months ago that he had a message to deliver to Doctor Lopez from the Count Fuentes, and an Abrasjo, which he did desire to deliver to him. And coming to Doctor Lopez's house, failing to find the Doctor there, Manoel Lowys did write a letter to the Doctor, which this Examinate did deliver to him. The contents of the letter was that the Count of Fuentes did send an inbracing to Doctor Lopez, and did bid him to tell the Doctor that he was glad that the Doctor was a good servant [f.33v] to the King, and to assure him he should be very well recompensed, and did wish him to procure some thing under my Treasurer's hand, to renew the treaty of peace, and that the King was now desirous of it, and that there might men of quality be sent to intreat of it. . . . He further doth confess that Andrada sent by Manuel Lowis a little Ticket to Doctor Lopez, to give credit unto Manoel Lowys, which this Examinate did deliver to the Doctor' (Harl. Mss 871, ff.33r–v).

184:1   Lopez and Ferreira in the garden at Wanstead, 31 May 1593, as described in Ferreira's confession of 22 January 1594: 'The assignation which the King Don Antonio made to Doctor Lopez, the said Doctor did deliver to this Examinate at Wanstead, this last summer about six or seven months ago. He doth confess that the acknowledgement of the receipt of the said assignation which he made to the Doctor was but to cover the matter' (Harl. Mss. 871, f.21r).

185:1   Ferreira to Fuentes: the *Baga de Secretis* (p.286) gives the date of 9 June 1593 for Ferreira's 'secret messages and intelligences' to both da Moura and Fuentes, but as Ferreira originally stated that he wrote to da Moura in the presence of Andrada at Mountjoy's Inn before Andrada's final departure on 24 April , this may be discounted; the prosecution in Lopez's trial chose to ignore the Don Emanuel issue entirely, and consequently condensed the sequence of events and dates. Ferreira wrote to Fuentes on either 8 or 9 June, having received Don Antonio's assignation from Lopez at Wanstead just over a week before.

186:1   The forging of Tinoco's passport is described in Ferreira's confession of 30 January 1594: 'He doth confess that he did cause the passport, which Her Majesty did grant to him two years sithence at the suit of the King Don Antonio, to be altered in the date, by one Monox, an Englishman, and he gave him twenty shillings for his labor' (Harl. Mss 871, f.33v).

186:3   'gunpowder, brimstone, and saltpetre': the confession of John Annias, late January 1594 (PRO/SP12/247/33; see CSPD 1591–4, p.421).

The commissioning of Patrick Collen and John Annias to kill Antonio Perez for £30: Collen's 'examination' of 6 February 1594 (CSPD 1591–4, p.427).

The full story of the Collen Plot is in CSPD 1591–4, pp.421–31, arts.33–64; Collen's trial is in *Baga de Secretis*, pp.283–4.

187:3   Caldera in the Vidame's house at East Molesey: Harl. Mss 871, f.13r.

Ferreira's dealings with Francis Caldera are described in Caldera's confession of just after 9 February 1594: 'He (amongst other things) did confess that, being in extremity of sickness and destitute of all means, he was relieved by Ferreira who, having bound him by his kind relief in his great necessity, thought he might repose trust in him, and so brake with him in some sort in respect of the means he had about the Vidame and the French Ambassador, to concur with D. Lopez to serve the King of Spain. Caldera replied he would not have to do with Doctor Lopez, being a Jew, and his Enemy for, by reason of a quarrel Caldera had with Andrada, Doctor Lopez had conceived displeasure against him.

'Hereupon, Ferreira told this party (the more to assure him) that he need not doubt the Doctor, for he had his foot upon his throat, which words were mark, and kept well in mind. This companion was brought up with the king Don Antonio of a child, and by this kindness and persuasion of Ferreira's was won both to betray His Majesty, and very treacherously did yield to hold correspondence with D. Lopez. So by his means, and the embrace and credit he had in the house of the Vidame (who had trusted him with matters of service) and the French Ambassador, he should advertise all matters concerning both these kingdoms, which he did very maliciously and spitefully, delivering often times his observations to Manuel Lowys [Tinoco], who was the ledger to make and send away the dispatches' (Harl. Mss 871, ff.34r–35v).

11. The Projector

190:Q   Your mind is tossing upon the ocean: Salerio to Antonio, *The Merchant*, I.i.7–13.

196:3   Tinoco at Mountjoy's Inn, 24 July 1593: *Baga de Secretis*, p.286.

Tinoco departed from London with the 'letter of submission' on 26 July 1593 (PRO/SP12/248/17).

199:1   Lopez's gossip about Essex's 'diseases': Goodman, pp.152–3.

199:2   Valentine Russwurin of Schmalkald: Harkness, p.145–6; see Clowes, *Briefe and necessarie Treatise*, f.11r.

Lord Burghley's urine: BL Ms. Landsdowne 101/4, f.12r. Russwurin found the sample to be 'eight ounces and a little more, wherein it hath no difference from a sound man his water at all'.

200:2   Girolamo Fracastoro and his *Syphilis* poem: Porter, *The Greatest Benefit to Mankind*, pp.174–5.

201:1   Syphilis treatments: Porter, *The Greatest Benefit . . .*, p.175.

201:2   Essex and syphilis: a case advanced by Robert Lacey, *Robert, Earl of Essex*, pp.79, 201–2, 261.

202:1   The two Antonios tell Essex: Goodman, p.153.

202:2   There are two sets of possible dates for Tinoco's visit. A calendar of the conspiracy dated 10 March 1594, prepared for Lord Burghley and annotated by him, reads (Burghley's addition in italics): 'Manuel Louis

[Tinoco] came again hither in the end of August 1593 or beginning of September, and stayed one day and went back again. *In this way were M. Lowys* [Tinoco's] *letters of Andrada*' (PRO/SP12/248/17). Wade's version in Harl. Mss 871, f.55r concurs with this: 'Manoel Lowis . . . at his being here . . . the 31 of August'. Alternatively, Sir Edward Coke's prosecution gave the dates of 4–5 September for Tinoco's visit (*Baga de Secretis*, p.286). I have followed the weight of evidence and used the earlier date.

202:3   Tinoco in London, 31 August to 1 September 1593: PRO/SP12/248/17 (10 March 1594). The *Baga de Secretis* account gives the dates of 4–5 September (p.286).

Da Moura's letter to Lopez and Ferreira was dated 4 August (*Baga de Secretis*, p.286).

204:2   Gomez d'Avila 'dwelling hard by Lopez's house': Francis Bacon's *True Report*, in Spedding, I, 282.

The commissioning of Gomez d'Avila: PRO/SP12/247/100 and 101; PRO/SP12/248/17; see also *Baga de Secretis*, p.285.

Gomez not meeting Lopez is described in Ferreira da Gama's first confession of 8 March 1594: 'Doctor Lopez was the occasion that I sent Gomez d'Avila with a message into the Low Countries, and he [Lopez]would not speak to him directly. . . .The said Gomez d'Avila and I went to his [Lopez's] house and found him not there' (PRO/SP12/248/12). See also Harl. Mss 871, f.55v: 'The Doctor was so wary in the carriage of this practise, as in no wise he would speak with Gomes d'Avila until his return.'

Gomez's verbal instructions were described in Ferreira's second confession of 8 March 1594: 'And when the said Gomez d'Avila went hence I told him by word of mouth that he should tell the Count of Fuentes and Stephen d'Ibarra that Dr. R. Lopez was ready to perform all that they from hence should demand of him, for which cause they should advertise by himself [Gomez] what they would have done here, for that was the D.'s own request; and so the Doctor required it should be done' (PRO/SP12/248/12; see also Harl. Mss 871, f.55v for a slightly altered version, substituting 'command' for 'demand').

Lopez's requests to Ferreira for a reply to the mails carried by Gomez d'Avila (PRO/SP12/247/100 and 101).

The prosecution appear to have misdated the Ferreira–Gomez meeting of 17 September to 30 October. By then, such an encounter would have been impossible, as Ferreira was imprisoned at Eton on 18 October (see PRO/SP12/248/17 and 18).

206:3   The arrest of Ferreira da Gama: PRO/SP12/248/17; Harl. Mss 871, f.7r confirms that it was 'about the middest of October'.

12. The Huddler Underhand

209:Q   'He that sinneth against his Maker . . .': Wisdom of Ben-Sira (Ecclesiasticus), 38.

209:1   Essex leads the investigation: Harl. Mss 871, ff.7r–v.

210:2   'whole rest of favour and credit': Anthony Bacon to Anne Cooke Bacon, 18 July 1593 (LPL Ms 649, art.15; see Birch, I, p.254).

Essex's 'amnestia' appeal and Burghley's reply to Lady Bacon: Essex to Francis Bacon, late August 1593 and 29 August 1593: LPL Ms. 649, art.168; see Birch, I, pp.120–1.

The Cecils' response to Francis Bacon, 27 September 1593: LPL Ms 649, f.299v, art.197.

210:3   Anthony Bacon's illnesses prevent him from attending at Court, 9 and 13 October 1593: Anthony Bacon to Francis Bacon, 10 October 1593, (LPL Ms. 649, f.334r, art.227); and Anthony Bacon to Anne Cooke Bacon, 19 October 1593 (LPL Ms 649, f.337r, art.230).

211:1   Essex's audience with the Queen, the night of 13 October 1593: Essex to Anthony Bacon, LPL Ms 653, art.172; see Birch, I, pp.126–7.

211:4   'I have made a great draught . . .': Harl. Mss 871, f.8v.

212:1   Torres to Fernandes (Tinoco to Ferreira da Gama) by the ordinary post: Harl. Mss 871, ff.7v–10r.

213:2   Ferreira's engagement of Pedro Ferrera the jailer is described in Pedro's undated confession: 'He sayeth that Ferreira at the beginning used to him the speeches following: "I mean to do you good, and do pray you that the first thing you do for me be, that you go to Francis Caldera and desire him from me that he will vouchsafe to passe along under the window of the chamber where the said Ferrera lodged in the King's lodging." This message this Examinate delivered to Caldera. And Caldera answered he would not so do, fearing therby to overthrow both Ferrera and himself.' (Harl. Mss 871, f.36v).

213:3   Ferreira da Gama's letter to Francis Caldera, just after 4 November 1593: 'All the diligence that hath been used doth not condemn Doctor

Lopez as yet any whit, for I have bravely shifted my body from that notwith-standing there is a carrier looked for who bringeth all things. Therefore it behoveth to advertise with all possible hast in such sort as they may under-stand, I am taken and also Gomes d'Avila, for he doth offer to help them to those letters in which he sayeth all the declarations come at large, and they speak of him in all matters.

'Constance Ruis hath a sister, who hath a son that speaketh well Spanish or any else you shall like better, and he may go by word of mouth to adver-tise if they will find remedy, for the King himself cannot help him if the Secretary get the letters, because they come written in Spanish, and then he doth not use to bring them hither, and the rather when he hath his Ears open.

'And herein is not sent above twenty Ducats, and he that will have dili-gence is there in five days. And let them not say that I have not given warning in time, and let there be no forslowing in that which importeth that the King doth likewise his part. And making this diligence, he shall safe for all. And God help us, for all the rest I take upon myself. And consider there be not matters to leave to adventure, sithence you for what diligence they make here, and how not so much as one paper doth scape from them, be that you send must go into Antwerp, and advertise the Secretary [Ibarra] or Manuel Luis [Tinoco]; and if he meet the post by the way, let him see if he bring any letters from Domingo Fernandes, and take them, or for Jeronimo Lopez, because it may be they may come in his packet; and the surest way is to take all the letters that come to any Portugal. And if they come not in them, they may be in the packet of Rizo, an Italian, or in those for Osterbrich, a Fleming.'

'The Lord be with us.' (Harl. Mss. 871, ff.16r–17r).

213:4   Francis Caldera to Pedro the jailer: Harl. Mss 871, f.37r.

214:1   Lopez gives Ferreira's second letter to Don Antonio: 'After this, Ferreira gave to this Examinate another letter, addressed to a priest in the King of Portugal's house, which he this Examinate delivered, wrapped up in a handerkerchief. And this letter the priest delivered to Doctor Lopez, who afterward shewed the same to the King [Don Antonio]. Upon the sight of which letter the said Ferreira was more straightly restrained than before' (Harl. Mss f.37r).

214:3   F. Bacon to Essex, 10 November (?) 1593: LPL Ms. 649, art.283.

A. Standen to A. Bacon, 11 November 1593: LPL Ms 649, f.390r (art.268); see Birch, I, p.130.

215:1   Ferreira on Gomez d'Avila's assistance to the inquiry: Harl. Mss 871, f.17r.

216:2   'Recover' and 'Huddler' definitions: *Britannica World Language Edition of the Oxford Dictionary* (2 vols; Oxford, OUP, 1933).

Antonio's losses: *The Merchant*, IV.i.28–9.

Claudius on Polonius's secret burial: *Hamlet*, IV.v.84.

217:1   Ferreira's confession of 11 November 1593: Harl. Mss 871, ff.17r–18v.

218:1   Essex denounces Lopez to Elizabeth and her sceptical response: Harl. Mss 871, ff.8r–8v. The 'interpretation': ibid., f.13r–v.

219:2   Tinoco (Torres) to Ferreira (Fernandes), 26 October 1593: *A True Report . . .*, p.30. The *True Report* misdates this letter as having been couriered by Gomez d'Avila from 'Brussels, in Decemb. 1593'. Even allowing for adjustment to Old Style dating, in which 5 November in Brussels was 26 October in London, this is impossible. It would mean that the letter was written more than three weeks after Gomez was arrested in England on 4 November 1593. *Baga de Secretis*, p.287, which reprints the letter with minor changes and without the last two sentences, gives the letter's date of writing as 26 October 1593. The *True Report* dating can be assumed to be a copyist's or printer's error. Such a slip was easy, given that the letters which came from Brussels in December were of a similar tone and content to this one.

220:3   The 'honest gentleman' and Gomez d'Avila: Harl. Mss 871, f.12r.

Anne Bacon on A. Standen: Anne Bacon to Anthony Bacon, 26 June 1593 (LPL Ms 649, art.100); see also Birch, I p.107.

Anne Bacon on Antonio Perez: Anne Bacon to Anthony Bacon, undated, probably 1594 (LPL Ms 653, art.177).

220:4   Lopez hears the 'news of Gomez d'Avila's arrest; and a woman that Gomez d'Avila 'hath kept as his wife': Harl. Mss 871, ff.12r–v.

221:2   The release of Gomez d'Avila: 'And this was the Coming of the Doctor, for he feared if he should not work the delivery of this Fellow [Gomez], being a most impudent Varlet, a shifting Companion and a Jew, Gomez would no longer conceal him, and desired it should be solicited by his woman, being a cunning peer; and under colour of his [Lopez's] importuning, he [Lopez] himself moved Her Majesty for the enlargement of his

[Gomez's] person, that was sent by his [Lopez's] order' (Harl. Mss 871, f.12v).

223:1   'Whether a deceiver might be deceived': Francis Bacon, in Spedding, I, p.283.

223:2   Lopez's confession to Elizabeth and the Cecils: 'The Doctor in the meanwhile did bestir him in giving hard informations to Her Majesty and other honourable persons about Her Highness: of the King Don Antonio and [how] cruelly he had dealt with Ferreira, a gentleman that had lost, for the affection he bare to the King, great Revenue and his Country, prosecuted with such extremity and Rigour by the King of Spain as both himself and his wife were executed in picture.

'[Lopez] provideth what service might be drawn by Ferreira's means if he were let escape, that there was a fitter instrument in the world to work a peace between the two kingdoms. And sayeth already they two had layeth a good foundation to work upon for that matter, which Ferreira touched also by way of his declaration. He [Lopez] sheweth extraordinary courtesy and all compliments to those that by Her Majesty's order dealt in this matter, and would not stick. Such was his impudency, to propound to Her Majesty what a good deed it were to cosen the King of Spain. Which speech uttered by him purposely, Her Majesty in her princely disposition did both greatly mislike, and sharpely reprehend.

'He devised also very lewd suggestions against some he doubted, would display his Treachery to make an impression, beforehand to diminish the credit wherein the accusation might come' (Harl. Mss 871, ff.13v–14r).

224:1   Lopez's 'heavy wit' and dissembling: Francis Bacon, in Spedding, I, p.283.

224:2   Anthony Standen to Anthony Bacon, 25 November 1593: LPL Ms 649, art.261; see Birch, I, pp.134–5.

225:1   Anthony Standen to Anthony Bacon, 11 December 1593: LPL Ms 649, art.295; see Birch, I, p.138.

On rumours of Essex's flight to Dover and the Queen's reaction, Standen to A. Bacon, 18 December 1593: LPL Ms 649, f.425r (art.294); see Birch, I, p.139.

13. The Treasurer's Defence

227:Q   One of them showed me a ring that he has of your daughter for a monkey' . . .: Tubal and Shylock, *The Merchant*, III.i.107–13.

227:1 Tinoco at Calais: 'He, being come so far as Calais, was there advertised from Antwerp from Diego Lopez Soeiro, with whom the Doctor had intercourse (and to whom he hath sent letters a little before, as is confessed), of the apprehension and restraint of Ferreira, and that Gomez d'Avila had been committed, but was set again at Liberty, and the King Don Antonio was gone for France' (Harl. Mss 871, f.19v).

Prior to this, he had been at Brussels in December 1593. He met with Ibarra and Fuentes on 2–12 December. Fuentes wrote to Lopez on 2–12 December, and Ibarra wrote to Ferreira da Gama on 4–14 December (PRO/SP12/248/17; see *Baga de Secretis*, p.287).

228:1 'Shadows': Fuentes to Ferreira and Lopez, 2–12 December 1593 (Harl. Mss 871, f.28r).

228:2 Tinoco's request to Burghley from Calais: 'At my coming into this kingdom, I had had that which so much in my letters from Calais I did so earnestly desire. In the which I requested nothing else but brevity and much service' (PRO/SP12/248/20, part I).

229:1 'The memorials of E. de L., translated out of Portuguese', 16 January 1594: PRO/SP12/247/12 (see CSPD 1591–4 pp.413–4).

231:2 'I embarked with a servant of Thomas Jeffries . . .': Tinoco to Burghley, 10 March 1594 (PRO/SP12/248/20, part 1).

Tinoco's arrival in England: 'Manuel Louis [Tinoco] came last 14 January 1594 *and brought ye resolution of Spayne*' (PRO/SP12/248/17; Burghley's addition in italics).

231:3 'And I and Thomas Jeffries' man . . .': Tinoco to Burghley, 10 March 1594 (PRO/SP12/248/20, art. 1).

232:1 Tinoco's two interviews with Sir Robert Cecil, 15 and 16 January 1594: PRO/SP12/248/20 part I. Harl. Mss 871, f.24r–v concurs with this: 'It is to be understood, upon the coming to the court of Manoel Lowis [Tinoco], Her Majesty appointed Sir Robert Cecil to reveal these advertisments he did offer, and to acquaint Her Majesty with the same. Amongst the which were some things of good Importance.'

232:3 Sir Robert Cecil to Essex and the Queen regarding Tinoco: Harl. Mss 871, f.24v.

233:1 Lopez's reaction to the news about Tinoco and his burning of his papers: 'A present resolution to burn all his writings at his chamber in the Court' (Harl. Mss 871, f.20r).

Burghley's interview with Essex, and Lopez's burning of his papers at court probably took place on 17 January, immediately after Tinoco's first interview with Cecil.

233:2   Tinoco's interrogation by Cecil and Essex at Hampton Court, probably 18 January 1594: 'He was brought to the Lodge in the Park at Hampton Court, where first (as before he had done) he did declare his coming over to be of mere zeal and affection to do Her Majesty service, and to advance a matter which by his privity had been broken before to the Earl of Essex, wherein he protested he and Ferreira meant all sincerity. But being convinced by his own letters that were produced, he changed hue and excused the matter as though he would be loath to accuse Ferreira, whom he understood already to be in some trouble. But did exceedingly set forth what greate means and oppportunity he had to do notable service to Her Majesty, so as he might be secretly and speedily despatched, and said the only way to give him credit was to promitt him to speak with Doctor Lopez, and to have two or three lines from him under his hand, to shew when he should arrive on the other side, which he before and at other times still did vehemently and suspiciously request' (Harl. Mss 871, ff.25r–26r).

234:2   'A matter which by his privity had been broken before to the Earl of Essex': Tinoco, probably on 19 January 1594 (Harl. Mss 871, f.25r).

'I have made a great draught . . .': Harl. Mss 871, f.8v.

235:2   Tinoco's second interrogation by Essex and Cecil, probably on 19 January 1594: 'And therefore Manoel Lowys [Tinoco] was by the Earl of Essex and Sir Robert Cecil dealt withall, to expound the meaning and secret sense of those letters, seeing it appeared by the same that he was made acquainted with the contents, fully instructed in the business, and expressly sent to direct and advance this practise, and to him all things were referred to be ordered. But he held his mouth so close, and had his lesson so well conned, as a man might easier pluck out his teeth than the truth by any persuasion. And yet, in spite of his obstinate Resolution, by the course of his examinations and the direction and diligence that was used, there was always some hold taken of him, so as he could not slip [written: sleep] away, for he confessed that the letters Steven Ferreira had sent by Gomez d'Avila, by the report of Secretary Ibarra to himself, did contain very great and special matter, importing the good, the quiet and establishment of all. He came also a point further, that he thought whatsoever that matter might be (for he affirmed with great oaths that he never saw those letters), it was to be done by Doctor Lopez, and when he was urged, seeing the letters, accused him to be instructed in these matters to declare the charge given him, and to expound the secret sense and meaning. He said they gave him instructions in one sort and wrote in another manner. But always he urged (if he might be trusted), he would do great services, both in the discovery of this matter, and other things of great importance. Still with this pleasant bait of the means he had to do service, thinking to have allured their Honours that he might have wrought his delivery' (Harl. Mss 871, ff.29r–30r).

235:4   'Some long arguing this afternoon . . .': Edward Stanhope to Francis Bacon, 20 January 1594 (LPL Ms 650, f.45r, art.29).

237:1   Lopez burns his papers at Mountjoy's Inn, and his 'favourable' interrogation: Harl. Mss 871, ff.19r–20v.

Essex 'opposed' in his enquiry: Birch, I, p.150.

Lopez interrogated at Burghley House, imprisoned at Essex House: Birch, I, p.150.

237:2   Cecil to Elizabeth about Lopez's innocence: Birch, I, p.150.

237:4   Ferreira's second confession, 22 January 1594: 'To the first, he doth answer that the assignation which the King Don Antonio made to Doctor Lopez, the said Doctor did deliver to this Examinate at Wanstead, this last summer about six or seven months ago. He doth confess that the acknowledgement of the receipt of the said assignation which he made to the Doctor was but to cover the matter.

'To the second, he sayeth that the said Doctor did give the said assignation unto this Examinate to the end [that] he should [send] it to the King of Spain, and by that means draw of the said King so much as he could in respect of the Service D. Lopez had done to the King. He further doth avow that the D. told him how he had done divers services unto the King of Spain by means of Andrada and of Vega, and that he had been once in the Tower in time of the Earl of Leicester, for doing service to the King of Spain; and hereof they have had conference divers times, both at Wanstead in the Garden and in D. Lopez's house.

'To the [third], he sayeth the said Doctor did declare that contained in the said article to this Examinate two several times in his own Garden at London.

'He doth confess that Manuel Andrada did know and was privy to all these practises, and that he hath written three or four times letters to the Doctor, and the Doctor also hath delivered three or four times letters to this Examinate concerning these causes which Andrada wrote to his Examinate, and he did communicate the same always to the Doctor.

'He doth confess that Doctor Lopez, this Examinate and Andrada have had often conferences together about these causes, and that there was a letter written from Don Emanuel unto the King of Spain, which was sent by Manuel Luis [Tinoco], which letter was shewed unto the Doctor, and he read the same in the presence of this Examinate and of Andrada.

'Being asked if ever he did shew the said Doctor the letters he received from the Count of Fuentes and Xtofero da Moura, he saith he did shew the same unto the said Doctor, in the Garden at Wanstead, and the said Doctor did read the same' (Harl. Mss 871, ff.21r–v).

239:2 Lopez's first confession, 22 January 1594: Harl. Mss 871, ff.23r–v.

239:6 Tinoco's confession of 23 January 1594: SP12/247/19; see CSPD 1591–4, p.416.

Burghley to Robert Cecil, 23 January 1594: 'In Lopez's folly, I see no point of treason to the Queen', (Cambridge University Library Ms. E.e.3–56, no.15; see Read, *Lord Burghley and Queen Elizabeth*, p.586. Cecil scratched out Lopez's name. (See Chapter 15, footnote 273:4).

240:1 Burghley 'indisposed': Birch, I p.147.

240:5 Essex's 'rash and temarious' audience with Elizabeth, and his two-day sulk, 25–27 January 1594: Birch, I, pp.149–51; see LPL Ms 650/f.80 (art. 50).

241:2 Essex to Bacon re poison, 28 January 1594: Birch, I, p.152.

241:5 Essex alleges Lopez planned to poison the Queen, 28 January 1594: Goodman, p.153.

241:6 Lopez to the Tower, 29 January 1594: Standen to A. Bacon, 3 February 1594, LPL Ms 650, f.80r (art.50).

14. The Jew of Malta

242:Q 'Were you the doctor, and I knew you not?': Bassanio to Portia, *The Merchant*, V.i.280.

242:1 Bags of fiery opals, sapphires, amethysts,

Jacinths, hard topaz, grass-green emeralds,

Beauteous rubies, sparkling diamonds.

>(Barabas, *The Jew of Malta*, I.i.25–8.)

'infinite riches in a little room': ibid., I.i.37.

'scattered nation': ibid., I.i.119.

243:2 Ten thousand Portagues, besides great pearls,

Rich, costly jewels, and stones infinite

>(Barabas, *The Jew of Malta*, I.ii.245–6.)

245:1 Performances of *The Jew of Malta*: listed in *Henslowe's Diary*, 1592: pp.16–19; February – August 1594, pp.19–23.

Most-performed plays at the Rose, with number of performances: February 1593 – January 1594:

Jeronimo	20
Henry VI	16
Muly Morocco	14
Jew of Malta	12
Friar Bacon . . .	6

Machiavel and *Don Horatio* had three performances each; *Titus Andronicus* had two.

February – September 1594:

Jew of Malta	14 (February: 2; April: 2; May: 1; June: 4; July: 2; August: 2; September: 1)
Cutlake	12
Rangers' Comedy	9
Massacre at Paris	7
Venetian Comedy	6 (September only)
Tamburlaine	5
Mahomet	5
Titus Andronicus	4
Doctor Faustus	2
King Lear	2
Hester and Ahasuerus	2
Friar Bacon . . .	2
Taming of the Shrew	1

Of note: *The French Doctor* was added in September, as *The Jew of Malta* dropped back to low rotation.

246:1 Lopez's appeal to the Queen from the Tower, after 29 January 1594: Goodman, pp.153–4.

246:5 Lopez interrogated in the Tower, 7a.m. Wednesday, 30 January 1594: 'The Wednesday following at seven in the morning was examined before the Earl and Sir Robert Cecil and hither confessed more than proveth' (Anthony Standen to Anthony Bacon, 3 February 1594, LPL Ms 650, ff.80r–v/art.50).

Lopez and Ferreira interrogated in the Tower: their confessions of 30 January 1594 (Harl. Mss 871, ff.32r–34v).

249:4 Cecil's and Essex's argument in the coach on 30 January 1594, as told by Essex to Anthony Standen, was reported by Standen to Anthony Bacon on 3 February 1594: LPL Ms 650, ff.80v–81r (art.50). See also Birch, I, pp.152–3.

249:6 Anthony Standen's audience with Essex at 11 p.m. on 2 February 1594, reported by Standen to Anthony Bacon in a letter of 3 February 1594: LPL Ms 650, f.80r (art.50).

250:3 'The King of Spain hath determined . . .': Tinoco to Burghley, 16 January 1594, PRO/SP12/247/12; see CSPD 91–4, pp.413–4.

251:1 For the examinations of John Annias, Patrick Collen and their co-conspirator William Polwhele, see CSPD 1591–4, pp.421–31. For Collen's trial, see *Baga de Secretis*, pp.283–4.

John Annias's jewel: PRO/SP12/247/38; see CSPD 1591–4, p.423.

251:3 Lopez's passport to Antwerp: Annias was accused of 'procuring a passport from Count Mansfeldt for Lopez to Holland, under colour that it was for two merchants professing to do good service'. (PRO/SP12/247/38; see CSPD 1591–4, p.423).

Robert Draper's confession, 5 February 1594: PRO/SP12/247/41; see CSPD 1591–4, p.425.

252:2 Annias admits that he knew Tinoco: 'Examination of John Annias, 5 February 1594 (PRO/SP12/247/44; see CSPD 1591–4, pp.425–7).

15. The Spanish Prisoner

256:Q 'My deeds upon my head!': Shylock, *The Merchant*, IV.i.202.

257:1 'That villain Wade': Lord Cobham, after Wade's investigation of the Main and Bye Plots of 1603 (DNB, Waad; the alternate spelling).

Wade's inquiry into the Gunpowder Plot: see generally Fraser, *The Gunpowder Plot*.

258:1   Armagil Wade on religious change: Read, *Mr Secretary Cecil and Queen Elizabeth*, pp.127–8.

258:3   The pinching of Tinoco: 'And Yr. Honour can remember how when Ferreira avowed his confession to his [Tinoco's] face, he stood in denial, and after he was a little pinched, so under his own hand did avow' (Wade to Sir Robert Cecil, 12 March 1594, PRO/SP12/248/22; see CSPD 1591–4, p.458).

259:2   Tinoco's confession that 'under the peace was understood the death of the Queen's Majesty', 8 February 1594: PRO/SP12/247/51; see CSPD 1591–4, p.428.

261:5   'But for Antonio Perez . . .': 'Examination of D. Loppes, taken the ix of February 1594', Harl. Mss 871, f.34v.

262:3   Caldera's arrest, taken from Ditton Park to the Counter and 'often times and examined upon soundry interrogatories': Harl. Mss 871, ff.36v–39r.

263:1   Wade 'especially in credit' with the Cecils, and 'trusted in these services of weight': Nicholas Faunt to Anthony Bacon, 11 February 1594 (LPL Ms 650, f.114, art.67; see Birch, I, pp.155–6).

264:3   William Wade to Nicholas Faunt on the night of 10 February 1594, as told to Anthony Bacon in a letter of the next day: 'The parties taken are one Stranger and two other men sent by the choice of Sir William Stanley, two of them not yet found make 5 in all. One of the prisoners apprehended hath twice been near Her Majesty as she went to the chapel. The Stranger and the rest had undertaken the destruction of Her Majesty, . . . having letters from the Count Fuentes to Lopus for his assistance, which cannot yet be wrested from them, though otherwise discovered. This party is found to confess that indeed he came to kill Don Perez, but another circumstance reacheth further, that indeed should be done also, but the other, it is principally intended, in no case be left undone, and so it is likely to fall out in proof' (LPL Ms 650, f.114, art.67; see Birch, I, pp.155–6.)

265:1   Francis Bacon's case before the King's Bench, 10 February 1594: Anthony Bacon to Anne Cooke Bacon, LPL Ms 649, f.47r, art.29.

'A choke pear to praters': Anthony Standen to Anthony Bacon, 3 February 1594, LPL Ms 650, ff.80r–v, art.50.

Henry Gosnold's report: Gosnold to Anthony Bacon, undated, LPL Ms 653, f.187r, art.101.

266:1 Pedro Ferrera accuses Ferreira da Gama about Lopez and the 'syrup': Harl. Mss 871, f.37r.

266:8 Ferreira's allegation that Lopez plotted to poison the Queen: his confession of 18 February 1594, Harl. Mss 871, ff.39v–40r; see Yetswirt, *A True Report*, pp.27–8. It is noticeable that Ferreira did not specify the method of poisoning in this confession. The reference to Lopez having offered 'to give the Queen a syrup' of poisoned medicine – the first confession to refer to poisoning and the first reference to this method – was made prior to this confession and not expanded upon in subsequent confessions.

268:1 'like a resty jade, loath to go forward but as he was spurred': Harl. Mss 871, f.40v.

268:4 'There is no law to warrant torture in this land': Coke, *Third Institute* (1594) (Fraser, p.176).

The rack: Fraser, pp.177–8.

'Ay, but I fear you speak upon the rack . . .': Portia to Bassanio, *The Merchant*, III.ii.32–3.

269:1 The manacles: Fraser, p.178.

269:4 Tinoco 'brought to the manacles': Harl. Mss 871, f.42v. His confession of 22 February 1594: Harl. Mss 871, ff.42v–44r; see also Yetswirt, *A True Report*, pp.28–30.

269:5 Tinoco and Ferreira 'contending' to outdo one another: Harl. Mss 871, f.46v.

269:6 Wade's interrogation techniques: Harl. Mss 871, f.36r.

Ferreira's confession of 22 February 1594, made in two parts: Harl. Mss 871, ff.40v–42r.

272:2 Lopez's interrogation and confession of 25 February 1594, before Burghley, Cecil, Essex and Howard: Harl. Mss 871, ff.49r–50v.

272:4 The 'great consultation' at Burghley House, and 'exceeding great haste': Nicholas Faunt to Anthony Bacon, 25 February 1594 (LPL Ms 650, f.112, art.66).

273:2 Summoning of jurors, 26 February 1594: *Baga de Secretis*, p.285.

Writ of habeas corpus: ibid., p.286.

Lopez's indictment, 27 February 1594: ibid., p.286.

273:4 'In Lopez's folly, I see no point of treason to the Queen, but a readiness to make some gain to the hurt of Don Antonio.': Burghley to Sir Robert Cecil, 23 January 1594: (University Library Cambridge Ms.E.e.3–56, no.15; see Read, *Lord Burghley and Queen Elizabeth*, p.586). Cecil scratched out the names of Lopez and Don Antonio.

16. The Queen's Pawn

275:Q DUKE: Go one and call the Jew into the court.

SALERIO: He is ready at the door – he comes, my Lord': *The Merchant*, IV.i.14–5.

277:1 Composition of the jury: 'Cuthbert Buckle, Mayor of the City of London; John Puckering, Knight, Keeper of the Great Seal; William, Lord Burghley, Lord Treasurer of England; Robert, Earl of Essex, Master of the Horse; Charles, Lord Howard, Lord High Admiral of England; Thomas, Lord Buckhurst; Robert, Lord Rich; Thomas Heneage, Knight, Vice-Chamberlain; John Popham, Knight, Chief Justice of the Queen's Bench; Robert Cecil, Knight; John Fortescue, Knight, Chancellor of the Exchequer; Edward Fenner, one of the Justices of the Queen's Bench; Thomas Owen, one of the Justices of the Court of the Common Pleas; Ralph Rookeby, one of the Masters of the Court of Requests; Richard Martin, Knight; John Hart, Knight; William Webb, Knight; Edward Stanhope, one of the masters of the Court of Chancery; William Daniel, William Wade and Richard Young, Esquires' (*Baga de Secretis*, p.285).

277:4 Lopez's trial, 28 February 1594: *Baga de Secretis*, p.288.

277:6 Coke's indictment of Collen, 22 February 1594: The record of Collen's trial and conviction is in the *Baga de Secretis*, pp.283–4. Collen was tried the day after Lopez, on 1 March.

278:1 Sir Edward Coke's prosecution, 28 February 1594: Coke's preliminary notes, entitled 'Heads of the Indictments against D. Lopez' are PRO/SP12/247/100 and 247/101. 247/101 is a copy of 247/100, but minus a list of dates; it is endorsed in Lord Burghley's hand as 'A report from Mr. Attorney and Solicitor General of the treason of Dr. Lopez'. As they are both in the same hand, it would appear that 247/101 was a copy sent from the Solicitor-General's office to Lord Burghley before the trial of 28 February, summarising the prosecution's case against Lopez for Burghley's approval. The *Baga de Secretis* account of Coke's prosecution follows 247/100 closely, only adding material relating to the Lopez–Ferreira–Andrada meeting of 20 February 1593 and Andrada's courier run to Brussels of 30 April 1593.

278:2   'Insurrection and rebellion': *Baga de Secretis*, p.285.

279:2   Andrada paid to supply 'such news as he found in the streets' of Calais and to 'run with the Count of Fuentes': Tinoco to Sir Robert Cecil, 26 February 1594 (PRO/SP12/247/83).

282:3   Lopez's claim that he had been pressured into a confession, and the 'applause of the world': Cecil to Thomas Windebank, from The Strand, 4 p.m., 28 February 1594: PRO/SP12/247/97; see CSPD 1591–4, p.444.

282:4   Sir Robert Cecil gathers Tinoco's papers from Calais: Lord Cobham to Cecil, 4 March 1594, Salis. IV, p.488. Cobham reports, 'What is in the portmanteaux, Jeffrey knoweth not, for that Luis [Tinoco] brought the key with him.'

Burghley directs Wade to assemble a 'short narration': Wade to Sir Robert Cecil, 4 March 1594, 'I have drawn a short narration of the treasons of D. Loppez in such sort as I was directed by His L., which occasion hath kept me from the Court, and an Inclination to an Ague' (PRO/SP12/248/7; see Salis. IV, p.487).

283:2   Wade and Jeronimo Lopez: Essex to Sir Robert Cecil, 4 March 1594, 'Sends a letter of the party Cecil spoke with the other day; received in a letter from Mr. Wade to himself. Would confer with Cecil to satisfy him in all his demands' (Salis. IV, p.487).

Wade and Bartholomew Quiney: Wade to Sir Robert Cecil, 4, 7 and 9 March 1594 (Salis. IV, pp.488–9).

284:1   Burghley annotating plot chronology: his notes to PRO/SP12/248/18; see CSPD Eliz. 1591–4, p.456.

284:2   Ferreira da Gama's clarifications, 8 March 1594: PRO/SP12/248/12; see CSPD Eliz. 1591–4, p.455, and Harl. Mss 871, f.55v.

Wade on Gomez d'Avila: Wade to Essex, 10 March 1594 (PRO/SP12/248/19; see CSPD 1591–4, p.456).

Tinoco's 'explication': Wade to Essex, 10 March 1594 – (PRO/SP12/248/19), and to Sir Robert Cecil, 12 March 1594 (PRO/SP12/248/22; see CSPD Eliz. 1591–4, p.458).

284:4   Tinoco names Jeronimo Lopez: Tinoco to Burghley, 10 March 1594

(PRO/SP12/248/20.I; see CSPD Eliz. 1591–4. p.456).

Jeronimo Lopez escorted to Gravesend: Wade to Sir Robert Cecil, 12 March 1594, 'I have dismissed my guest, and given him twenty pound in gold as he desired. . . .Your Honour shall hear from him so soon as he shall be on the other side. I sent one of my servants to bear him company to Gravesend'. (PRO/SP12/248/22; see CSPD 1591–4, p.458). Wade also told Cecil, 'I send Your Honour herewith all the letters that came to D. Lopez from Constantinople; there is no matter in them of any moment.'

285:2   Lopez in bed since his trial: Lord Keeper Puckering to Sir Robert Cecil, 14 March 1594 (SP12/248/29.I; see CSPD Eliz. 1591–4, p.460).

286:2   Sir John Puckering to Sir Robert Cecil, and Sir Thomas Egerton to Sir John Puckering: PRO/SP12/248/26 and 26.I; see CSPD Eliz. 1591–4, pp.459–60.

286:5   Memorandum to Coke, before 14 March 1594: SP12/248/16; see CSPD Eliz. 1591–4, pp.455–6.

287:3   Sir Edward Coke's notes for the trials of Ferreira da Gama and Tinoco: SP12/ 248/27; see CSPD Eliz. 1591–4, p.462.

Zopyrus's self-mutilation: Herodotus, *Histories*, Book III, Chapters 153–160, (Everyman ed., 1997, pp.297–301).

289:3   False evidence in Tinoco's indictment of 12 March 1594: 'Tinoco took his journey from Brussels to London, and afterwards, viz., 16 January, 36 Eliz. [1594], came to London, and delivered the same letters to da Gama in the parish before mentioned' (*Baga de Secretis*, p.287).

17. The Pound of Flesh

292:Q   'But is it true, Salerio . . .?': Bassanio to Salerio, *The Merchant*, III.ii.265–9.

293:1   Lopez appeals to Elizabeth after his conviction: Goodman, p.154.

293:3   Ferreira da Gama's will, 25 March 1594: Salis. IV, pp.493–4.

294:1   Contarini, Venetian ambassador to Prague, to the Doge and Senate, 22 March 1594: CSP Venetian, vol.IX, p.123 (art.261). For this news to have reached Prague on or before 22 March, this mail would have been sent from London just after Essex's announcement of the poison plot on 28 January.

295:1   Judah Serfatim's embassy, February–March 1594: Serfatim wrote to Burghley on 7 February 1594 (Wolf, *Jews in Elizabethan England*, pp.76–7), and twice to the Privy Council in March (Harl. Mss 871, ff.65–71 and f.71 etc.; also, Wolf, ibid., pp.77–84). In the first of the March letters, he named David Passi as a Spanish agent, described how Lopez and Alvaro Mendes had worked together against Spanish spies. Mendes's mails had reached Lopez 'by way of Ragusa to Venice, where his factor Simon Chavaron had forwarded them to Doctor Lopez'. In his second letter to the Privy Council, Serfatim gave a twenty-seven point reply to the Council's queries. Point 25 reported, 'The discords between Monsieur Don Salomon [Alvaro Mendes] and the King Don Antonio; the letters which the aforementioned Lord [Mendes] has written to Doctor Lopez, which I have passed to Sir Robert Cecil, told the truth.'

Wade reported to Burghley on 19 March 1594; he enclosed a letter from Serfatim. In this letter Serfatim denounced Edward Barton, English ambassador to Constantinople, for keeping company with Spanish spies; and reported that as 'My Lord [Mendes] had been advertised by Doctor Lopez that Don Antonio had talked very badly of Her Majesty to him', he had despatched Serfatim to obtain her 'good grace and opinion' (see Wolf, *Jews in Elizabethan England*, pp. 85–8).

Serfatim sent a final letter to Burghley on 10 April 1594, reporting that Wade had treated him suspiciously: 'I have written to Mr. Wade, as permitted, what I had to declare from my Lord to Doctor Lopez, if at liberty . . . I was only sent for the Queen's service, because for her great renown, my Lord thinks my service cannot be better employed . . . I have been examined as to my commission, owing to Doctor Lopez's fall.' (PRO/SP12/248/64; see CSPD 1591–4, p.482, which does not identify Serfatim as the letter's author).

296:2   Bacon on Lopez: Spedding, I, p.278.

297:2   Bacon's conclusion: ibid..

298:1   Sir Robert Cecil's recommendation of Francis Bacon to Sir Thomas Egerton, 27 March 1594: LPL Ms 649, f.92, art.60.

298:2   The Queen rebuffs Essex: Essex to Francis Bacon, 29 March 1594 (LPL Ms 650, f.147r, art.89; see Birch, I, p.167).

298:3   Bacon abandons politics: Francis Bacon to Essex, 29 March 1594 (LPL Ms 650, f.147r, art.89; see Birch, I, p.167).

299:1   The death of Lord Strange: Stow, p.767.

299:3   Order sent to Sir Michael Blount, 17 April 1594: Salis. IV, p.513.

300:1   The delay ordered by the Queen: Sir Michael Blount to Sir Thomas Heneage and Sir Robert Cecil, 25 April 1594: Salis. IV, p.515.

304:3   'We have therefore to sway your Lordships': Essex and Howard to Puckering and Buckhurst, 4 June 1594 (Harl. Mss. 6996, f.160r).

'And so we take leave of your Lordships': Essex and Howard to Puckering and Buckhurst, 4 June 1594 (Harl. Mss. 6996, f.162r).

305:1   The Queen's progress, June 1594: letter of 7 June 1594, from Philip Gawdy to his brother (*HMC, 7th Report*, p.523). Gawdy wrote, 'This day Lopus was executed, and two Portugalls more, at Tyburn.'

305:5   Prosecution of Lopez in Queen's Bench trial, 7 June 1594: PRO/SP12/247/102.

306:1   Stow's account of the Queen's Bench trial: Stow, p.768.

307:3   *The Venetian Comedy*:   dates and receipts:

25 August 1594	50 shillings and sixpence
5 September 1594	46 shillings and sixpence
15 September 1594	46 shillings and sixpence
22 September 1594	45 shillings
3 October 1594	17 shillings
11 October 1594	16 shillings
11 November 1594	21 shillings
26 November 1594	13 shillings
10 February 1595	20 shillings
25 February 1595	20 shillings
8 May 1595	30 shillings

(*Henslowe's Diary* (it.), pp.23–25, 27–28)

307:4   'Sold unto Steven Magett, the 20th of January 1596, a doublet of fustian plain, and a pair of Venetians of braid cloth . . .': *Henslowe's Diary*, p.37. Fustian was thick twilled, short napped cotton cloth, usually dyed dark.

309:1   Henry Carey, Lord Chamberlain to Cuthbert Buckle, 8 October 1594: Holden, p.134.

309:3   Coke's annotations to the *True Report*, pub. Yetswirt: his copy in the British Library, shelfmark BL.599.b.5.

Epilogue

313:1   Sara Lopez's appeal to the Queen: Salis. IV, p.601.

313:2   The Queen's lifting of the attainder against the Lopez estate: *Signet Office Docket Books*, PRO/SO3/1/f.516v.

314:1   Coryate in Constantinople: see Shapiro, p.71.

Jeronimo Lopez as Essex agent: LPL Ms. 661, f.239, a letter to Anthony Bacon from Jeronimo in French, from 1597.

315:3   Allington marriage, 1597: *Register of Marriages, St Andrew's, Holborn*, (GL/MS.6668/1/1618).

Lease of Lopez's garden to Sir Thomas Savage; and then to the Earl of Warwick: *The Pension Book of Gray's Inn*, I, pp.165–6 and p.447.

The building of Warwick Court: ibid., Vol. II, pp.51, 95, 117–9, 368.

316:2   Don Antonio's death and burial: De Faria, p.1; the Daughters of Ave Maria was in the Rue des Barrés, behind the Quai Saint-Paul. De Faria describes Carlos as 'cousin-germain' to Antonio.

Don Antonio's descendants: De Faria, pp.8–10.

The van Troostwijks had two children at the time of de Faria's genealogical inquiry, Frederica Augusta Doude van Troostwijk (born 26 January 1899) and Lodewijk Willem Doude van Troostwijk (born 17 September 1901).

316:4   'I chanced to be walking near the gates of the City': Antonio Perez, in Marañon, p.319.

318:1   'The traitor in faction': Bacon, 'On Faction', *Essays*, p.212.

318:3   Bacon's death: see Jardine and Stewart.

322:1   Elizabeth I's last words: Black, p.496.

323:2   Jeronimo Lopez's *seder*, 1605: Samuel, *Passover in Shakespeare's London*. Furtado's confession, dated 6 March 1609, is in Processo 3333, Lisbon Inquisition, Portuguese National Archives. In 1606, the *Returns of Aliens* recorded Jeronimo as being exempt from the subsidy charge, along with 'Widow Añes', (most probably Constance Ruis, widow of Dunstan Añes) and 'Gabriel Fernando' (*Returns of Aliens*, iii, p.124).

Bibliography

A Note on Sources

There are five contemporary accounts of the plot. They all emanate from William Wade's original account of March 1594 which, over more than 20,000 words, included all the confessions and most of the intercepted letters. Despite the urgency with which it had been prepared, it was not published. As Wade's unguarded admissions and plethora of evidence have been my main source for the unknotting of the plot, and the tracking of how Lopez was framed as a regicide, it is easy to see why Burghley preferred to present a less malleable account. Wade's account survives in two versions, both in the British Library. Each has its own history.

The most original version seems to be BL Add. Mss 48029, ff.147–84 (Yelverton Mss XXIII): *A Discourse of the Treasons of D. Lopes and his Treasons, gathered by Sir William Ward, one of the Clerks of Her Majesty's most honourable Privy Council.* It is bound with *Letters from Jesuits to Other Papists* and papers relating to various other Elizabethan Catholic plots, including the trial of the Earl of Arundel. It is written in the hand of Essex's secretary William Temple. Another version, Harleian Manuscript 871, is also in Temple's hand. It is virtually identical, but adds Tinoco's account of his meeting with Andrada in St Stephen's, Lille, and part of the Solomon Cormano correspondence.

Immediately after Lopez's conviction, Sir Robert Cecil ordered the production of a second, condensed narrative. Drawn from Wade's account, it is preserved in the Public Record Office (PRO/SP12/247/7.I); the first page of the manuscript is a frontispiece design for publication. However, this second account was also not considered suitable for publication; subsequently it was reprinted in Murdin, pp.669–75.

At the same time the Essex camp produced their version of events, adding a third narrative. Wade's account, either in its Yelverton or Harleian variation, seems to have been the basis for the Essex camp's position paper on the Lopez affair, written by Francis Bacon before the end of March 1594: *A True Report of the Detestable Treason, Intended by Dr. Roderigo Lopez, A Physician Attending upon the Person of the Queen's Majesty*. It was subsequently printed in the *Resuscitatio* of 1657 and in Spedding, I.

After Sir Robert Cecil and Francis Bacon had prepared their versions, Lord Burghley wrote a fourth version, which became the basis of the final government publication. It combined a brief treatment of the Lopez plot with two other plots involving Brussels and religious nonconformity: the Collen plot, and a third plot involving Sir William Stanley, the exiled Jesuit Cardinal Allen and a chaplain called Thomas Worthington. They were accused of engaging one Richard Hesketh to persuade Ferdinando, Lord Strange to declare himself King of England. The manuscript, bearing heavy annotation from Burghley and lighter annotation from Sir Robert Cecil, also survives (PRO/SP12/250/10). The resulting corporate Cecil version was sent to Wade for assessment; a letter of 27 October 1594 from Wade to Burghley records Wade's contribution of his 'opinion' to the Lopez account and his suggestion that letters whose interpretation might lead to 'doubtfulness' should be excluded. The resulting hybrid, the annotated fourth version, was published in November 1594 under the unwieldy title of *A True Report of Sundry Horrible Conspiracies of late time detected to have (by barbarous murders) taken away the life of the Queen's Majesty, whom Almighty God hath miraculously conserved against the treacheries of her Rebels, and the violences of her most puissant Enemies*. The only name given was that of the publisher, Charles Yetswirt who, as Clerk of the Signet Office, had assisted Burghley throughout the case. Any doubts as to its ultimate authorship must be resolved by Sir Edward Coke's note on the frontispiece of his personal copy (now in the British Library, shelfmark BL.599.b.5), that Burghley had thought it best to describe the case 'personally'.*

---

* Wade to Burghley, 27 October 1594: Murdin, p.680.

Primary Sources

Acts of the Privy Council of England (New Series), vols. III, *1550–52*; IX, *1578–80; and* XVIII, *1589–90*, ed. J. R. Dasent (London: HMSO, 1891; and Norwich: HMSO, 1898 and 1899)

Agas, Ralph *A View of London about the year 1560* (facsimile by Blades, East & Blades; London: E. Bonser & Sons, 1875)

Bacon, Francis, *A True Report of the Detestable Treason, Intended by Dr Roderigo Lopez* (see: Spedding, J., vol. I, pp.274–87)

——— *The Essays*, ed. J. Pitcher (London: Penguin, 1985)

——— *The Bacon Papers* (Lambeth Palace Library Mss)

Baga de Secretis: *Inventory and Calendar of the Baga de Secretis, Edward IV – George III, from the 3rd, 4th and 5th Reports of the Deputy Keeper of the Public Record Office* (London: HMSO, 1912; PRO ref. KB8/52)

Birch, Thomas, *Memoirs of the Reign of Queen Elizabeth From the Year 1581 till her Death, In Which the Secret Intrigues of her Court and the Conduct of her Favourite, Robert, Earl of Essex, both at Home and Abroad, are particularly Illustrated* 2 vols (London: A. Millar, 1754)

The Book of Plans (1617; Ms HC19, Archives, The Clerk's House, St Bartholomew's Hospital)

British Library Add. Ms 48029 (Yelverton Mss XXIII); a copy of Wade's account, in the hand of William Temple

Calendar of the Manuscripts of the Most Honourable the Marquess of Bath, vol. V: Talbot, Dudley and Devereux Papers, 1533–1659, ed. G. D. Owen (London: HMSO, 1980)

Calendar of the Manuscripts of the Most Honourable the Marquis of Salisbury, preserved at Hatfield House, Herts., vols. II, IV, V, VI, VII and VIII (The Cecil Papers); (London: HMSO, 1888, 1892, 1894, 1895, 1899 and 1899)

Calendar of the Patent Rolls, Elizabeth I, vol. IX, 1580–82, ed. Ann Morton (London: HMSO, 1986)

Calendar of Letters and Papers, Foreign and Domestic, of the Reign of Henry VIII, vol. 2, part ii, ed. J. S. Brewer (London: Longman, Green, Longmans, Roberts & Green, 1864)

Calendar of State Papers, Domestic Series, Edward VI, Mary and Elizabeth, 1547–80, ed. R. Lemon (London: Longmans, Brown, Green, Longmans & Roberts, 1856)

Calendar of State Papers, Domestic Series, of the Reign of Elizabeth, 1581–1590, (CSPD), ed. R. Lemon (London: HMSO, 1865)

Calendar of State Papers, Domestic Series, of the Reign of Elizabeth, 1591–4, and 1595–7 (CSPD), ed. M.A.E. Green, (London: Longmans, Green, Reader and Dyer, 1867 and 1869)

Calendar of State Papers, Domestic Series, (CSPD), Addenda 1566–1579, and *Addenda 1580–1625,* both vols. ed. M.A.E. Green, (London: Longmans & Co., 1871 and 1872)

Calendar of State Papers, Foreign Series, of the Reign of Elizabeth I, (CSPF), 1579–1580; and *January 1581-April 1582,* both vols. ed. A.J. Butler, (London: HMSO, 1904 and 1907)

Calendar of State Papers, Foreign Series, of the Reign of Elizabeth I, (CSPF), January-June 1583 and Addenda, ed. A.J. Butler and S.C. Lomas, (London: HMSO, 1913)

List and Analysis of Calendar of State Papers, Foreign, Vol. I, August 1589-June 1590; Vol. II, July 1590-May 1591; Vol. III, June 1591-April 1592; Vol. IV, May 1592-June 1593; Vol. V, July 1593-December 1594; Vol. VI, January to December 1595, (LASP F), all vols. ed. R.B. Wernham, (London: HMSO, 1964, 1969, 1980, 1984, 1989 and 1993)

Calendar of Letters, etc., Relating to English Affairs, Preserved Principally in the Archives of Simancas, (CSP SP) vol. II *Elizabeth, 1568–79;* vol. III *Elizabeth, 1580–86;* and *vol. IV, 1587–1625,* all vols ed. M. A. S. Hume (London: HMSO, 1894, 1896 and 1898)

Calendar of State Papers and Manuscripts Existing in the Archives and Collections of Venice (CSP Venetian), vols VIII, *1581–91;* and IX, *1592–1603;* ed. H. F. Brown (London: HMSO, 1894 and 1897)

Camden, W., *Annales, the True and Royall History of the Famous Empress Elizabeth, Queene of England . . .* (translation of *Annales rerum Anglicarum . . .;* London, 1625)

Carleton, George, *A Thankfull Remembrance of God's Mercy, in a Historicall Collection of the great and mercifull Deliverances of the Church and State of England, since the Gospell began here to flourish, from the beginning of Queene Elizabeth* (London, 1606; 2nd ed. of 1627 includes engravings)

Englander, D., ed., with Norman, D., O'Day, R. and Owens, W. R.,

Culture and Belief in Europe, 1450–1600: An Anthology of Sources (1990; Blackwell, Oxford, 1994)

The Explanation of the True and Lawfull Right and Tytle of the Most Excellent Prince, Anthonie, the first of that name, King of Portugall (Leyden: Christopher Plantyn, 1585; BL shelfmark 1060.c.33)

Goodman, Godfrey, *The Court of King James the First*, 2 vols, ed. J. S. Brewer (London: Richard Bentley, 1839)

Harleian Manuscript no. 871, ff.7r–64r; expanded version of Wade's account of the Lopez conspiracy and trial; copied by William Temple.

Harleian Manuscript no. 6996, ff. 160r and 162r; Letters from the Council to Lord Keeper Puckering and Lord Buckhurst regarding Lopez's execution.

Harvey, Gabriel, notes to frontispiece of *In Iudaeorum Medicastrorum calumnias & homicidia*, by G. Meier (1570; BL shelfmark C.60.h.18)

Henslowe's Diary, eds R. A. Foakes and R. T. Rickert (Cambridge: CUP, 1961)

Historical Manuscripts Commission, 4th Report, 2 vols., (London: HMSO, 1874)

Historical Manuscripts Commission, 7th Report, 2 vols, (London: Eyre and Spottiswoode, 1879)

Historical Manuscripts Commission, 8th Report (London, Eyre and Spottiswoode, 1881)

Index to the Calendar of the Patent Rolls, 31–7 Eliz. I (PRO/O12)

Jones, P. G., *Private Correspondence with the Archivist, St Bartholomew's Hospital, regarding Ph.D. thesis, 1979–85* (Archives, The Clerk's House, St Bartholomew's Hospital)

Jonson, Ben, *The Alchemist*, ed. J. B. Steane (1610; Cambridge University Press, 1967)

The Journal of St Bartholomew's Hospital, vols. II and III (Mss HC1/2 and HC1/3, Archives, The Clerk's House, St Bartholomew's Hospital)

The Ledger of St Bartholomew's Hospital, vol. II (Ms HC1/2, Archives, The Clerk's House, St Bartholomew's Hospital)

Leicester's Commonwealth, aka *The Copie of a Letter, Wryten by a Master of Arte of Cambridge, to his Friend in London, concerning some talk past of late between two worshipful and grave men, about the present state, and some proceedings of the Erle of Leycester and his friendes in England*, probably written by Father Robert Persons (1584; BL shelfmark 292.b.17)

Leicester's Ghost, prob. author Father Robert Persons (reprinted London, 1641 with verse; BL shelfmark 599.a.30)

Lodge, *Illustrations of British History, Biography, and Manners in the Reigns of Henry VIII, Edward VI, Mary, Elizabeth and James I*, 3 vols (London: G. Nicol, 1791)

Manuscripts of Lord De L'Isle and Dudley, vol. II, ed. C. L. Kingsford (London: Hist. Mss Comm., 1935)

Marlowe, Christopher, *Doctor Faustus and Other Plays* (Oxford: OUP, 1998)

Meres, Francis, *Palladis Tamia (Wit's Treasury)*, (London: P. Short for Cuthbert Burble, 1598)

Murdin, W., ed., *A Collection of State Papers Relating to the Affairs in the Reign of Queen Elizabeth from the Year 1571 to 1597, Transcribed from Original papers and other Authentic Memorials never before Published, left by William Cecil, Lord Burghley, and reposited at Hatfield House* (London: William Bowyer, 1759)

The Ordre of the Hospital of S. Bartholomewes in West-smythfielde in London (London, 1552; reprinted A. G. Bishop & Sons, Orpington, 1997)

The Pension Book of Gray's Inn (Records of the Honourable Society), 1569–1669, 2 vols, ed. Reginald J. Fletcher (London: Chiswick Press, 1910)

Ralph Treswell's Survey (1587, Ms HC10/1, Archives, The Clerk's House, St Bartholomew's Hospital)

The Register of Admissions to Gray's Inn, 1521–1889, Together with the Register of Marriages in Gray's Inn Chapel, 1695–1754, ed. Joseph Foster (London: Hansard, 1889)

The Register of St. Bartholomew's the Less, West Smithfield (Ms SBL10/1, Archives, Clerk's House, St Bartholomew's Hospital; reprinted as *Transcript of Baptisms 1547–1894* and *Transcript of Burials 1547–1848*, both vols transcribed and indexed by M. Spearman)

The Registers of St Andrew's, Holborn (Guildhall Library, London): *Baptisms 1558–1623* (GL/Ms 6667/1); *Marriages 1558–1623* (GL/Ms 6668/1); *Burials 1558–1623* (GL/Ms 6673/1)

Returns of Aliens Dwelling in the City and Suburbs of London from the Reign of Henry VIII to that of James I, X, pts i–iv, Eds. R. E. G. Kirk and Ernest F. Kirk Aberdeen: Huguenot Society of London, 1908)

The Roll of the Royal College of Physicians, ed. W. Munk (London: Longmans, Green, Longham & Roberts, 1861)

The Royal Penitent, or The Psalmes of King Antonio, in Which a Sinner Confesses his Faults, and Implores the Grace of God (BL.C.183.ac.6, trans. 'Fr. Ch. Esq.', i.e. Francis Chamberleyne; London, 1596)

Shakespeare, William, *The Merchant of Venice*, ed. J. R. Brown (London: Arden, 1955)

Signet Office Docket Books (PRO/SO3)

Stow, John, *Annals of England* (London, 1631, ed. J. Strype, 1755)

Thane, J., (ed.), *British Autography: A Collection of the Handwriting of Royal and Illustrious Personages, with their Authentic Portraits* (3 vols; London: J. Thane, 1788–93)

A True Report of Sundry Horrible Conspiracies (London: Charles Yetswirt, 1594); BL shelf mark 599.b.5

Usque, Samuel, *A Consolation for the Tribulations of Israel*, trans., ed. and commentary Gershon I. Gelbart (New York: Bloch, 1962)

Walsingham, Sir Francis, *The Journal of Sir Francis Walsingham, December 1570 – April 1583*, ed. C. T. Martin (reprinted London: Camden Society, 1870)

Wriothesley, Charles, *A Chronicle of England During the Reigns of the Tudors from 1485 to 1559* (reprinted in Camden Society NS, xx, vol. II, pp.36–7, London: Camden Society, 1877)

Secondary Sources

Akrigg, G. P. V., *Shakespeare and the Earl of Southampton*, (London: Hamish Hamilton, 1968)

Allen, Arthur B., *The Spacious Days of Queen Elizabeth* (London: Rockliff, 1959)

Archer, John Michael, *Sovereignty and Intelligence: Spying and Court Culture in the English Renaissance* (Stanford, California: Stanford University Press, 1993)

Baiao, *Inquisicão en Portugal no seculo XVI*, 2 vols (Porto, 1919)

Baptista, A. V., *Os Acôres e o Rei D. Antonio, Prior do Crato* (Barcelos: Portucalense Editora, 1962)

Barnard, E. A. B., 'Shakespeare and Shylock' (Letter to *Times Lit. Supp.*, 12.5.50, in Archives, Clerk's House, St Bartholomew's Hospital)

Barron, Caroline, *The Parish of St Andrew, Holborn* (London: Diamond Trading Company, 1979)

Besant, Sir Walter, *London in the Time of the Tudors* (London: Adam & Charles Black, 1904)

Black, J. B., *The Reign of Elizabeth* (Oxford: OUP, 1959)

Bowen, Catherine D., *The Lion and the Throne: The Life and Times of Sir Edward Coke, 1552–1634* (London: Hamish Hamilton, 1957)

Burgess, Anthony, *Shakespeare* (1970; London: Vintage, 1996)

Cohen, Mark R., *Under Crescent and Cross: The Jews in the Middle Ages* (Princeton N.J.: Princeton University Press, 1994)

Cowper, Francis, *A Prospect of Gray's Inn* (London: Graya, 1985)

Davies, C. S. L., *Peace, Print and Protestantism: 1450–1558* (1977; London: Paladin, 1986)

Dedijer, Stevan, *The Rainbow Scheme: British Secret Service and Pax Britannica*, in *Clio Goes Spying: Eight Essays on the History of Intelligence*, pp.10–63, (Lund Studies in International History, 17; Malmo: Infotryck, 1983)

Devereux, W. B., *Lives and Letters of the Devereux, Earls of Essex in the Reigns of Elizabeth, James I and Charles I*, 2 vols (London: John Murray, 1853)

Dictionary of National Biography, ed. L. Stephen (London: Smith, Elder and Co., 1885)

Elliot, J. H., *Europe Divided: 1559–1598* (1968; London: Fontana, 1971)

Elton, G.R., *The Tudor Constitution: Documents and Commentary*, (Cambridge: CUP, 1965)

Epstein, Maurice, *The Early History of the Levant Company* (London, George Routledge, 1908)

Fenn, P. J., 'Queen Elizabeth's Poisoner', in *SBH Journal*, February 1957, pp.49–55.

Feuer, Lewis S., 'Francis Bacon and the Jews: Who was the Jew in the New Atlantis?' in *TJHSE* XXIX (1982–6), pp.1–25, (London: JHSE, 1988)

Gerber, Mark, *The Jews of Spain* (New York: Free Press, 1992)

Goris, *Étude sur les Colonies Marchandes Meridionales – Portugais, Espagnols, Italiens – à Anvers de 1488 à 1567* (Louvain, 1925)

Greenblatt, Stephen, *Renaissance Self-Fashioning: From More to Shakespeare* (Chicago and London: University of Chicago, 1980)

Griffith, A., 'Dr Roderigo Lopez', in *SBH Journal*, November 1964, pp.449–52.

Gross, John, *Shylock: Four Hundred Years in the Life of a Legend* (1992; London: Vintage, 1994)

Guy, John, *Tudor England* (1988; Oxford: OUP, 1990)

Gwyer, John, 'The Case of Dr Lopez', in *TJHSE*, XV: 1939–45 (London: Edward Goldston, 1946)

Hammer, Paul J., *The Polarisation of Elizabethan Politics: The Political Career of Robert Devereux, 2nd Earl of Essex, 1585–1597* (Cambridge: Cambridge University Press, 1999)

Harvey, Gabriel, *Gabriel Harvey's Marginalia*, ed. G. C. Moore Smith (Stratford-upon-Avon: Shakespeare Head, 1913)

Haynes, Alan, *The Elizabethan Secret Services* (Stroud: Sutton, 2000)

Hibbert, Christopher, *The Virgin Queen: The Personal History of Elizabeth I* (1990; London: Penguin, 1992)

Hilton, Claire, 'St Bartholomew's Hospital and its Jewish Connections', in *TJHSE* XXX (1982–6), pp.21–51 (JHSE, 1989)

Holden, Anthony, *William Shakespeare: His Life and Work* (London: Abacus, 1999)

Hume, Martin, 'The So-Called Conspiracy of Dr Ruy Lopez', in *TJHSE*, (Edinburgh & London: Ballantyne, Hanson & Co., 1912)

———— *The Year After the Armada* (London: T. E. Unwin, 1896)

Inalcik, Halil, *The Ottoman Empire – The Classical Age 1300–1600* (1973; London: Phoenix, 2000)

Israel, Jonathan I., *Empires and Entrepôts – The Dutch, the Spanish Monarchy and the Jews, 1585–1713* (London and Ronceverte: Hambledon Press, 1990)

———— *European Jewry in the Age of Mercantilism, 1550–1750* (London: Littman Library of Jewish Civilisation, 1988)

Jacobs, E. M., *In Pursuit of Pepper and Tea* (Amsterdam: Walburg Pers, 1991)

Jardine, Lisa and Stewart, Alan, *Hostage to Fortune: The Troubled Life of Francis Bacon, 1561–1626* (1998; London: Phoenix, 1999)

Jenkins, Elizabeth, *Elizabeth and Leicester* (London: Victor Gollancz, 1961)

Kadourie, Elie (ed.), *Spain and the Jews: The Sephardi Experience, 1492 and After* (London: Thames & Hudson, 1992)

Katz, David S., *The Jews in the History of England* (Oxford: Clarendon Press, 1996)

Keay, Anna, *The Elizabethan Tower of London: The Haiward and Gascoyne Plan of 1597* (London: London Topographical Society Publication No. 158, with Historic Royal Palaces, and The Society of Antiquaries of London, 2001)

Kohler, Max J., 'Dr Rodrigo Lopez, Queen Elizabeth's Jewish Physician, and his relations to America', in *Publications of the American Jewish Historical Society*, XVII, pp.9–25 (Baltimore: Lord Baltimore Press, 1909)

Lacey, Robert, *Robert, Earl of Essex: An Elizabethan Icarus* (London: Weidenfeld & Nicolson, 1971)

Lee, Sidney, 'The Original of Shylock', in *The Gentleman's Magazine*, CCXLVI, January to June 1880, pp.185–200 (London: Chatto & Windus, 1880)

——— 'Rodrigo Lopez', in *DNB*, XXXIV, pp.132 ff (London: Smith, Elder & Co., 1893)

Litvinoff, Barnet, *1492: The Year and the Era* (London: Constable, 1991)

Malvezin, Theophile, *Michael de Montaigne – Son Origine, Sa Famille* (Bordeaux: Charles Lefebvre, 1875)

Marañon, G., *Antonio Perez: Spanish Traitor*, (trans. C.D. Ley; London: Hollis & Carter, 1954)

Marcham, Frank, *Lopez The Jew: An Opinion by Gabriel Harvey* (Harrow Weald: Waterlow & Sons, 1927)

Maslen, R. W., *Elizabethan Fictions: Espionage, Counter-Espionage and the Duplicity of Fiction in Early Elizabethan Prose Narratives* (Oxford: Clarendon Press, 1997)

Matar, Nabil, *Turks, Moors and Englishmen in the Age of Discovery* (New York: Columbia University Press, 1999)

McBride, G. K., 'Elizabethan Foreign Policy in Microcosm: The Portuguese Pretender, 1580–89', in *Albion*, III (1973), p.194.

McCarthy, Justin, *The Ottoman Turks: An Introductory History to 1923* (London: Longman, 1997)

Medvei, V. C. and Thornton, J. L., *The Royal Hospital of St Bartholomew 1123–1973* (London: Royal Hospital of St Bartholomew, 1974)

Mencken, H. L., *H. L. Mencken's Dictionary of Quotations* (London: Collins, 1982)

Menendez Pival, Ramon, *Historia de España, Tomo XIX (XX:ii): España en Tiempo de Felipe II* (Madrid: Espasa-Calpe, 1958)

Meyers, Charles, 'Debt in Elizabethan England: The Adventures of Dr Hector Nuñez, Physician and Merchant', in *THJSE*, XXXIV (1994–6), pp.125–35 (London: JHSE, 1997)

———— 'Dr Hector Nuñez: Elizabethan Merchant', in *TJHSE*, XXVIII, pp.129–31 (London: JHSE, 1984)

Moore, Norman, *The History of St Bartholomew's Hospital* (London: C. Arthur Pearson, 1918)

————'The Physicians and Surgeons of St Bartholomew's Hospital Before the Time of Harvey', in *SBHR*, XVIII (London: Smith, Elder & Co., 1882)

Netanyahu, B., *The Marranos of Spain* (Cornell: Cornell University Press, 3rd ed., 1999)

Nicholl, Charles, *A Cup of News: The Life of Thomas Nashe* (London: Routledge, Kegan & Paul, 1984)

———— *The Reckoning: The Murder of Christopher Marlowe* (London: Jonathan Cape, 1992)

Oelman, Timothy, ed. and trans., *Marrano Poets of the 17th Century* (East Brunswick: Associated University Presses, 1982)

Parry, J. H., *The Age of Reconnaissance* (1963; London: Cardinal, 1973)

Porter, Roy, *The Greatest Benefit to Mankind: A Medical History of Humanity, from Antiquity to the Present Day* (London: HarperCollins, 1997)

———— *London: A Social History* (1994; London: Penguin, 2000)

Power, Sir D'Arcy, *A Short History of St Bartholomew's Hospital, 1213–1923* (London, 1923)

Prior, Roger, 'A Second Jewish Community in Tudor London', in *TJHSE*, XXXI, pp. 137–52 (London: JHSE, 1990)

Rabb, Theodore K., 'The Stirrings of the 1590s and the Return of the Jews to England', in *TJHSE*, XXVI (1974–8), pp.26–33 (London: JHSE, 1979)

Read, Conyers, *Lord Burghley and Queen Elizabeth* (London: Jonathan Cape, 1960)

—— *Mr Secretary Cecil and Queen Elizabeth* (London: Jonathan Cape, 1955)

—— *Mr Secretary Walsingham and the Policy of Queen Elizabeth*, 3 vols (Oxford: Clarendon Press, 1925)

Richler, Mordecai, *On Snooker* (London: Yellow Jersey Press, 2001)

Rodger, N. A. M., *The Safeguard of the Sea: A Naval History of Britain, Vol. I, 660–1649* (London: HarperCollins, 1997)

Rosedale, H. G., *Queen Elizabeth and the Levant Company* (London: Henry Frowde, 1904)

Rosenberg, Eleanor, *Leicester: Patron of Letters* (New York: Columbia University Press, 1955)

Rosner, Fred, *Medicine in the Bible and Talmud* (1977; Hoboken, N.J.: Ktav, 1995)

Roth, Cecil, *A History of the Jews in England* (Oxford: Clarendon Press, 1949)

—— *A History of the Marranos* (Philadelphia: Jewish Publication Society of America, 1932)

—— *Anglo-Jewish Letters* (London: Soncino, 1938)

—— *England in Jewish History* (London: JHSE, 1949)

Rowse, A. L., *The Elizabethan Renaissance: The Life of a Society* (1971; London: Penguin, 2000)

—— *The England of Elizabeth* (London: Macmillan, 1950)

—— *Shakespeare's Southampton: Patron of Virginia*, (London: Macmillan, 1965)

Samuel, Edgar, 'Dr Rodrigo Lopes' last speech from the scaffold at Tyburn', in *TJHSE* XXX (1982–6), pp.51–3 (London: JHSE, 1989)

—— 'Passover in London', in *THJSE*, XXVI (1974–8), pp.117–18 (London: JHSE, 1979)

Samuel, Edgar, *Portuguese Jews in Jacobean London*, in *TJHSE* XVIII, pp.171–230, (London: JHSE, 1989)

Scholem, Gershom, *Major Trends in Jewish Mysticism* (1946); New York: Schocken, 1996)

Shapiro, James, *Shakespeare and the Jews* (New York: Columbia University Press, 1996)

Shaw, W., 'The Parish Register of St Bartholomew the Less in Elizabethan Times', in *SBH Journal*, April 1940, pp.117–22, 136–41.

Smith, Lacey Baldwin, *English Treason Trials in the Sixteenth Century*, (Cambridge, Mass.: MIT, 1954)

Smith, Pamela and Findlen, Paula, eds, *Merchants & Marvels: Commerce, Science and Art in Early Modern Europe* (New York and London: Routledge, 2002)

Spedding, James, *The Letters and the Life of Francis Bacon, vol.I* (London: Longmans, Green & Co., 1890)

Stabel, P., Blonde, Bruno and Greve, Anke eds, *International Trade in the Low Countries (14th to 16th Centuries)* (Louvain: Garant, 2000)

Stewart, Alan, *Close Readers: Humanism and Sodomy in Early Modern England*, (Princeton: Princeton University Press, 1997)

—— *Philip Sidney: A Double Life* (2000; London: Pimlico, 2001)

Strachey, Lytton, *Elizabeth and Essex* (1928; London: Penguin, 2000)

Strong, Roy, *The Cult of Elizabeth: Elizabethan Portraiture and Pageantry* (1977; London: Pimlico, 1999)

Thomson, George Malcolm, *Sir Francis Drake* (BCA, 1973)

Trevelyan, G. M., *English Social History* (1944; London: Longman, 1978)

Ungerer, Gustav, 'The Printing of Spanish Books in Elizabethan England', in *The Library* (5th Series) vol. 20, pp.177–230 (1965)

—— *A Spaniard in Elizabethan England: The Correspondence of Antonio Perez's Exile* 2 vols (London: Tamesis, 1974)

Ward, A. C., *A History of the Levant Company* (Oxford: OUP, 1935)

Weinreb, Ben and Hibbert, Christopher, *The London Encyclopaedia* (London: Macmillan, 1992)

Wesker, Arnold, *The Birth of Shylock and the Death of Zero Mostel* (London: Quartet, 1997)

Wilson, F. P., *The Plague in Shakespeare's London*, (Oxford: Clarendon Press, 1927)

Wolf, Lucien, 'Jews in Elizabethan England', in *TJHSE* XI (London: Spottiswoode, Ballantyne & Co., 1928)

—— 'Jews in Tudor England', in *Essays in Jewish History* (London: JHSE, 1934)

Yates, Frances, *Astraea: The Imperial Theme in the 16th Century* (1975; London: Peregrine, 1977)

———— *The Occult Philosophy in the Elizabethan Age* (1979; London: Routledge, 2001)

Yeo, Geoffrey, *Images of Bart's – An Illustrated History of St Bartholomew's Hospital in the City of London* (London: Historical Publications, 1992).

Yerushalmi, Yosef Hayim, *Zakhor – Jewish History and Jewish Memory* (Washington: University of Washington Press, 1989)

Yovel, Yirmiyahu, *Spinoza and Other Heretics: The Marrano of Reason* (1989; Princeton N.J.: Princeton University Press, 1992)

Zeitlin, Solomon, *Maimonides: A Biography* (New York: Bloch, 1935)

Zeman, F. D., 'The Amazing Career of Doctor Roderigo Lopez', in *Bulletin of the History of Medicine*, XXXIX (July–August 1965), pp.295–308

Index

Index